NATIVE TREES OF CANADA

PACIFIC OCEAN

YUKON TERRITORY

NORTHWEST TERRITORIES

BRITISH COLUMBIA

ALBERTA

SASKATCHEWAN

MANITOBA

CANADA
U.S.A

LEGEND

FOREST REGIONS | **PRINCIPAL TREE SPECIES**

Boreal
  Predominantly Forest........White Spruce, Black Spruce, Balsam Fir, Jack Pine, White Birch, Trembling Aspen................
  Forest & Barren...............White Spruce, Black Spruce, Tamarack.................
  Forest & Grass...............Trembling Aspen, willow.................
Subalpine.....................Engelmann Spruce, Alpine Fir, Lodgepole Pine.................
Montane......................Douglas-fir, Lodgepole & Ponderosa Pine, Tr. Aspen.................
Coast........................W. Red Cedar, W. Hemlock, Sitka Spruce, Douglas-fir.................
Columbia.....................W. Red Cedar, W. Hemlock, Douglas-fir.................
Deciduous....................Beech, maple, Black Walnut, hickory, oak.................
Great Lakes-St. Lawrence.....Red Pine, E. White Pine, E. Hemlock, Yellow Birch, maple, oak
Acadian......................Red Spruce, Balsam Fir, maple, Yellow Birch.................
The Grasslands...............Trembling Aspen, willow, Bur Oak.................

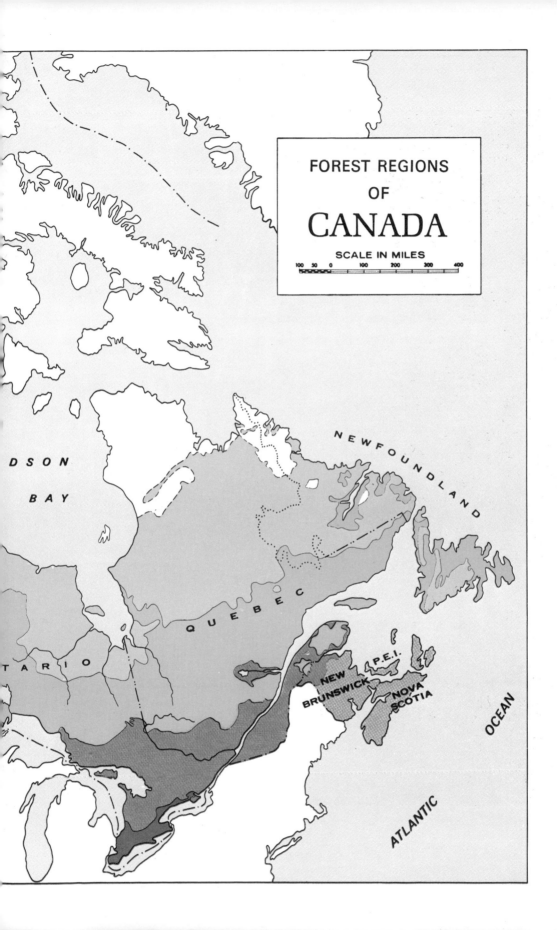

FOREST REGIONS
OF
CANADA

SCALE IN MILES

100 50 0   100   200   300   400

R.C.Hosie

NATIVE TREES OF CANADA

Eighth Edition

Published by Fitzhenry & Whiteside Ltd.
in co-operation with the Canadian Forestry Service
(Environment Canada) & the Canadian Government
Publishing Centre, Supply & Services, Canada

Eighth Edition

©1979, Minister of Supply and Services Canada

No part of this publication may be reproduced
in any form, or by any means, without permission
in writing from the publisher.

Fitzhenry & Whiteside Limited
150 Lesmill Road,
Don Mills, Ontario M3B 2T5

ISBN 0-88902-572-X (cloth)
     0-88902-550-9 (paper)

catalogue number Fo 45-61/1979

printed and bound in Canada.

Contents

Foreword

When *Native Trees of Canada* first appeared in 1917, it included descriptions of approximately 100 trees and large shrubs. During the past 50 years, several new species have been added in succeeding editions until, today, nearly 140 species are represented.

In 1917, the authors Messrs. Morton and Lewis commented that, "No distinct line can be drawn between trees and shrubs", and then agreed to describe species, "which grow in tree form in some part of their natural range'. By 1949 the list had been expanded to include, "certain common species . . . which generally occur in Canada as shrubs". In the 5th and 6th editions, this approach was perpetuated and *Native Trees of Canada* was expanded accordingly.

In the present edition, to prevent needless expansion, a "native" tree is defined as a *single-stemmed perennial woody plant growing to a height of more than ten feet, and which is indigenous to Canada*. Ornamental or "exotic" trees which are capable of growing in Canada may be mentioned within the text, but only in the context of a comparison or interesting phenomenon.

The text is completely new and was written by the late Mr. R. C. Hosie, Forestry Consultant to the Department of the Environment. His detailed descriptions and selection of illustrations are the product of a lifetime spent teaching dendrology to university students, and are designed to assist all who wish to identify native trees. The Keys, included as Appendix "D", were designed by Mr. Hosie, and he gave valuable advice on general arrangement and photography.

Dr. T. C. Brayshaw, formerly Research Scientist, Department of the Environment, Petawawa Forest Experiment Station, Chalk River, Ontario, prepared the research notes on which Mr. Hosie based his manuscript. Dr. Brayshaw's artistic talents are evident in many of the conifer silhouettes, and he was responsible for supplying most of the information on which the cartographers based the range maps.

Many other persons have been involved in preparing this publication. A few worked continually, most made a small contribution within a specialized area, but all were vital to the success of the book. Those members and former members of the Canadian Forestry Service, Department of the Environment, who carried a major share of responsibility are introduced below. Other contributors are listed on page 318. To all, the Department of the Environment extends sincere thanks.

Mr. Jas. B. M. Gibson acted as Project Officer and Editor for this edition. Mr. Gibson planned and co-ordinated the photographic program and wrote or compiled the material in the Introduction, Notes, Appendices A, B and C, and the Index.

Mr. W. K. Robins supervised the editorial production and was responsible for editorial policy.

Mr. M. Biddall took most of the new photographs. His skill is particularly evident in the lighting of those minute details so important to positive tree identification.

Mr. H. Schade supervised photography and photographed some species in the field. He and Mr. A. Craigmyle covered the western species and genus pages.

Graphic Services, under the direction of Mr. F. Gusella, created and produced the design, layout, cartography and photography.

Mr. D. Herwig performed the valuable role of locating many of the species growing in Ontario and Quebec, and was out in all weathers collecting botanical samples for photography.

Dr. J. S. Rowe provided initial guidance for the project and supplied the material for "The Forest Regions".

Mr. J. H. Cayford served as Technical Co-ordinator and established liaison with the many contributing organizations and individuals across Canada.

Introduction

"New" seems a strange word to use when describing the forests of Canada but, in relation to some other forests and the age of the Earth itself, "new" is quite appropriate. All except our west coast forests are new.

Only 15,000 years ago, most of Canada lay under a coating of ice, in some places well over 5,000-feet thick. Approximately 10,000 years ago — a mere second on the geological clock — the ice began to recede, releasing tremendous quantities of water. Vast lakes formed and emptied, valleys were carved by erosion and landscape patterns changed. The dry land that emerged was thus ready for an invasion by plants from the south and from parts of northwestern Canada that had escaped being enveloped in ice.

To some extent, the present distribution of species throughout Canada reflects the ability of various trees to migrate. Migration alone, however, was not sufficient; the trees had to be able to adapt to new soils and climate.

There were three types of migrants. First came the fast travellers — the spruces, larches, birches, poplars and willows — all the trees that are now crowding the northern tree limit. Next came those with less-easily transportable seeds — the pines, the maples and basswoods — all species not quite so adaptable to a colder environment. Last of all, and venturing only into the more temperate areas, came the oaks, hickories, walnuts and butternuts — the trees that depend on animals to spread their heavy seeds. Sometimes birds carried and disseminated seeds beyond the normal distribution range of a species, giving a tree a chance to establish well ahead of rival species.

Keeping in step with this northward movement was the process of natural selection. As soils weathered, nutrients changed and moisture levels fluctuated, tree populations flourished or withered. Competition sometimes prevented the slower movers from establishing, even in ideal soils. Fire, climate and landform all contributed to vegetation patterns and left their mark on the forests across the continent.

The Trees Of Canada

Native trees fall naturally into two groups — the coniferous trees and the deciduous trees. The first includes those with leaves that live on the tree for two seasons or longer, and the second includes those whose leaves change colour in autumn and are shed from the tree, usually before winter.

The forests of Canada are largely composed of coniferous trees from the first group, particularly in the northern and coastal areas, and especially on the west coast. Within this group there are nine species of pine, three larches, five spruces, three hemlocks, one Douglas-fir, four true firs, two cedars, one cypress, two junipers, and one yew, a total of 31 species, compared to over 100 deciduous species which make up the second group.

The Coniferous Trees

The first group — the conifers — are also known as evergreens, needle-leafed trees, or softwoods. Mature trees generally have a straight central trunk with short side branches which spread to form a distinctive conical or columnar crown. Their leaves are either very narrow compared to their length, or small and scale-like, with straight veins unconnected by cross veins. All except those of the larch retain their green colour over winter and live on the tree for two or more years. As seedlings, their seed-leaves are almost needle-like and usually there are more than two.

The reproductive organs of conifers are not looked upon as being part of a true flower. They are not accompanied by the greenish sepals and colourful petals of a normal flower, but are minute bodies borne in clusters on fleshy formations, called scales, which may eventually become woody. The scales are arranged like the leaves of a tree on a central axis, but are placed very close to one another to form a structure called a cone. The male organs consist of a number of small stamens, each bearing two or more pollen sacs or anthers. The female organs are few in number and usually consist of two ovules which are not enclosed in an ovary but which lie exposed on the scales that bear them. The stamens and ovules are found in separate cones with both kinds on the same tree, except in juniper and yew where they are on different trees. Pollination is by wind, the ovules maturing in the cones to form the seeds either in the same year or one or more years later.

The wood of most coniferous species is soft, resinous and non-porous. Viewed under a lens, the cross-section shows uninterrupted radial rows of cells between narrow dividers, called rays. These cells constitute the bulk of the tissue. They are long, tapered at the ends to fit closely together and their purpose is to transfer liquids through minute openings in their walls.

The Deciduous Trees

This second group is also known as the broad-leaved or broadleaf trees, or hardwoods. The form of the deciduous trees varies a great deal, but the commonest has a broad rounded crown with branches often as long or longer than the short tapered trunk. Their leaves are broad compared to their length, are net veined and (with the exception of the Arbutus) are retained on the tree for only one season before being shed. In the seedling stage they have two seed-leaves; these are usually broad and not needle-shaped.

Their reproductive organs are usually grouped in the form of true flowers, each flower consisting of four concentric whorls of specialized parts. The outer whorl is composed of small green, leaf-like sepals inside which are the petals, sometimes colourful, although not usually so on trees. Within the petals are the reproductive organs, first the stamens each with two anthers and, in the centre, the pistil with its ovary enclosing the ovules. Although both kinds of organs are commonly borne in the same flower, occasionally they may be in separate flowers, either on the same tree, or on different trees. Pollination is by insects or wind, the seeds maturing in the ovaries in a relatively short time and usually within the growing season. The ovary may open to shed the ripe seeds if it is a pod, or it may remain closed to form a nut, berry, or — if winged — a samara, or other kind of fruit.

The wood is hard, heavy and non-resinous in most species, and is partly composed of vessels. These are cells with open ends set one above the other to form continuous vertical conducting tubes. The tubes are visible in the cross-section of the wood as pores; on many species they can be seen without a lens. In some species, the cells formed during the spring are larger than those formed later in the year and, when the change from one size to the other is abrupt, a conspicuous band appears within the growth ring. Such wood is classed as ring porous. Where the pores do not vary noticeably in size throughout the growth ring, the wood is classed as diffuse porous. The growth rings are shown on page 27.

The Forest Regions

The forests of Canada can be divided into nine regions based on marked differences caused by terrain, soil and climate. A composite map of the regions is reproduced on the end leaves.

The Boreal Forest Region

This Region comprises the greater part of the forested area of Canada. It forms a continuous belt from Newfoundland and the Labrador coast westward to the

Rocky Mountains and northwestward to Alaska. White Spruce and Black Spruce are characteristic species; other prominent conifers are Tamarack which generally ranges throughout, Balsam Fir and Jack Pine in the eastern and central portions, and Alpine Fir and Lodgepole Pine in the western and northwestern parts. Although the Boreal forests are primarily coniferous, there is a general admixture of deciduous trees such as White Birch and poplar; these are important in the central and south-central portions, particularly along the edge of the prairie. In turn, the proportion of spruce and larch increases to the north and, with the more rigorous climate, the close forest gives way to an open lichen-woodland which finally changes into tundra. In the eastern section, along the southern border of the Region, there is a considerable intermixture of species from the Great Lakes-St. Lawrence forest, such as Eastern White Pine, Red Pine, Yellow Birch, Sugar Maple, Black Ash and Eastern White Cedar.

The Coast Forest Region

This Region is part of the Pacific Coast forest of North America. Essentially coniferous, it consists principally of Western Red Cedar and Western Hemlock, with Sitka Spruce abundant in the north and Douglas-fir in the south. Amabilis Fir and Yellow Cypress are represented throughout the Region and, together with Mountain Hemlock and Alpine Fir, are common at the higher altitudes. Western White Pine is found in the southern parts, while Western Yew is in widely scattered groups. Deciduous trees, such as Black Cottonwood, Red Alder and Bigleaf Maple, have a limited distribution. Arbutus and Garry Oak grow only on the southeast coast of Vancouver Island, the adjacent islands and mainland. The Arbutus is a broadleaved evergreen. Both are species whose centres of population lie southward in the United States.

17

A

B

C

D

E

F

G

FOREST REGIONS

A The Grasslands	**E** Deciduous
B Boreal	**F** Coast
C Great Lakes-St. Lawrence	**G** Subalpine
	H Acadian
D Columbia	**I** Montane

H

I

The Subalpine Forest Region

This is a coniferous forest located on the mountain uplands of Alberta and British Columbia, from the Rocky Mountain range through the Interior of British Columbia to the Pacific Coast inlets. The characteristic species are Engelmann Spruce, Alpine Fir and Lodgepole Pine. There is a close relationship between the Subalpine Forest Region and the Boreal Forest Region, which also shares Black Spruce, White Spruce and Trembling Aspen. There is also some penetration of Interior Douglas-fir from the Montane forest, and Western Hemlock, Western Red Cedar and Amabilis Fir from the coastal forests. Other species are Western Larch, Whitebark Pine, Limber Pine and, on the coastal mountains, Yellow Cypress and Mountain Hemlock.

The Montane Forest Region

The Region occupies a large part of the interior uplands of British Columbia, as well as a part of the Kootenay Valley and a small area on the east side of the Rocky Mountains. It is a northern extension of the typical forest of much of the western mountain system in the United States, and comes in contact with the Coast, Columbia, and Subalpine Forest regions. Ponderosa Pine is a characteristic species of the southern portions. Interior Douglas-fir is found throughout, but more particularly in the central and southern parts; Lodgepole Pine and Trembling Aspen are generally present, the latter being particularly well represented in the north-central portions. Engelmann Spruce and Alpine Fir from the Subalpine Forest Region, together with White Birch, are important constituents in the northern parts. White Spruce, although primarily Boreal in affinity, also grows here. Extensive prairie communities of bunch-grasses and herbs are found in many of the river valleys.

The Columbia Forest Region

A large part of the Kootenay Valley, the upper valleys of the Thompson and Fraser rivers and the Quesnel Lake area of British Columbia contain a coniferous forest, called the Columbia Forest Region, which closely resembles the Coast Forest Region. Western Red Cedar and Western Hemlock are the characteristic species in this interior "wet belt". Associated trees are the Interior Douglas-fir which has general distribution and, in the southern parts, Western White Pine, Western Larch, Grand Fir and Western Yew. Engelmann Spruce from the Subalpine Forest Region is important in the upper Fraser Valley and is found to some extent at the upper levels of the forest in the remainder of the Region. At lower elevations in the west and in parts of the Kootenay Valley, the forest merges into the Montane Forest Region and in a few places into prairie grasslands.

The Deciduous Forest Region

A small portion of the deciduous forest, which is widespread in the eastern United States, extends into southwestern Ontario between lakes Huron, Erie and Ontario. Here, with the deciduous trees common to the Great Lakes-St. Lawrence Forest Region, such as Sugar Maple, Beech, White Elm, Basswood, Red Ash, White Oak and Butternut, are scattered a number of other deciduous species which have their northern limits in this locality. Among these are the Tulip-tree, Cucumber-tree, Pawpaw, Red Mulberry, Kentucky Coffee-tree, Redbud, Black Gum, Blue Ash, Sassafras, Mockernut Hickory, Pignut Hickory, Black Oak and Pin Oak. In addition, Black Walnut, Sycamore and Swamp White Oak are confined largely to this Region. Conifers are few, but there is a scattered distribution of Eastern White Pine, Tamarack, Eastern Red Cedar and Eastern Hemlock.

The Great Lakes-St. Lawrence Forest Region

Extending inland from the edges of the Great Lakes and the St. Lawrence River lies a forest of a very mixed nature which is characterized by Eastern White Pine, Red Pine, Eastern Hemlock and Yellow Birch. With these are associated certain dominant broad-leaved species common to the Deciduous Forest Region, including Sugar Maple, Red Maple, Red Oak, Basswood and White Elm. Other species with wide ranges are the Eastern White Cedar and Largetooth Aspen and, to a lesser extent, Beech, White Oak, Butternut and White Ash. Boreal species such as White Spruce, Black Spruce, Balsam Fir, Jack Pine, poplars, and White Birch are intermixed, and Red Spruce is abundant in certain central and eastern portions. This Region extends in a westward direction into southeastern Manitoba, but, as shown on the map, does not include the area north of Lake Superior.

The Acadian Forest Region

Over the greater part of the maritime provinces (excluding Newfoundland) there is a forest closely related to the Great Lakes-St. Lawrence forest and, to a lesser extent, to the Boreal forest. Red Spruce is a characteristic though not exclusive species, and associated with it are Balsam Fir, Yellow Birch and Sugar Maple, with some Red Pine, Eastern White Pine and Eastern Hemlock. Beech was formerly a more important forest constituent than at present, but beech bark disease has drastically reduced Beech representation in Nova Scotia, Prince Edward Island and southern New Brunswick. Other species of wide distribution are White Spruce, Black Spruce, Red Oak, White Elm, Black Ash, Red Maple, White Birch, Grey Birch and poplars. Eastern White Cedar, though present in New Brunswick, is extremely rare elsewhere within the Region. Jack Pine, a common native of this Region, is apparently absent from the upper St. John River Valley and the southern part of Nova Scotia.

The Grasslands

Although not a forest region, the prairies of Manitoba, Saskatchewan and Alberta support several species of trees in great numbers. Trembling Aspen forms groves or "bluffs" around wet depressions, and continuous dense stands along the northern boundary. Several other species of poplar are usually found along rivers and in moist locations, along with willows and some White Spruce. There are sporadic stands of White Birch, Manitoba Maple, Bur Oak and ash. In British Columbia, where the grasslands are confined to deep valleys and low areas of the Interior, there are scattered representations of Ponderosa Pine, birches, poplars, spruce and Mountain Alder.

How Trees Are Named

The common names which most people use when referring to trees have been handed down from generation to generation and can be traced to one of several origins. For example, Swamp White Oak got its name from the type of soil in which it grows, that is, its habitat; Trembling Aspen describes a distinctive feature of the leaves; Engelmann Spruce was named after George Engelmann, a famous American botanist; the Sugar Maple is identified by its product; the Manitoba Maple takes its name from a geographical location; and the Chinquapin Oak is an Indian name. Sometimes common names vary according to locality. For example, the tree called "Yellow Birch", on page 156, is also known as either Curly Birch, Hard Birch, Black Birch, Gold Birch, Silver Birch, Tall Birch or Red Birch in various places throughout its range in eastern Canada. These are called "local names".

In this edition of *Native Trees,* only the most widely used local names are included and the most appropriate predominates. Local names which tend to perpetuate an incorrect identification, or which almost duplicate names already given, have been purposely omitted to avoid confusing the reader.

Botanists use a scientific name to ensure positive identification of a tree. This consists basically of *two words* — the generic name and the specific name. Recognition of the person who first named the tree is normally indicated in abbreviated form and, when a variety is identified, its name is also added, preceded by the word "variety", or "var.". Thus, to the botanist, the variety of White Birch, called Western Paper Birch, becomes *Betula papyrifera* Marsh. var. *commutata* (Reg.) Fern. Here is an explanation of its parts.

Betula — is the generic name, and means that the tree is one of the birches.

papyrifera — the specific name, meaning "papery", refers to the bark.

Marsh. — the abbreviated form of Humphry Marshall (1722-1801) the American botanist who first described this birch. (Usually in writing out the name of a variety, the original author's name is omitted, but it has been inserted in this example to show all the possible components.)

var. — indicates that this tree is a variety of *Betula papyrifera.*

commutata — meaning "changeable", is the given name of the variety.

(Reg.) — refers to Eduard von Regel (1815-1892) who first identified this particular tree and recognized it as being different from the tree that Marshall had described. He classified it as a distinct species, *Betula commutata* Regel.

Fern. — refers to Merritt Fernald (1873-1950) who re-classified Regel's identification and reduced it to a variety of the White Birch.

For those who wish to know more about trees, the botanical names are given in the text and also in the index. Appendix "A" comprises short biographical sketches of the botanical authors mentioned throughout the book, while Appendix "B" lists the meanings of the botanical names given by these authors. Appendix "C" includes Little's "Check List of Native and Naturalized Trees of the United States (including Alaska)" which has been the reference for all botanical names used in this edition of *Native Trees of Canada.*

Arrangement Of The Species

A botanical arrangement has been used to group the various kinds of trees according to a recognized system of classification. To those who are unfamiliar with botanical systems of classification, it may seem peculiar to start with the pines and deal with the ashes near the end of the book, but the alternative, an alphabetical arrangement, is not practical because it puts unlike trees together and separates those that are closely related.

When there is more than one representative of a family native to Canada, a complete page is devoted to a general description of the family (genus). This description should be read in conjunction with any of the related species' descriptions. A single representative of a family has been treated with as much detail as possible within the allotted space. More information will be found in several of the reference books listed in Appendix "C".

The illustrations accompanying the species' descriptions have been chosen to show the main identifying features of the trees. Usually, the salient points have been given prominence, but the illustrations are intended to supplement the text, not substitute for it. Both text and illustrations should be used to properly identify a tree.

Silhouettes are included only as a guide to the general outline and appearance of each tree species, but are not necessarily representative of individual trees.

The range of each main species is shown in colour on the range maps. Where closely related species or varieties are shown on the same map they are identified by a code, which also indicates overlapping ranges.

What To Look For

Even when a person's knowledge of trees is confined to recognizing the difference between a Christmas tree and an apple tree, a step has been made towards tree identification. There is an awareness of the two groups of trees — the ones with needle-like leaves and the ones with broad leaves. Leaves alone, however, are not always a clue to a tree's identity — especially the leaves of evergreens. The flowers, fruit, twigs and bark, all have to be examined to ensure positive identification.

The simplest way to describe important features and introduce new terms is to draw a picture. In the following illustrations, the main points vital to tree recognition are shown. Although mostly deciduous tree features have been used in the drawings because of the greater variety of leaf shapes, the terms apply equally well to coniferous species. There are several important features or terms which could not be illustrated, however, and they have been listed separately under the heading "definitions". The twigs in the drawings and also in the descriptions throughout the book are given as they would appear in winter. Bark descriptions are of the mature tree unless otherwise noted.

For those who have difficulty in telling a spruce from a fir or an elm from a basswood, identifying keys to the families are provided in Appendix "D" on page 347.

Tree Terminology

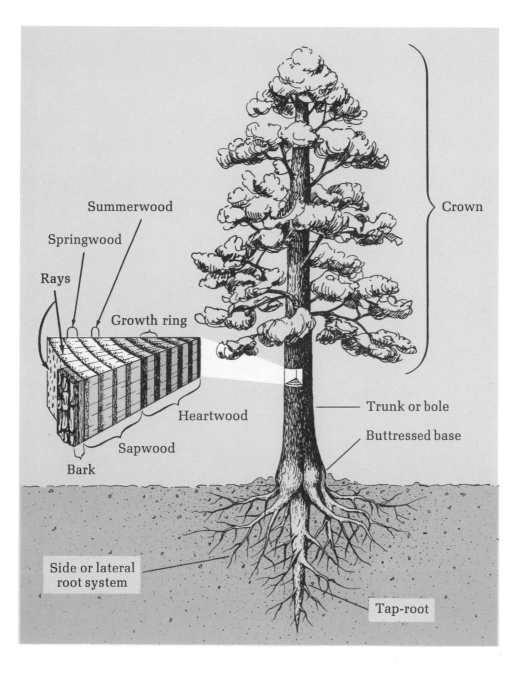

Summerwood

Springwood

Rays

Growth ring

Heartwood

Sapwood

Bark

Crown

Trunk or bole

Buttressed base

Side or lateral root system

Tap-root

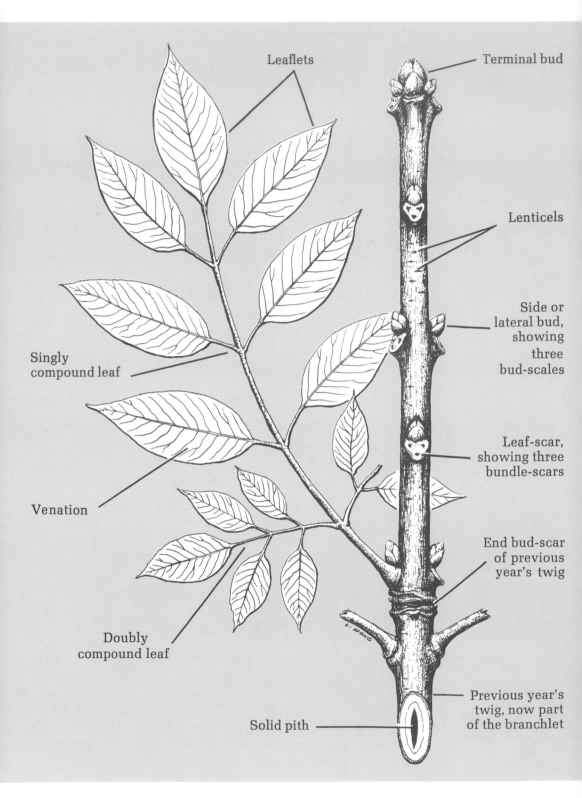

Leaflets

Singly
compound leaf

Venation

Doubly
compound leaf

Solid pith

Terminal bud

Lenticels

Side or
lateral bud,
showing
three
bud-scales

Leaf-scar,
showing three
bundle-scars

End bud-scar
of previous
year's twig

Previous year's
twig, now part
of the branchlet

L. WONG

A COMPOUND LEAF DIVIDED
INTO LEAFLETS

WINTER TWIG WITH OPPOSITE
BUD ARRANGEMENT

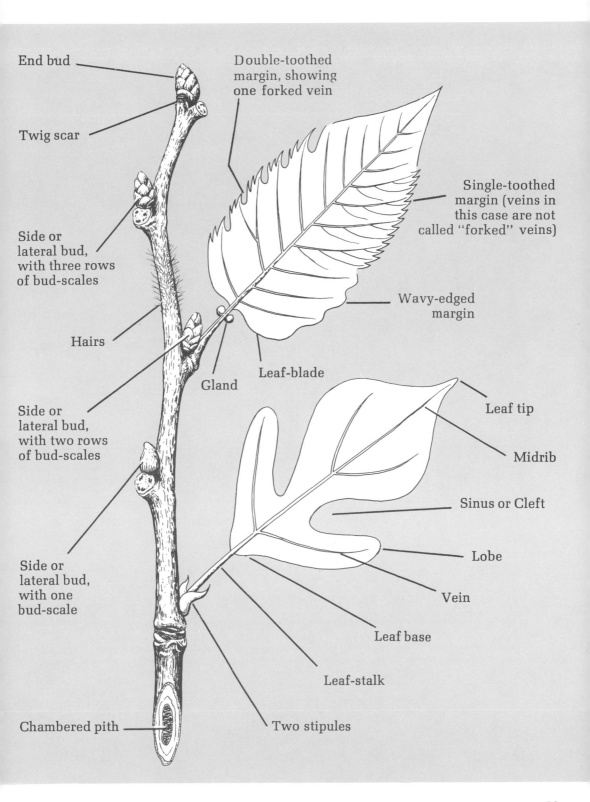

End bud

Twig scar

Side or
lateral bud,
with three rows
of bud-scales

Hairs

Side or
lateral bud,
with two rows
of bud-scales

Side or
lateral bud,
with one
bud-scale

Chambered pith

Gland

Double-toothed
margin, showing
one forked vein

Single-toothed
margin (veins in
this case are not
called "forked" veins)

Wavy-edged
margin

Leaf-blade

Leaf tip

Midrib

Sinus or Cleft

Lobe

Vein

Leaf base

Leaf-stalk

Two stipules

WINTER TWIG WITH ALTERNATE
BUD ARRANGEMENT

TWO SIMPLE LEAVES SHOWING IMPORTANT
IDENTIFYING FEATURES

29

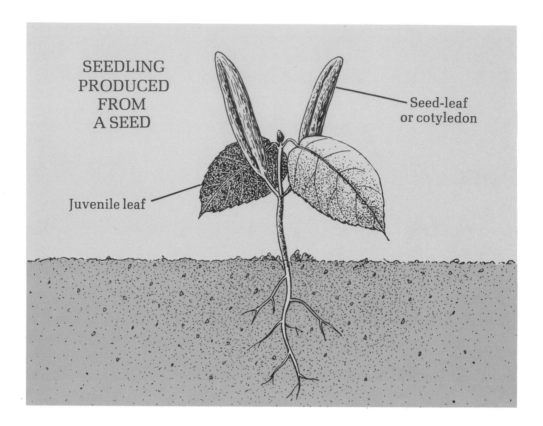

SEEDLING
PRODUCED
FROM
A SEED

Seed-leaf
or cotyledon

Juvenile leaf

DEFINITIONS

CATKIN ———————— a slender, flexible, simple, compact cluster of unisexual, stalkless flowers without petals.

HUSK ———————— the outer covering of certain fruits (e.g. walnut).

NODE ———————— the place on the stems where leaves normally originate.

NUT ———————— a hard woody fruit containing a single seed.

NUTLET ———————— a very small nut.

POD ———————— a dry fruit that splits into two or more parts to release the seeds.

RACEME ———————— a cluster of stalked flowers or fruits arranged along a central stem.

RESIN CANAL ——— an elongated duct containing resin.

SAMARA ———————— a nutlet with a wing.

UMBEL ———————— a cluster of flowers with stalks all arising from one place.

EXAMPLE OF A "PERFECT" FLOWER
CONTAINING BOTH MALE AND FEMALE ORGANS

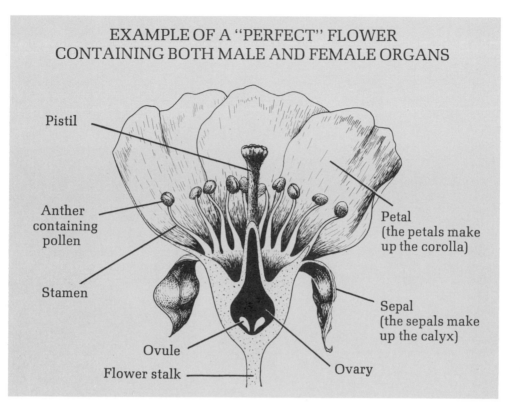

Pistil

Anther
containing
pollen

Stamen

Petal
(the petals make
up the corolla)

Sepal
(the sepals make
up the calyx)

Ovule

Flower stalk

Ovary

CONE PARTS

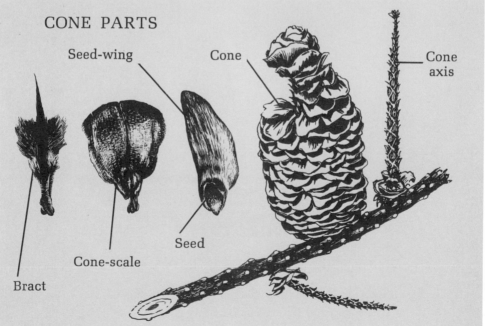

Seed-wing

Cone

Cone
axis

Bract

Cone-scale

Seed

CONIFEROUS TREES

PINE

Pinus L.

The pines comprise 80 to 90 species of trees, or occasionally shrubs, of the northern hemisphere. About 35 are native to North America; nine of them, all trees, grow in various parts of Canada.

The pines are divided into two groups — the SOFT PINES and the HARD PINES. The soft pines, also called white pines or five-needle pines, include Eastern White Pine, Western White Pine, Limber Pine and White-bark Pine. They have leaves in clusters of five, with deciduous basal sheaths; their cone-scales are mostly without prickles. The hard pines, also called yellow pines or pitch pines, include Ponderosa Pine, Pitch Pine, Red Pine, Jack Pine and Lodgepole Pine. They have leaves in clusters of two or three, with persistent basal sheaths, and cone-scales which are often armed with prickles.

The leaves of pines are evergreen, needle-shaped, or linear. Each cluster arises at the base of a brown papery scale, or primary leaf, that is usually shed early in the growing season. The clusters are spirally arranged on the twigs and branchlets. Around the base of each are the bud-scales elongated into a chaff-like sheath which in some of the species is shed early, but in others remains attached.

The reproductive organs are minute bodies borne on scales arranged spirally around central axes to form cone-shaped clusters. Each cone is composed of organs of one sex only, with both sexes on the same tree (monoecious). The male cones, containing many stalkless stamens, are clustered at the base of the new spring growth, and disintegrate soon after the pollen is released. The female cones, bearing two ovules on the upper side and at the base of each scale, occur singly, or a few in a whorl, either terminally or laterally on the new growth. The cones take two years to mature, and three years in the case of Austrian Pine. At maturity their scales are woody, and each bears two terminally winged or wingless seeds which are soon shed, except in a few species where they remain in the cones for long periods. The cones usually fall soon after maturing, but in some species remain on the trees for many years.

Pine seedlings have a variable number of needle-shaped seed-leaves (cotyledons). Adult leaves in clusters typical of the species appear in the second growing season, or in some cases not until after several seasons. In describing the species, it is customary to refer only to the adult leaves.

Among the many foreign species of pine commonly planted in Canada are Scots Pine (*Pinus sylvestris* L.) also known as Scotch Pine or Scotch Fir; Austrian Pine (*Pinus nigra* Arnold); and Mugho Pine (*Pinus mugo* Turra var. *mughus* Zenari) a dwarf form of the variable Swiss Mountain Pine. All have leaves in pairs. Those of the Scots Pine are bluish-green and twisted, so that both surfaces can be seen without rotating the leaf. The other two have dark green straight leaves; those of the Austrian Pine are 5- to 6-ins. long, very rigid, with needle-sharp tips, while those of Mugho Pine are flexible, relatively blunt tipped and seldom over 2 ins. in length. In the Scots Pine, the bark is an unusual orangey-red which is very noticeable in the upper part of the tree, where it keeps flaking off in ragged pieces. The bark is dark in the other two species.

The pines have been held in high esteem ever since Canadian forests began to be exploited. They have been of great importance in the past and are still important in the economic and industrial development of the nation. Undoubtedly they will continue to be important, not only because of the quality of their wood and other products, but perhaps to a greater degree because of their ability to grow on the poorer soils and drier sites. Pines are essentially trees with meagre requirements and this alone will reserve them a place on many of the sites too poor for other growth.

EASTERN WHITE PINE

Pinus strobus L.

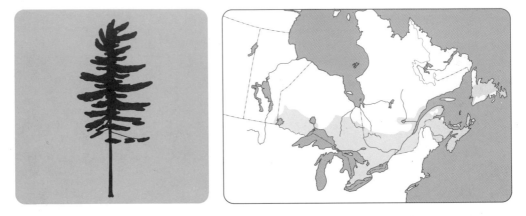

FORM—The crown of a mature tree growing in the open is composed of wide-spreading branches at approximately right angles to the trunk in its mid-portion. In the upper part of the tree the branches ascend, giving a broadly oval outline which often becomes irregular, or asymmetrical, owing to the effect of the prevailing wind. In closed stands, the tree is often clear of branches over the lower two-thirds and the crown is columnar. The root system is wide-spreading, moderately deep, without a distinct tap-root, and the tree is quite windfirm.

HABITAT—Eastern White Pine is a characteristic tree in the Great Lakes-St. Lawrence Forest Region, but its range also extends into the southeastern parts of the Boreal Forest Region, eastward into the Acadian Forest Region and south throughout the Deciduous Forest Region. It is thus seen throughout most of eastern Canada. Eastern White Pine is found on many different soils, from dry sandy and rocky ridges to sphagnum bogs, but it makes its best growth on moist sandy or loamy soils. It may grow in pure stands or in association with other conifers and hardwoods.

SIZE—The tallest conifer in eastern Canada, commonly reaching heights of 100 ft. and diameters of 3 ft.; on favourable soils, it may attain heights of 175 ft. and diameters of 5 ft.

LEAVES—In five's, 2½- to 5-ins. long, needle-shaped, slender, straight, flexible and soft to touch, bluish-green, the edges finely toothed; mature clusters without basal sheaths.

CONES — Mature in September and fall during the winter; cylindrical when closed, 3- to 8-ins. long, 1-in. across, on ¾-in. stalk, pendulous; scales 50 to 80, usually in five spiral rows, thin-tipped, without prickles, opening soon after maturing to release the seeds; seed-wing about ¾-in. long.

TWIGS—Green, downy, becoming free of hairs and changing to orangey-brown; buds slender, ½-in. long, sharp pointed, with overlapping reddish-brown scales.

BARK—Thin, smooth, greyish-green when young, becoming darker with age; dark greyish-brown on old trunks and deeply furrowed longitudinally into broad scaly ridges, 1- to 2-ins. thick.

WOOD—Light, moderately low in strength, soft; creamy-white to yellow, sapwood white; moderately decay resistant.

SEEDLINGS—Seven to ten needle-shaped, minutely toothed seed-leaves.

IMPORTANCE — This species produces the most valuable softwood lumber in eastern Canada. Because of its low shrinkage and uniform texture, it is used extensively for patterns, window sashes and frames. Other important uses are for doors, mouldings, trim, siding, panelling and cabinet work.

NOTES—The name Weymouth Pine comes from Lord Weymouth who planted large areas of his estate in Wiltshire, England, with seedlings which he imported into England during the 18th century.

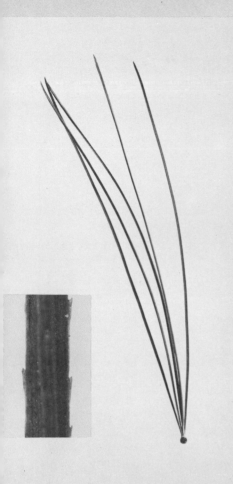

UNOPENED CONES AT THE TOP OF A TREE

MINUTE TEETH CAN BE FELT ON LEAF MARGIN

MATURE BARK DEEPLY FURROWED

CONES ARE SHED SOON
AFTER MATURITY

A MATURE TREE

WESTERN WHITE PINE

Silver Pine

Pinus monticola Dougl.

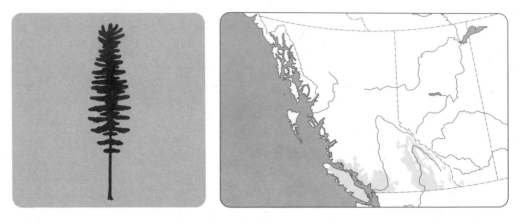

FORM—In general, when growing in the open, Western White Pine tends to have a more slender columnar crown than its eastern counterpart, with short, conspicuously whorled branches; but in exposed situations the crown is often asymmetrical like that of the eastern species. In closed stands, it has a short, open, usually symmetrical crown with a trunk which is free of branches up to 90 ft. from the ground, and which shows little taper. The root system is wide-spreading, with a tendency to develop a few deep roots which make the tree very windfirm.

HABITAT—Western White Pine grows in the southern parts of the Coast and Columbia Forest regions. It thrives on a wide variety of soils, ranging from peat bogs to dry sandy and rocky earth, but it makes its best growth on the fertile well-drained soils in moist valleys, and on gentle slopes with northern exposures. It may form nearly pure stands, but is usually found in mixture with other species.

SIZE—Generally reaches heights of 90 to 110 ft. and diameters of 2 to 3 ft.; an exceptional tree may attain a height of 200 ft. or more, and have a diameter of up to 8 ft.

LEAVES—In five's, 2- to 4-ins. long, needle-shaped, slender, straight, moderately flexible and soft to touch, bluish-green with a whitish bloom, the edges finely toothed; mature clusters without basal sheaths.

CONES—Mature in late summer and fall during the winter or early spring; cylindrical when closed, 4- to 10-ins. long, 1- to 1½-ins. across with a ¾-in. stalk, pendulous; scales, 90 to 160 or more, often reflexed when dry, in seven to nine spiral rows, thin-tipped, without prickles, opening soon after maturing to release the seeds; seed-wing about 1¼-ins. long.

TWIGS—Green, downy, changing to brownish and becoming free of hairs with age; buds slender, ½-in. long, blunt, with overlapping, closely fitting, brownish scales.

BARK—Thin, smooth, greyish-green when young, turning darker with age; dark grey to nearly black on old trunks and broken into small, squarish to rectangular, thick, scaly plates separated by deep, longitudinal furrows and horizontal crevices; bark on old trees 1- to 1½-ins. thick.

WOOD—Light, moderately low in strength, soft; creamy-white to yellow, sapwood white; moderately decay resistant.

SEEDLINGS—Seven to ten needle-shaped, minutely toothed seed-leaves.

IMPORTANCE—The wood is very similar to that of Eastern White Pine. It is used for window sashes, frames, doors, patterns, siding, panelling, trim, wooden matches and for many other purposes which require a soft pine wood.

NOTES—Discovered and named by David Douglas in 1825 during his journey of exploration up the west coast of North America.

WESTERN WHITE PINE

LEAVES ARE SIMILAR TO THOSE OF EASTERN WHITE PINE

CONES MUCH LARGER THAN THOSE OF EASTERN WHITE PINE

MATURE TREES
HOLYOAK LAKE, B.C.

RIDGES BROKEN ACROSS INTO THICK PLATES

LIMBER PINE

Rocky Mountain White Pine

Pinus flexilis James

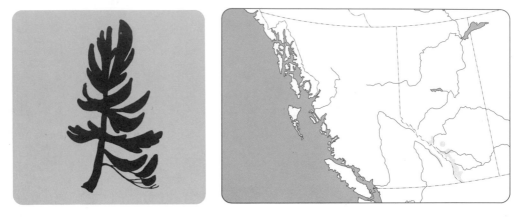

FORM—On mature trees, the trunk is short, thick, markedly tapered, usually crooked and irregularly limbed, with a large uneven crown extending over most of the tree's length. On old trees, some of the lower branches become very long, sometimes longer than the height of the tree. The branches tend to droop, but with their tips upturned. Young branches are very tough and flexible, hence the name "limber" pine. This species is sometimes confused with the Whitebark Pine, both having very similar foliage and nut-like almost wing-less seeds. By some authors, they are classed as stone pines; by others they are placed with the nut pines, or pinyons. They can be distinguished by their cones and the way in which the seeds are released from them.

HABITAT—The Limber Pine grows on the eastern and western foothills of the Rocky Mountains at altitudes between 3,000 and 6,000 ft. It occurs as a single scattered tree, or in small open groves of a few widely spaced trees, or in small stands, on dry rocky exposed situations, but it will grow on a wide variety of soils. In southern Alberta, it forms forest outliers on rocky outcrops along the edge of the prairies.

SIZE—A small tree 25 to 40 ft. in height and from 1 to 2 ft. in diameter. It is often reduced to a low-spreading prostrate form when growing at high elevations in situations exposed to strong winds.

LEAVES—In five's, 1½- to 3½-ins. long, needle-shaped, stout, stiff, slightly curved, bluish-green, the edges not toothed, clustered towards the ends of the branchlets.

CONES—Mature in September and fall during the winter; cylindrical to narrowly oval when closed, 3- to 8-ins. long, 1½- to 2¼-ins. across, very short-stalked and not pendulous; scales 40 to 70 in five to eight irregular, spiral rows, slightly thickened at the ends, without prickles, often with reflexed tips, opening when mature to release the seeds; seeds about ⅜-in. long, nearly or quite wingless.

TWIGS—Stout, tough, at first hairy, later smooth; greenish-yellow becoming grey; buds oval, pointed, with overlapping loose scales.

BARK—On young stems, smooth, pale grey; with age becoming thick, rough, dark brown to nearly black and fissured into wide scaly plates; on old trees 1- to 2-ins. thick.

WOOD—Light, close-grained, moderately soft; heartwood lemon-yellow, sapwood nearly white; very heavy when green, but when completely dry weighs under 20 lb. to the cubic foot.

SEEDLINGS—Nine to eleven seed-leaves, without teeth.

IMPORTANCE—Limber Pine has no commercial importance, although it is used locally for fuel.

NOTES—Limber Pine grows slowly but can live for several hundred years.

CONES BEAR ALMOST WINGLESS SEEDS

IMMATURE BARK IS
SMOOTH

MATURE BARK IS BROKEN
INTO SCALY PLATES

NOTE THE CURVED LEAVES

TREE IS STUNTED WHEN EXPOSED

WHITEBARK PINE

Scrub Pine

Pinus albicaulis Engelm.

FORM—This is an alpine tree which usually has a short rapidly tapering trunk and a wide-spreading crown. In some stands, especially when in association with narrow-crowned conifers, it develops a long slightly tapered trunk and a narrow crown which, on old trees, may widen, but only at the top. When exposed to strong winds, it is often reduced to a shrub with wide-spreading, irregularly disposed and twisted branches that lie almost flat on the ground. It is so similar to Limber Pine in its foliage and general appearance that the two are often mistaken for each other. When bearing cones, however, Whitebark Pine is readily distinguishable since its cones are so distinctly different from those of the other species of pines.

HABITAT—The normal habitat of this species is on exposed slopes and rocky ridges in the Subalpine Forest Region at altitudes from 3,000 ft. near the coast and from 6,000 ft. inland, usually near the upper tree line. It can grow on very thin soils, often appearing on rock ledges, rock faces and cliffs with scarcely visible soil coverings. Under such conditions its growth is very slow, but on well-drained soils which are deep enough to remain relatively moist, it makes good growth. It may form pure stands or grow in association with other species.

SIZE—Seldom more than 40 ft. in height by 2 ft. in diameter; in favourable locations, may reach a height of over 80 ft. with diameters above 3 ft. At high altitudes it often grows as a low shrub.

LEAVES—In five's, 1½- to 3½-ins. long, needle-shaped, stout, stiff, slightly curved, bluish-green, the edges not toothed, clustered towards the ends of the branchlets.

CONES—Mature in August or September; egg-shaped to almost globular, 1½- to 3-ins. long, not stalked, growing at right angles to the branch; scales 30 to 50 in about five spiral rows, thick and tough with stout pointed ends but no prickles, permanently closed; the cones fall at maturity and decay to release the seeds; since birds and rodents often tear them open, intact cones are seldom found on the ground; seeds about ⅜-in. long, wingless.

TWIGS—Stout, tough, usually hairy, reddish-brown to chalky-white; buds oval, sharp pointed, with overlapping loose scales.

BARK—On young stems thin, smooth, chalky-white; on old trees rarely more than ½-in. thick, in narrow, brown, scaly plates (similar in appearance to Limber Pine).

WOOD—Light, close-grained, moderately soft; heartwood pale brown, sapwood narrow and nearly white.

SEEDLINGS—Nine to eleven seed-leaves, without teeth.

IMPORTANCE—Of little commercial importance; the wood is cut locally for lumber and for mine timbers.

WHITEBARK PINE

AVES ARE SIMILAR TO THOSE
LIMBER PINE

CONE EGG-SHAPED TO ALMOST
GLOBULAR

THICK-TIPPED CONE-SCALE; SEED
WINGLESS

REE IS STUNTED IN EXPOSED SITUATION

TREE HAS GOOD FORM WHEN PROTECTED

PONDEROSA PINE

Pinus ponderosa Laws.

FORM—Mature trees have straight trunks with little taper and are often clear of branches over most of their length. The crown is irregularly cylindrical and narrow, with numerous short stout branches, the lower ones often drooping. Old trees commonly have short flat-topped crowns. The root system has very wide-spreading shallow lateral roots and, where the soil permits, develops a deep massive tap-root which makes the tree very windfirm.

HABITAT—Ponderosa Pine will grow on a wide variety of soils from extremely dry ones to well-drained, relatively deep, moist soils, where it makes its best growth. It is a characteristic tree in the southern parts of the Montane Forest Region in British Columbia, where it forms pure, but open, park-like stands at the dry, lower forest margin down to altitudes of 1,000 ft. It also grows in association with the Interior form of Douglas-fir at altitudes up to 4,000 ft.

SIZE—Under very favourable conditions, Ponderosa Pine may attain heights of 160 to 170 ft. and diameters of 5 to 6 ft. or more, but heights of 75 to 100 ft. and diameters of 2 to 3 ft. are more usual.

LEAVES—In three's (occasionally in two's and three's on the same tree), 5- to 11-ins. long, needle-shaped, straight, slender, flexible, very sharp, dark yellowish-green, the edges sharply toothed; clusters with persistent sheaths at the base.

CONES—Cylindrical to narrowly oval when closed, 3- to 6-ins. long, almost stalkless; scales thickened at the tips, bearing rigid sharp prickles, opening in autumn at maturity; cones have usually fallen from the tree by spring, leaving their stalks with a few basal cone-scales attached to the branchlets; seeds ¼-in. long with a terminal wing ¾-in. long.

TWIGS—Stout, hairless, yellowish-green changing to orange; buds ½- to 1-in. long, sharp pointed, usually resinous.

BARK—On young trees blackish, rough and scaly; on mature trees ½- to 4-ins. thick, pink to orangey-brown, deeply fissured into broad, elongated, flat, flaky, ridge-like plates.

WOOD—Relatively light, moderately strong; heartwood yellowish to reddish-brown, moderately resistant to decay; sapwood very wide, ranging from nearly white to pale yellow.

SEEDLINGS—Eight to ten seed-leaves, finely pointed, without teeth, 1½- to 2-ins. long; juvenile leaves greyish-green, 1- to 1¼-ins. long.

IMPORTANCE—Second only to Douglas-fir as a timber-producing tree in western North America, Ponderosa Pine is used for sashes, frames, door mouldings, panelling, patterns, cabinet work, boxes and crates.

NOTES—In some parts of its range, Ponderosa Pine lumber is sold under the name "Pondosa" and is used where Western White Pine might otherwise be preferred.

CLOSED AND OPEN CONES; NOTE PRICKLES

LEAVES ARE LONGEST OF THE PINES

MALE CONES (LEFT); FEMALE CONES (RIGHT)

LARGE, ELONGATED, SCALY PLATES MATURE BARK

REMNANTS OF CONE REMAIN ATTACHED TO BRANCH

PITCH PINE

Pinus rigida Mill.

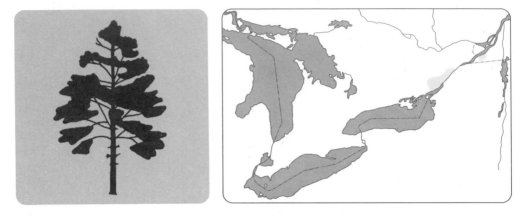

FORM—Pitch Pine is of very variable form. Open-grown trees on exposed sites have irregular crowns with many twisted, gnarled, drooping branches, most of them dead and covered with clusters of old weathered cones. The trunks commonly show clusters of closely packed leaves, borne on twigs that seldom exceed 1 or 2 ins. in length. New and old weathered cones mingle with the leaves and appear as if they are attached directly to the trunk of the tree. On good soils, when growing in close association with other trees, the trunks are straight with very little taper and support small open, but fairly uniform, crowns. The root system is not wide-spreading, and usually there is a short tap-root; old trees are commonly windthrown. This is the only native conifer that produces sprouts from the stumps of trees that have been cut, or severely injured by fire.

HABITAT—This pine is most frequently found on dry sandy and gravelly slopes and rocky ridges. It grows in sparsely stocked woodlands as a widely scattered tree, usually with hardwoods such as Grey Birch and low quality white oaks. Although Pitch Pine can survive in extremely dry situations, it makes its best growth on well-drained sandy loams. It is confined to two small areas in the upper St. Lawrence River Valley.

SIZE—Under the most favourable conditions, it reaches a height of 60 ft. and a diameter of 2 ft., but is usually about 30 ft. in height and less than 1 ft. in diameter.

LEAVES—In three's, 3- to 5-ins. long, needle-shaped, moderately stiff, twisted, blunt tipped, yellowish-green, the edges sharply toothed, often in tufts along the trunk; clusters with persistent sheaths at the base.

CONES — Egg-shaped, 2- to 3½-ins. long, almost stalkless; scales thickened at the tips, bearing rigid sharp prickles, opening when mature in autumn· and at irregular intervals throughout the winter; seeds ³⁄₁₆-in. long with a wing ½-in. long; cones usually remain on the trees for many years.

TWIGS—Stout, hairless, greenish to orange or dark brown, often in clusters on the tree-trunk; buds ½-in. long, sharp pointed, often resinous, covered with chestnut-brown, loose, overlapping scales.

BARK—Reddish-brown, smooth, becoming scaly, eventually furrowed into large, thick, irregular, flat-topped, often blackish plates.

WOOD—Moderately heavy, relatively hard, resinous; heartwood light reddish-brown, sapwood varying from nearly white to pale yellow.

IMPORTANCE—This tree is usually scrubby in Canada and is not too common; it is seldom suitable for anything but fuelwood.

NOTES—The ability of the wood to withstand alternate soaking and drying made it much sought after in sizes suitable for mill water-wheels and sluice-boxes.

OPEN AND CLOSED CONES; SCALE-TIPS
HAVE RIGID PRICKLES

NOTE THE SPIRAL TWIST

TREE
HAS AN UNKEMPT
APPEARANCE

IRREGULAR FLAT-TOPPED PLATES ON MATURE BARK

LEAVES OFTEN IN TUFTS ON THE TRUNK

RED PINE

Norway Pine

Pinus resinosa Ait.

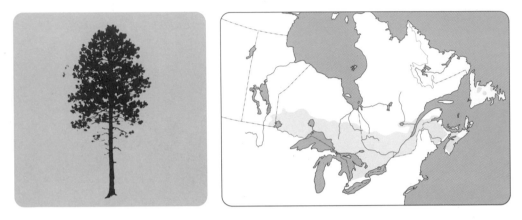

FORM—Red Pine has a straight limbless trunk with little taper and a short oval crown when growing in closed stands; the tree may be clear of branches for as much as three-quarters of its length. In open stands, leafy branches are usually retained over almost the full length of the tree, and the trunk is noticeably tapered. The crown of the open-grown tree, which is usually broadly oval or short cylindrical, is often quite irregular and has horizontally spreading or somewhat drooping branches with the foliage tufted towards the ends. The root system, which is moderately deep and wide-spreading, seldom has a well-developed tap-root.

HABITAT—This species is very uniform in its growth habits and usually does well in plantations, where it is often preferred to Eastern White Pine because of its freedom from blister rust and weevil damage; also, it will grow on soils too poor for Eastern White Pine. It is found from the Atlantic Coast to southern Manitoba, and is a characteristically dominant tree on sandy or gravelly soils in the Great Lakes-St. Lawrence Forest Region. It may form pure stands, or mix with Eastern White Pine and Jack Pine.

SIZE—Under favourable conditions, Red Pine may reach heights of 75 to 125 ft. and diameters up to 3 ft., but the usual heights are between 60 and 80 ft. with diameters from 1 to 2 ft.

LEAVES—In two's, 4- to 6½-ins. long, needle-shaped, straight, flexible, somewhat sharp pointed, shiny, dark green, the edges finely and sharply toothed; clusters with a persistent sheath at the base.

CONES—Egg-shaped, 1½- to 2½-ins. long, almost without stalks; scales slightly thickened at the tips and without prickles, opening in autumn at maturity to discharge the seeds; cones shed the following year, sometimes leaving a few basal scales on the branchlet; seeds ³⁄₁₆-in. long, dull, often mottled; seed-wing about ⅜-in. long.

TWIGS—Stout, orange to reddish-brown, shiny; buds ½- to ¾-in. long, sharp pointed, resinous with chestnut-brown, loosely overlapping, hairy scales.

BARK—Reddish to pinkish, scaly; on old trunks furrowed into long, flat, scaly ridges.

WOOD—Relatively light, moderately hard, straight-grained; heartwood pale brown to reddish-brown, sapwood relatively wide, yellowish-white.

SEEDLINGS—Six to nine seed-leaves, without teeth.

IMPORTANCE—The wood is somewhat heavier and harder than that of Eastern White Pine, and is used as structural timber. The lumber is used for the same purposes as that of Eastern White Pine. The thick sapwood is readily penetrated by preservatives; therefore Red Pine is suitable for poles, piling and railway ties. Other uses are planing-mill products and pulp.

CONES HAVE THICKENED SCALE-TIPS WITHOUT PRICKLES

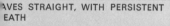

TWO SEEDS
LIE ON THE INNER
SURFACE OF THE CONE-SCALE.
(SEEDS GREATLY ENLARGED.)

...AVES STRAIGHT, WITH PERSISTENT
...EATH

...TURE BARK HAS LONG, FLAT, SCALY RIDGES

FOREST-GROWN TREES HAVE STRAIGHT LIMBLESS TRUNKS

JACK PINE

Pinus banksiana Lamb.

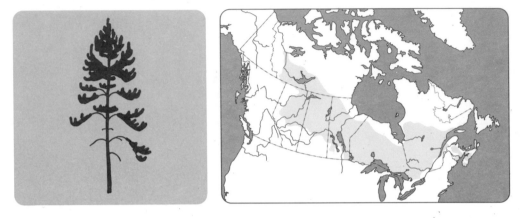

FORM—Jack Pine is quite variable in form. In the open, it has a conical open crown of ascending and arching branches and a tapered trunk. In a closed stand, the live-crown becomes greatly reduced, usually covering less than one-fifth of the length of the tree; the trunk is slender, straight, and with little taper. On poor soils and rocky sites, the tree is short, often twisted, with wide-spreading, lightly foliaged branches, some of them dead or dying, which gives the crown an unkempt appearance. In western Canada where the range of Jack Pine overlaps that of the closely related Lodgepole Pine, the two are often difficult to separate because of the many hybrids between them. The root system is wide-spreading, moderately deep and without a tap-root, except on deep porous soils.

HABITAT—Characteristically, Jack Pine is a tree of the Boreal Forest Region and grows in pure stands or in mixture with Black Spruce. Also in mixed conifer/hardwood stands it is found with White Spruce, Black Spruce, Balsam Fir, Trembling Aspen, Balsam Poplar, and White Birch. It reaches its best development on the sandy soils in a wide area north and west of Lake Superior.

SIZE—In closed stands on favourable sites, it reaches 80 ft. in height, with a straight trunk 2 ft. in diameter but, normally, it is 40 to 60 ft. in height and 8 to 12 ins. in diameter.

LEAVES—In two's, ¾- to 2-ins. long, needle-shaped, straight, or slightly twisted, stiff, sharp pointed, light yellowish-green, spread apart, the edges toothed; clusters with persistent basal sheaths.

CONES—Variable in shape, oblong to conical, asymmetrical, straight or curved inwards, 1- to 3-ins. long, stalkless, often whorled, usually pointing forward; scales with thickened tips, smooth or with a minute prickle, usually remaining closed, but occasionally opening on some trees; cones persistent on the tree; seeds ⅛-in. long, black, often ridged; seed-wing about ⅜-in. long.

TWIGS—Slender, yellowish-green becoming dark greyish-brown; buds pale reddish-brown, rounded, ¼-in. long.

BARK—Thin, reddish-brown to grey on young stems, becoming dark brown and flaky; on old trunks furrowed into irregular thick plates.

WOOD—Moderately hard and heavy, not strong; heartwood light brown, sapwood nearly white.

SEEDLINGS—Four or five seed-leaves, without teeth.

IMPORTANCE—Used in general construction and for pulp; other uses are railway ties, poles, pilings and mine timbers.

NOTES—Parboiling the male flower clusters to remove excess resin makes them suitable for eating.

Early settlers considered the Jack Pine to be an evil tree — probably because their crops failed to survive on the poor soil in which this tree sometimes grows.

LEAVES NOT TWISTED, BUT
SPREAD APART

COMMON CONE SHAPES

OCCASIONALLY,
CONES OPEN
ON SOME TREES

BARK OF MATURE TREE IS FLAKY

STAND OF JACK PINE

LODGEPOLE PINE

Shore Pine

Pinus contorta **Dougl.**

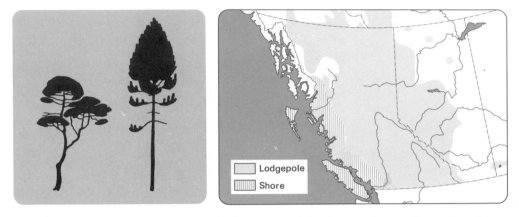

Lodgepole
Shore

FORM—This species occurs in two distinct forms: a short, scrubby, often crooked tree growing in a relatively narrow area along the coast of British Columbia; and an inland tree, tall, slender and straight, ranging over most of British Columbia, much of Alberta and in parts of southwestern Saskatchewan. Some authors consider the two to be varieties of Lodgepole Pine, the coast form being *Pinus contorta* var. *contorta*, and called Shore Pine, while the tall inland form is *Pinus contorta* var. *latifolia* Engelm., called Lodgepole Pine. Since the two have almost identical leaves, reproductive organs and cones and cannot be satisfactorily separated, they are treated here as a single species.

HABITAT—The tree grows on a wide variety of sites from gravelly and stony ridges to swamps and coastal dunes, but it makes its best growth on well-drained loams. It may be found in pure stands or in association with other species.

SIZE—The coast form reaches heights of 15 to 50 ft. and diameters of 1 to 1½ ft. The inland form is much larger and attains heights of 50 to 100 ft. and diameters of up to 2 ft.

LEAVES—In two's, 1- to 3-ins. long, often spirally twisted, needle-shaped, stiff, very sharp pointed, dark green to yellowish-green, the edges sharply toothed; clusters with persistent basal sheaths.

CONES—Variable in shape from short-cylindrical to egg-shaped and usually asymmetrical, 1- to 2-ins. long, without stalks; scales thickened at the tips, bearing curved prickles that may be shed early, usually remaining closed when mature, but occasionally opening in the autumn; cones often persisting on the tree for many years; seeds about ⅛-in. long, brownish, often mottled and ridged on one side; seed-wing about ⅜-in. long.

TWIGS—Orange or reddish-brown to nearly black; buds about ¼-in. long, resinous, reddish-brown.

BARK—On coast trees, becomes deeply furrowed into flat, coarse, flaky, dark reddish-brown plates, ¾- to 1-in. thick; on inland trees less than ½-in. thick, orangey-brown to grey, finely scaled.

WOOD—Light and soft to moderately hard and heavy, sometimes spiral-grained, often prominently dimpled on the flat grain surface; heartwood light yellow to yellowish-brown, sapwood nearly white.

SEEDLINGS—Three to six seed-leaves, ½- to 1¼-ins. long; juvenile leaves toothed on the edges.

IMPORTANCE—The inland form is an important timber-producing tree used in general construction, siding and pulp. Preservative-treated, it is used for railway ties, poles and mine timbers. The coast form is of negligible commercial importance, but is used locally for fuel.

NOTES—The Indians boiled the inner bark for food, and used this tree for wigwam poles.

LODGEPOLE PINE

TE THE SPIRAL TWIST

CONES SHOWING THICKENED SCALE-TIPS WITH PRICKLES; MALE
REPRODUCTIVE ORGANS VISIBLE ON THE RIGHT

NSE STAND OF LODGEPOLE PINE

MATURE BARK OF LODGEPOLE PINE

LARCH

Larix Mill.

This is a genus of the northern hemisphere consisting of about 10 species, three of which grow in Canada. Alpine Larch and Western Larch are western species and the Tamarack is a northern species which grows in each of the provinces across Canada. In association with Black Spruce, White Spruce, Trembling Aspen and White Birch, it forms the most northerly forests. Also prevalent in various municipalities throughout Canada are three exotics: European Larch (*Larix decidua* Mill.) and its variety *pendula* Henk. & Hochst.; Siberian Larch (*Larix sibirica* Ledeb.); and the Japanese Larch (*Larix leptolepis* (Sieb. & Zucc.) Gord.). These are planted as ornamental trees, although the European Larch has also been used to a limited extent in plantations in eastern Canada.

Generally, the larches are tall slender trees with straight, gradually tapering trunks and narrow open crowns of many irregularly arranged, slender, somewhat horizontal branches. They differ from all other native conifers in not retaining their foliage over winter. Each year their leaves turn yellow late in the autumn and are shed before winter sets in. They differ also from most other trees in that their leaves appear on the trees in two different ways on two kinds of twigs. Towards the ends of the branches and branchlets, the twigs elongate in the regular way and bear single leaves distinctly separated from each other. Farther back on the branches, many of the twigs fail to elongate and scarcely attain ⅟₁₆ in. in length; on these dwarf twigs the leaves crowd so closely that they appear to be in clusters. The annual recurrence of dwarf twigs builds up the short, stout, spur-like growths (dwarf branches) that are a characteristic feature of all larches. The only other group of Canadian trees with this characteristic is the birches, but they could never be mistaken for larch.

The leaves of the larches are spirally arranged, needle-shaped, slender, flexible and soft to touch, ¾- to 1¾-ins. long; the number in the clusters varies from 10 to 50.

The reproductive organs are of the pine type, with both male and female organs in separate cones, and with both kinds on the same tree. Unlike the pines, the cones mature in a single season. Their bracts are not fused to the scales, and may be seen extending beyond the scale-edges or, if concealed by the scales, they may be seen at the base of the cone. The cones are borne on the dwarf twigs, stand erect on short stalks and open when mature to release the winged seeds.

The bark is scaly, resembling that of a spruce tree, but, unlike spruce bark, the inner bark of larch is a vivid reddish-purple. Hemlock has similarly coloured inner bark, but its outer bark is deeply grooved and ridged, rather than being scaly.

The twigs are mostly brittle, with prominent, rounded, non-resinous, reddish buds and quite small leaf-scars, each of which shows only one bundle-scar, when examined with a lens.

The three exotic species are distinguishable from the native larches by their mature cones. These are about the same size as those of the two western species (1 to 2 ins.), but differ from them in having bracts that do not project beyond the cone-scales. The cone of the Tamarack also has short bracts that do not project beyond the scales, but its small size (½ in.) prevents it from being confused with the cones of either the western species or the exotics.

The exotics can also be separated from each other by their cones. There are 40 to 50 cone-scales on the cone of the European Larch and the seed-wings extend to their outer edges. On the Siberian Larch and Japanese Larch there are only about 30 scales to a cone, and the seed-wings are so short that they do not reach the outer edges of the scales. The scale-ends are bent back on the Japanese Larch, but are straight on the other two species.

TAMARACK

Larix laricina (Du Roi) K. Koch

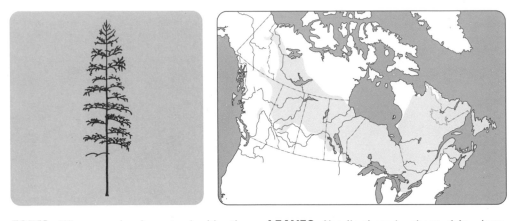

FORM—When growing in a stand with other species, this tree has a straight trunk with little taper and a small, narrow, open, conical crown with slightly ascending branches. It is not considered to be self pruning, but with the aid of other species may develop a branch-free trunk. On open-grown trees, the crown extends over most of the trunk and becomes quite irregular and often ragged looking. The root system is shallow, but wide-spreading, and provides moderate windfirmness. In the far north, Tamarack is often a stunted tree with a much reduced crown, very short leaves, and cones with quite narrow scales. This form of the species is recognized by some as var. *alaskensis* (Wight) Raup, and is called Alaska Larch. The separation of the two has not received general acceptance.

HABITAT—Tamarack is a tree of cold, wet, poorly drained places, but makes better growth on moist, well-drained, light soils. Being very intolerant of shade, it requires well-lighted situations and is rarely found in pure stands. Within its wide range it is generally restricted to sphagnum bogs and swamps, where it associates with other swamp species. Frequently it will grow in open muskegs along with Black Spruce. On better-drained areas, its associates are Trembling Aspen, White Birch, and Balsam Fir, but, as a widely spaced tree in mixture with other species, it may grow in almost any open stand.

SIZE—A small to medium-sized tree, 30 to 70 ft. in height and 1 to 2 ft. in diameter.

LEAVES—Needle-shaped, about 1-in. long, slender, soft, flexible, light green, turning yellow in late autumn, spirally arranged, single on elongated twigs, appearing in clusters of 10 to 20 on dwarf twigs, shed each autumn.

CONES—About $\frac{1}{2}$-in. long, slightly longer than they are broad, erect, on stout, short, curved stalks, approximately 20 smooth scales, light brown when mature, opening in autumn, persisting on the tree throughout the winter and the following summer; bracts shorter than the scales, visible only at the base of the cone; seeds $\frac{1}{8}$-in. long, seed-wing $\frac{1}{4}$-in. long.

TWIGS—Slender, orangey-brown, hairless; buds small, rounded, smooth, dark red.

BARK—Thin, smooth, grey when young, becoming reddish-brown and scaly; inner bark dark reddish-purple.

WOOD—Moderately hard and heavy, somewhat oily; heartwood yellowish-brown, decay resistant, sapwood whitish; frequently spiral-grained.

SEEDLINGS—Four to six slender seed-leaves.

IMPORTANCE—Used for railway ties, poles, posts, piling, boxes, crates, boat-building, and pulpwood.

NOTES—Tannin for use in tanning leather can be extracted from the bark.

In the days of wooden ships, the ship-builders prized Tamarack roots for joining ribs to deck timbers.

LEAVES HAVE TWO ARRANGEMENTS

LEAF-SCAR
ON REMAINS
OF LEAF-BASE WHICH
IS PRESSED AGAINST
THE HAIRLESS TWIG HAS
ONLY ONE BUNDLE-SCAR

BRACTS VISIBLE AT BASE OF CONE

THREE MATURE CONES; MALE ORGANS (TOP LEFT);
FEMALE ORGANS (TOP RIGHT)

BRACT MUCH SHORTER
THAN CONE-SCALE

WESTERN LARCH

Western Tamarack

Larix occidentalis Nutt.

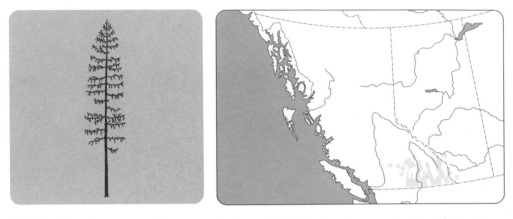

FORM—When in a stand, Western Larch develops a long, tapering, branch-free trunk over most of its height, and has a short, narrow, open pyramidal crown of nearly horizontal branches. Occasionally the crown is composed of drooping branches which extend over half the height of the tree. Open-grown trees retain foliage branches to within a few feet of the ground, but have open crowns. A deep widespreading root system with many branching laterals makes the tree quite windfirm.

HABITAT—Western Larch is a characteristic tree of the southern part of the Columbia Forest Region and is also found in adjacent parts of the Montane Forest Region within British Columbia. It grows at altitudes between 1,400 and 4,000 ft., and has been reported as far northwest as the Barriere Valley near Kamloops; a few trees are also found in the Kananaskis Valley and southward in the foothills of Alberta. The best growth is made on deep, porous, moist soils where occasionally small pure stands may form. More often, it is mixed with other species, As with all species of larch, Western Larch is very intolerant of shade and requires a well-lighted habitat for its full development; therefore, it does well in open stands. Some of its common associates are Douglas-fir, Western White Pine, Lodgepole Pine, Engelmann Spruce, Alpine Fir, Western Hemlock and Ponderosa Pine.

SIZE—This is the largest of the larches. Heights of 100 to 180 ft. and diameters up to 4 ft., or greater, are common.

LEAVES—Needle-shaped, 1- to 1¾-ins. long, slender, soft, flexible, pale yellowish-green turning yellow in autumn, spirally arranged, single on elongated twigs, appearing in clusters of 15 to 30 on dwarf twigs, shed each autumn.

CONES— Oval when closed, somewhat egg-shaped when open, 1- to 1½-ins. long, on short, stout, curved stalks, reddish-brown at maturity; cone-scales bent slightly downwards when fully open, covered with whitish hairs below; bracts with long slender points extending straight out beyond the scales; seeds ³⁄₁₆-in. long, seed-wing ⁵⁄₁₆-in. long.

TWIGS—Stout, brittle, orangey-brown, at first slightly downy, but becoming almost hairless; buds small, rounded, hairless, dark brown.

BARK—On young trees, reddish-brown, scaly, becoming deeply furrowed into flat flaky ridges; on mature trunks 3- to 6-ins. thick.

WOOD—Heavy, hard and strong; heartwood brown, moderately resistant to decay; sapwood yellowish-white, narrow.

SEEDLINGS—Usually six seed-leaves.

IMPORTANCE— Western Larch is the most important of the larches and is one of the most important timber-producing trees in western Canada. It is used mainly in building construction. Other uses are railway ties, pilings, flooring, interior and exterior finishing and pulp.

TOP LEFT: CONE-SCALE INNER SURFACE; TOP RIGHT: CONE-SCALE OUTER SURFACE;
BOTTOM LEFT: WINGED SEED; BOTTOM RIGHT: BRACT HAS LONG TIP WHICH EXTENDS
BEYOND THE EDGE OF THE CONE-SCALE

TURE BARK BREAKS UP INTO FLAT SCALY PLATES

LARCHES REPLACE THEIR LEAVES EACH SPRING

ALPINE LARCH

Larix lyallii Parl.

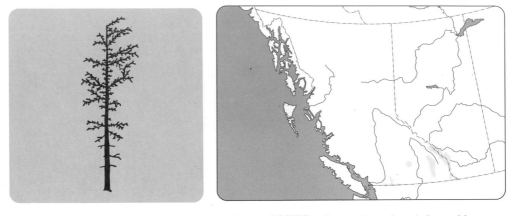

FORM—Alpine Larch is a typical timber-line tree. Generally it has a short sturdy trunk that tapers rapidly into a ragged-looking crown of irregularly spaced, gnarled branches. Many of the branches are short, some being only a few inches long, others are long, thick near the trunk and wide-spreading. On some trees, the branches may droop and have turned up ends; most are sparsely foliaged, with the leaves confined to the outer branchlets. Also, scattered along the trunk are many dead branch stubs and parts of branches, or complete branches that appear to be dead or dying, and this helps to give the tree its very ragged and unkempt look.

HABITAT—This is a tree of the high slopes in the southern parts of the Subalpine Forest Region. It is found at altitudes of 6,000 to 7,000 ft., and sometimes forms the upper timber line in the Rocky Mountains. It grows on rocky and gravelly soils in small, open, pure stands or mixed with a few other species. Some of its common associates are Alpine Fir, Engelmann Spruce, Mountain Hemlock, and the two high-altitude pines, Whitebark Pine and Limber Pine.

SIZE—A small tree seldom over 30 to 40 ft. in height and 1 to 2 ft. in diameter.

LEAVES—Needle-shaped, 1- to 1½-ins. long, slender, soft and flexible, pale bluish-green turning yellowish before falling, spirally arranged, single on the elongated twigs, appearing in clusters of 30 to 40 on dwarf twigs, shed each autumn.

CONES—Oval when closed, but with somewhat parallel sides when open, 1½- to 2-ins. long, on very short, slender, usually curved stalks (or without stalks), dark brown at maturity; cone-scales fringed with white hair and covered with whitish matted hairs below, often bent downwards when fully open; bracts with long slender points extending beyond the scales, their tips often curved back towards the scale-edges; seeds about ⅛-in. long with wings ¼-in. long.

TWIGS—Stout, tough, covered with dense, whitish, woolly down which may persist for two or more years and which ultimately becomes black; buds prominent, with long, white, matted hairs fringing the scale-edges and often completely hiding the bud.

BARK—On young trees and on the branches of older trees, thin, smooth greyish to yellowish-grey, becoming scaly as the tree ages; on old trees ½- to ¾-in. thick, divided into irregularly shaped, reddish, scaly plates.

WOOD—Heavy, hard; heartwood reddish-brown, sapwood nearly white.

SEEDLINGS—Usually six seed-leaves.

IMPORTANCE—Because of inaccessibility, Alpine Larch has no commercial value, but is of some importance in controlling run-off and erosion in the high mountains.

NOTES—Soup can be made from the young twigs of Alpine Larch.

ALPINE LARCH

BRANCHLETS AND TWIGS,
INCLUDING DWARF TWIGS,
ARE DENSELY HAIRY

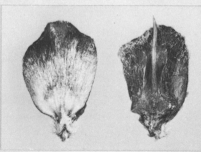

INNER AND OUTER
SURFACE OF CONE-SCALE

ALY BARK RESEMBLES THAT
SPRUCE

CONES HAVE PROTRUDING BRACTS; SPUR-LIKE GROWTHS
ARE DWARF BRANCHES

SPRUCE

Picea A. Dietr.

About 40 species of spruce have been named; seven are found in North America — five of them in Canada. Several varieties have been reported in different parts of Canada and a few of these have been named. Hybrids are commonly found among the individuals of Sitka Spruce, White Spruce and Engelmann Spruce, where their ranges overlap. Black Spruce and Red Spruce also develop intermediate forms where these two grow together, but there are no records of cross-breeding between White Spruce and Black Spruce, nor between White Spruce and Red Spruce.

In addition to the native species, two foreign species may be found in some localities. Norway Spruce (*Picea abies* (L.) Karst.) from Europe can be identified by its large cones (about 5-ins. long), its somewhat flattened leaves, and branchlets which hang vertically from the main branches. The other is Blue Spruce (*Picea pungens* Engelm.) from the Rocky Mountains in the United States, so easily recognized by its bluish, often silvery, extremely stiff, needle-pointed leaves which radiate at right angles from the twigs. Blue Spruce is used mainly for ornamental purposes, but Norway Spruce has been used widely in plantations and to some extent in reforestation programs in eastern Canada.

The spruces have long straight trunks with scaly bark, and dense narrow crowns of many pliable branches that often extend to the ground — particularly on open-grown trees. In dense stands, old trees may be clear of branches for more than half of their height, but spruce, being very tolerant of shade, is not considered to be self-pruning and often retains some live branches below the upper crown. The root system is shallow and the tree is not usually windfirm.

The leaves of all species are evergreen and remain on the tree for five or more years. They are mostly under 1-in. long, stiff, very narrow, almost needle-shaped, singly and spirally arranged on woody peg-like bases which remain on the branchlets when the leaves are shed. The leaves are four-sided in cross-section and roll easily between the thumb and forefinger (except in Sitka Spruce and some forms of the introduced Norway Spruce which have leaves that are flattened and, although remaining four-sided in cross-section, will not roll between the thumb and forefinger). The projections on the leafless branchlets are a useful means of differentiating spruce from the other conifers. Only the hemlocks and yews have somewhat similar leaf bases, but their leaves are flat or semi-circular in cross-section. Other conifers with flat leaves are the Douglas-fir (*Pseudotsuga*) and the true firs (*Abies*), but both of these have branchlets without rough projections.

The reproductive organs are similar to those of the pines, with both male and female organs in separate cones on the same tree. Unlike the pines, the cones mature in one season, have very thin scales which are not fused to the bracts and, in all species, hang from the branches. The seeds are under $\frac{3}{16}$-in. long and have a single terminal wing which detaches completely from the seed, leaving it the same colour on both sides — usually blackish. In this feature of wing-detachment, spruce seeds differ from those of the other conifers, with the possible exception of some pines.

The twigs of spruces are slender, tough, whitish to dark greyish-brown, with conical, pointed, scaly buds which are usually shorter than $\frac{3}{16}$ in. and sometimes resinous.

The wood of the different species is very similar in its properties, being light in weight, soft, moderately strong, and without a distinct heartwood. It is of great commercial importance. In volume of production of sawn lumber, spruce is first among the timber producers. It is used for general construction, mill work, interior finishing, plywood, boxes and crating. Because spruce wood is almost tasteless and odourless, it is the preferred material for food containers. Its natural light colour, low resin content, and desirable fibre characteristics make spruce the foremost species in the world for the production of pulpwood.

WHITE SPRUCE

Cat Spruce

Picea glauca (Moench) Voss

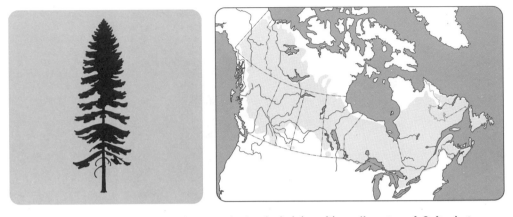

FORM—White Spruce has a uniform conical crown with branches that spread or droop slightly and extend to the ground, concealing a trunk with a pronounced taper and thin scaly bark. Quite tolerant of shade, the tree retains its leaves and branches low on the trunk but, in dense stands where there is little light, it gradually sheds its lower branches. In these conditions, the tree develops a long, slightly tapering trunk, almost free of branches, with the crown occupying about half of the tree's height. The root system is shallow with many tough, pliable, wide-spreading laterals, but the tree has only moderate resistance to wind-throw. Two western varieties have been named: Western White Spruce (*Picea glauca* var. *albertiana* (S. Brown) Sarg.) which has shorter and broader cones than those of White Spruce and a very narrow columnar crown; and Porsild Spruce (*Picea glauca* var. *porsildii* Raup) which has quite smooth bark covered with many resin blisters.

HABITAT—White Spruce is a characteristic tree of the Boreal Forest Region, although it can be found almost everywhere in Canada. With such a wide distribution, it grows in a variety of soils and climates, yet it rarely forms pure stands. The best examples of the tree are found in mixed stands on well-drained but moist, silty soils. The commonest associates are Trembling Aspen, White Birch and Balsam Fir, but it grows in mixture with other conifers and broad-leaved trees.

SIZE—On the average, White Spruce is 80 ft. in height with a diameter of 2 ft., but some trees attain heights of 120 ft. and diameters of up to 4 ft.

LEAVES—Broad needle-shaped, about ¾-in. long, stiff, with blunt ends, straight, four-sided in cross-section, green to bluish-green but often with a whitish bloom, aromatic when crushed.

CONES — About 2-ins. long, slender, cylindrical, with stiff, smooth-margined, often indented, roundish, close-fitting, light-brown scales which spread almost at right angles on open cones and are easily crushed. Cones open in autumn and fall during the winter or the following spring.

TWIGS—Usually without hairs, whitish-grey to yellowish; outer bud-scales pointed, but not projecting beyond the tip of the bud.

BARK—Thin, scaly, light greyish-brown; inner bark silvery-white.

WOOD—Light, soft, resilient, straight-grained; white, with little contrast between sapwood and heartwood.

SEEDLINGS—Five to seven thick seed-leaves; juvenile leaves toothed.

IMPORTANCE—One of the most important trees in Canada for pulpwood and lumber.

NOTES—The roots of this tree are so pliable that the Indians often used them for lacing the birch bark on canoes.

White Spruce is too aromatic for use in making spruce tea, but most of the other spruces make a palatable brew.

WHITE SPRUCE

VES ARE STRAIGHT

CLOSE-FITTING SCALES HAVE SMOOTH MARGINS

TURE BARK HAS THIN SCALES

BUD-SCALES
SHORTER THAN BUD

LEAF-BASES STAND
OUT FROM HAIRLESS TWIG

ENGELMANN SPRUCE

Mountain Spruce

Picea engelmannii Parry

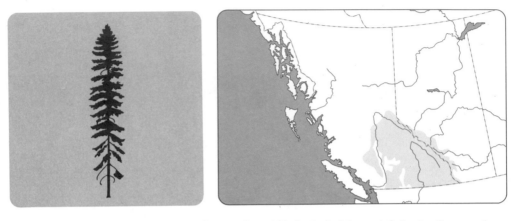

FORM—The crown of Engelmann Spruce is generally symmetrical, narrow and spire-like. The tree, being quite tolerant of shade, may have branches extending over nearly its whole length, especially in open stands and on steep hillsides. The lower branches are often drooping. In dense stands, the trees become relatively clear of branches for up to half their length, and the trunk develops without much taper. Intermediate forms between this species and White Spruce may be found where the ranges of the two overlap, and the trees in some stands may appear to be a mixture of species. Some trees seem to satisfy the description for Engelmann Spruce, others that for White Spruce, but still others — often the majority — cannot be clearly assigned to either species. These are the forms that have resulted from interbreeding, and they should be referred to simply as hybrids without any attempt being made to name them.

HABITAT—Engelmann Spruce is characteristic of the southern part of the Subalpine Forest Region, except at the coast. It usually grows at elevations of between 3,000 and 6,000 ft., but is often found along streams further down the mountains, where it makes its best growth on deep, rich, moist loamy soils. It may form pure stands, but more often is in mixture with other conifers such as firs, hemlocks, larches and pines.

SIZE— Normally reaches a height of 100 to 120 ft. and a diameter of 1 to 3 ft., but trees 180 ft. in height and 6 ft. in diameter have been reported.

LEAVES—Broad needle-shaped, about ¾-in. long, stiff, blunt or sharp pointed, curved, four-sided in cross-section, bluish-green but often with a whitish bloom, aromatic when crushed; a strong tendency to point towards the upper side and end of the twig.

CONES— Cylindrical to narrowly oval, 1- to 3-ins. long, with finely toothed, often notched, flexible, yellowish-brown, loosely fitting scales that are tapered at both ends and have rather prominent bracts. Cones open in autumn and fall during the winter or following spring.

TWIGS—More or less hairy, greyish to light brown; outer bud-scales shorter than the bud, not usually projecting beyond its tip.

BARK—Thin, broken into rather large, loose, coarse, brownish scales; inner bark silvery-white.

WOOD— Light, soft, resilient, straight-grained; white, with little contrast between heartwood and sapwood.

IMPORTANCE—One of the most important species in the Interior of British Columbia. The wood, similar in its properties to that of White Spruce, is used for the same purposes.

NOTES—The Engelmann Spruce tree has a pungent, unpleasant odour which is so distinctive that once the smell has been experienced it is a good identifying feature for future use.

ENGELMANN SPRUCE

NOTE LOOSE-FITTING SCALES ON CLOSED CONE

BRANCHLET SHOWING CURVED LEAVES

CONE-SCALE IS TAPERED AT BOTH ENDS

CROWN IS NARROW AND SPIRE-LIKE

MATURE BARK BREAKS INTO LARGE
LOOSE SCALES

SITKA SPRUCE

Tideland Spruce

Picea sitchensis (Bong.) Carr.

FORM—In the forest, this tree produces a long, branch-free, cylindrical trunk often buttressed at the base, and a short rather open crown of horizontal branches, with the uppermost ones ascending and drooping at the ends. The root system is shallow and wide-spreading. In the northern inland parts of its range, Sitka Spruce mingles with White Spruce, and hybrids between the two have been found in the Nass and Skeena valleys. Also, in the Skagit Valley in southern British Columbia, there are hybrids between Sitka Spruce and Engelmann Spruce. Some of these hybrids have been named.

HABITAT—Sitka Spruce is a tree of the Coast Forest Region. It is mostly confined to a belt along the coast — seldom wider than 50 miles — and to the borders of a few streams in the Coast and Cascade mountains for distances inland of about 100 miles, and to elevations of 2,300 ft. It is most abundant in the northern coastal forest, and on the Queen Charlotte Islands, where it makes its best growth on deep well-drained soils near streams. Sitka Spruce grows in pure stands, and in mixture with other species. Some common associates are Douglas-fir, Western Red Cedar, Grand Fir, Red Alder and Black Cottonwood.

SIZE—This is the largest of the spruces. Commonly it attains heights of 125 to 175 ft., and diameters of 3 to 6 ft., but trees up to 280 ft. in height and over 13 ft. in diameter have been reported.

LEAVES—Broad needle-shaped, about 1-in. long, stiff, very sharp pointed, straight, four-sided in cross-section but flattened (will not roll between thumb and forefinger), yellowish-green above, whitened beneath, tending to radiate at right angles from the twig.

CONES—Broad cylindrical, 2¼- to 4-ins. long, opening at maturity and falling during late autumn and winter; scales thin, stiff, elongated, rectangular, loose-fitting, pale-brown, wavy surfaced and irregularly toothed on the margin.

TWIGS—Hairless, whitish-grey to yellowish-brown; outer bud-scales blunt tipped, shorter than the bud.

BARK—Thin, broken into large, loose, reddish-brown scales; inner bark silvery-grey.

WOOD—Light, soft, resilient, relatively strong; heartwood light pinkish-brown with gradual transition into a creamy-white sapwood.

IMPORTANCE—This is one of the most important timber-producing species in British Columbia. Its great size yields a large proportion of clear lumber when sawn. It is used in general construction, ship-building, plywood, boxes, crates, sounding boards for musical instruments and for pulp. Years ago, Sitka Spruce was used for aircraft construction.

NOTES—The Indians on the west coast made baskets and household articles from the very pliable roots and smaller branches of young Sitka Spruce.

SITKA SPRUCE

UNLIKE OTHER
NATIVE SPRUCES,
THE LEAVES
ARE FLAT

BARK BREAKING
INTO
LOOSE SCALES

FEMALE CONES (LEFT); MALE CONES (RIGHT)

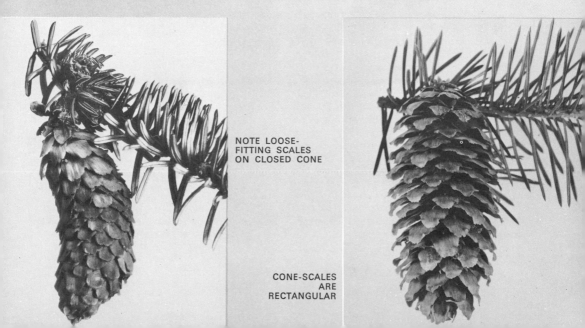

NOTE LOOSE-
FITTING SCALES
ON CLOSED CONE

CONE-SCALES
ARE
RECTANGULAR

RED SPRUCE

Yellow Spruce

Picea rubens Sarg.

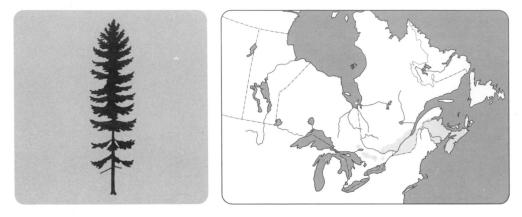

FORM—Open-grown Red Spruce develops a wide columnar or conical crown that extends almost to the ground, but in stands, the crown becomes confined to the upper third of the tree and remains widely conical. The lowest branches spread horizontally and have up-turned ends. The trunk below becomes almost clear of branches and has little taper. The root system is shallow and wide-spreading, which makes the tree only moderately windfirm. Where Red Spruce grows in mixture with Black Spruce, there are intermediate forms that result from interbreeding. These cannot always be clearly assigned to either species.

HABITAT—Red Spruce is characteristic of the Acadian Forest Region and has some representation in the eastern part of the Great Lakes-St. Lawrence Forest Region. Intermediate between White Spruce and Black Spruce in its tolerance to competition, it grows on soils mid-way between well-drained uplands and bogs. Occasionally it forms pure stands, but is more often mixed with other species. Common associates on wet lands are Black Spruce, Tamarack and White Birch. On moist but drained soils, where it makes its best growth, the usual associates are White Spruce, Eastern White Pine, Balsam Fir, Eastern Hemlock, Yellow Birch and Sugar Maple. In mixed stands, it usually grows in scattered clumps, or as widely scattered individuals.

SIZE—On the average a smaller tree than White Spruce, Red Spruce attains a height of 70 to 80 ft. and diameters of 1 to 2 ft.

Occasionally, trees may reach heights above 100 ft. and diameters of up to 3 ft.

LEAVES—Broad needle-shaped, ½- to ¾-in. long, stiff, with blunt ends, often curved, four-sided in cross-section, bright yellowish-green and shiny as though freshly varnished.

CONES—Narrow egg-shaped, pointed, 1½- to 2-ins. long, pendulous; scales stiff, toothed or rough margined, rounded or slightly pointed, brownish, close fitting but spread almost at right angles on open cones, firm and difficult to crush. The cones open in autumn and usually remain attached to the tree until late summer of the following year.

TWIGS—Covered with dense short hairs, orangey-brown; outer bud-scales shiny, reddish-brown, long pointed, sometimes extending beyond the tip of the bud.

BARK—Thin, scaly, light reddish-brown; inner bark pale olive-green.

WOOD—Light, soft, resilient, straight-grained; nearly white, with little contrast between sapwood and heartwood.

SEEDLINGS—Six or seven seed-leaves; juvenile leaves without teeth.

IMPORTANCE—The wood is similar to White Spruce and is marketed with it and Black Spruce under the common name "spruce".

NOTES—A cure for scurvy was made by boiling young twigs, adding molasses, honey or maple sugar and allowing the liquid to ferment.

RED SPRUCE

CLOSED CONE POINTED; SCALES OF OPEN CONE STIFF

LEAVES ARE SHINY

TWIG HAIRY; BUD-
SCALES LONGER
THAN BUD

BRANCHES GROW
HORIZONTALLY

MATURE BARK IS SCALY

BLACK SPRUCE

Bog Spruce
Swamp Spruce

Picea mariana (Mill.) B.S.P.

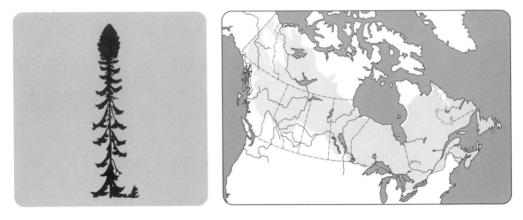

FORM—In stands, Black Spruce develops a straight trunk with little taper and without branches for much of its length. It has a narrow crown of drooping branches with up-turned ends. On many trees, cone-clipping by squirrels combined with very slow branch growth gives the top of the crown a compact somewhat club-like shape which is a distinctive feature. In the far north and in extremely cold bogs, the leaves are greatly reduced in length and the cones are about half their normal size. This form of the species is referred to by some authors as *Picea mariana* var. *brevifolia* (Peck) Rehd. The root system is shallow and the tree is windfirm only when growing in stands.

HABITAT—Black Spruce grows in many different soils and climates. In the south, it is generally confined to sphagnum bogs, while farther north it often grows on well-drained slopes and flats. It has one great advantage over many species in that, besides being able to reproduce from seed, it can reproduce by "layering". This means that the lower live branches on becoming covered by mosses or litter develop roots, and the branches eventually become new trees. Sometimes this is the only way that Black Spruce reproduces itself.

SIZE—Usually a slow-growing tree which averages 30 to 50 ft. in height and 6 to 10 ins. in diameter. Under favourable conditions it may reach heights of 100 ft. and diameters of 3 ft. In the tundra it may be dwarfed to a shrub.

LEAVES—Broad needle-shaped, ½-in. long, stiff, blunt, four-sided in cross-section, dark bluish-green, without lustre.

CONES—About 1-in. long, egg-shaped, pointed, almost spherical when open; scales close fitting, roughly toothed, purplish to dark brown, spread outwards only slightly when open, firm and difficult to crush; the cones are not shed from the tree, but open at intervals to release the seeds gradually throughout the winter; some seeds are retained within the cones for years.

TWIGS—Dark brown, covered with dense short hairs; outer bud-scales greyish, finely hairy, with long slender points that project well beyond the tip of the bud.

BARK—Thin, scaly, dark greyish-brown; inner bark deep olive-green.

WOOD—Moderately light, soft, relatively strong, resilient, straight-grained; nearly white, with little contrast between sapwood and heartwood.

SEEDLINGS—Three to five seed-leaves; juvenile leaves slender, without teeth.

IMPORTANCE—The wood, like that of White Spruce and Red Spruce, is of great importance to the pulpwood industry.

NOTES—The long fibres in Black Spruce, which add strength, make this tree a favoured pulpwood for the manufacture of facial tissues and other paper products.

LEAVES ARE STRAIGHT WITH A BLUNT TIP

TOOTHED CONE-SCALES SPREAD ONLY SLIGHTLY
ON OPEN CONE (RIGHT)

SEED IS NEARLY BLACK

TE DENSE HAIRINESS OF TWIG
D PEG-LIKE BASES OF LEAVES

MATURE BARK IS THIN AND SCALY

FOREST-GROWN BLACK SPRUCE SHOWING
SEVERAL CLUB-LIKE TOPS

HEMLOCK

Tsuga (Endl.) Carr.

The genus *Tsuga* comprises about 10 species of coniferous trees distributed in the forests of North America and of eastern Asia, from Japan and Taiwan to the Himalayas. In North America there are four species, three of which are found in Canada; of these the Western Hemlock and Mountain Hemlock grow only in British Columbia, while the Eastern Hemlock ranges from Lake Superior to Cape Breton Island. Hemlocks are not found naturally in Europe, although there is evidence that they grew there in an earlier time. Hemlock pollen has been found in peat bogs in Poland and France, and hemlock-wood fossils have been found in other parts of Europe.

Hemlock is a graceful tree when young, with a pyramidal or columnar crown, slender, heavily foliaged, horizontal or slightly drooping branches that grow at intervals along the trunk, and a flexible leader that curves away from the prevailing winds and usually droops at the tip. The crown of older trees becomes uneven, often with a few, irregular, wide-spreading branches interspersed among numerous shorter ones, some of which may have lost their foliage but remain attached to the tree for years. The trunk is rough with deeply furrowed bark and is seldom clear of branches even when the tree is growing in stands or is old; usually it has a pronounced taper. The root system is shallow but wide-spreading, and the tree is susceptible to windthrow. Seedlings have from three to six seed-leaves.

Hemlock is usually found in moist locations such as northern slopes, the borders of streams and lakes and near swampy areas. It will grow in pure stands or in mixture with other species.

The leaves of all species are evergreen and remain on the trees for three or more years. They are of different lengths on the same twig — those on the upper side being the shortest. On all species the leaves are less than ⅞-in. long, linear, flat or semi-circular in cross-section, rounded or indented at the tip, narrowing abruptly at the base to thread-like stalks that are attached to raised swellings.

The stalks are arranged spirally, but on the upper and lower sides are usually curved to make the leaves appear to be in two ranks. The way in which hemlock leaves are attached to the bases is unlike that of any other conifer, except spruce — but spruce leaves are not stalked. When the leaves fall, the woody bases remain closely pressed against the twig or branchlet, with the leaf-scars pointing forward in hemlock, but spreading at almost right angles to the twig in spruce. Hemlock and spruce trees are thus easily distinguishable by their leaf-bases, and both are readily identified by this feature.

The reproductive organs are of the pine type with male and female organs in separate cones on the same tree. Unlike pines, the cones mature in a single season and have minute bracts which are not fused to the scales. In these two features, they resemble larch, spruce, Douglas-fir and the true firs. In all hemlocks, the cones hang from the branches, open when mature to spread their scales at right angles, and release seeds which are terminally winged and dotted with minute resin blisters. The resin blisters help to make hemlock seeds distinguishable from spruce seeds.

The twigs are slender and hairy, with small, rounded, non-resinous buds.

The bark of hemlock trees is rich in tannin. Eastern Hemlock was for years one of the main commercial sources of this product. The inner bark is strikingly cinnamon-red or purplish, and the outer bark shows purplish streaks when freshly cut.

The wood is slightly harder than that of most conifers, and is non-resinous, with a distinctive fragrance when freshly sawn. The sapwood is not sharply distinct from the heartwood.

Hemlocks are among the most tolerant of trees. They can grow successfully in competition with, and in the shade of, other trees. They will stand a considerable amount of pruning, and are popular for ornamental planting in city parks.

74

EASTERN HEMLOCK

Tsuga canadensis (L.) Carr.

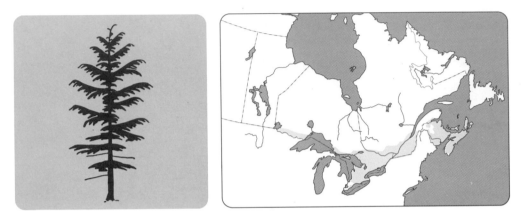

FORM—When young, this is Canada's most graceful conifer. Its branches are slender and flexible, with the branchlets forming flat sprays that spread horizontally from the trunk and droop towards their ends. The leader is generally bent away from the prevailing wind and droops slightly. The branches are heavily foliaged, extend to the ground and form a narrow pyramidal or conical tree. In contrast, the crown of old trees is generally very ragged. Even when shaded by surrounding trees in a stand, few branches fall; they remain, some alive, some dead, to give a rugged persevering appearance. The knots in the wood that result from these branches are responsible for lowering the quality of the lumber cut from older trees. This, and the rather brittle character of the wood, accounts for the relatively low value placed on Eastern Hemlock by the lumber trade. The trunk shows a pronounced taper, except in young trees. The root system is wide-spreading and shallow, and the tree is not usually windfirm.

HABITAT—Eastern Hemlock grows in different types of soil, but requires a moist cool location. It is found throughout the Great Lakes-St. Lawrence Forest Region and the Acadian Forest Region, and is often one of the dominant trees in Acadian forests. It may grow in pure stands, but more often is distributed in mixture with other species. One of its most common associates is Yellow Birch; other associates are Eastern White Pine, Red Spruce, White Spruce, Sugar Maple and Beech.

SIZE—Commonly 60 to 70 ft. in height, with a trunk 2 to 4 ft. in diameter.

LEAVES—Flat, rounded or indented at the tip, narrowing abruptly at the base to a thread-like stalk, tapering slightly from base to tip, a whitish band on each side of the midrib on the underside, variable in length on the same twig, $\frac{1}{3}$- to $\frac{2}{3}$-in. long, appearing as if two-ranked on the twig.

CONES—About $\frac{3}{4}$-in. long, widest about the middle when closed, pointed, short stalked; scales as broad as they are long, thin, rounded, smooth margined or faintly toothed, opening slightly at maturity in autumn, shedding the seeds during winter; cones remain on the tree into the following spring.

TWIGS—Slender, yellowish-brown, hairy; buds $\frac{1}{16}$-in. long, blunt, brownish.

BARK—Scaly when young, becoming deeply furrowed into broad flat-topped ridges. Freshly cut bark streaked with reddish-purple.

WOOD—Moderately light, fairly hard, low in strength; heartwood light flesh-coloured, sapwood lighter in colour.

IMPORTANCE—Used for coarse lumber, rough dimension stock, general construction, boxes, crates, railway ties and pulp.

NOTES—Hemlock is not suitable for campfires since it throws off sparks. The knots are extremely hard and will dull an axe.

LEAVES TAPER SLIGHTLY

CONE SCALES ROUNDED; SEED TRIANGULAR

LEAVES ARE STALKED

MALE FLOWERS (LEFT); FEMALE FLOWERS (RIGHT)

WOODY LEAF-BASES PROJECT
AND POINT FORWARD

YOUNG LEAVES OF NEW GROWTH

WESTERN HEMLOCK

Tsuga heterophylla (Raf.) Sarg.

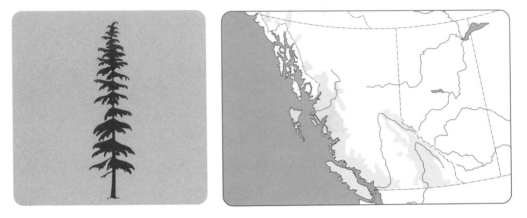

FORM—Western Hemlock attains a long branch-free trunk with a short, open, pyramidal crown when growing in the forest. In the open, the columnar crown extends from the ground to the top of the tree (with a few, coarse, spreading branches giving some irregularity) and conceals a strongly tapered, rugged trunk. The branches are slender towards the outer area of the crown, with branchlets that form flattened and drooping sprays which give a pleasingly graceful appearance. As with all hemlocks, the leader is whip-like, bends away from the prevailing wind and droops. The root system is shallow and wide-spreading, and the trees are susceptible to windthrow.

HABITAT—This tree grows throughout the Coast and Columbia Forest regions, and in the Interior ascends into the lower levels of the Subalpine Forest Region up to altitudes of 5,000 ft. It is often a dominant tree in the coastal forest, seldom grows in pure stands, and is often mixed with Western Red Cedar, Douglas-fir, Grand Fir, Black Cottonwood and Red Alder. It can regenerate well under a closed canopy and its seedlings are commonly found on rotten logs, or in partially decomposed forest litter where there is sufficient moisture. In addition to shelter from direct sunlight, plentiful moisture in both soil and atmosphere appears to be a requirement for regeneration and good growth.

SIZE—Commonly reaches heights of 120 to 160 ft. and diameters of 3 to 4 ft., but exceptional trees attain greater sizes.

LEAVES—Flat, blunt tipped or indented at the tip, narrowed abruptly at the base to a thread-like stalk, very variable in length, ¼- to ¾-in. long on the same twig, without taper from base to tip, two whitish bands below, one on each side of the midrib, appearing as if in two ranks on the twig.

CONES — About ¾-in. long, with parallel sides when closed, blunt tipped, short stalked; scales elongated, narrow, rounded at the ends, smooth margined or faintly toothed, spreading widely on opening to release the seeds in autumn; cones shed during winter.

TWIGS—Slender, brownish, hairy; buds ¹⁄₁₆-in. long, blunt.

BARK—Scaly when young, russet-brown, becoming darker with age and deeply furrowed into flat-topped scaly ridges.

WOOD—Moderately light, fairly hard and strong; whitish to dull pale brown, with little difference between sapwood and heartwood.

IMPORTANCE—Western Hemlock is one of the most important timber-producing species in western Canada. The wood is used in general construction, for siding, flooring, plywood, railway ties, boxes and crates. It is also a valuable pulpwood species.

NOTES—The early settlers named the hemlock after a European weed because of the similar odour when the needles are crushed.

CONE-SCALES ARE RECTANGULAR AND OPEN WIDELY

DROOPING LEADER IS
CHARACTERISTIC FEATURE OF ALL HEMLOCKS

E LEAVES HAVE NO TAPER

URE BARK IS
PLY FURROWED INTO FLAT-TOPPED SCALY RIDGES

MOUNTAIN HEMLOCK

Tsuga mertensiana (Bong.) Carr.

FORM—This species of hemlock varies from a low-spreading shrub-like form on exposed ridges at high elevations to a small tree, and sometimes even to a large tree when growing in favourable situations. In the open, it develops a strongly tapered trunk bearing slender branches almost to the ground; the branches usually droop and often have ascending tips. The outline of the crown is narrowly conical or pyramidal beneath a slender drooping leader, but becomes irregular and bent or twisted on old trees. In dense stands, the crown covers only the upper half or less of the tree, and the trunk below develops with a more gradual taper, and becomes virtually clear of branches. The root system is shallow and wide-spreading.

HABITAT—Mountain Hemlock is found in the wetter areas of the Subalpine Forest Region, above the Coast and Columbia Forest regions, at altitudes between 2,500 and 6,000 ft., but descends into the northern part of the coastal forest nearly to sea level. It makes its best growth on deep moist soils on slopes and sides of ravines with northern exposures. It may form pure stands or grow in association with other conifers. Some common associates are Alpine Fir, Engelmann Spruce, Alpine Larch, Whitebark Pine, Lodgepole Pine and Amabilis Fir.

SIZE—Usually from 25 to 50 ft. in height and 10 to 20 ins. in diameter, but under very favourable conditions will grow much larger.

LEAVES—Semi-circular in cross-section; about ¾-in. long, blunt tipped; upper surface often ridged or grooved; bluish-green on both surfaces; narrowing abruptly at the base to a slender stalk; of about equal length on a twig and extending all round, but usually crowded to the upper side; not appearing to spread in two ranks like the other hemlocks.

CONES—Broad cylindrical, ½- to 3-ins. long; scales slightly thickened, broad, fan-shaped with slightly roughened or toothed margins, opening widely at maturity in autumn, becoming bent back towards the cone-base after shedding the seeds during winter; cones shed during the spring or early summer.

TWIGS—Slender to stoutish, downy, reddish-brown; buds ⅛-in. long, reddish-brown, outer scales with awl-like tips.

BARK—Dark reddish-brown, divided into hard, narrow, flat-topped ridges.

WOOD—Moderately light, relatively hard and strong, close-grained; heartwood pale reddish-brown, sapwood nearly white, not distinctly separated from the heartwood.

IMPORTANCE—Mountain Hemlock is of less importance than Western Hemlock owing to its relative inaccessibility. Usually the wood is marketed with Western Hemlock and is used for the same purposes. It has some importance also in protecting steep slopes against erosion.

NOTES—Unlike most other conifers, the Mountain Hemlock does not provide shelter from the rain because some of its branches slant downwards towards the trunk.

VES ROUNDED ON THE UPPER SURFACE

CONE-SCALES BEND
TOWARDS THE BASE
ON OPEN CONE

JRE BARK HAS NARROW FLAT-TOPPED RIDGES

SOME MOUNTAIN HEMLOCKS ARE SCRUBBY

DOUGLAS-FIR

Pseudotsuga Carr.

Two species of *Pseudotsuga* are native to western North America, but there are others in eastern Asia. Only one species is found in Canada, but two forms of Douglas-fir are now generally recognized. The Coast form, which is the largest and most important species of all the Douglas-firs, grows on the islands and mainland of the west coast.

The Interior form is distributed throughout the Rocky Mountain area from southwestern Alberta and central British Columbia, south through the western United States into Mexico. It has been classified as *Pseudotsuga menziesii* var. *glauca* (Beissn.) Franco, and is sometimes known as the Blue Douglas-fir. It is characteristic of the Montane Forest Region and often dominates stands in the central and southern parts — occasionally in pure stands — but more often mixed with Ponderosa Pine, Lodgepole Pine, Engelmann Spruce, Western Red Cedar, Alpine Fir, Western Larch or Western White Pine. In the drier parts, Ponderosa Pine may be its only associate.

Although they do interbreed, there are well-marked differences between the Coast and Interior forms. The Interior form is much stockier, and seldom exceeds 140 ft. in height compared to the 150 to 200 ft. and even 300 ft. of the Coast form. It has a short tapering trunk and a long limby crown. The foliage is decidedly bluish-green and the cones, which are usually shorter than 3 ins., have bracts that are often reflexed.

Young open-grown Douglas-firs, regardless of their location, have typical narrow conical crowns extending over their whole length; but on older trees, particularly when growing in stands, the trunk is branch-free over most of its length. The relative scarcity of branches depends on the proximity of associating trees. The root system is strong and wide-spreading, which makes the tree generally windfirm, and some trees survive for over 1,000 years.

Douglas-firs are evergreen trees with single leaves arranged spirally around the branchlets. The leaves often appear to be in two ranks because the bases of the lower and upper leaves twist and spread the leaves laterally. They are linear, flat, usually grooved above and whitened beneath by several rows of closely spaced markings (stomata), and narrow at the base into slender short stalks. In cross-section, there are two resin canals on the lower side, but not within the tissue of the leaf. When shed, the stalks fall with the leaves and the branchlets show flat, somewhat oval leaf-scars that are smooth to the touch.

The reproductive organs are of the pine type, with both male and female organs in separate cones on the same tree. Unlike pines, the female cones mature in one season and their bracts are not fused to the scales, but have three prominent prongs extending beyond the scale-edges. The cones hang from the branches on stout stalks and open when mature to release the terminally winged seeds.

On young trees the bark is thin and smooth with conspicuous resin blisters. On mature trees it becomes thick and broken vertically into irregular broad ridges that are separated by deep V-shaped crevices.

Originally the Douglas-firs were classified with the *Abies* because of the similarity of their leaves to those of true firs. The accepted botanical name *Pseudotsuga* (literally "false hemlock") indicates a relationship to the hemlock, but actually there is little similarity between them. Also, in some localities the Douglas-fir species have the common names "Douglas Spruce" and "Bigcone Spruce" suggesting a similarity to spruces; but spruce is even less like Douglas-fir than hemlock. Further, Douglas-fir wood has been marketed as "Oregon Pine" — yet none of the species resemble pines.

The following easily recognized features set Douglas-fir apart from any of the other conifers. Their twigs and branchlets are smooth after leaf-fall, which should prevent them from being mistaken for spruce or hemlock. Their sharp-pointed non-resinous buds set them apart from any true fir. Their single leaves prevent them from being confused with any of the pines.

DOUGLAS-FIR

Pseudotsuga menziesii (Mirb.) Franco

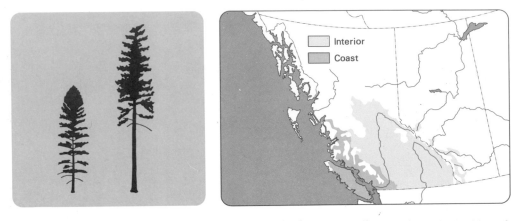

Interior
Coast

FORM—The tree is characterized by a long, branch-free, cylindrical trunk and a short, columnar and flat-topped crown. Young trees are very attractive, with narrowly conical crowns that extend to the ground. (This was the first-recognized form of the species. In some texts, it is designated as *Pseudotsuga menziesii* var. *menziesii*, following the rule adopted by botanists in 1950 that a species is the sum of its varieties and, when these are named, the species itself becomes a variety. With many species for which varieties have been proposed, the rule has not had general acceptance by botanists throughout the world, and for that reason the splitting of species into varieties has not been adopted here.)

HABITAT—Douglas-fir is found on a variety of soils, but makes its best growth on deep well-drained, sandy loams where both soil moisture and atmospheric moisture are plentiful. It is commonly a pioneer in the wetter parts of the Coast Forest Region, but, being more intolerant of shade than most other species with which it associates, is later replaced by some of the following species: Western Hemlock, Amabilis Fir, Western Red Cedar, Sitka Spruce, Grand Fir or Western White Pine.

SIZE—Mature trees reach heights of 150 to 200 ft. and diameters of up to 9 ft.; occasionally, trees may attain heights above 300 ft. and diameters of 15 ft. or more.

LEAVES—Linear, ¾- to 1¼-ins. long, often sharp pointed, soft, bright yellowish-green,

paler below, standing out from three sides of the twig and appearing two-ranked.

CONES—When mature, narrowly oval, 2- to 4-ins. long, falling after seed dispersal; scales rounded, usually exceeded by the three-pronged bracts; seeds terminally winged, two on each scale.

BARK—When young, thin, smooth, grey, resin-blistered; becoming deeply furrowed into dark reddish-brown ridges, 4- to 12-ins. thick.

TWIGS—Slender, flexible; buds conical, sharp pointed, shiny reddish-brown.

WOOD—Moderately light to heavy, hard, strong; heartwood reddish-brown, sapwood yellowish-white; marked contrast between spring and summer wood.

SEEDLINGS—Five to nine seed-leaves, ½- to 1-in. long, without teeth.

IMPORTANCE—One of the best known timber-producing trees in the world market, not only used for structural purposes (for which it is noted) but also for ship-building, interior and exterior finishing, box making, flooring, silos, veneer, plywood, railway ties, poles, piling, hardboard, pulp and barrel-making, to mention only a few of the many uses of this valuable tree.

NOTES—Descriptions on this page cover the Coast form. See page 82 for the differences between the Interior form and Coast form.

    Creosote-protected Douglas-fir piles and decking are used extensively in marine structures in Canada's coastal waters.

THREE-PRONGED BRACTS PROMINENT ON MATURE CONES

LK AND LEAF FALL TOGETHER LEAVING SMOOTH
GS

MALE CONES (LEFT); FEMALE CONES (RIGHT)

MATURE BARK DEEPLY FURROWED
INTO THICK RIDGES

FIR

Abies Mill.

The firs are a genus of trees of the north temperate regions and comprise about 40 species of which nine grow in North America. Four of these nine species grow in Canada. Balsam Fir has the most widespread range and can be found in every province; Amabilis Fir and Grand Fir are found only in British Columbia; Alpine Fir is distributed throughout British Columbia and western Alberta.

In addition to the native species, three foreign trees are often planted as ornamentals. The most common is the White Fir (*Abies concolor* (Gord. & Glend.) Lindl.) which can be recognized by its 2- to 3-ins. long, silvery-green leaves (approximately double the length of those on any native species, or either of the other foreign species). The Shasta Fir (*Abies magnifica* var. *shastensis* Lemm.) is usually planted only in British Columbia. It is identified by its four-sided leaves, and by its cones which are about 8-ins. long. The Spanish Fir (*Abies pinsapo* Boiss.) is a strikingly beautiful tree with short flat leaves about ¾-in. long, spreading at right angles round the twig in much the same way as those of the Blue Spruce (Page 62). The recognition feature for the Spanish Fir is its short flat leaves.

Firs are stately evergreen trees, with single straight trunks and narrow pyramidal crowns. The branches are regularly whorled, spread horizontally and bear branchlets in two rows to form flat sprays that droop slightly at the ends. Since the leaves are retained for several years, the crowns become quite dense and, if growing in the open, the lower branches commonly extend to the ground. In this form they have a most pleasing appearance and rank among the most imposing of the conifers. In stands, the leaves are shed slowly and usually some dead branches are retained along the trunk below the live crown — even when the trees are mature. Owing to their tolerance of shade, firs can survive as small trees for many years in the shade of other trees and still have great ability to recover from this oppression when the opportunity arises, either through the natural death or the cutting down of the dominating trees during lumbering operations.

The leaves are single, spirally arranged, mostly appearing to be in two rows along the twig (caused by a twisting of the leaf-bases); linear, flattened, sharp pointed, rounded or notched at the tip, without stalks, leaving flat circular leaf-scars when shed; two resin canals are visible in the cross-section of the leaf.

The reproductive organs are similar to those of the pines, with both male and female organs in separate cones on the same tree. Unlike the pines, the female fir cones mature in one season and have bracts that are not fused to their scales. On the mature cone, these are useful in the identification of the species. The cones stand erect on the branches and, at maturity, the scales, bracts and terminally winged seeds are shed from the central cone-axis, which remains upright on the tree into the next summer, or longer. No other native evergreen tree sheds its cones in this way.

The bark is smooth and thin, with conspicuous resin blisters on young trees; later it becomes scaly, or thick and furrowed on old trees.

The twigs are stout and somewhat brittle. They have rounded buds which are mostly covered with a waxy substance.

Usually, firs grow in stands intermixed with spruce, and often the two are cut and marketed without differentiation. Although in many respects fir is considered to be an inferior wood to that of spruce, fir trees are important in a number of ways. The wood of all the Canadian species is similar in its properties and is used extensively for pulp. In addition to its importance as a timber-producing tree, in some parts of Canada the liquid from the resin blisters on the bark is collected and marketed under the name of "Canada balsam". Various leaf oils are also valuable in the manufacture of some medicinal products.

BALSAM FIR

Abies balsamea (L.) Mill.

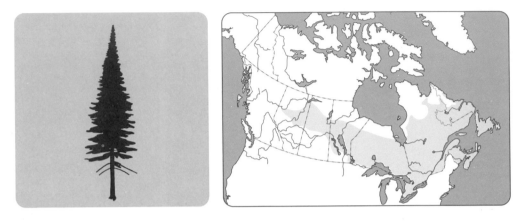

FORM—This is one of the most distinctive trees in Canada. It is nearly always symmetrical in outline, with a narrow pyramidal crown of slender horizontal branches that gradually ascend into an upper spire-like portion which is the basis for the tree being aptly referred to in some localities as "the church steeple". The slightly tapering trunk below the crown is usually covered with dead branches which persist for years. On open-grown trees, the lower branches remain alive and green foliage extends to the ground. The root system is shallow and the tree is not windfirm. One variety, Bracted Balsam Fir (*Abies balsamea* var. *phanerolepis* Fern.), grows in eastern Canada. In Newfoundland, Bracted Balsam Fir is more common than the other type and is easily recognized by its shorter leaves and protruding bracts on the mature closed cones.

HABITAT—Balsam Fir is prominent in the Acadian Forest Region, the Great Lakes-St. Lawrence Forest Region, and the eastern and central portions of the Boreal Forest Region. In western Canada it merges with Alpine Fir. With such a wide range, it is obvious that the tree is adaptable to a variety of soils and climates. It forms pure stands, particularly in areas subjected to severe budworm damage. After a budworm attack has ravaged a stand, the young Balsam Fir seedlings (which are nearly always plentiful) have a chance to flourish, and pure stands of young Balsam Fir are common in many parts of eastern Canada. The tree is also found in mixture with other

species, and is one of the most conspicuous inhabitants of the northern pulpwood forests of central and eastern Canada. Its common associates are Trembling Aspen, White Birch, White Spruce and Black Spruce.

SIZE—Usually from 50 to 70 ft. in height and 1 to 2 ft. in diameter; occasionally, trees are somewhat larger.

LEAVES—Two-ranked, ¾- to 1¼-ins. long, rounded or notched at the tip, dark shiny green above, sometimes without markings (stomata) or occasionally with a few dotting the tip, numerous lines of stomata in white bands beneath; resin canals in the internal tissue.

CONES—Oblong, 2- to 4-ins. long; bracts shorter than the scales, with rounded shoulders and a central needle-shaped tip.

TWIGS—Smooth, slightly hairy, greenish; buds ³⁄₁₆-in. long, rounded, and covered with a wax-like resin.

BARK—Smooth, greyish, dotted with raised resin blisters when young, with age becoming broken into irregular brownish scales.

WOOD—Light, soft, weak, somewhat brittle, odourless; white with no contrast between heartwood and sapwood.

SEEDLINGS—Four blunt-tipped seed-leaves, without teeth.

IMPORTANCE—Besides being important in the pulpwood industry, Balsam Fir is sawn and marketed as "spruce", and is also used as a Christmas tree.

BALSAM FIR

LVES ALTERNATE; TWIGS
STLY OPPOSITE

TWIG; LEAFLESS TWIG SHOWS FLAT ROUNDISH LEAF-SCARS

MALE (LEFT) AND FEMALE CONES

N BLISTERS CONSPICUOUS
YOUNG BARK

CONE OF THE VARIETY, BRACTED
BALSAM FIR

BRACTS OF SPECIES NOT VISIBLE
UNTIL CONE BREAKS UP

ALPINE FIR

Abies lasiocarpa (Hook.) Nutt.

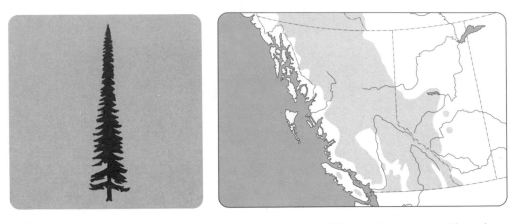

FORM—This tree is a relative of Balsam Fir and in several ways resembles it closely. By some botanists it is classified as *Abies balsamea* (L.) Mill. ssp. *lasiocarpa* (Hook.) Boivin. On open-grown trees the crown is extremely narrow and dense, with short branches that have a tendency to droop and extend down to the ground. The upper part ends in a long spire-like top. When the tree is growing in the forest, the crown is narrowly conical with a much elongated and extremely narrow top. The trunk is only slightly tapered and may be clear of branches for half or more of the tree's height. The root system is shallow and wide-spreading, and the tree is not windfirm.

HABITAT—Alpine Fir is a high-altitude tree, and is characteristic of the Subalpine Forest Region and of the northwestern parts of the Boreal Forest Region at elevations ranging from 2,000 to 7,500 ft. It is not found on the Queen Charlotte Islands and is scarce on Vancouver Island. This tree does best on well-drained loamy soils and, although it may grow in pure stands, it is usually mixed with other species. Its principal associate is Engelmann Spruce, but it can also be found with Alpine Larch, Lodgepole Pine and, in some parts, with Trembling Aspen.

SIZE—Forest trees attain heights of 65 to 100 ft. and diameters of 1 to 2½ ft., but, on exposed ridges at the timber line, it may be reduced to shrub size.

LEAVES—Greyish-green to pale bluish-green above and below, with many markings (stomata) on both surfaces, 1- to 1¾-ins. long, rounded or notched at the tip, curved upwards to stand almost erect along the twig, crowded, seldom two-ranked; resin canals in the internal tissue as viewed in the cross-section of the leaf.

CONES—Oblong, 2½- to 4-ins. long; bracts shorter than the scales with shoulders sloping away from a long, central, needle-shaped tip.

TWIGS—Stout, hairy, brownish, becoming greyish, but retaining the hairiness usually for several years; buds 3/16-in. long, rounded and covered with a wax-like resin.

BARK—Smooth, ash-grey, blotched with raised resin blisters when young, becoming broken into irregular greyish-brown scales.

WOOD—Light, soft, relatively low in strength, odourless; white with no contrast between heartwood and sapwood.

SEEDLINGS—Four seed-leaves ½-in. long, blunt tipped, without teeth.

IMPORTANCE—Used mainly for general construction and pulp; also suitable for boxes and crates. Often included in shipments of Engelmann Spruce and White Spruce.

NOTES—The Alpine Fir is a favourite tree for squirrels who tear open the clusters of large cones when the seeds ripen in September.

ALPINE FIR

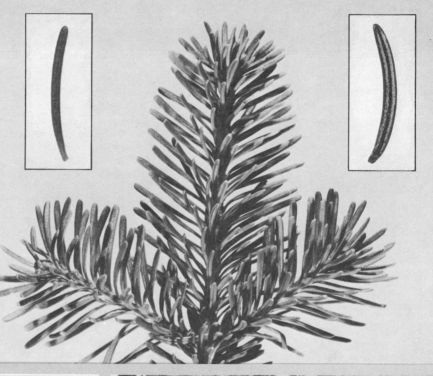

LEAVES STALKLESS
WITH MANY STOMATA
ON BOTH SURFACES

OTE NEEDLE-LIKE TIP ON BRACT

NOTE RESIN BLISTERS TYPICAL
OF YOUNG FIR BARK

MATURE BARK IS SCALY

CROWN NARROW AND SPIRE-LIKE

AMABILIS FIR

Abies amabilis (Dougl.) Forbes

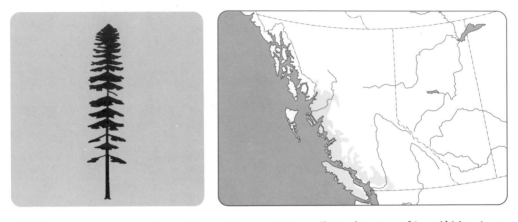

FORM—This is a slender tree with a narrow conical crown of horizontal or drooping branches and a long gradually tapering top. Mature forest trees produce long slender trunks free of foliage for half or more of the tree's height, and have cylindrical crowns that terminate in spire-like tops. As with all firs, the leaves are tolerant of shade and, since they remain on the branches for several years, the crown becomes dense. Also, the branches are shed slowly and the trunks, even in closed stands, usually have some dead branches below the live crown. The root system is moderately deep and wide-spreading, and to some extent the trees are windfirm.

HABITAT—This fir is confined to the Coast Forest Region and coastal parts of the Subalpine Forest Region. It grows on a variety of soils, occasionally in pure stands, but more often in mixture with other species. Some common associates are Sitka Spruce, Western Hemlock, Douglas-fir, Western White Pine, Engelmann Spruce and Alpine Larch. In the wetter parts of the coastal forest (except on the Queen Charlotte Islands where it does not grow) it is often a dominant tree.

SIZE—Mature trees reach heights of 80 to 125 ft. and diameters of 2 to 3 ft. Exceptional trees may attain greater sizes.

LEAVES—Shiny dark green above without markings (stomata), or with a few towards the tip (these usually only on leaves from cone-bearing branches), white-banded beneath by numerous lines of stomata; ¾- to 1¼-ins. long; those on the lower surface and sides of the twig spread horizontally, those on the upper surface pressed along the top and pointing forward; resin canals against the lower side (not in the tissue) as viewed in cross-section.

CONES—Broad at the middle and barrel-shaped, 3½- to 5-ins. long; scales as wide as they are long; bracts shorter than the scales, with shoulders sloping away from the broad base of a long wedge-shaped tip.

TWIGS—Stout, minutely hairy, dark orangey-brown; buds ¼-in. long, rounded, resinous.

BARK—Smooth, pale grey, blotched with resin blisters, eventually scaly on old trees.

WOOD—Light, soft, low in strength; creamy-white to yellowish-brown, with no contrast between heartwood and sapwood.

SEEDLINGS—Five to seven, short, blunt, smooth-edged seed-leaves.

IMPORTANCE—The wood is used mainly for pulpwood, general construction and plywood. Because of the symmetrical shape of the young tree and its attractive shiny foliage, it is sometimes planted as an ornamental.

NOTES—Amabilis Fir grows very slowly and requires up to 100 years to reach sawlog size. A tree 2 ft. in diameter is probably at least 200-years old.

NOTE THE ARRANGEMENT OF THE LEAVES

SCALY BARK IS STARTING TO SHOW

MATURE CONE ABOUT TO SHED CONE-SCALES

CONE-AXIS REMAINS AFTER SCALES ARE SHED

GRAND FIR

Lowland Fir

Abies grandis (Dougl.) Lindl.

FORM—On mature forest trees of this species, the crown is cylindrical or oval in outline with horizontally spreading branches that tend to bend downwards, but with up-turning tips. The top of the crown is roundish or dome-like. The trunk, which is only slightly tapered, is long compared to the length of the crown and is usually clear of dead branches. On open-grown trees, the trunk is completely hidden by the branches that extend to the ground and, except on very old trees, the top of the crown is pointed. The roots are deep and wide-spreading, and the tree is windfirm.

HABITAT—Grand Fir is confined to relatively low elevations in the southern parts of the Coast and Columbia Forest regions. Occasionally, it is found in pure stands but, since it grows best on deep, well-drained, alluvial soils where other species also thrive, it is usually mixed with several different types of trees. Prominent amongst these are Western Red Cedar, Black Cottonwood, Western Hemlock, Douglas-fir, Red Alder and, occasionally, Sitka Spruce.

SIZE—This is the largest of the Canadian firs. In the coastal forests, heights of 100 to 125 ft. and diameters of 2 to 3 ft. are normal, with some trees on Vancouver Island having been recorded at heights of 240 ft. In the Interior, the trees are usually under 120 ft. in height.

LEAVES—Shiny dark green above without markings (stomata), or with a few scattered towards the tip (usually only on leaves from cone-bearing branches), white-banded beneath by numerous lines of stomata; 1- to 2-ins. long, horizontally spreading in two distinct ranks on sterile branches, resin canals against the lower side (not in the tissue) as viewed in the cross-section of the leaf.

CONES—Cylindrical to narrowly oval, 2- to 4½-ins. long; scales much wider than they are long; bracts shorter than the scales, with broad shoulders that slope inwards to the base of the central tip which is little more than a small tooth and is no higher than the tops of the shoulders.

TWIGS—Slender, minutely hairy, dark orangey-brown; buds ¼-in. long, round, resinous.

BARK—Smooth, greyish-brown, blotched with resin blisters, becoming scaly; on mature trees 2- to 3-ins. thick, broken into dark-grey flat ridges.

WOOD—Light, soft, relatively low in strength, odourless; white to pale yellowish-brown, no contrast between heartwood and sapwood.

SEEDLINGS—Four to six, flat, blunt-tipped seed-leaves which are grooved on top.

IMPORTANCE—This tree is not of great commercial importance in Canada. It is used for lumber, pulpwood, plywood, boxes and crates, when in sufficient supply.

NOTES—Originally named *Abies aromatica* because of the odour from its crushed leaves.

NOTE TWIST IN LEAF-
BASES TO BRING LEAVES
INTO TWO RANKS

ALY BARK BREAKING INTO FLAT RIDGES

TWO STATELY LOOKING YOUNG GRAND FIRS
AT LANGFORD, B.C.

ARBOR-VITAE

*Thuja** L.

Of the six known species of arbor-vitae, two are native to North America and the remainder grow in eastern Asia. In Canada, trees belonging to this genus are more often called "cedar" than arbor-vitae, but the true cedars belong to the genus *Cedrus*, of which there are no species native to North America.

One Asiatic species, the Oriental Cedar (*Thuja orientalis* L.), is commonly planted as an ornamental tree because of its narrow, conical, compact form. It is distinguishable from the Canadian species by its branchlets, which are displayed in vertical planes, its thick fleshy cone-scales with the conspicuous projecting points on their backs, and its wingless seeds.

The arbor-vitae grow on a variety of soils from bogs to relatively dry ground. The best examples are rooted in moist soil that has some drainage. Since the roots are shallow and wide-spreading, however, these trees depend for support largely on the intermingling of their roots with those of other trees.

The arbor-vitae are evergreen trees with stout trunks, short branches, fibrous bark and opposite (usually scale-like) leaves. On seedlings, the first leaves produced after the two flat seed-leaves are needle-like, sharp pointed, about ⅜-in. long, and widely diverging from the stem and twig which remain visible through the leaves. After the seedling stage, the juvenile forms are replaced by leaves that seldom exceed ⅛ in. in length, are almost as broad as they are long, and appear to be pressed so close to the twig that it is completely hidden from view. These leaves are of two kinds, in alternating pairs, each pair being placed at right angles to the pair below so that they appear to be in four rows along the twig. The pair on the upper and under sides are flat and have their tips overlapping the next higher pair. The pair on the sides are folded, so that their edges clasp the two flat leaves at their level on the twig, and partially cover them.

Thuja is also spelled *Thuya*

The leaf-covered twig is thus flattened and, since the lateral twigs on a branchlet are in the same horizontal plane, the branches are formed in flat sprays. The leaves at the tips of these sprays and on vigorous leaders are not always of two kinds, are often longer than ⅛ in., and have their tips elongated into slender points.

The reproductive organs are of the pine type, with both male and female organs in separate cones on the same tree. Unlike the pines, their arrangement in the cones is opposite (rather than spiral) and in alternating pairs, like the leaf arrangement. The young cones are tiny and inconspicuous at the ends of the twigs, with the sexes usually on different branches. They have few scales; the males have four to six pairs of stamens, each one a scale-like structure consisting of two to four roundish pollen cells; the females have four to six pairs of scales, but only the middle ones bear ovules which become the seeds — usually two to a scale. The female cones mature in one season and the seeds have two lateral wings which almost surround them.

The bark is smooth and thin on young trees, but is furrowed on older trees into long, thin, flat-topped, fibrous strips.

No visible buds are formed on the twigs, which show only scale-like leaves until the cones appear. Individual leaves are not shed, but the lateral branchlets on old parts of the branches are shed with the leaves on them.

The wood is light, soft, aromatic, non-resinous, and quite resistant to decay in adult trees, but not in saplings; consequently, many trees have hollow trunks.

Arbor-vitae trees are important in many ways. They are a most valuable group for ornamental purposes, and for years have been a popular hedge plant in many parts of the country. Because of the durability of the wood, they are useful for purposes where excessive moisture is liable to cause decay.

EASTERN WHITE CEDAR

Arbor-vitae

Thuja occidentalis L.

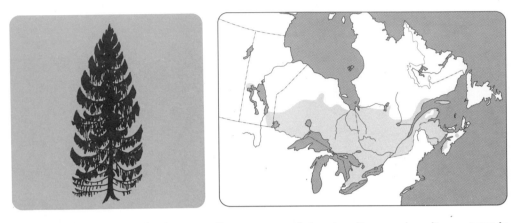

FORM—When growing in the open, Eastern White Cedar has a narrow, conical, almost columnar crown which extends to the ground. The branches bend slightly downwards before arching gradually upwards towards their tips. The foliage is dense, with an outline that has a somewhat pruned appearance. The rapidly tapering trunk is often twisted, and has a rugged appearance. The shallow wide-spreading root system is assisted in holding the tree erect by a pronounced swelling or broadening of the trunk at its base, and very often by a trunk divided into two or more secondary limbs of about equal size. When growing in a stand, the trunk is exposed for up to half the height of the tree, but usually has the stubs of some dead branches remaining well below the live crown. The crown is often irregular and, except in its upper part, is separated horizontally, which exposes uneven portions of the main trunk.

HABITAT—Eastern White Cedar is found throughout the Great Lakes-St. Lawrence Forest Region, most of the Acadian Forest Region, and in the central and eastern parts of the Boreal Forest Region approximately as far north as James Bay. It grows in swampy areas, usually where the water is not too acid, but where the underlying rock is limestone. It occurs also on very shallow dry soils that commonly cover flat limestone rock in various places within its range. It is also a common associate of Black Spruce and Tamarack in shallow sphagnum bog areas, but, there, its growth is generally very slow. It may grow in pure stands or in mixture with other species. On the moist soils, where it makes its best growth, some common associates are Eastern White Pine, Yellow Birch, Eastern Hemlock, Silver Maple, Black Ash and White Elm.

SIZE—Averaging about 45 ft. in height and 1 ft. in diameter, this tree may sometimes attain a height of 80 ft. and a diameter of 3 ft.

LEAVES — Yellowish-green, dull, ⅛-in. long, to ¼-in. long on vigorously growing twigs; show conspicuous glandular spots.

CONES — Oval, ⅓- to ½-in. long, ripening in late summer and shedding the following year.

TWIGS—Yellowish-green on both sides, in broad fan-shaped sprays.

BARK—Thin, reddish-brown, shreddy, forming narrow flat ridges on old trunks.

WOOD—Very light, soft, low in strength, with a characteristic odour; heartwood light brown, resistant to decay; sapwood nearly white.

IMPORTANCE—Valuable for posts, poles, shingles, boat-building, canoes and other uses where timber is exposed to decay, but where there is little likelihood of mechanical wear.

NOTES—On the advice of friendly Indians, *Arbor-vitae*, the tree of life, was used by Jacques Cartier to treat scurvy among his crew.

E ARE THREE LEAF SHAPES

CONE-SCALES IN OPPOSITE PAIRS, SEED HAS TWO WINGS

RE BARK BREAKS INTO LONG THIN SHREDS

OPEN-GROWN TREE HAS CROWN EXTENDING TO GROUND

WESTERN RED CEDAR

Giant Arbor-vitae

Thuja plicata Donn

FORM—This massive tree has a long narrowly conical and typically irregular crown with spreading and drooping branches that turn upwards at the ends. The trunk tapers rapidly and is flaring and buttressed at the base. The root system is shallow and wide-spreading, but strong. Old trees commonly have many dead branches in the crown and often show dead tops. Open-grown trees have foliage which extends to the ground, and which is so dense and compact on numerous branches that it hides the trunk of the tree. The crown has a neatly pruned appearance.

HABITAT—A characteristic tree in the forests of the Coast and Columbia Forest regions, Western Red Cedar is also found in the wet parts of the Montane and Subalpine Forest regions, where it is a rather stunted tree. At altitudes above 4,500 ft., it is reduced to a shrub. The best growth is made on moist areas, or alluvial sites, but the tree may be found in shallow sphagnum bogs or in drier situations on richer soils. It seldom grows in pure stands of any great extent, but generally mixes with other species. A few common associates are Douglas-fir, Sitka Spruce, Western Hemlock, Black Cottonwood and Red Alder, and, at higher elevations, Engelmann Spruce and Western Larch.

SIZE—Forest trees may attain heights of 150 to 200 ft. and diameters of 8 ft. or more.

LEAVES— Yellowish-green, shiny, ⅛-in. long, to ¼-in. long on vigorously growing twigs; usually without glandular spots.

CONES — Oval, ½- to ¾-in. long, ripening in late summer and shedding the following year; cone-scales often have minute, weak, sharp points on their backs near the tips.

TWIGS—In narrow, elongated and tapering sprays, drooping from the branches, yellowish-green with an often whitened underside.

BARK—Thin, reddish-brown, shreddy, forming narrow flat ridges on old trunks.

WOOD—Very light, soft, relatively low in strength, very straight-grained, with a characteristic odour; heartwood pinkish or reddish-brown to deep brown, resistant to decay; sapwood nearly white.

IMPORTANCE—This species is one of the important timber producers of British Columbia. The wood is suitable for use in situations favourable to decay. It is particularly valued for shingles, poles, posts, boat-building, greenhouse construction and exterior siding. It is used also for doors, window sashes, millwork and interior finishing.

NOTES—Western Red Cedar is a long-lived tree — one specimen on record was 800-years old when cut.

The Indians of the Pacific northwest carved totem poles out of this tree and used the wood to build canoes and lodges. There are records of hollowed-out canoes being over 60-ft. long and 8-ft. wide; one on display in the National Museum is over 54-ft. long and 6-ft. wide.

CONE-SCALES HAVE SHARP POINTS NEAR THE TIP

ILAR TO EASTERN WHITE CEDAR BUT USUALLY
GLANDULAR SPOTS

TWO LATERAL WINGS
ALMOST SURROUND SEED

JRE BARK SHREDDY IN NARROW FLAT RIDGES

CROWN NARROW, CONICAL AND IRREGULAR

YELLOW CYPRESS

Alaska Cedar

Chamaecyparis nootkatensis (D. Don) Spach

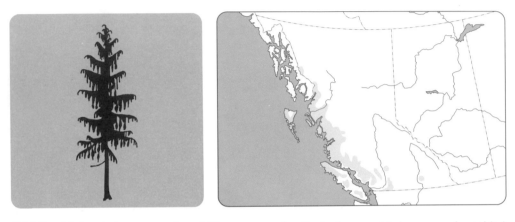

FORM—Of the six known species of *Chamaecyparis*, three are found in eastern Asia, and three in North America of which one grows in western Canada. Mature trees have a broadly buttressed and often fluted base, with a tapered trunk and sharply conical crown of spreading and drooping branches bearing loosely hanging branchlets. The tip of the crown is slender and often bent over. Above 4,500 ft., it is usually reduced to a shrub. The root system varies from shallow to deep.

HABITAT—Yellow Cypress is found in the Coast Forest Region and in the coastal parts of the Subalpine Forest Region. North of Knight Inlet it grows down to sea level, but south from there its normal habitat is higher. Near the ocean it makes its best growth in deep soil where there is plenty of moisture, and in these circumstances will usually grow singly or in small clumps in mixture with other conifers. There have been reports of its growing in the Interior of British Columbia, near Lake Slocan in the Selkirk Mountains.

SIZE—A medium-sized tree, 60 to 80 ft. in height by 2 to 3 ft. in diameter. Occasionally, trees reach 100 ft. in height, with diameters up to 5 ft.

LEAVES—Dark bluish-green, $\frac{1}{8}$- to $\frac{1}{4}$-in. long, pointed, scale-like, with the tips often diverging, sometimes pitted with glands on the surface. Unlike the arbor-vitae, the leaves are all alike; there is not a flat pair alternating with a folded pair — all are partially folded — which

makes the leaf-covered twigs appear four-sided rather than flat.

CONES — Of the pine type in general, with the male and female organs in separate cones on the same tree. Unlike the pines, the arrangement of the organs in the cones is not spiral, but opposite; the pairs alternate at right angles. Female cones are spherical, $\frac{1}{4}$ to $\frac{1}{2}$ in. in diameter when mature at the end of the second season; scales thick, four to six, umbrella-shaped; seeds with two lateral wings about twice as wide as the seeds.

TWIGS—Slender, four-sided but slightly flattened, unpleasant to touch because of the sharp spreading leaf-tips.

BARK—Thin, greyish-brown, scaly on young trees; with narrow intersecting ridges on more mature trunks.

WOOD—Light, hard, strong, close-grained, even textured, non-resinous, mild characteristic odour; pale yellow, with thin whitish sapwood not clearly distinct from the heartwood.

IMPORTANCE—The wood is used in boat-building, greenhouse construction, and for other purposes where its resistance to decay is advantageous. Used also for carving, pattern-making, hobby poker-work and canoe paddles.

NOTES—The Yellow Cypress grows so slowly that it requires over 200 years to reach a marketable size.

...VES OF ONE TYPE; TWIG NOT FLAT; CONES ROUND
...H PRICKLE-TIPPED SCALES

ON SOME BRANCHLETS LEAF-TIPS OFTEN DIVERGE

...EED HAS TWO WINGS

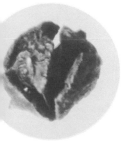

...NE-SCALES MEET ALONG
THEIR EDGES

TYPICAL MATURE BARK; NOTE
BUTTRESSED BASE

BRANCHLETS HANG LIMPLY

JUNIPER

Juniperus L.

This genus consists of about 50 species of evergreen trees and shrubs distributed throughout the northern hemisphere. The majority are of little commercial importance because of their small size and irregular trunks. About 15 species are native to North America; four of them grow in Canada.

Of the Canadian species only two reach tree size. One of them, the Rocky Mountain Juniper, is confined to the mountainous area of the west; the other, the Eastern Red Cedar, is found in the southern parts of Ontario and Quebec. These trees are difficult to tell apart but, since their ranges are so widely separated in Canada, they are not likely to be mistaken. The other Canadian junipers, although only of shrub size, are liable to be confused with the tree species since they are distributed across Canada from coast to coast. For that reason, their main identifying features are included here. The Common Juniper (*Juniperus communis* L.), which is a very variable species, differs from the others in having needle-like leaves that are about ½-in. long and arranged in three's. Usually its fruit takes three years to ripen. Creeping Juniper (*Juniperus horizontalis* Moench) has very long wide-spreading branches that trail over the ground, and most of the leaves are scale-like.

The two tree species have compact, narrowly conical or pyramidal crowns with irregular branches, and branchlets that do not form flat sprays like the arbor-vitae. The leaves on young trees, and on fast-growing shoots of older trees and seedlings, are awl-shaped with needle-like points, similar to those of the shrub *Juniperus communis*. They are opposite in pairs, or in three's, with their tips spreading widely from the twigs so that the branches bearing them are very prickly to handle, particularly when the leaves are dry. When the needle-shaped leaves have numerous closely spaced markings (stomata), they appear silvery and give the branches that bear them a whitish-green hue. The mature leaf is scale-like, $\frac{1}{16}$- to $\frac{1}{8}$-in. long; usually each has a resin gland or pit on its outer surface. These leaves are all alike — partially folded. They are in opposite, alternating pairs covering the twigs completely; each twig is four-sided like the *Chamaecyparis*, but without any flatness. They are quite unlike the flat twigs of the arbor-vitae.

The reproductive organs are of one sex; the male and female organs are in different cones and are similar in the arrangement of their parts to those of the arbor-vitae. Unlike the arbor-vitae and most other conifers, the two kinds of cones are usually on separate trees. The female cones mature into pea-sized, fleshy, berry-like fruits containing wingless seeds — quite unlike any other conifer. The "berries" are borne in large numbers on vigorous shoots of the female trees and ripen in one to three seasons, depending on the species. They are distinctly bluish or blue-black, often with a whitish bloom, and remain on the branches throughout the winter. They have a unique, sweetish, resinous taste and are used in flavouring some foods. They also provide winter food for various kinds of birds, which in turn assist in the distribution of the seeds.

The bark of most species is thin and fibrous and separates into long narrow strips or scales. The wood varies from soft to hard, is finely textured, durable, pleasantly fragrant and easy to work. It is used mainly for chests, wardrobe closet lining, pencils and carving. Locally it may be used for fence posts.

The fruit of certain species is used to flavour gin, which apparently gets its name from *genièvre* — a French word meaning "juniper berry". In India a species of juniper is burned as incense, and the berries of at least three North American junipers are quite palatable when used in cakes.

A great many horticultural varieties from both native and foreign species have been developed and are planted for ornamental purposes. Many of them are noted for their ability to survive and grow on dry sites.

EASTERN RED CEDAR

Juniper

Juniperus virginiana L.

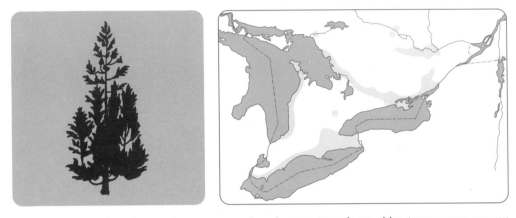

FORM—This juniper has a dense crown of short, slender, ascending branches and a narrowly pyramidal or columnar shape. On old trees, the crown becomes open and irregular. The trunk tapers rapidly, and has an irregular cross-sectional outline. The root system is usually deep where soil depth permits. The commonest form of Eastern Red Cedar in Canada is *Juniperus virginiana* var. *crebra* Fern. & Griscom; a columnar type with strongly ascending branches and noticeably pointed leaves that overlap slightly.

HABITAT—Eastern Red Cedar grows sparingly in the Deciduous Forest Region and in the southern parts of the Great Lakes-St. Lawrence Forest Region, where it is usually found on rocky and gravelly ridges or on dry sandy soils. In some places within its range, it will invade relatively poor abandoned farmland and grow there as a scattered tree or in varying-sized clumps. Although it grows well on poor farmland, the Eastern Red Cedar makes its best growth on sandy loams of limestone origin. Occasionally it can be found in rather small pure stands.

SIZE—Seldom more than 30 ft. in height and 8 ins. in diameter. In exposed situations, reduced to a low shrub.

LEAVES—Scale-like, with or without glandular pits on the back, $\frac{1}{16}$-in. long, dark bluish-green, successive pairs alike, overlapping and covering the twigs in four rows and forming four-sided branchlets. On young trees and on

vigorous growth on older trees, some narrow needle-like leaves of about $\frac{1}{2}$ in. in length and not overlapping may be scattered in whorls of three, or in two's; this type has no glandular pitting on the back.

CONES—Almost circular, $\frac{1}{8}$ to $\frac{1}{4}$ in. in diameter, green and fleshy when fully grown, ripen the first autumn, dark blue with a whitish bloom and firm when mature, containing one or two wingless seeds, rarely more, not opening nor breaking up to release the seeds.

TWIGS—Slender, not flattened, bluish-green on all four sides (not forming flat sprays); winter buds minute, without scales; branchlets turn coppery or yellowish-brown in winter.

BARK—Thin, fibrous, reddish-brown, separating into long, narrow, shreddy strips.

WOOD—Moderately heavy and moderately hard, low in strength, strongly aromatic; heartwood bright purplish-red to dull red, resistant to decay; sapwood nearly white.

IMPORTANCE—The wood is usually of small dimensions and knotty, used mainly for cedar chests, closet lining, pencils, carving and small ornamental work. The foliage is sometimes distilled for the production of "cedar oils". The tree is often cultivated in various forms for use as an ornamental.

NOTES—French settlers called this tree *baton rouge*, meaning "red stick". Finding the same tree in Louisiana, they applied the name to the state capital.

TYPICAL BRANCH WITH TWO TYPES OF LEAVES

LARGEMENT OF SCALE-LIKE LEAVES   ENLARGEMENT OF NEEDLE-LIKE LEAVES   SECTIONED FRUIT SHOWING WINGLESS SEEDS

FRUIT COVERED WITH A WHITISH BLOOM

THE TRUNK TAPERS RAPIDLY

ROCKY MOUNTAIN JUNIPER

Juniperus scopulorum Sarg.

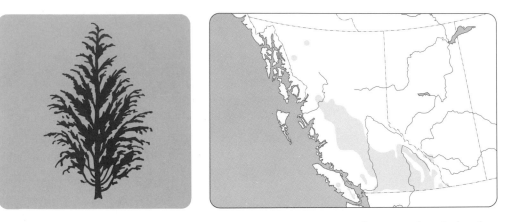

FORM—The Rocky Mountain Juniper, when growing in the open, has a rather open coarsely branched crown with long ascending lower branches coming from near the base of the trunk, and short partly horizontal and partly ascending ones in the upper part of the crown. The outline is irregularly conical with a shaggy appearance, and the tree is often rather scrubby looking. The trunk is short and often divided at the base into two or more stems. On protected sites, and when growing in a stand, the crown is slender, often with drooping branches, with its lower part made up of many dead and partially shed branches.

HABITAT—This tree is found in the foothills of southern Alberta and westward into southern British Columbia in the Montane Forest Region and the driest parts of the Coast Forest Region. Generally looked upon as a mountain tree, it also grows near sea level within the coastal forest. It is most commonly found on dry rocky or sandy soils but, like most trees, makes better growth on the moist, well-drained, loamy soils within its range. It does well in moist rocky canyon bottoms and along shores of streams and lakes when there is little competition from other trees. It may form pure but open stands, or grow in mixture with other species such as Douglas-fir and Ponderosa Pine.

SIZE—The largest of the Canadian junipers, although usually a small tree up to 30 ft. in height and 1 ft. in diameter, it has been known to exceed 70 ft. in height and reach

3 ft. in diameter. On poor sites it is often reduced to shrub size.

LEAVES—Scale-like, faintly glandular on the back, ⅛-in. long, usually pale yellowish-green, successive pairs alike, barely overlapping but covering the twigs in four rows. On vigorously growing branches some needle-like leaves about ½-in. long may be scattered in two's or whorls of three, but these leaves do not have glandular pitting on the back.

CONES—Ripen in the second autumn; thus two generations of cones may be on the same tree. Mature cones slightly larger than those of Eastern Red Cedar and up to ⅓ in. in diameter.

TWIGS—Rather coarse, pale yellowish-green to whitish-green; branchlets not greatly different in colour in winter than in summer.

BARK—Thin, fibrous, reddish- or greyish-brown, divided into flat-topped, interlacing, shreddy strips.

WOOD—Moderately heavy and moderately hard, low in strength, strongly aromatic; heartwood reddish-brown, often streaked with white, resistant to decay; sapwood nearly white.

IMPORTANCE—This tree is too scattered to be of any commercial importance in Canada. It is useful in preventing erosion on rocky and gravelly slopes and is suitable for ornamental planting on dry sites.

NOTES—The wood is excellent for the manufacture of pencils.

ROCKY MOUNTAIN JUNIPER

DETAIL OF GLANDULAR PITTING

NCH WITH MANY LEAF-
COVERED TWIGS

ENLARGEMENT OF SCALE-LIKE
LEAVES AND FRUIT

BARK DIVIDING INTO THIN SHREDDY STRIPS

GENERATIONS OF CONES ARE EVIDENT; INSERT SHOWS
OSITE ARRANGEMENT OF SCALES

LOWER BRANCHES SPREADING WIDELY BELOW
IRREGULAR CROWN

WESTERN YEW

Pacific Yew

Taxus brevifolia Nutt.

FORM—Two species are native: the Canada Yew, commonly known as Ground Hemlock (*Taxus canadensis* Marsh.); and Western Yew. The former is a low-spreading shrub of the forest floor, which grows in colonies but never reaches tree size. It is mentioned here only because of its widespread occurrence and similarity in foliage and fruit to the tree species. Both may be found as shrubs, but the two are not liable to be confused since Ground Hemlock does not grow west of Manitoba. In the tree form, Western Yew has a conical crown composed of slender horizontally spreading branches with flat or slightly drooping branchlets, and a trunk that is often twisted and fluted. Two foreign species often seen in ornamental settings are English Yew (*Taxus baccata* L.) and Japanese Yew (*Taxus cuspidata* Sieb. & Zucc.). Both have very dark green leaves that are slightly broader than the native species.

HABITAT—Western Yew does not form pure stands. It thrives generally as a scattered tree in the understory of the larger conifers of the Coast and Columbia forests. It grows best on moist flats along streams. At higher elevations, it is reduced to a low-spreading shrub.

SIZE—Usually a small tree 15- to 25-ft. high and with diameters of 4 to 6 ins., Western Yew has been reported reaching heights of up to 45 ft.

LEAVES—Linear, flat, about 1-in. long, spirally arranged, twisted to appear two-ranked, dark yellowish-green above, paler green below, sharp pointed, tapered at the base to a short slender stalk; remain attached and function as leaves for more than one year.

CONES—One-sexed; male and female usually on separate trees; males minute, in stalked, round clusters of six to twelve thread-like stamens; females, a single ovule at the top of several small scales, ripening the same autumn into a single dark-bluish seed, ⅓-in. long, surrounded but not completely covered by a red cup-shaped fleshy body.

TWIGS—Slender, hairless, green, becoming dark reddish-brown in their second season; buds minute, rounded, with thin, closely overlapping scales.

BARK—Very thin, scaly, dark reddish or purplish.

WOOD—Reddish to orange with yellow sapwood; heavy, hard, strong, resilient, nonresinous, decay-resistant.

SEEDLINGS—Two short, flat, sharp-pointed seed-leaves.

IMPORTANCE—Although of only minor commercial importance, yew is used for canoe paddles, tool handles and carving; it is prized for bows used in archery.

NOTES—The leaves of yew are poisonous to horses and cattle, especially when cut and piled and allowed to rot.

Branches of the yew were used in ancient times to symbolize bereavement.

The stringy supple underbark is sometimes used for braiding and weaving.

WESTERN YEW

NOTE TWIST
ON LEAF-STALKS

OPEN-TOPPED FLESHY
BODY SURROUNDS SINGLE SEED

NCHES SPREAD HORIZONTALLY

DECIDUOUS TREES

WILLOW

Salix L.

This is a genus of over 250 species which are generally confined to the northern hemisphere. About 75 species grow in North America and most can be found in Canada. The group includes tiny arctic plants, a large representation of shrubs, and several trees. A few of the native species that regularly reach tree size may fail to get beyond shrub size in many places within their range.

Willows are usually thought of as having an association with swamps, riverbanks and streams. As a group they do require ample moisture, but a few are regularly found on well-drained upland soils.

The willows are easily separated from all other native broad-leaved trees. With few exceptions, their leaves are long and narrow, pointed at both ends, and have short stalks in relation to the length of the leaf-blades. At the base of the leaf-stalks, there are two small leaf-like structures (stipules) which may remain attached throughout the summer. The leaves are mostly toothed with fine single teeth, and are arranged alternately on the twigs. In winter, willows can be identified by their bud-scales. Willows, and the Sycamore (*Platanus occidentalis* L.), are the only native trees among those with alternately arranged leaf-scars having buds with only one bud-scale. In addition, the bark of a willow has a peculiarly bitter taste.

The species are often difficult to separate however, because definite identification is usually based on differences in the flowers and fruit. Not only are these features found on the tree for a short time, but the flowers are of two sexes, with males and females on different trees. A given tree, therefore, has only one kind of flower, and the trees that have male flowers never bear fruit. In addition, there are many hybrids among the species.

The flowers appear in early spring before or with the leaves. They are arranged along slender stems (like the flowers of the poplars) but with stems erect, not hanging limply as they do on poplars.

The fruits are also similar to those of the poplars. Each is a small pod that splits into two parts, when mature, to release minute seeds surrounded by tufts of long, white, silky hairs.

The twigs are usually slender and flexible, or often quite brittle and easily broken. In a few species they are long, whip-like and tough. Both the twigs and the buds are variable in colour, with muted yellow and orange predominating. The twigs bear only lateral buds, and these are pressed against the stems.

Willow roots are close to the surface of the soil and divide into a multitude of rootlets.

The wood is light and soft, but tough and shock-resistant, which makes it suitable for the manufacture of many useful products, though few trees attain a large enough size to achieve commercial importance. A few species are used locally in basket making. In reclamation work, however, willows achieve some recognition, because they can be propagated easily from cuttings and grow rapidly. Both are attributes which make them eminently suitable for ornamental planting—but exotic rather than native species are favoured by most landscape gardeners.

Among the commonest introduced species are the Golden Willow (*Salix alba* var. *vitellina* (L.) Stokes) with its bright yellow branchlets in winter and its narrow, long-pointed, silver-green leaves in summer; Weeping Willow (*Salix babylonica* L.) readily identified by its handsome weeping mantle of slender drooping branchlets; Crack Willow (*Salix fragilis* L.) named for the ease with which its branchlets break off and litter the ground following storms; and Bayleaf Willow (*Salix pentandra* L.) one of the handsomest trees with its shiny dark green foliage and golden-yellow flower clusters in spring. All are of European origin.

The Russian-olive (*Elaeagnus angustifolia* L.), a member of the *Oleaster* family, is sometimes mistaken for a willow. It is distinguishable by the dense coating of glistening silvery scales on its leaves and branchlets, and by the single dash-like mark on the leaf-scar, in contrast to the three marks on willow leaf-scars.

WILLOWS

Salix L.

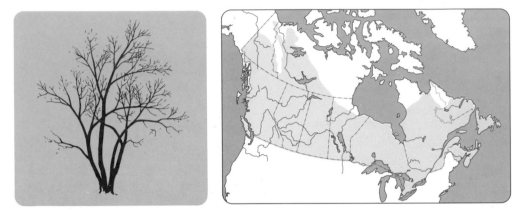

INTRODUCTION—Although there are approximately 75 different species of willow in Canada, only eight normally attain tree size, and one of these is only shrub size in all but two provinces.

BLACK WILLOW—*Salix nigra* Marsh. is the common willow of moist ground in the forests of Ontario and east to the Atlantic Coast. By some authors, it is considered to be the largest North American species. The leaf is about 3-ins. long by ½-in. wide and narrows gradually from above the middle to a long point, green on both surfaces, very finely toothed.

SHINING WILLOW—*Salix lucida* Mühl. is a small tree which is found from central Saskatchewan eastwards to Newfoundland. The leaf is about 4½-ins. long by 1¼-ins. wide, finely toothed, with a long drawn-out tip; leaf surfaces, like the twigs, are bright shiny green.

PEACHLEAF WILLOW—*Salix amygdaloides* Anderss. is perhaps the largest of the native willows. In Manitoba and Ontario, it attains heights of up to 40 ft., but elsewhere across Canada it is usually a shrub. The leaf is about 4-ins. long by 1-in. wide, with a long tip, yellowish-green above, much paler beneath, finely toothed.

BEBB or BEAKED WILLOW—*Salix bebbiana* Sarg. is probably the commonest of the tree-size willows, since its range extends all across Canada. The leaf is notably variable, about 2½-ins. long and, for its length, broadest

of all the willows, blunt or short tipped, with fine hairs, conspicuously veined beneath, sparsely toothed or without teeth.

PUSSY WILLOW—*Salix discolor* Mühl. is a small tree which usually grows in clumps from Alberta eastwards to Newfoundland. The leaf is about 3½-ins. long by 1¼-ins. wide, with a short tip, whitened and hairless beneath except when unfolding; may have a few rounded teeth, or be almost without teeth.

PACIFIC WILLOW—*Salix lasiandra* Benth. is a small tree which is distributed from Alberta to the Pacific Coast. The leaf is about 4½-ins. long by 1-in. wide, with a long drawn-out tip, dark green and shiny above, pale below, sometimes slightly hairy, finely toothed.

SCOULER WILLOW—*Salix scouleriana* Barratt is a small tree which can reach heights of 30 ft. over parts of its range from Saskatchewan to British Columbia. The leaf is blunt tipped, about 3-ins. long, tapering from above the middle to the base, a few teeth.

HOOKER WILLOW—*Salix hookeriana* Barratt is a small tree which grows to heights of 30 ft. and diameters of up to 1 ft. on Vancouver Island, adjacent shores and southward. The leaf is about 3-ins. long by 1½-ins. wide, with a blunt or rounded tip, whitish hairy beneath, obscurely toothed.

NOTES—The wood of the Black Willow is used for making polo balls.

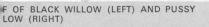

F OF BLACK WILLOW (LEFT) AND PUSSY
LOW (RIGHT)

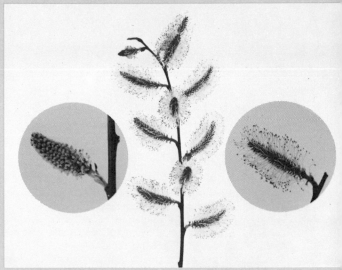

MALE FLOWERS; IMMATURE (LEFT); MATURE (RIGHT)

FEMALE FLOWERS;
IMMATURE (LEFT);
MATURE (RIGHT)

MMER TWIG SHOWING LEAF STIPULES
BUD ARRANGEMENT

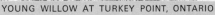

YOUNG WILLOW AT TURKEY POINT, ONTARIO

POPLAR

Cottonwood, Aspen

Populus L.

Poplars are widely distributed throughout the northern hemisphere, chiefly in the temperate zone. About 35 species have been named, of which six are native to Canada. Previous editions have usually included a seventh, Lanceleaf Cottonwood (*Populus* X *acuminata* Rydb.), but, being a hybrid, it is now deleted. The poplars are among the best-known trees because they grow in every province; in parts of the prairies, they are the only trees.

In addition to the native species, some introductions and a few hybrids are widely planted for ornamental purposes, wood production, or (especially in the prairie provinces) for windbreaks. Of these, one of the commonest is European White, or Silver, Poplar (*Populus alba* L.) which appears in several varieties. It is known by the dense, white, woolly hairs that cover the undersurface of its lobed leaves and coat the twigs and buds. Another distinctive introduction is the Lombardy Poplar (*Populus nigra* var. *italica* Muenchh.) with its spire-like crown and almost vertical branches. The Carolina Poplar (*Populus* X *canadensis* Moench), a fast-growing hybrid often planted along city streets and to a limited extent in plantations, is another common introduction. In many of its features, it appears to be midway between the Lombardy Poplar and the Eastern Cottonwood (*Populus deltoides* Bartr.) which grows in eastern Canada. In form of tree and shape of leaf, it resembles the Eastern Cottonwood, but its twigs and buds more closely resemble those of the Lombardy Poplar. A less well-known poplar is Balm-of-Gilead (*Populus candicans* Ait.) which is occasionally found as an ornamental. It resembles the native Balsam Poplar, but has a much broader crown and leaves that are almost heart-shaped, hairy beneath, with the hairs spreading down the leaf-stalks.

Poplars are fast-growing short-lived trees which shed their leaves each autumn. They are supported by wide-spreading shallow root systems. Most of the species propagate chiefly by means of suckers that arise from roots near the surface of the ground — a characteristic that is of great importance in the natural regeneration of poplar on cut-over and burned-over areas. A few species sprout readily from stumps. Vegetative reproduction results in the development of large numbers of individuals with identical characteristics. When nurseries require a poplar that is difficult to reproduce from seed or is of an unusual variety, cuttings taken from the roots, twigs or branchlets of the desired type are used as new stock.

The leaves of the native species are alternate, simple, single toothed, long-stalked, and usually have a few variable-sized, seldom straight, irregularly spaced veins spreading from a prominent midrib. Leaves on adult trees are generally reliable for identifying the different species, but juvenile trees often have a different form of leaf which makes identification by leaves alone less reliable.

The flowers are quite small, almost stalkless and of one sex on an individual tree. Several flowers are arranged along flexible stems to form single-stemmed clusters that hang limply like caterpillars from the branchlets. They appear before the leaves unfold and, when shed, whole clusters fall — not the individuals within the clusters.

The fruit is mature by the time the leaves are fully grown. It consists of a tiny pod that splits into two, three or four parts to release minute seeds bearing long, white buoying hairs that assist them along when airborne.

Poplars are easily recognized in winter by their buds. The lateral ones are arranged in several rows along the twig and, unlike any other native tree with alternate leaf-scars, have their lowest bud-scale placed directly above the leaf-scar — not off to the side.

The bark on young trees is whitish-green or yellowish-green and smooth. On older trees it becomes greyish-green to brownish, and is furrowed on most species.

The wood is light in weight, soft and with inconspicuous growth rings. It is used for veneer, lumber, boxes, small woodenware and barrels for dry goods. As a pulpwood species, poplar ranks high among the broadleaf trees.

TREMBLING ASPEN

Populus tremuloides Michx.

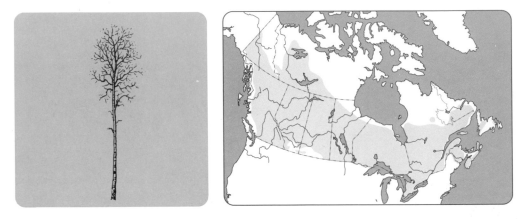

FORM—This is a slender and graceful tree with a long cylindrical trunk and a short rounded crown. The trunk has little taper and for most of its length is branch-free and smooth. The root system is shallow, very wide-spreading, and commonly produces root suckers. Following disturbances that are favourable to the development of root suckers (such as fire or logging) the Trembling Aspen may produce suckers in great abundance. Reproduction by root suckers is the main natural method of propagation of this species, and extensive forests composed mainly of Trembling Aspen have been developed in this way.

HABITAT—Trembling Aspen grows throughout the forested areas of Canada. It is found on almost all soils, but makes its best growth on well-drained, moist, sandy or gravelly loams. As a young tree, it grows in pure stands in many areas but, being quite intolerant of shade, is usually succeeded by more tolerant conifers and hardwoods. In many places Trembling Aspen has acted as a "nurse tree" to the species that later replaced it. It occurs also in mixed stands, and is a prominent constituent of the northern pulpwood forest in which White Spruce, Black Spruce, Balsam Fir, White Birch, Balsam Poplar and Jack Pine are common associates.

SIZE—A tree averaging 40 to 60 ft. in height and 8 to 10 ins. in diameter, but may attain heights of 90 ft. and diameters of 2 ft., or more.

LEAVES—Nearly circular, with an abrupt short sharp tip, 1½ to 2 ins. in diameter, fine irregular teeth on the margin, rounded at the base, deep green above, paler below, without hairs; stalk flattened, slender, usually longer than the leaf-blade which trembles in a breeze.

FRUIT—Pods narrowly conical, without hairs, about ¼-in. long, splitting into two parts to discharge the seeds, crowded on slender flexible stems.

TWIGS—Slender, shiny, brownish-grey, round in cross-section; end bud ¼-in. long, slender, conical, sharp pointed, dark reddish-brown, without hairs; lateral buds similar to the end bud but slightly smaller and with the tips curving inwards, not gummy or fragrant.

BARK—Smooth with a waxy appearance, pale green to almost white, with age becoming grey and furrowed into long flat ridges.

WOOD—Moderately light, soft, relatively low in strength; heartwood greyish-white, not clearly defined; sapwood nearly white.

IMPORTANCE—Used mainly for pulpwood. Occasionally, lumber is cut for boxes, crates, excelsior and matches; some selected logs are used for veneer and plywood.

NOTES—In several languages, the local name for Trembling Aspen translates as "woman's tongue"! The Indians call it "noisy leaf".
There are records of the early settlers having extracted a quinine-type drug from the intensely bitter-tasting inner bark.

STALK USUALLY LONGER THAN ROUNDED
LEAF-BLADE

MALE (LEFT) AND FEMALE FLOWER CLUSTERS

FRUIT PODS RELEASE BUOYANT SEEDS (INSERT)

TYPICAL STAND

TWIG WITH OPENING FLOWER BUDS;
LOWEST BUD-SCALE ABOVE
LEAF-SCAR (INSERT)

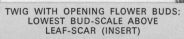

BARK OF OVER-MATURE TREE

LARGETOOTH ASPEN

Populus grandidentata Michx.

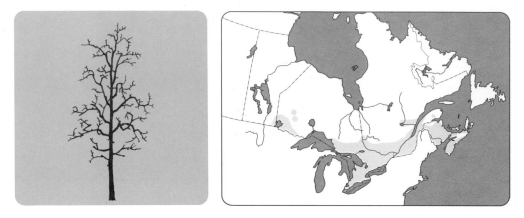

FORM—The crown of this tree is oval, but is usually quite uneven with a few irregular, coarse branches. The trunk is short and tapered. When crowded, the trunk is straight and slender and may extend over two-thirds of the height of the tree; the crown then becomes short and rounded. The Largetooth Aspen has a shallow root system, and root suckers are produced in abundance when conditions for their development are favourable. Like Trembling Aspen, the Largetooth Aspen depends mainly on root suckers for reproduction.

HABITAT—The range of Largetooth Aspen is not as widespread as that of Trembling Aspen, Largetooth Aspen being confined to the moister soils within the Great Lakes-St. Lawrence, Acadian, and Deciduous Forest regions. It will grow on dry, sandy or gravelly soils, but generally as a rather scrubby and small tree. It makes its best growth on moist fertile soils. Pure stands of limited size are found, but more often the tree grows in mixture with Trembling Aspen, White Birch, Eastern White Pine, Balsam Fir, White Spruce, willows and alders. Being intolerant of shade, it eventually loses its position in a mixed stand unless there is some disturbance (such as a fire or logging) to provide an opportunity for regeneration.

SIZE—Heights of 50 to 60 ft. and diameters of 1 to 2 ft. are usual; occasionally, a tree may reach 100 ft. in height and a diameter of up to 3 ft. on the best sites.

LEAVES—Vary from egg-shaped with short sharp tips to broadly oval, or almost circular with blunt tips, 2- to 4-ins. long, with three to four uneven teeth to each inch of margin and with both sides of each tooth curved inwards; dark green above, paler beneath, with a downy underside when unfolding in spring; stalk flattened, shorter than the leaf-blade which quivers with the slightest breeze.

FRUIT—Pods narrowly conical, downy, about ¼-in. long, splitting into two parts to discharge the seeds, closely spaced on flexible stems.

TWIGS—Moderately stout, dull, brownish-grey, downy when the leaves are unfolding, some hairiness often remaining; end bud about ⅜-in. long, covered with a greyish down; tips on lateral buds not turned inwards, not gummy or fragrant, similar to the end bud.

BARK—Smooth, pale green to yellowish-grey, usually with an orange cast; dark grey and furrowed on old trunks.

WOOD—Light, soft, low in strength; heartwood greyish-white to light greyish-brown, not clearly differentiated from the nearly white sapwood.

IMPORTANCE—The wood is used for pulp, boxes, crates, excelsior, matches, veneer and the manufacture of plywood.

NOTES—Some authorities believe that the wood will outlast many of the so-called "durable" varieties, provided it is kept dry.

BUDS HAIRY; LATERALS SPIRAL ROUND TWIG

-STALK SHORTER THAN LEAF-BLADE

URE BARK DEEPLY FURROWED

FLOWER BUDS ARE PLUMP

BALSAM POPLAR

Tacamahac

Populus balsamifera L.

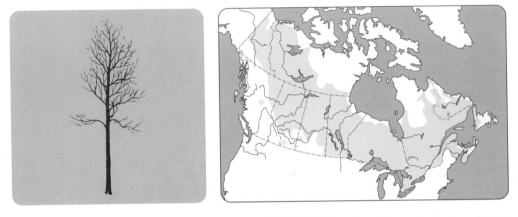

FORM—Balsam Poplar has a long, straight, cylindrical trunk with a narrow open crown of a few stout, ascending branches, and a shallow root system. There are many different forms of the tree throughout its wide range. In western Canada, where it merges with Black Cottonwood, there are many individuals intermediate between the two species. This interbreeding has led some botanists to accept the variations as responses to differences in geography, and to designate the parents as subspecies. In this book, they are treated as separate species. Throughout the prairies there are also different forms of Balsam Poplar, one of which has been called Heartleaf Balsam Poplar and classified as *Populus balsamifera* var. *subcordata* Hylander. It has leaves that are broad at the base, almost heart-shaped, and distinctly hairy on the undersurface and on the leaf-stalk. The Balm-of-Gilead (*Populus candicans* Ait.) is said to have been derived from cuttings of a female tree of the Heartleaf Balsam Poplar, or a hybrid of it.

HABITAT—Balsam Poplar grows across Canada throughout the Boreal, Great Lakes-St. Lawrence, and Acadian Forest regions. It does best on moist, rich, low-lying ground and may grow in pure stands or in mixture with alders, willows, Balsam Fir, Black Spruce, White Spruce, White Birch and other species of the northern forests.

SIZE—A medium-sized tree, 60 to 80 ft. in height by 1 to 2 ft. in diameter; occasionally, it reaches heights of 100 ft. and diameters of 4 ft. or more.

LEAVES—Egg-shaped, gradually tapering to a sharp tip, 3- to 5-ins. long, finely toothed with many low rounded teeth that turn inwards at their tips, slightly rounded at the base, shiny dark green above, whitish-green below, often stained with brownish resin blotches, mostly hairless; stalk round in cross-section (can be rolled between thumb and forefinger), often bears glands below the base of the leaf-blade.

FRUIT—Pods egg-shaped, without hairs, ¼- to ⅓-in. long, splitting into two parts to discharge the seeds, closely spaced on flexible stems.

TWIGS—Stout, smooth, reddish-brown, round in cross-section; end bud ¾-in. long, slender, long pointed, not angled, very resinous, fragrant, reddish-brown; lateral buds pressed against the twig.

BARK—On young trees smooth, greenish-brown, turning dark greyish and becoming furrowed into flat-topped rough ridges separated by irregular V-shaped crevices.

WOOD—Light, soft, low in strength; heartwood greyish-brown, sometimes tinged with red; sapwood nearly white.

IMPORTANCE—Useful on the western prairies for windbreaks. The wood is used for plywood, excelsior and pulpwood.

NOTES—A piece of bark cut from the base of a mature tree can be shaped to serve as an excellent fishing float.

124

BALSAM POPLAR

POPLARS DISCHARGE MANY AIRBORNE SEEDS

T LEAVES HAVE LONG TAPERING TIPS

MATURE BARK HAS DEEP FLAT-TOPPED RIDGES

S-SECTIONS OF TWIG AND BUD ARE ROUND

NARROW CROWN WITH ASCENDING BRANCHES

EASTERN COTTONWOOD

Populus deltoides Bartr.

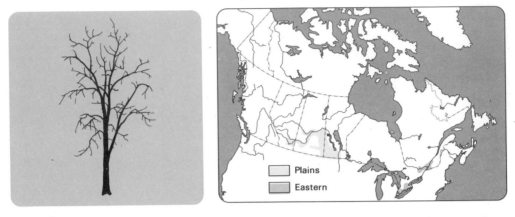

Plains
Eastern

FORM—One of the larger poplars, this species when growing in the open develops quite a massive short trunk which divides near the ground into a few large, wide-spreading branches to form a broad, irregularly-shaped, open crown. When crowded by other trees, the Eastern Cottonwood has a long, straight, branch-free trunk with a small and rounded crown. The root system is usually quite shallow and wide-spreading, but in some locations the tree may develop deep roots. Like most poplars, the Eastern Cottonwood is quite variable in form within its wide range, and several varieties and hybrids have been recognized and named. One western form, given the name *Populus sargentii* Dode by some authors, and by others classified as a variety, *Populus deltoides* var. *occidentalis* Rydb., deserves mention. It is known as the Plains Cottonwood. Its leaves have a few coarse teeth, a longer toothless tip, and winter buds that are covered with minute hairs.

HABITAT—Under favourable conditions, the cottonwoods grow rapidly and are often planted where fast growth is the main requirement. Their eastern range is within the Deciduous Forest Region and the southern and eastern parts of the Great Lakes-St. Lawrence Forest Region. There are also forms growing near Lake-of-the-Woods and on the prairies. They may form pure stands of limited size on the banks of streams, or mix in open stands with species having similar requirements.

SIZE—A medium-sized to large tree, attaining heights of 75 to 100 ft. and diameters of 2 to 4 ft.

LEAVES—Roughly an equilateral triangle in shape, 2- to 4-ins. long, approximately six rounded teeth to an inch of margin, a short tip without teeth, bright shiny green above, slightly paler beneath, without hairs on either surface; often hanging vertically on long, smooth, flattened stalks that frequently bear glands below the base of the leaf-blade.

FRUIT—Pods on flexible stems, oval, tapering to both ends, ¼- to ⅓-in. long, splitting into three or four parts to discharge the seeds.

TWIGS—Stoutish, smooth, yellowish-brown, angled in cross-section; end bud ¾-in. long, slender, long pointed, angled, slightly resinous, yellowish-brown, without hairs.

BARK—Smooth, yellowish-grey on young trees; dark grey and deeply furrowed on mature trunks.

WOOD—Light, soft, low in strength; heartwood greyish-white to pale brown, sapwood nearly white.

IMPORTANCE—Used in western Canada for shelterbelts and fuel. The wood is also useful for lumber and veneer, but the supply of good-quality lumber for these purposes is somewhat limited.

NOTES—Growth is so rapid that some trees are known to have reached maximum height within 15 years.

The Indians used the roots for making fire by friction.

126

TRIANGULAR; GLANDS OFTEN AT THE BASE

CLUSTER OF UNOPENED FRUIT PODS

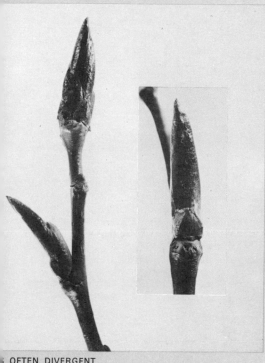

OFTEN DIVERGENT

BARK FURROWED INTO DEEP RIDGES

BLACK COTTONWOOD

Western Balsam Poplar

Populus trichocarpa Torr. & Gray

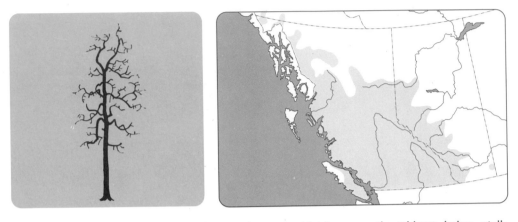

FORM—This tree is very similar in form and in many other features to Balsam Poplar. It develops a straight cylindrical trunk with a narrow, but somewhat columnar, open crown of a few stout, ascending branches. The root system is shallow and wide-spreading. There are many examples of interbreeding between Black Cottonwood and Balsam Poplar, and a few of the results of their crossing have been named as varieties or hybrids. The identity of these offspring is still rather uncertain however, and none of them is included here.

HABITAT—Black Cottonwood grows throughout most of British Columbia and in the western part of Alberta. It is usually confined to low-lying damp areas, where the tree grows mostly on loose, porous, sandy or gravelly soils. Sometimes there may be pure stands on riverbanks or on other types of moist soil, but more often the tree grows in mixture with other species having similar growth requirements.

SIZE—This is the largest of the native poplars and the largest broad-leaved tree native to British Columbia. It attains heights of 80 to 125 ft. and diameters of 3 to 5 ft.

LEAVES—Broadly egg-shaped, gradually tapering from below the middle to a long drawn-out tip, 3- to 5-ins. long, very finely toothed with many low, rounded teeth that turn inwards at their tips (often part of the margin may be without teeth), rounded or slightly heart-shaped at the base, dark green above, silvery-green below and frequently stained with brownish resin blotches, mostly without hairs; stalk round in cross-section (can be rolled between thumb and forefinger); almost indistinguishable from Balsam Poplar.

FRUIT—Pods nearly circular, with short tips, covered with short hairs, ⅓- to ½-in. long, splitting into three parts to discharge the seeds, closely spaced on long slender stems.

TWIGS—Moderately stout, smooth, orangey-brown, round to slightly angled in cross-section; end bud ¾-in. long, slender, long pointed, slightly angled, very resinous, fragrant, orangey-brown, with scales that may be indistinctly fringed with hairs; lateral buds usually pressed against the twig.

BARK—On young trees, smooth, yellowish-grey turning dark greyish-brown and becoming furrowed into flat-topped ridges separated by irregular V-shaped crevices.

WOOD—Light, soft, low in strength; heartwood greyish-brown, sapwood nearly white.

IMPORTANCE—Black Cottonwood is the most important broad-leaved tree in British Columbia. Logs produce wide boards of knot-free lumber used for furniture making, boxes, crates, veneer and plywood.

NOTES—Black Cottonwood cuttings have been exported from Canada to Europe where they are expected to thrive and provide fast-growing trees for windbreaks, fuel, and raw material for exploitation by new industries.

BLACK COTTONWOOD

IS VERY BROAD BELOW THE MIDDLE

FRUIT PODS SPLIT INTO THREE PARTS

TWIG AND BUDS
SIMILAR TO THOSE OF
BALSAM POPLAR

A GROVE OF BLACK
COTTONWOOD,
DUNCAN, B.C.

MATURE BARK DEEPLY FURROWED

NARROWLEAF COTTONWOOD

Populus angustifolia James.

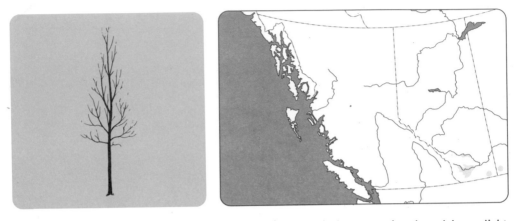

FORM—Typically a small slender tree with a narrowly conical crown of ascending slender branches and appearing more like a willow than a poplar, partly because of the long, narrow, willow-like leaves. Narrowleaf Cottonwood is scarce in its typical form in Canada because it is outnumbered by hybrids. Cross-breeding with other poplars produces many strains which are similar to both parents and are difficult to identify. The tree is said to cross readily with Black Cottonwood (*Populus trichocarpa* Torr. & Gray) and less frequently with the Plains Cottonwood (*Populus deltoides* var. *occidentalis* Rydb.). In winter, the bright white branches and twigs make it distinguishable from other trees.

HABITAT—Narrowleaf Cottonwood grows in southwestern Saskatchewan and in a few river valleys in the prairies of Alberta, from the Bow River southward. Often it will be one of the first plants to establish on gravel and sand bars but, being intolerant of shade, it is seldom found in stands or groves midway in their development. This tree is not sufficiently important in Canada to have received special scientific attention, but available evidence indicates a need for moist soils. No pure stands have been found within its known range.

SIZE—The smallest native poplar, usually less than 40 ft. in height and 1 ft. in diameter.

LEAVES—Narrow, 2- to 3-ins. long and ½- to ¾-in. wide, widest near or below the middle and in their narrowness unlike the shape of any other native poplar leaf; finely toothed to the tip, narrowed to a wedge-shaped base, light yellowish-green above, slightly paler and often resin-stained below; stalk very short, stiff, hairless and glandless, almost circular in cross-section, flattened near the base of the blade.

FRUIT—Pods broadly egg-shaped with short tips, hairless, ¼-in. long, splitting into two parts to discharge the seeds, widely spaced on flexible stems.

TWIGS—Slender, yellowish-brown becoming a bright whitish-to-ivory shade by the second year; buds shiny brown, moderately resinous, without hairs; terminal bud ¼- to ¾-in. long, long pointed, brownish, shiny; lateral buds slightly smaller.

BARK—Whitish or yellowish-green, smooth, becoming slightly furrowed at the base of mature trunks.

WOOD—Light, soft, low in strength; heartwood greyish-white, sapwood nearly white.

IMPORTANCE—Owing to its small size and scarcity, Narrowleaf Cottonwood has no commercial value. Locally, it is used for fuel and fence posts.

NOTES—In some parts of Canada, and most particularly in the southwestern portion of the prairies, positive identification of poplars becomes almost impossible for the amateur. Narrowleaf Cottonwood, although having distinctive leaves, is one of the species that most non-professional botanists will be content to record simply as a "poplar", without attempting to separate the hybrids.

NARROWLEAF COTTONWOOD

LEAVES WILLOW-LIKE

TWIG SLENDER; BUDS HAVE
LONG, POINTED TIPS

JRE BARK IS FURROWED INTO LOW RIDGES

FRUIT POD SPLITS INTO TWO WHEN MATURE

WALNUT

Juglans L.

About 15 species of this genus are widely distributed in North and South America and in the Old World, from southeastern Europe to eastern Asia. In North America, there are six species of which two, the Butternut and the Black Walnut, are found in eastern Canada. None grow in western Canada.

The walnuts are conspicuous trees throughout the year. In winter, the small number of branches with relatively few stout twigs make them stand out from other trees. In summer, their open crowns of long divided leaves give them a very attractive appearance. The photographs opposite illustrate this point well, although the growing conditions differ from those of a tree in the natural state.

In addition to the two native species, two introduced species are planted in Canada. The English Walnut or Persian Walnut (*Juglans regia* L.), of Asia and southeastern Europe, produces the valuable English Walnut wood or "Circassian Walnut" that has been used so extensively in the manufacture of furniture and fine cabinets. This tree is also the source of the edible walnuts of commerce, but it is not hardy in Canada, except in the mildest districts. A few of the several named varieties of this species have been introduced. The Japanese Walnut (*Juglans sieboldiana* Maxim.) is a hardy species which is occasionally planted in Canada as an ornamental tree.

Walnut trees are intolerant of competition. In natural stands, walnut is usually a scattered tree; no known pure plantations have been successful. In the shade of large walnut trees, the growth of walnut seedlings and other plants is inhibited, probably because of toxic substances produced in the soil by the roots.

The leaves appear singly and are arranged alternately on the twigs. They are about 1 ft., or more, in length by 5- to 8-ins. wide and have from 11 to 23 toothed and almost stalkless leaflets arranged along each side of the leaf-stalk.

The first leaves of the seedlings are not divided, but are coarsely toothed. During the first year, divided leaves are produced, initially with only three leaflets, but later with progressively larger numbers until the typical adult leaves are formed.

The flowers appear as the trees are leafing out. They are of one sex, with the males and females in separate clusters, but both kinds develop on the same tree. The male flower cluster consists of short spikes of from two to ten flowers attached along an unbranched flexible stem about 4-ins. long. The clusters arise from lateral buds on the twigs and hang limply from them. The female flowers appear singly or in small groups of two or three that arise towards the end of the twig and remain ascending until the weight of the fruit causes them to bend downwards.

The fruit is a large, edible, hard-shelled nut enclosed in a firm somewhat fleshy covering (husk). It ripens in one season and is shed in the autumn. The outer husk does not split to release the nut, but turns brown and with weathering gradually rots away.

The twigs are stout, with lateral buds arranged in five rows lengthwise. (Sassafras, poplars, hickories and oaks have a similar bud arrangement, but they can be recognized by other features.) There is a true terminal bud which has few scales, and often appears without scales. The lateral buds are smaller, and there is often more than one of them above a leaf-scar. The leaf-scars are conspicuous because of their three U-shaped bundle-scars or bundle-scar groups. The pith is the most useful recognition feature, however, because, after the first season, it shows cavities alternating with partitions.

The wood is valuable, but the supply from the native species is too small to give the genus much commercial importance.

The native walnuts are distinguishable from their relatives, the hickories, by their chambered pith, leaves with 11 or more leaflets, and a fruit husk that does not split open at maturity.

The two native species are easily separated by comparison of such characteristics as leaves, fruits, twigs and bark.

BUTTERNUT

White Walnut

Juglans cinerea L.

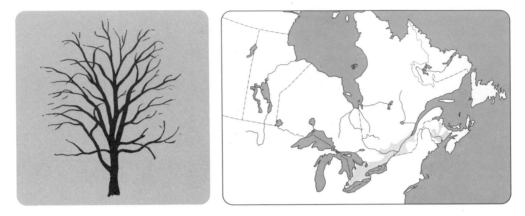

FORM—This tree usually has a rather short trunk which is divided into a few ascending limbs with large, spreading, sparsely forked branches. The smaller branches tend to bend downwards and then turn up at the ends. The crown is rather open and broad, but is quite irregular in outline and is rounded on top. The root system is composed of a number of wide-spreading laterals that grow to quite a depth; usually a tap-root develops in deep soils.

HABITAT—Butternut is a short-lived tree which seldom survives longer than 80 years. It is found sparingly in the Deciduous Forest Region, the southeastern portion of the Great Lakes-St. Lawrence Forest Region and the western section of the Acadian Forest Region. It grows in a variety of locations, including dry rocky soils (particularly those of limestone origin) but it makes its best growth on moist, well-drained, fertile soils in shallow valleys and on gradual slopes. Butternut is commonly found as a scattered tree, or in small groups among other species of hardwoods and conifers. Its usual associates are Beech, Sugar Maple, White Ash, White Elm, Slippery Elm, Black Cherry, Black Oak, Red Oak, White Oak, Basswood, Shagbark Hickory, Bitternut Hickory, Yellow Birch, Eastern Hemlock and Eastern White Pine.

SIZE—A small to medium-sized tree seldom exceeding 70 ft. in height or 3 ft. in diameter.

LEAVES—About 15-ins. long, composed of 11 to 17 almost stalkless leaflets on a stout central stalk; terminal leaflet usually present and about the same size as the larger leaflets; lowest two or three pairs of lateral leaflets small in relation to the others, yellowish-green and rough above, paler and hairy below; dense hairiness also along the stalk and on the twig.

FRUIT—About twice as long as they are broad, pointed, 2½-ins. long; husk with dense sticky hairs; surface of nut cut into irregular jagged grooves.

TWIGS—Stout, hairy, buff-coloured; terminal bud hairy, elongated, about ½-in. long, somewhat flattened, blunt tipped, with lobed outer scales; lateral buds much smaller, rounded, often more than one bud above a leaf-scar; upper margin of leaf-scars straight across and bordered with hair.

BARK—Ash-grey, smooth, becoming separated by narrow, shallow, dark crevices into wide, irregular, flat-topped, intersecting ridges.

WOOD—Light, soft, low in strength, coarse-grained; heartwood light chestnut-brown, sapwood nearly white to light greyish-brown.

IMPORTANCE—The Butternut is not an important timber species. The wood is soft and suitable only for a few uses such as interior finishing, furniture, cabinet work and small household woodenware.

NOTES—An iodine-like yellow dye can be extracted from the fruit husks and bark, and the root bark provides a laxative.

.FLETS STALKLESS WITH DENSELY-HAIRY
DERSURFACE; TERMINAL LEAFLET
OMINENT

MALE FLOWER CLUSTERS

A GROUP OF FEMALE FLOWERS

TOP OF LEAF-SCAR
BORDERED WITH HAIRS;
TWIG HAS CHAMBERED
PITH

HUSK SMOOTH, HAIRY
AND STICKY; SHELL OF NUT JAGGED

MATURE BARK
HAS IRREGULAR, FLAT-
TOPPED, INTERSECTING RIDGES

BLACK WALNUT

Juglans nigra L.

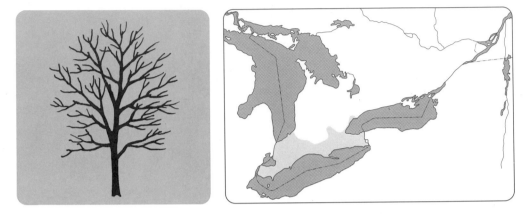

FORM—Black Walnut develops a long clear trunk with little taper, and a small rounded crown, when growing in the forest. In the open, the trunk forks low down into large limbs with a few ascending and spreading coarse branches; the crown covers most of the height of the tree, but is open. The open crown is an indication of the tree's intolerance of shade, since the inner leaves have failed to survive in the shade of the outer ones. The root system usually includes a deep tap-root and several wide-spreading and deeply set lateral roots.

HABITAT—This species is found in the warmer parts of Ontario, mainly in the Deciduous Forest Region and slightly north of it, and along the north shore of Lake Ontario to just beyond Kingston. For good growth it requires a deep, rich, well-drained loam. The Black Walnut does not grow in pure stands, although there are small groves within the mixed southern hardwood forest. Its common associates are White Ash, Black Cherry, Basswood, Shagbark Hickory, Beech, Black Oak, White Oak, Yellow Birch and other southern species. As with other "nut trees", squirrels play an important role in the natural reproduction of Black Walnut by gathering the fruits and hiding them in the soil. The germination of some of these buried walnuts is the principal means of distributing the species throughout the forest.

SIZE—Medium-sized, reaching heights of up to 90 ft. and diameters of 2 to 3 ft.

LEAVES—About 1-ft. long, composed of 15 to 23 slightly stalked leaflets on a moderately stout stalk; terminal leaflet much smaller than the lateral leaflets, or often absent; upper and lower leaflets small relative to the middle ones, yellowish-green and smooth above, faintly hairy beneath; a slight hairiness also along the stalk and twig.

FRUIT—Round, about 2 ins. in diameter; husk hairy; surface of nut deeply grooved — not jagged like the Butternut.

TWIGS—Stout, faintly hairy, orangey-brown; terminal bud blunt, about ¼-in. long and ¼-in. broad, slightly hairy; lateral buds smaller, often more than one above the leaf-scars which are deeply notched on the upper margins and without hairy borders.

BARK—Light brown, scaly when young but becoming darker, with rounded, almost black, intersecting ridges on the mature tree.

WOOD—Heavy, hard, strong; heartwood light brown to chocolate-coloured or purplish-brown, resistant to decay; sapwood nearly white.

IMPORTANCE—One of the most valuable hardwood species in North America, but in Canada the supply is almost exhausted. The wood is used mainly in the form of veneer for furniture, cabinets, interior finishing and boats.

NOTES—There is some indication that the roots of the Black Walnut make the soil unsuitable for certain garden vegetables.

FRUIT HUSK ROUND; NUT GROOVED—
NOT JAGGED

MINAL LEAFLET SMALLER;
FLETS STALKED

MATURE BARK HAS ROUNDED
INTERSECTING RIDGES

TOP OF LEAF-SCAR INDENTED—
NO PAD OF HAIRS AS IN
BUTTERNUT

E FLOWER CLUSTERS

GROUP OF FEMALE FLOWERS

HICKORY

Carya Nutt.

The hickory is typically a tree of eastern North America, since only two species are found elsewhere in the world. The actual number of species is variously reported as being from 16 to 22 and, of these, six have ranges which extend into Canada.

Of the six Canadian species, Bitternut Hickory belongs in the "pecan hickory" group, and the remaining five species are "true hickories". The pecan hickories differ in having leaves with a greater number of somewhat scythe-shaped leaflets; the fruit husks are four-winged above the middle, and the winter buds have scales that meet along their edges without overlapping. In the "true hickory" group, Red Hickory (*Carya ovalis* (Wang.) Sarg.) is a questionable species. By some botanical authors it is classified as a hybrid between Pignut Hickory and Shagbark Hickory, while other authors consider it to be only a form of Pignut Hickory. Published descriptions of Red Hickory, however, suggest some differences between it and Pignut Hickory, particularly in the fruit, but like so many doubtful species, these differences are not always apparent in any given selection of samples. A few recognition features of Red Hickory are given under the heading "NOTES" on the page dealing with the Pignut Hickory.

Species identification is complicated by a number of other varieties and hybrids which are often difficult to relate to their proper species. Also, within any of the species, the leaves vary considerably in size and number of leaflets and, if used alone, can be unreliable for identifying a particular tree. The fruit is also quite variable in size and appearance. These variations are partly caused by differences in environment, but mostly stem from the tendency of the species to cross with one another to produce forms that have characteristics of two species. Pignut Hickory and the doubtful Red Hickory are good examples of these difficulties. Therefore, in the identification of hickories, it is not practical to rely on leaves alone, nor on fruits alone. All available features should be examined and the possibility of the specimen being a hybrid should not be overlooked. One helpful hint relating to Canadian species is that Shagbark Hickory and Bitternut Hickory are the two most common hickories. Other species are relatively rare and are confined to the most southerly parts of the Deciduous Forest Region.

The hickories are medium-sized to large trees with mostly coarse branching, and alternate leaves that are shed each autumn and replaced in the spring. The leaves are divided, with five to eleven stalkless, or nearly stalkless, leaflets arranged along a stiff stalk, and a terminal leaflet as large as, or often larger than, the largest of the lateral leaflets. The lowest pair is always the smallest.

The flowers appear as the trees are leafing out. They are of one sex, with the males and females in separate clusters on the same tree (similar to those of the walnuts), but the male flower clusters are three-branched, not single as in the walnuts.

The fruits also are similar to those of the walnuts, but differ from them in having a husk that splits (as the fruit matures) all the way to the base in the Shagbark, Big Shellbark and Mockernut hickories, and usually to above the middle in the Bitternut and Pignut hickories. The shell of the nut is relatively smooth — not deeply grooved as in the walnuts.

Hickory twigs are stout to moderately slender, with a continuous pith that is usually angled when viewed in cross-section. The leaf-scars are in five rows along the twig (as in the walnuts) and are conspicuous. They are dotted with numerous small bundle-scars. The terminal buds are much larger than the laterals, and except on Bitternut Hickory are covered with overlapping scales.

The wood of the different species is very similar. It is one of the toughest, hardest and strongest of Canadian hardwoods, and is unequalled for a few special products such as sporting goods and tool handles. The native supply is very small however, and requirements of the wood-using industries are met almost entirely by importation from the U.S.A.

SHAGBARK HICKORY

Carya ovata (Mill.) K. Koch

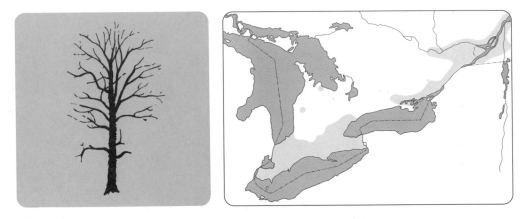

FORM—In the forest, Shagbark Hickory develops a straight, slender, scarcely tapering trunk which is free of branches for about three-quarters, or more, of its length. The crown is composed of short ascending and spreading branches, and widens out at the top to become almost flattened. In the open, the crown covers three-quarters, or more, of the tree's height, is oblong in outline and is supported by a short branch-free trunk which is noticeably tapered at the base. As with all native hickories, a deep tap-root is developed and the tree is very windfirm. Varieties and hybrids of hickories are not unusual, but one variety of this species, var. *fraxinifolia* Sarg., which is sometimes called Ashleaf Hickory, deserves some mention here. It has been reported in the Kingston and Wallaceburg areas of Ontario and is identifiable by its leaves. They are smaller than those of the species, and average 7- to 9-ins. long. The leaflets are very narrow, being two to three times as long as they are wide, and they grow on slender leaf-stalks.

HABITAT—Shagbark Hickory is found in the Deciduous Forest Region and in the southern parts of the Great Lakes-St. Lawrence Forest Region where it occupies the same type of soil as the Bitternut Hickory. It grows on rich moist soils in valleys, on hillsides and at the edges of some swamps. Generally, it associates with the common hardwoods found in the southern part of Ontario.

SIZE—A medium-sized to large tree, attaining heights of 60 to 80 ft. and diameters of up to approximately 2 ft.

LEAVES—About 10-ins. long; five to seven leaflets (usually five), broadest at the middle, long pointed at both ends, finely toothed, fringed with hairs, sparsely hairy beneath, dark yellowish-green above, paler below; terminal leaflet normally the largest of all the leaflets.

FRUIT—About 1½-ins. long, almost round (but shorter than it is wide); husk thick, woody, splitting to the base when the fruit is ripe; shell moderately thick, hard; kernel sweet and edible.

TWIGS—Stout, shiny, reddish-brown to greyish-brown; terminal bud ½- to ¾-in. long, greenish-brown, pointed; scales overlapping, the outer ones loosely spreading, the inner ones densely hairy.

BARK—Dark grey; on mature trunks separating into long shaggy plates, free at their lower ends or at both ends, giving the trunk an untidy look.

WOOD—Heavy, hard, tough, strong; heartwood reddish-brown, moderately resistant to decay; sapwood nearly white.

IMPORTANCE—This species is the source of edible hickory nuts; the wood is in demand for sporting goods and handles.

NOTES—For many years, wheelwrights used Shagbark Hickory to form the spokes of wooden wheels for carriages and carts and, subsequently, for the automobile.

SHAGBARK HICKORY

LEAVES USUALLY HAVE FIVE LEAFLETS

FRUIT HUSK SPLITS ALONG THE GROOVES

ALE FLOWER CLUSTERS ARE THREE-BRANCHED

FEMALE FLOWERS OFTEN IN CLUSTERS OF THREE

AL BUD (INSERT) SMALLER
TERMINAL BUD

TRUNK LOOKS UNTIDY

THICK WOODY HUSK (LEFT) SPLITS TO RELEASE
NUT (RIGHT)

BIG SHELLBARK HICKORY

Kingnut

Carya laciniosa (Michx. f.) Loud.

FORM—This tree is very similar to Shagbark Hickory in that its recognition features differ mainly in their greater size. In the forest, Big Shellbark Hickory develops a slightly tapering trunk which may be free of branches for more than half of its length; the crown is narrow and open and is composed of short, sturdy, ascending branches which widen out towards the top of the tree. In the open, the tree carries a much longer crown which covers most of its length and takes on a fairly uniform oblong shape. The portion of the trunk that is free of branches is short and sturdy, and is noticeably tapered at the base. A deep strong tap-root is developed and the tree is windfirm.

HABITAT—Big Shellbark Hickory is an inhabitant of the Deciduous Forest Region, but is never abundant within its range in Canada. Like its close relative, Shagbark Hickory, the few widely scattered examples of Big Shellbark Hickory do best on moist, well-drained, rich, loamy soils in valleys and on gradual slopes of low hills, and on the banks of streams. When encountered, it is usually in association with other southern species including some maples (particularly Red Maple and Silver Maple), White Ash, White Oak, White Elm and other hickories.

SIZE—A medium-sized to large tree, attaining heights of 60 to 90 ft. and diameters of 2 to 3 ft. Larger sizes have been recorded.

LEAVES—About 1 ft. in length, with seven to nine leaflets (usually seven), finely toothed, fringed with hair, dark yellowish-green above, paler below, sparsely hairy beneath, the terminal leaflet 5- to 10-ins. long, larger than the other leaflets.

FRUIT—About 2- to 2½-ins. long and as wide; husk ¼- to ½-in. thick, woody, splitting all the way to the base when the fruit is ripe; shell moderately thick, hard; kernel sweet and edible.

TWIGS—Simply a Shagbark Hickory twig on an enlarged scale; tan-coloured, slightly hairy; buds large, somewhat spreading; terminal bud ¾- to 1-in. long.

BARK—Dark grey; on mature trunks separating into long shaggy plates free at their lower ends or at both ends; trunk often shaggy in appearance and untidy.

WOOD—Heavy, hard, very tough and strong; heartwood reddish-brown, moderately resistant to decay; sapwood nearly white.

IMPORTANCE—The tree is scarce in Canada and where cut and used would be considered as Shagbark Hickory. It was used on farms for making ladders, wagon shafts and axles; the nuts are sometimes gathered for local use.

NOTES—The wood is particularly suitable for making skis, but the supply is much too limited to support an industry.

Like the other hickories, this tree takes up to 200 years to reach maturity.

142

BIG SHELLBARK HICKORY

USUALLY SEVEN LEAFLETS

FRUIT LARGEST OF THE HICKORIES

FRUIT; INSERTS: THICK HUSK (LEFT) SPLITTING ALL THE WAY TO BASE; NUT (RIGHT)

BUDS SLIGHTLY
HAIRY; LATERALS
LESS SPREADING
THAN SHAGBARK

HICKORY LEAF-
SCARS HAVE MANY
BUNDLE-SCARS

MOCKERNUT HICKORY

Carya tomentosa **Nutt.**

FORM—When growing in association with other trees, this species develops a long, slender, straight trunk which is free of branches for about half the height of the tree. The crown is open, quite narrow and round-topped. In the open, the crown covers much more of the length of the tree and is generally oblong, with branches that bear stout branchlets. Sometimes the branches droop. The trunk is often swollen at the base. As with other hickory species, a deep strong tap-root is usual, and the tree is quite windfirm.

HABITAT—Mockernut Hickory is scarce and is found only in the Deciduous Forest Region where it is confined to areas around the eastern and western ends of Lake Erie and the southeastern end of Lake St. Clair. It grows on a wide variety of soils, but thrives best on rich well-drained slopes where there is a plentiful supply of moisture. It is intolerant of shade and requires the good lighting found in moderately open stands. Usually associating with it are such southern hardwoods as White Oak, White Ash, soft maples, Pignut Hickory, Black Walnut, Yellow Birch and other broad-leaved species.

SIZE—A medium-sized to large tree attaining heights of 75 to 90 ft. and diameters of up to 2½ ft.

LEAVES—About 10-ins. long; seven to nine leaflets (occasionally only five), narrow and broadest above the middle, up to 6 ins. in length with a long tapered point at each end,

finely toothed to coarsely toothed, resinous, very fragant when crushed, dark shiny green above, paler and distinctly hairy beneath; terminal leaflet usually the largest.

FRUIT—About 1½-ins. long, almost as wide, somewhat flattened, broadest above the middle; husk ⅛- to ¼-in. thick, splitting to the base to release an extremely thick-shelled nut; kernel sweet, edible, but small.

TWIGS—Stout, reddish-brown, hairy; terminal bud about ¾-in. long, very broad and blunt, the outer bud-scales dark reddish-brown, hairy, shed early in autumn and leaving a plump, pale, densely hairy bud through the winter; lateral buds similar but smaller, and spreading from the twig.

BARK—Dark grey, thin (up to ¾-in. thick), close, firm, shallowly ridged with narrow flat ridges criss-crossing the shallow furrows.

WOOD—Heavy, hard, very tough and strong; heartwood dark brown, moderately resistant to decay; sapwood thick, almost white.

IMPORTANCE—The wood, often considered superior to that of other hickories, has the same uses, but the tree is too rare to be of commercial importance in Canada.

NOTES—The early settlers of the Niagara Peninsula were able to extract a black dye from the bark of the Mockernut Hickory, probably by boiling small pieces of bark in a vinegar solution.

...NG STOUT; OUTER TERMINAL BUD-SCALE IS SHED EARLY;
...TERAL BUDS DIVERGE; LEAF-SCAR HAS MANY BUNDLE-SCARS

MATURE BARK HAS CRISS-CROSSING RIDGES

MALE (LEFT) AND FEMALE FLOWERS ARE ON SAME TREE

THICK HUSK SPLITS TO THE BASE

PIGNUT HICKORY

Carya glabra (Mill.) Sweet

Pignut

Red

FORM—This is a very variable species which appears in several different forms throughout its wide range in eastern North America. Several of the forms have been classified as varieties of this species or of the closely related and somewhat doubtful species Red Hickory (*Carya ovalis* (Wang.) Sarg.). The crown on trees grown in the open is irregularly narrow and is composed of short crooked branches with the tips and lower branchlets usually drooping. The longest and heaviest branches develop near the top of the tree and give it a top-heavy appearance. In stands, the crown is restricted to a short narrow cylinder which spreads out at the top. The trunk is mostly free of branches and without much taper. Like other hickories, the root system is deep, with a long tap-root that gives good support to the heavily branched crown.

HABITAT—Pignut Hickory is restricted to the southern portion of the Deciduous Forest Region, mainly in the extreme southwestern part of Ontario and in the area lying south of Lake Ontario. It is typically an upland species and is rather intolerant of shade, but can be found in association with other southern hardwoods such as the white oaks, soft maples, other species of hickory, Tulip-tree, Red Mulberry, Sassafras and elms.

SIZE—A medium-sized tree, usually 40 to 60 ft. in height and 1 to 3 ft. in diameter.

LEAVES—About 10-ins. long, usually with seven rather narrow leaflets about 5-ins. long,

dark yellowish-green above, paler below, often hairy beneath on the main veins, finely toothed margins, unequal wedge-shaped bases and long, narrow, pointed tips.

FRUIT—About 1½-ins. long, pear-shaped, borne in clusters, enclosed in thin, friable, four-ridged husks which split from the top to about the mid-portion; nut slightly flattened, 1-in. long with a moderately thick shell; kernel usually bitter, not edible.

TWIGS—Slender, shiny, grey to reddish-brown, without hairs; buds variable, laterals broad and blunt tipped, ⅛- to ¼-in. long; terminal bud larger but under ½-in. long and more pointed, outer scales shed in early autumn leaving a small, stout, densely hairy bud.

BARK—Thin, grey, becoming shallowly fissured and forming narrow criss-cross ridges.

WOOD—Light brown, almost white sapwood.

IMPORTANCE—The wood is similar to that of the other hickories and is used for sporting goods and tool handles.

NOTES—The difference between this species and Red Hickory is most apparent in the fruit. The fruit husk of the Red Hickory is somewhat thicker and splits readily to the base; also, the kernel of the nut is sweet.

Tool handles made of hickory can be identified by their bell-like tone when dropped on end on a hard surface.

LEAVES USUALLY HAVE SEVEN LEAFLETS

LATERAL BUDS BLUNT; TERMINAL BUD POINTED

THIN HUSK SPLITS ABOUT HALFWAY DOWN

MATURE BARK HAS THIN
CRISS-CROSS RIDGES

OPEN-GROWN TREES HAVE IRREGULAR NARROW CROWNS

BITTERNUT HICKORY

Carya cordiformis (Wang.) K. Koch

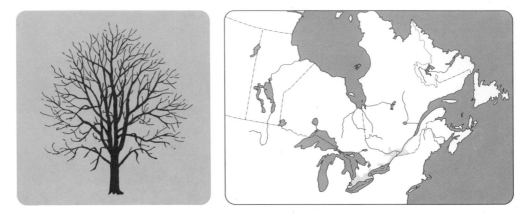

FORM—This is the only member of the group classified as "pecan hickories" that is native to Canada, but, unlike the real pecan of the southern United States, its fruits are inedible. In the forest, it develops a long branch-free trunk with little taper, and a short rounded crown of slender ascending branches that broaden the crown towards the top. The branchlets, which are rather sparse, tend to droop slightly from the main ascending branches.

HABITAT—Bitternut Hickory inhabits the Deciduous Forest Region and southern parts of the Great Lakes-St. Lawrence Forest Region, where it grows in low moist situations and on rich soils of higher ground. It is the commonest hickory in Canada and, being fairly tolerant of shade, is generally found in mixed stands in association with Silver Maple, Beech, Shagbark Hickory, Black Ash, White Elm, Black Oak, White Oak, Black Cherry and other deciduous species.

SIZE—A medium-sized tree attaining heights of 50 to 60 ft. and diameters of 1 to 1½ ft.

LEAVES—About 9-ins. long; seven to eleven long, narrow leaflets tending to be scythe-shaped, finely toothed, shiny dark green above, paler below; terminal leaflet seldom larger than the upper lateral leaflets.

FRUIT—About 1-in. long, almost round, often broadest above the middle and slightly broader than it is long; husk very thin, friable, four-winged from the tip to about the middle, usually splitting partly towards the middle

when the fruit is ripe; shell thin, can be cut easily with a knife; kernel very bitter.

TWIGS—Slender, smooth, shiny, often slightly hairy, greenish to greyish-brown; buds slender, tapering, flattened, sulphur-yellow; bud-scales not overlapping but placed edge to edge; usually more than one lateral bud above a leaf-scar, some lateral buds have the appearance of being stalked and angular.

BARK—Greenish-grey on young trees, remaining smooth for many years, gradually splitting into shallow fissures with almost line-like crevices, always tight-fitting and not peeling or shagging off in large loose scales like that of the Shagbark or Big Shellbark hickories. Becomes somewhat furrowed and broken into scales on mature trees.

WOOD—Dark brown, heavy, hard, strong (but not as strong as the other hickories), diffuse porous to semi-ring porous, moderately resistant to decay; sapwood nearly white.

IMPORTANCE—Perhaps the most important of the Canadian hickories because of its common occurrence and wide distribution. Although the wood is weaker than that of some of the other species, it has the main characteristics of hickory wood and is valuable for such items as sporting goods and tool handles.

NOTES—The wood of the Bitternut Hickory is the best type for producing the smoke required to give hams and bacon that true "hickory smoked" flavour.

LEAVES
USUALLY HAVE
NINE LEAFLETS

E FLOWERS

FEMALE FLOWERS

TWIG; BUD-SCALES DO
NOT OVERLAP

, TIGHT-FITTING, SHALLOW
ES ON BARK

FRUIT HAS FOUR WINGS AT THE TIP

HUSK IS THIN

HOP-HORNBEAM

Ironwood

Ostrya virginiana (Mill.) K. Koch

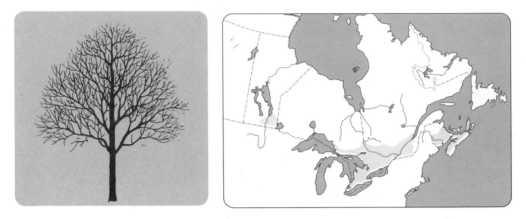

FORM—Of the seven known species of *Ostrya*, three are native to North America and one, the Hop-hornbeam, grows in Canada. It develops an upright trunk which extends almost to the top of the tree, and has long slender branches that form a wide-spreading crown. The crown is often as wide as it is high, and the branchlets tend to droop at their ends.

HABITAT—Hop-hornbeam is found in the Deciduous, Great Lakes-St. Lawrence and Acadian Forest regions. In the north, it enters the southern fringe of the Boreal Forest Region and to the west the eastern fringe of the Grasslands. It makes its best growth on well-drained slopes and ridges and, being tolerant of shade, is commonly found in the shade of larger hardwoods in the southern hardwood forests of eastern Canada.

SIZE—Averages 25 to 40 ft. in height and 6 to 10 ins. in diameter, but may occasionally reach 60 ft. in height and 2 ft. in diameter.

LEAVES—Alternate, simple, in two rows along the twigs, 2½- to 5-ins. long, 1- to 2-ins. wide, successively larger up the twig, gradually tapering to a narrowly rounded or indented base, tapering from the middle to a long sharp tip; dark yellowish-green above and below, turning dull yellow in autumn, soft downy beneath, sharply toothed, teeth indistinctly of two sizes, the larger teeth at the ends of the straight veins; usually one or more veins fork and extend to two or more of the larger teeth; texture soft and fragile.

FLOWERS—Fully developed as the leaves begin to appear; male and female in separate clusters with both kinds on the same tree, cluster consists of a slender flexible stem with closely spaced flowers; male flowers visible in winter as slender cylindrical structures about 1-in. long.

FRUIT—A flattish nut about ¼-in. long enclosed at the bottom of an inflated sac ¾-in. long, several together on a short drooping stem; the sacs fall during winter, leaving their stems attached to the ends of the branchlets.

TWIGS—Slender, dark reddish-brown; buds spreading from the twig, pointed, faintly hairy, uniform greenish-brown; scales in more than two rows up the bud; no true terminal bud.

BARK—Greyish-brown, broken into longitudinal narrow strips, free at both ends.

WOOD—One of the hardest and toughest native woods, heavy, close-grained, light-brown; sapwood nearly white.

IMPORTANCE—The wood is used locally for tool handles and other purposes where a strong tough wood is required. The tree's scattered occurrence and small size, however, prevent the Hop-hornbeam from becoming important as a commercial species.

NOTES—Up to the turn of the century, Hop-hornbeam was used for runners on sleighs.

THE VEINS FORK NEAR THE MARGIN

MALE FLOWERS ARE AT THE END OF THE TWIG

THE TWIGS HAVE UNDEVELOPED
THE FLOWERS

MATURE BARK
BREAKS INTO
NARROW VERTICAL STRIPS

FRUIT GROWS IN A CLUSTER; INFLATED FRUIT
SAC (LEFT) NUT (RIGHT)

BLUE-BEECH

Hornbeam, Ironwood

Carpinus caroliniana Walt.

FORM—The local names Hornbeam and Iron-wood are applied to this species as well as to the Hop-hornbeam (*Ostrya virginiana* (Mill.) K. Koch). It seems better, therefore, to give first place here to the name Blue-beech, even though this species is not truly a beech. Of the 26 known species of *Carpinus*, this is the only one native to North America. It usually has a short, crooked and fluted trunk with a low, wide-spreading, poorly formed crown composed of a few irregular and slightly zigzag branches bearing fine twigs in flat sprays.

HABITAT—Blue-beech is scattered throughout the southern part of the Great Lakes-St. Lawrence Forest Region and the Deciduous Forest Region. It is very tolerant of shade, and is commonly found growing in the shade of hardwoods, generally on deep, rich, moist soils on lower slopes in valleys and along the borders of streams and swamps.

SIZE—It is a small tree seldom over 20 ft. in height and 10 ins. in diameter.

LEAVES—Alternate, in two rows on the twigs, simple, 2- to 4-ins. long by ¾- to 1¾-ins. wide, becoming successively larger up the twig, fully rounded at the base, tapered from above the middle to a short sharp tip, bluish-green above and below, turning red in autumn, almost free of hairs, occasionally tufts of pale hairs in the vein-axils of the undersurface, sharply toothed around the margin with teeth of two distinct sizes, each large tooth at the end of a straight vein with one or two smaller intervening teeth; veins straight without forking at the ends; texture firm between the fingers.

FLOWERS—Fully developed as the leaves begin to appear; male and female in separate clusters with both kinds on the same tree, cluster consists of a slender flexible stem with closely spaced stalkless flowers; male flowers not visible until spring.

FRUIT—A small ribbed nut at the base of a three-lobed leaf-like structure about 1 in. in length, the middle lobe toothed only on one side; each arranged along a flexible stem about 2½-ins. long.

TWIGS—Slender, as narrow as the leaf-buds, reddish-brown; buds pressed against the twig, blunt, slightly hairy; scales in more than two rows up the bud and with a whitish margin; no true terminal bud.

BARK—Thin, unbroken, smooth, slate grey; conspicuous because of the muscle-like longitudinal ridges which give the trunk a wavy outline when viewed in cross-section.

WOOD—Very heavy, hard and strong.

IMPORTANCE—This tree is too small to have commercial importance in Canada.

NOTES—Since the wood is extremely hard, the early settlers fashioned wedges from it for use in splitting other logs.

S SELDOM FORK; TEETH DISTINCTLY OF TWO SIZES

MALE FLOWER CLUSTERS (LEFT)
FEMALE FLOWER CLUSTERS (RIGHT)

TS HANG ON A FLEXIBLE STEM

NUT LIES ON A LEAF-LIKE STRUCTURE

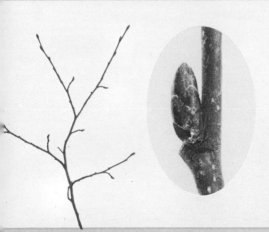

GS ON BRANCHLET ARE SLENDER; BUD-SCALES
E WHITISH MARGIN

BARK HAS MUSCLE-LIKE RIDGES

BIRCH

Betula L.

Probably 50 or more species of birch, varying from dwarf shrubs to trees, grow in the north temperate and arctic regions of the world. The actual number has still not been ascertained, because relationships are not completely understood and distinctions between species are often obscured by hybridization. About 10 species are distributed in Canada, six of which are trees. Previous editions have usually included Blueleaf Birch (*Betula caerulea-grandis* Blanch.), but being considered a hybrid, it is now deleted.

Two European species are commonly planted. The best known is the Silver, or Weeping, Birch (*Betula pendula* Roth) which has small coarsely toothed leaves and chalky-white bark that becomes black and deeply furrowed on the trunk. The other, and perhaps the more wide-spread, is *Betula alba* L., also known as *Betula pubescens* Ehrh. This tree has leaves resembling those of the native White Birch but which are smaller and more ascending on the twigs. It can be identified by its fruit which is about 1-in. long.

Young trees have slender ascending branches which form relatively narrow symmetrical crowns of somewhat oval outline, but which are usually widest below the middle. On older trees, the branches tend to become more nearly horizontal, sometimes drooping, and the crown outline becomes pyramidal. Since birches are intolerant of shade, their crowns are always open. In stands, the lower branches are shed early and the trees develop branch-free trunks. The root system is generally shallow, but in some species is quite deep.

Birches are perhaps best known for their paper-like bark. On most species, the bark is smooth when the trees are young, and peels off in thin papery layers. It has conspicuous, long, horizontal markings called lenticels. Generally the bark is whitish which, in combination with the light green foliage and open crown, make the trees most attractive. On old trees, the bark becomes thick and broken into irregular rough segments.

The leaves are alternate but, unlike most trees with alternate leaves, they appear to be in pairs on the older parts of the branchlets and become single towards the ends. This results from the trees having two distinct kinds of twigs. The usual type develops towards the outer part of the tree, where the lighting is best; there, the twigs elongate in the ordinary way so that their leaves become widely spaced. Farther back on the branch, the twigs do not elongate; they seldom exceed $\frac{1}{8}$ in. in length and, because of their shortness, have only two leaves (or at most three) growing so close together that they appear to be in pairs. This gives the appearance of a two-leaf arrangement.

The leaf-buds are another distinctive feature of birches. The buds on the elongated twigs show only three bud-scales, whereas the bud on the dwarf twig (there is only room for one) has from five to seven scales. The most common number is seven. This is an infallible recognition feature for a birch during the leafless stage of its annual cycle.

The flowers are fully developed as the leaves begin to appear. They are of one sex, with only one kind in a cluster, and each cluster consists of a slender flexible stem with closely spaced stalkless flowers. Both male and female clusters develop on the same tree. The male flower clusters, which are visible in late summer or autumn before the leaves fall, are conspicuous on the twigs throughout the winter, although they do not unfold until just before the leaves appear in spring.

The fruit is a very small flat nut with a thin wing on each side and is borne on minute, three-lobed, leaf-like scales. Many of these are attached to slender stems, since they are the mature form of the female flower cluster, and they form the fruiting-bodies that appear on birch trees from spring until early autumn. On some species the fruiting-bodies remain on the tree into winter.

The wood of the birches is important in the lumber, plywood and pulpwood industries of the country; some species are also important for landscaping, particularly White Birch.

YELLOW BIRCH

Betula alleghaniensis Britton (*Betula lutea* Michx. f.)

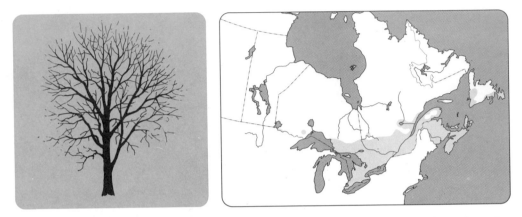

FORM—In the forest, this tree develops a short irregularly rounded crown, but in the open the crown is long and wide-spreading. Normally, the trunk breaks into a few spreading branches, but, when the tree is shaded on the sides, it extends almost to the top of the tree. In stands, the trunk is free of branches for over half of the tree's height, has little taper, but is seldom of great length. The root system is quite deep and wide-spreading.

HABITAT—Yellow Birch is a very important and characteristic component of the southern hardwood forests in the Great Lakes-St. Lawrence, Deciduous, and Acadian Forest regions, and extends into the Boreal Forest Region in eastern Canada. Although it grows on a variety of soils, the best growth is made on rich moist soils in association with other hardwoods. The commonest associates are Beech, Sugar Maple, Basswood, Eastern Hemlock, Balsam Fir, Eastern White Pine, White Spruce and Red Spruce.

SIZE—The largest of the native birches, normally attaining heights of 60 to 75 ft. and diameters of up to 2 ft., but occasionally trees reach 100 ft. in height and 3 to 4 ft. in diameter on the best sites.

LEAVES—Oval, tapering gradually from about the middle to a slender sharp point at the top and to a narrow base which is often somewhat heart-shaped, toothed all round the margin with two sizes of teeth; 12 or more pairs of veins each extending to one of the large teeth on the margin, with two or three smaller intervening teeth; deep yellowish-green above,

paler with soft down below where the veins join the midrib.

FRUIT—Broad fruiting-bodies about 1¼-ins. long by ⅝-in. wide, erect on the branches, often retained on the tree over winter; scales with three narrow ascending lobes, densely hairy; seed-wings narrow, not wider than the seed portion.

TWIGS—Slender, usually slightly hairy, uniformly brown, with a strong wintergreen taste when broken; buds sharp pointed, chestnut-brown.

BARK—Thin on small trunks, dark reddish, shiny, becoming yellowish or bronze on young trees and producing thin papery shreds, but not peeling easily; gradually darkening on mature trunks and breaking into large ragged-edged plates.

WOOD—Heavy, hard, strong, fine-grained (often wavy-grained); heartwood golden-brown to reddish-brown with sapwood that is whitish to pale yellow.

IMPORTANCE—The wood stains well, takes on a high polish and has an extensive use for furniture, cabinet work, interior trim in houses and public buildings, flooring, doors, veneer and plywood. It is also used in the hardwood distillation industry.

NOTES—Yellow Birch is distinguishable from Cherry Birch by the scales on the fruits. Yellow Birch has hairy scales, while those of Cherry Birch are hairless.

YELLOW BIRCH

... IS DOUBLE TOOTHED ALL
... ND THE MARGIN

MALE AND FEMALE FLOWERS (INSERT: FEMALE)

... FRUITING BODIES ARE ERECT

FRUIT WITH HAIRY FRUIT-SCALE (LEFT) SEED WITH NARROW
SEED-WING (RIGHT)

... HREE BUD-SCALES

FIVE BUD-SCALES

BARK DOES NOT PEEL EASILY

... ER TWIG; UNDEVELOPED MALE FLOWERS (LEFT); LATERAL BUD (ARROW).
... RF TWIG (RIGHT), BUDS HAVE FIVE TO SEVEN SCALES

CHERRY BIRCH

Sweet Birch
Black Birch

Betula lenta L.

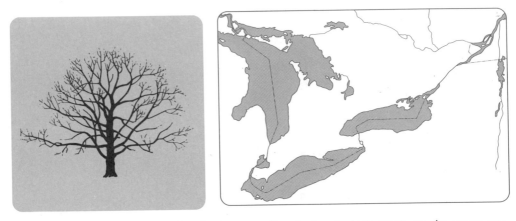

FORM—In the forest, this species develops a long branch-free trunk that supports a short rounded crown. When the tree is growing in the open, the crown is wide-spreading, irregular, and extends almost to the ground. The root system is fairly deep and wide-spreading. The tree resembles Yellow Birch in many of its leaf, flower, and fruit characteristics.

HABITAT—For many years, there have been reports of Cherry Birch growing naturally in Ontario, but no proof of its existence had been available until some trees were examined in 1967. The tree is now known to be growing in a small grove west of Port Dalhousie, near the top of a long steep slope of deep rich soil facing Lake Ontario. There are approximately 50 trees of different ages and sizes at this location. Several medium-sized trees are dead, a few others appear to be dying, but a good number are healthy. Two or three of the probable originators of the grove have been growing along the top of the slope for at least 75 years. Although it is not definite that these Cherry Birch arrived in Canada without man's help, there is also no evidence that they were planted on this site.

SIZE—Medium-sized, attaining heights of 40 to 50 ft. and diameters of 1 to 2½ ft.

LEAVES—Oval, about 3-ins. long, finely toothed all round the margin, often heart-shaped at the base; 12 or more pairs of veins each extending to one of the large teeth on the margin, with two or three smaller intervening teeth; firm textured, deep green on the upper surface, paler and soft downy on the undersurface.

FRUIT—Fruiting-bodies 1- to 1¼-ins. long by ½-in. wide, very short stalked, erect on the branchlets, often retained on the tree over winter; fruit-scales with three ascending lobes, without hairs; seed-wings narrow, not wider than the seed portion.

TWIGS—Slender, slightly hairy, uniformly reddish-brown, with a very strong wintergreen taste when broken; buds sharp pointed, uniformly reddish-brown.

BARK—Reddish-brown to almost black on young trees and until the bark breaks up into irregular plates; becoming thick and greyish.

WOOD—Heavy, hard, strong, fine-grained; heartwood golden-brown to deep reddish-brown, sapwood paler.

IMPORTANCE—The wood has the same properties as that of Yellow Birch and is favoured for furniture, cabinet work, interior trim, flooring, doors and veneer. The tree is too rare to have any economic value.

NOTES—A feature of Cherry Birch is the strong wintergreen taste from a broken twig. Wintergreen can be distilled from the twigs and inner bark, and a salve for minor injuries can be made by grinding boiled bark. A medicinal drink can be brewed from the twigs.

LEAVES AND FRUIT SIMILAR TO YELLOW BIRCH

LATERAL BUDS,
IN TWO ROWS,
HAVE THREE
BUD-SCALES

SMOOTH BARK AGES INTO THICK IRREGULAR PLATES

WHITE BIRCH

Paper Birch,
Canoe Birch

Betula papyrifera Marsh.

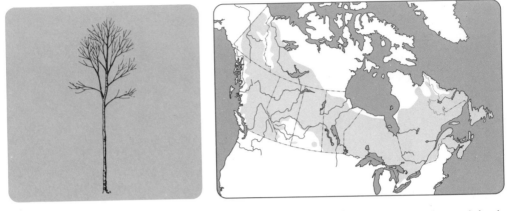

FORM—White Birch is a variable species with numerous forms and several recognized varieties. As a forest tree, it normally has a slender trunk which often curves, before extending almost to the top of the narrowly oval open crown. The crown is usually composed of many ascending branches which end in brushes of fine branchlets. On open-grown trees, the crown is pyramidal, with an irregularly rounded outline, and comprises the greater part of the tree's height. Of the many varieties that have been named, the following are the most distinctive. Mountain Paper Birch (var. *cordifolia* (Reg.) Fern.) inhabits eastern Canada and has leaves that are heart-shaped at the base. Western Paper Birch (var. *commutata* (Reg.) Fern.) is transcontinental in range and has leaves that are longer than normal. The third is variety *subcordata* (Rydb.) Sarg. which grows in western Canada and which has a small almost-circular leaf.

HABITAT—White Birch is distributed throughout most of Canada. It grows on a wide variety of soils, but does best on well-drained sandy or silty loams. Being intolerant of shade, it thrives on burned-over and cut-over areas where it often forms pure stands; later it becomes restricted to openings, as the forest matures. The tree has a very thin inflammable bark and is easily killed by fire, but it can reproduce itself quickly by developing sprouts around the base of the trunk. By this means White Birch has been able to maintain itself as

a prominent occupant of the forested lands within its range in Canada.

SIZE—A medium-sized tree, up to 80 ft. in height by 2 ft. in diameter.

LEAVES—Triangular or egg-shaped, about 3¼-ins. long, without teeth for about ½ in. on either side of the stalk; nine, or fewer, pairs of veins each extending to one of the large teeth on the margin, with smaller intervening teeth; dull green above, paler with soft down below.

FRUIT—Narrow fruiting-bodies about 1½-ins. long by ¼-in. wide, hanging from the branches, shed when ripe; scales with two rounded lobes pointing away from a short central lobe, hairy; seed-wings much wider than the seed portion.

TWIGS—Slender, sometimes hairy, dark reddish-brown, no wintergreen taste (characteristic of Cherry Birch and Yellow Birch); buds blunt (or sometimes pointed), greenish-brown, darker on the scale-tips, often gummy.

BARK—Thin, smooth, reddish-brown on young trunks, becoming creamy-white; peels easily into large sheets to expose a reddish-orange inner bark which gradually turns black with age.

WOOD—Moderately heavy, hard, strong, not durable when in contact with soil; pale brown with nearly white sapwood.

IMPORTANCE—White Birch is an important hardwood tree and is used for special products, turnery, pulpwood and veneer stock.

WHITE BIRCH

MALE AND FEMALE FLOWERS
(FEMALE THINNER)

CAL LEAF LACKS TEETH
R LEAF-STALK

FRUIT: SCALE (LEFT)
SEED (RIGHT) ARE SHED
EARLY IN FALL

BARK PEELS READILY

WINTER TWIGS; SOME HAVE UNDEVELOPED MALE FLOWERS AT THE END

ALASKA BIRCH

Betula neoalaskana Sarg.

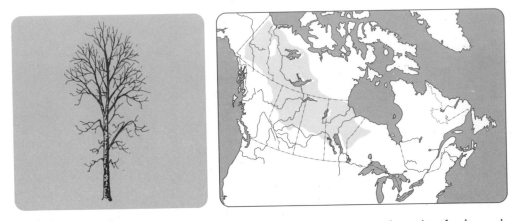

FORM—This species is still poorly under-stood. In previous editions, it has been re-ferred to under various names, or as a variety of White Birch having the botanical name *Betula papyrifera* var. *humilis* (Reg.) Fern. & Raup. Some other authors have described it under the name *Betula resinifera* (Reg.) Britton, while still others have used *Betula alaskana* Sarg., or *Betula papyrifera* var. *neoalaskana* (Sarg.) Raup. All of the published descriptions refer to it as a small tree which, from a dis-tance, resembles a White Birch, and which, when growing in association with White Birch, interbreeds to produce populations of small trees that are mixtures of the two. This tends to add to the difficulty of describing a typical form. Botanists who have identified Alaska Birch claim that it is a slender stiffly upright tree with a narrow oval crown of ascending branches, as shown in the illustration.

HABITAT—Alaska Birch is found throughout the western area of the Boreal Forest Region from the Severn River in northwestern Ontario to the Bering Sea. It characteristically inhabits bogs and poorly drained soils, where it may form pure stands or grow in association with other species, such as Black Spruce.

SIZE—A very small tree, attaining heights of 20 to 40 ft. and diameters of up to 7 ins.

LEAVES—Triangular to broadly oval, with a long taper to a sharp tip and a broad wedge-shaped base, about 2½-ins. long, teeth often glandular but none near the stalk, distinctly of two sizes; fewer than nine pairs of veins each extending to a large tooth on the margin, with smaller intervening teeth; dark green and shiny above, pale and yellowish-green below with tiny resin dots, almost or entirely hairless.

FRUIT—Narrow fruiting-bodies about 1¼-ins. long by ⅜-in. wide, blunt tipped, hanging or slightly spreading from the branches, shed when ripe; scales with two rounded lobes pointing away from a short central lobe or curved slightly downwards, hairy; seed-wings much wider than the seed portion.

TWIGS—Slender, with an abundance of fine short hairs, bright reddish-brown, covered with resin-glands that may be large and crystalline and so dense that they conceal the twig surface (no wintergreen taste); buds blunt, greenish-brown, gummy and slightly hairy.

BARK—Thin, smooth, dark reddish-brown on young trunks, becoming creamy-white or slightly pinkish; peels off in papery layers (but not as freely as on White Birch).

WOOD—Similar to that of White Birch; but the trees seldom become large enough to provide merchantable wood.

IMPORTANCE—The tree does not reach commercial size; therefore the wood is of little use, except for fuel.

NOTES—Birches were among the first trees to move north in the wake of the receding ice.

LEAF IS ALMOST
TRIANGULAR

BRANCH WITH FRUIT; INSERTS: SCALES (LEFT) HAVE ROUNDED,
DOWN-POINTING SIDE LOBES; SEED-WING (RIGHT)
IS MUCH BROADER THAN SEED

GS ARE COVERED WITH
RESIN-GLANDS

BARK PEELS OFF IN PAPERY
LAYERS

TREE HAS A NARROW CROWN WITH
UPRIGHT BRANCHES

WATER BIRCH

Betula occidentalis **Hook.** (*Betula fontinalis* **Sarg.**)

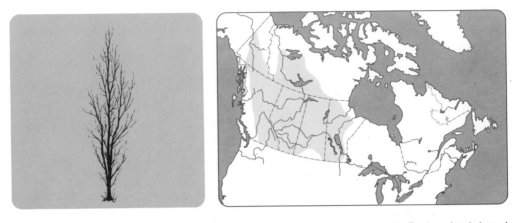

FORM—This species, when of tree size, has a short, usually curved or leaning trunk and an irregular, broad, open crown of ascending slender branches, with somewhat drooping branchlets. It is more commonly shrubby, with several spreading trunks. The natural diversity of the species is enhanced by its occasional crossbreeding with White Birch. Several of the forms that have been produced in this way have been named, but more work is needed before there can be an exact determination of the results of interbreeding. To avoid complications, none of these forms have been included in this edition.

HABITAT—Water Birch ranges through most of the forested areas of western Canada (except the coastal forest). Occasionally, it grows on dry soils, but the best growth is on moist soils along streams, or around springs, where it associates with poplars, willows, alders and other species with similar growth requirements. Dense pure thickets are common.

SIZE—Generally a tall shrub of up to 20-ft. high, but, on favourable sites, may become a tree attaining heights of up to 35 ft. and diameters of up to 14 ins.

LEAVES—Broadly oval, but usually broadest below the middle, with a short taper to a blunt or sharp tip, rounded or wedge-shaped at the base, ¾- to 2-ins. long, teeth sharp and distinctly of two sizes, but absent near the stalk; fewer than six pairs of veins each extending to a large tooth on the margin, with smaller intervening teeth; deep yellowish-green and shiny above, paler and finely gland-dotted beneath, usually without tufts of hairs at the junctions of the veins.

FRUIT—Narrow fruiting-bodies, 1- to 1½-ins. long by ³⁄₁₆- to ⅜-in. wide, blunt tipped, hanging or slightly spreading from the branches, shed when ripe; scales with two, sharp-pointed, ascending lobes shorter than the narrow middle lobe (which is also sharp pointed), hairy; seed-wings about as wide as, or wider than, the hairy seed portion.

TWIGS—Very slender, usually abundantly glandular, reddish-brown, sometimes with fine hairs; buds pointed, slightly gummy, greenish-brown, with fine hairs or hairless.

BARK—Thin, lustrous, dark reddish-brown to nearly black on young trunks, with conspicuous horizontal markings (lenticels); does not peel readily like the bark of most birch species.

WOOD—Relatively light and soft, low in strength; light brown to creamy-white.

IMPORTANCE—This tree seldom reaches commercial size; therefore its wood is of little importance. It is sometimes used locally for fuel and fence posts.

NOTES—The punishment known to schoolboys of another era as "The Birch" originated in Rome where a bundle of birch twigs was the symbol of authority. History does not record the name of the first teacher who turned the symbol into a more striking reminder of his authority, nor the name of the first victim.

WATER BIRCH

SMALL; TEETH LARGE

MALE AND FEMALE FLOWERS (INSERT: FEMALE)

T; FRUIT-SCALES POINTED; SEED-WING
SEED OF EQUAL WIDTH

NG BARK IS VERY DARK

BUDS POINTED; TWIG DENSELY GLANDULAR

GREY BIRCH

Wire Birch

Betula populifolia **Marsh.**

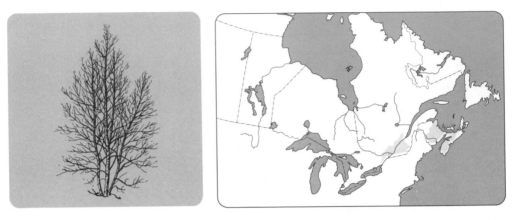

FORM—Grey Birch is commonly found growing in clumps. It has a narrow, irregularly open, conical crown with slender branches ending in fine twigs that have a tendency to droop. The trunk is usually curved and extends almost to the top of the crown. The root system of this tree is shallow.

HABITAT—Primarily a tree of the Atlantic seaboard, Grey Birch ranges through most of the Acadian Forest Region and the eastern parts of the Great Lakes-St. Lawrence Forest Region. It grows on wet or dry, sandy or gravelly soils. Since this tree is intolerant of competition, it tends to form pure stands on burned-over areas, cut overs and abandoned or worn-out pastures, but is soon largely replaced by other species and becomes confined to the openings. Aided by the increasingly wide-spread occurrence of such sites, Grey Birch is actively extending its range northward and westward. Like the White Birch, it can regenerate itself after cutting or fire by producing sprouts around the base of the trunk.

SIZE—One of the smallest of the birches, this species seldom exceeds 35 ft. in height or 6 ins. in diameter. It is a short-lived tree and rarely survives for more than 50 years.

LEAVES—Triangular with a long drawn-out tip, almost straight across at the base, about $2\frac{1}{2}$-ins. long, teeth distinctly of two sizes, the larger ones being almost shallow lobes, no teeth near the stalk; fewer than nine pairs of veins each extending to a large tooth on the margin, with smaller intervening teeth; dark green above, shiny and paler below without hairs; slender stalks allow the vertically hanging leaves to quiver in the slightest breeze.

FRUIT—Narrow fruiting-bodies about $\frac{7}{8}$-in. long by $\frac{3}{16}$-in. wide, blunt tipped, semi-erect on the branches, shed in early winter; scales less than $\frac{1}{16}$-in. long with two, broad, recurving lobes and a very short central one, hairy; seed-wings much wider than the seed portion which is hairless or almost so.

TWIGS—Slender, orangey-brown to grey, with pale warty glands (no wintergreen taste); buds uniform light brownish-grey, resinous, pointed, often hairy.

BARK—Thin, smooth, reddish-brown on young trunks, becoming chalky-white with prominent black patches below the bases of the branches; not peeling readily.

WOOD—Relatively light and soft, not strong; light reddish-brown, creamy-white sapwood.

IMPORTANCE—This tree rarely reaches commercial size in Canada. Its wood is most often used only for fuel. The species has some value as a "nurse tree" for more valuable conifers when these are young and require protection to get established.

NOTES—Grey Birch wood is excellent for turning and, although not available in commercial quantities, provides a workable wood for the craftsman when obtainable locally.

HAS A LONG DRAWN-OUT TIP

MALE FLOWERS GROW
AT THE END OF THE
TWIG

FRUIT; CENTRAL SCALE-TIP SHORT; SEED-WINGS
VERY BROAD

GREY BIRCH OFTEN GROWS IN CLUMPS

RESINOUS; BUDS
AND POINTED

BLACK PATCHES ON BARK ARE READILY
APPARENT

ALDER

Alnus B. Ehrh.

The exact number of species of this genus is not known with certainty, but about 30 have been recognized in the north temperate regions and in parts of Central and South America. Of the eight species in North America, five are found in Canada and, of these, four reach tree size; only one, the Red Alder of British Columbia, becomes a large tree, while two others, the Mountain Alder and Sitka Alder, are usually shrubs. Tag Alder or Speckled Alder (*Alnus rugosa* (Du Roi) Spreng., or *Alnus incana* (L.) Moench), the commonest alder in Canada, is distributed from the prairie provinces to the Atlantic Coast.

White Alder (*Alnus rhombifolia* Nutt.) has been omitted from this edition of *Native Trees*, because there has been no confirmation of reports that it grows in British Columbia.

The Black Alder (*Alnus glutinosa* (L.) Gaertn.), from Europe, is commonly planted in Canada as an ornamental. In Ontario conifer plantations, it is a useful supplement for soil improvement. It is easily distinguishable from the native alders by its dark green, smooth, almost-circular, coarsely toothed leaves which are usually notched at the top, and by its larger fruiting-bodies.

The leaves of alders are alternate and grow singly in two or three ranks along the twigs. On some trees, a few may appear to be in two's, three's or four's on dwarf twigs, somewhat similar to the paired leaves found on the birches. They are simple, mostly oval, and usually toothed, with two sizes of teeth.

The reproductive organs are of the birch type. The male flower clusters are formed in late summer and appear as three to five slender, cylindrical structures on the twigs in early autumn and throughout the winter. The flowers open in spring before the leaves appear. The female flower clusters are also often preformed, and appear as two or three small, oval structures through the winter. Both male and female flowers are on the same tree.

The fruit, which ripens in one season, is a small nutlet with a wing on each side. Sometimes the wing may be circular and completely surround the nutlet or, in some species, the nutlet may be wingless. In any event, the fruits are borne on woody scales that are attached to a stiff central stem and which form an oval fruiting-body that looks like one of the smaller cones on an evergreen tree. The scales open to release the nutlets in autumn, but the fruiting-body remains on the tree, so that "cones" of one or more past seasons are prominent on the tree along with next year's flower clusters. Thus, in autumn, alders may display old open fruiting-bodies that have shed their seeds, new fruiting-bodies that have not quite matured, and immature flower clusters (usually both male and female).

The twigs are slender to moderately stout with a triangular pith, a terminal bud (usually stalked) and lateral buds. Normally the lateral buds are stalked, and both types of buds have two or three overlapping scales, or scales that meet along the edges. The leaf-scars are raised on thickened portions of the twig, are semi-circular or triangular, and generally show three bundle-scars. In this latter feature, they are similar to the willows, poplars, birches, Hop-hornbeam and Blue-beech.

Alders have shallow root systems and, unlike most native trees, bear on their rootlets clusters of swellings inhabited by micro-organisms that can convert nitrogen from the air into compounds useful to plants. These compounds are exploited by the alders as long as the roots remain alive, but ultimately are released to the soil by the decay of the rootlets and become available to other plants. In this way, alders contribute to the maintenance of fertility in forest soils.

The bark is smooth on young trees and conspicuously patterned by long horizontal markings (lenticels). There is a red pigment in the bark that may stain freshly cut wood, especially when it is wet.

The wood is light, soft and moderately low in strength; of local commercial importance.

RED ALDER

Oregon Alder
Western Alder

Alnus rubra Bong. (*Alnus oregona* Nutt.)

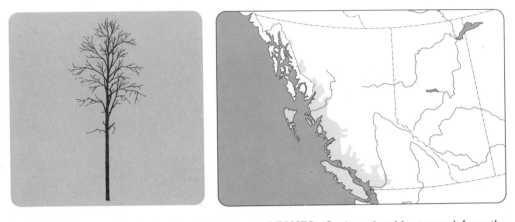

FORM—When growing in the forest, this species develops a straight slightly tapered trunk extending to the top of a narrow rounded crown. In the open, the crown starts almost at the ground, and is composed of spreading branches which give it a broadly conical shape. As with most alders, the root system is shallow and wide-spreading, but, in the protection of the taller trees with which it usually associates, the Red Alder is seldom windthrown. A form of this species with deeply lobed leaves has been recorded from Cowichan Lake, Vancouver Island, and is named *Alnus rubra* var. *pinnatisecta* Starker.

HABITAT—Red Alder is a tree of the Coast Forest Region of British Columbia. It is intolerant of shade and commonly grows in pure stands as an early occupant on cleared land. It is generally one of the first trees on burned-over and cut-over areas, but, like most pioneer species, does not survive for long and is soon succeeded by more tolerant species. The Red Alder is also found in association with Black Cottonwood, Grand Fir, Douglas-fir, Western Red Cedar, Western Hemlock, Western Yew, Bigleaf Maple, Vine Maple and various species of dogwoods, when these associates are growing in open stands.

SIZE—This is the largest of the native alders and regularly grows as a tree. It may reach heights of 80 ft. and diameters of 1 to 2 ft. It is a short-lived tree, old at 40 years, and seldom survives for more than 60 years.

LEAVES—Oval to rhombic, tapered from the middle to both ends, thick, not sticky, dull, dark green above, greyish beneath, hairy on the veins below; teeth noticeably of two sizes, the largest lobe-like with three to six inrolled teeth on each; veins impressed above, veinlets between veins form a ladder-like pattern.

FRUIT—Fruiting-body oval, ¾-in. long by ⅜-in. wide; nutlet narrowly winged or with the wing encircling it.

TWIGS—Moderately stout, triangular or roundish in cross-section, reddish-brown; buds reddish, with two or three hairy bud-scales meeting along their edges; pith indistinctly triangular in cross-section.

BARK—Smooth, light grey, sometimes almost white, occasionally shallowly furrowed in very old trees; breaking into irregular, flat plates; wounds turn red.

WOOD—Fine, even-textured, pale brown, often turning reddish after cutting.

IMPORTANCE—One of the most important hardwoods of the Pacific Coast forests. The wood takes stains well, works easily, and is used for cabinet work, furniture, core-stock, interior finishing, turnery and novelties.

NOTES—The Indians used to extract red dye from the inner bark.

The leaves of the alders are different from those of other deciduous trees in that they remain green in the fall.

NS ON UNDERSURFACE OF LEAF ARE HAIRY

MALE AND FEMALE (ARROW) FLOWER CLUSTERS
VISIBLE THROUGHOUT THE WINTER

NCHLETS ARE MODERATELY STOUT

TREES GROW IN DENSE THICKETS

SPECKLED ALDER

Tag Alder
Grey Alder
Hoary Alder

Alnus rugosa (Du Roi) Spreng. (*Alnus incana* (L.) Moench)

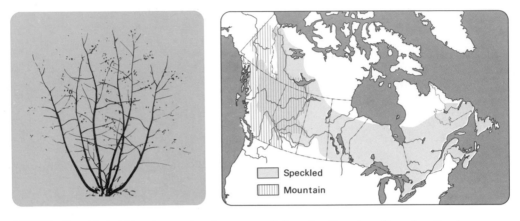

Speckled

Mountain

FORM—Speckled Alder is nearly always a coarse shrub with clumped and crooked trunks but, occasionally, under the most favourable conditions, it may take on an appearance approaching that of a tree. The trunk of the tree-form is also nearly always crooked, and is often bent in a wide curve at the base before rising to support a sparsely branched, round-topped, irregular crown. The curve at the base of the trunk results from the tree having a quite shallow and narrowly spreading root system, which, in a wet spongy soil, gives little support from the wind. When the tree is young, it may be flattened and lie on the ground so that it must rise from near the end of the trunk when straightening itself. Snow in the winter also plays a part in causing young trunks to curve, simply by the pressure of the snow's weight over prolonged periods. A species that is closely related is the Mountain, or Thinleaf, Alder (*Alnus tenuifolia* Nutt.).

HABITAT—Speckled Alder ranges across Canada, but is easily identified only from Saskatchewan eastwards. It is intolerant of shade and, in the forest, is confined to openings or to sparsely populated stands. It grows best in relatively wet situations, along streams, in gullies and in swamps that have some drainage. Mountain Alder grows from Saskatchewan westwards throughout the forested areas of Alberta and British Columbia. It is not found in the Coast Forest Region.

SIZE—When of tree size, Speckled Alder is usually from 20 to 30 ft. in height and under 6 ins. in diameter. Occasionally, trees may reach larger sizes. Mountain Alder is usually a shrub, but on the best sites may reach 45 ft. in height and 9 ins. in diameter.

LEAVES—On Speckled Alder, oval, 2- to 4-ins. long, thick-textured, not sticky, dull, upper surface wrinkled, lower surface hoary, teeth quite noticeably of two sizes; veins deeply impressed above, conspicuously projecting below, rusty-red, the veinlets forming a ladder-like pattern. The difference between Speckled Alder and Mountain Alder is most apparent in the leaves. Those of Mountain Alder are thinner and smoother and have veins that are not impressed above.

FRUIT—Fruiting-body oval, $\frac{5}{8}$-in. long by $\frac{5}{16}$-in. wide; small nutlet has narrow wings.

TWIGS—Moderately slender, reddish-brown; buds dark reddish-brown with two (or three) bud-scales meeting along their edges.

BARK—Smooth, reddish-brown with orange markings (lenticels).

WOOD—Pale brown, often turning reddish after cutting.

IMPORTANCE—Of no commercial importance; used locally for fuel.

NOTES — In areas of Saskatchewan, Speckled Alder and Mountain Alder overlap to the extent that their individuality disappears. Thus, Mountain Alder is a doubtful species and is best treated as a geographical variation of Speckled Alder, in this part of the country.

SPECKLED ALDER

LEAF
HAS PROMINENT
STRAIGHT VEINS,
IMPRESSED ABOVE,
PROJECTING
BELOW (RIGHT)

MALE FLOWER CLUSTER LARGER THAN FEMALE

; BUDS ARE
MINENTLY STALKED

BARK SMOOTH WITH
CONSPICUOUS MARKINGS

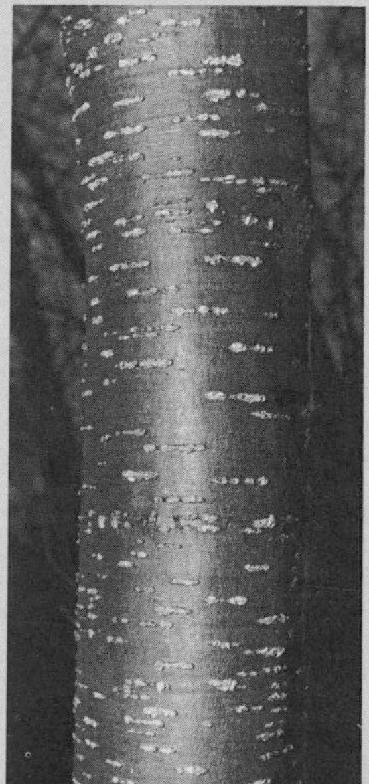

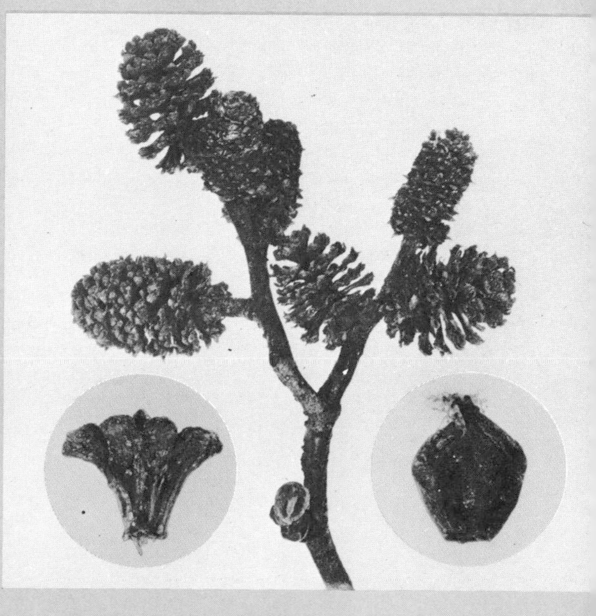

FRUITING BODIES
HAVE WOODY SCALES
(LEFT) AND NARROW-
WINGED SEEDS (RIGHT)

SITKA ALDER

Alnus sinuata (Reg.) Rydb.

FORM—When of tree size, Sitka Alder has a slender trunk and an open crown of short horizontal branches and usually a shallow root system. The species is described under a number of names. By some authors, Sitka Alder is considered to be a geographical variation of the American Green Alder (*Alnus crispa* (Ait.) Pursh), a trans-continental northern shrub with which it merges in northwestern Canada. Under this classification, Sitka Alder is a subspecies with the name *Alnus crispa* (Ait.) Pursh ssp. *sinuata* (Reg.) Hultén. Others recognize it as a distinct species under the name *Alnus sitchensis* (Reg.) Sarg. A form of Sitka Alder with deeply lobed leaves has been named *Alnus crispa* ssp. *sinuata* var. *laciniata* Hultén. It has also been grouped with a shrub of eastern Asia as *Alnus fruticosa* Rupr. var. *sinuata* (Reg.) Reg. ex Hultén. These, and other names under which Sitka Alder has been classified, give an indication of the uncertainty concerning its recognition as a distinct species. In this edition of *Native Trees*, Sitka Alder is recognized as a separate species under the most-used botanical name.

HABITAT—In Canada, this alder is found mainly on cool and moist situations at both high and low elevations in the western mountains. It is distributed from the Alaska border south through British Columbia and eastward to the Rocky Mountains, and in the northern area throughout the western portion of the Boreal Forest Region.

SIZE—Usually a shrub, but on the most favourable sites attains tree size, reaching heights of 40 ft. and diameters of 8 ins.

LEAVES—Broadly oval with a base almost straight across and without teeth near the stalk, abruptly tapered from above the middle to a short tip; thin, deep yellowish-green on both surfaces, shiny, sticky when young, mostly without hairs; teeth of two sizes, seven or more large ones on each side, with smaller intervening teeth which make the larger teeth look like shallow closely toothed lobes; a lateral vein extends to each large tooth, veinlets between lateral veins irregularly branched — not in ladder-like patterns.

FRUIT—Fruiting-bodies long-stalked, approximately ½-in. long, several in a cluster; nutlet with wings about as broad as, or broader than, the seed portion.

TWIGS—Slender, light reddish-brown or yellowish-brown with pale markings; buds without stalks, sharp pointed, reddish-brown, usually in two ranks along the twigs.

BARK—Reddish to greyish-brown, smooth, with long horizontal markings (lenticels).

WOOD—Light, soft, brittle; pale brown with whitish sapwood.

IMPORTANCE—The wood is used locally for fuel and occasionally for lumber when large enough. The tree has some use in preventing soil erosion and in controlling stream flow.

SITKA ALDER

LETS IRREGULAR BETWEEN VEINS

MALE FLOWER CLUSTERS ARE FORMED BEFORE
THE LEAVES FALL

TING BODIES ARE ON LONG STALKS

TREE IS USUALLY SHRUBBY

BEECH

American Beech

Fagus grandifolia Ehrh.

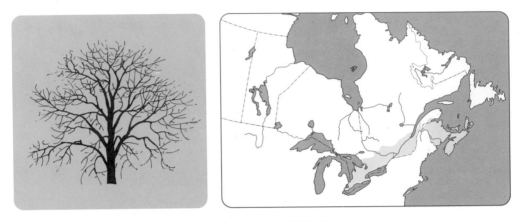

FORM—Of the 10 known species of beech, only one is native to North America. An open-grown Beech is a sturdy-looking tree with a short trunk and a wide-spreading crown. In the forest, it develops a straight clear trunk with a small crown. The root system is wide-spreading but shallow, and commonly produces sprouts when the tree is open grown. The European Beech (*Fagus sylvatica* L.) is planted in Canada, but only as an ornamental. Its leaf has fewer veins, is shorter and broader and minutely toothed in an irregular pattern, or almost without teeth. There are several varieties of European Beech, the commonest being the Copper Beech (*Fagus sylvatica* var. *purpurea* Ait.) with purple leaves; but there are weeping forms, cut-leaf forms, variegated leaf forms and others.

HABITAT—The Beech is a common tree throughout the Deciduous, southern Great Lakes-St. Lawrence, and Acadian Forest regions. It is usually found on moist well-drained slopes and rich bottomlands. Although it may grow in small pure stands, it is more often in mixture with Sugar Maple, Yellow Birch and Eastern Hemlock.

SIZE—It is a medium-sized tree, attaining heights of up to 80 ft. and diameters which range up to 4 ft.

LEAVES—Alternate, single, 2- to 5-ins. long, shaped like an elongated oval; dark bluish-green; straight veined, each vein ending in a prominent tooth with no teeth on the margin between the veins; texture almost leathery.

FLOWERS—Appear after the leaves unfold; males: together in a ball-like cluster at the end of a long drooping stalk; females: two to four in a small cluster; both kinds on the same tree.

FRUIT—A bristly reddish-brown husk which opens into four parts to release two sharply pyramidal, three-sided, edible nuts, each ½-in. long.

TWIGS—Slender, slightly zigzag; leaf-scars semi-circular with numerous indistinct bundle-scars; buds slender, ¾- to 1-in. long with many scales in four rows, each with a grey tip; lateral buds in two ranks along the twig, spreading from it at almost right angles.

BARK—Thin, smooth, light bluish-grey, often mottled; similar on mature trees, but darker.

WOOD—Heavy, hard, tough and strong with conspicuous rays; heartwood pale brown to reddish-brown, sapwood almost white.

SEEDLINGS—Display two fleshy, broadly notched seed-leaves; green above, white below; first juvenile leaves opposite, later ones have an alternate arrangement.

IMPORTANCE—The wood is used for flooring, furniture, containers, handles and wooden-ware; when treated with preservatives it is used for railway ties.

NOTES—The early settlers in southern Ontario often used dried Beech leaves as filling material for mattresses, because the leaves gave that certain springy comfort which was lacking with the universal material, straw.

STRAIGHT VEIN ENDS
TOOTH

MALE (LEFT) AND FEMALE FLOWERS IN SEPARATE CLUSTERS

HUSK OPENS TO RELEASE TWO PYRAMIDAL SEEDS

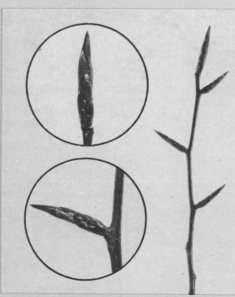

SMOOTH AND SILVERY

TWIG SLENDER; BUD-SCALES INCREASE IN SIZE TOWARDS TIP

CHESTNUT

Castanea dentata (Marsh.) Borkh.

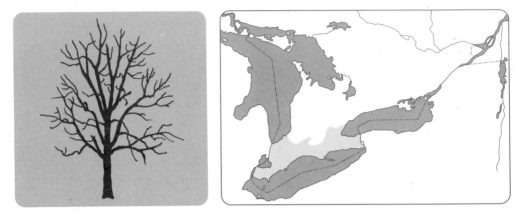

FORM—Of 10 known species of chestnut, five grow in North America, but only one is native to Canada. The Canadian species is a rare tree now, since most of the growing examples were destroyed by a blight, believed to have come to North America on stock imported from Asia towards the end of the last century. Some living roots remain however, and these sprout suckers which usually live long enough to produce a crop of seed, but the seedlings which develop are killed back to ground level, often before bearing seed. In their turn they produce suckers. Thus, the Chestnut maintains itself, although today it seldom reaches an appreciable size. The European Sweet Chestnut (*Castanea sativa* Mill.), occasionally planted as an ornamental, differs from the native species in having leaves that are rounded at the base and hairy beneath; it also has hairy winter-buds. Horse-chestnut (*Aesculus hippocastanum* L.), often seen on city streets, is not related to *Castanea* but is sometimes mistaken for it. It has opposite leaves divided into about seven radiating leaflets, each about the size of the native Chestnut leaf. The fruit is a large inedible nut.

HABITAT—The Chestnut is confined to the Deciduous Forest Region. Though growing in a variety of situations, it favours well-drained sands and gravels and is usually found in mixture with other southern hardwoods.

SIZE—Before the beginning of this century, the Chestnut grew to heights of 100 ft. and diameters of 3 ft. or more; now, usually less than 30 ft. with diameters under 6 ins.

LEAVES—Alternate, single, 6- to 9-ins. long by 2-ins. wide, gradually tapering to both ends, yellowish-green; veins extending beyond the teeth to form short bristles that curve upwards, no teeth on the margin between veins.

FLOWERS—Appear after the leaves are almost fully grown; males: on 6- to 8-ins. long flexible stems; females: solitary, or two to three in a cluster; both kinds on the same tree.

FRUIT—A spiny bur-like husk about 2-ins. across, splitting into four sections, releasing one to five smooth, dull, brownish, edible nuts; often remnants of male flowers at the top of the fruit husk.

TWIGS—Stout, shiny, reddish-brown; lateral buds in two or more rows and clustered at the end of the twig; two or three hairless bud-scales; pith five-pointed.

BARK—Smooth, dark brown, becoming separated into broad flat-topped ridges.

WOOD—Light, soft, not strong, straight-grained, very resistant to decay; greyish-brown, sapwood paler.

IMPORTANCE—Very little lumber was ever produced in Canada. It was used for interior finishing in large buildings, furniture, core-stock, posts and poles.

NOTES—Chestnut blight research is centred at Brooklyn Botanical Gardens, New York.

CHESTNUT

VEINS EXTEND THROUGH THE TEETH
FORM BRISTLES

LONG CLUSTERS OF MALE FLOWERS SURROUND THREE FEMALE
FLOWERS (ARROW)

TWIG AND BUDS
ARE HAIRLESS

NUTS ARE ENCASED IN SPINY BUR-LIKE HUSK

THE TREES ARE SELDOM SEEN

MATURE BARK
HAS BROAD FLAT-TOPPED RIDGES

OAK

Quercus L.

The oaks comprise a genus of over 200 species which are widely distributed in the north temperate regions, the tropics of Central and South America and southeastern Asia. There are 75 to 80 species in North America of which approximately 50 are trees; ten species grow in Canada. Earlier editions included 12 Canadian species, but Scarlet Oak (*Quercus coccinea* Muenchh.) and Northern Pin Oak (*Quercus ellipsoidalis* E. J. Hill) have been omitted because of a lack of identifiable material. Most of the native oaks are in eastern Canada; only Bur Oak (*Quercus macrocarpa* Michx.) ranges into the prairie provinces, and Garry Oak (*Quercus garryana* Dougl.) is confined to British Columbia. In Ontario, the Dwarf Chinquapin Oak (*Quercus prinoides* Willd.), is easily identified because it is a shrub that grows only near Lake Erie. It has small leaves which resemble those of the Chinquapin Oak (*Quercus muehlenbergii* Engelm.) but which usually have only six teeth to a side.

Two European species and their varieties are planted in Canada: English Oak (*Quercus robur* L.) and Durmast Oak (*Quercus petraea* (Mattuschka) Liebl.). Both have leaves with rounded lobes that do not have bristle tips, and in this feature they resemble Canadian white oaks. At the base of its leaf, the English Oak has two small projections that curve inwards to a short leaf-stalk. The Durmast Oak has rounded to heart-shaped leaf-bases and a leaf-stalk ½- to 1-in. long. Both have lobes that are usually without teeth.

The leaves of oaks are simple, alternate, and quite variable in shape and size. Although evergreen oaks (often called "live oaks") grow in warmer regions, all the native species shed their leaves each year and produce a new crop at the start of each growing season.

The flowers are minute. The males are arranged along slender flexible stems that hang in clusters; the females are solitary, or there may be a few on a stout stalk; both sexes appear on the same tree, usually after the leaves unfold.

The fruit is an acorn; a thin-shelled nut seated in a cup of overlapping scales.

The seedlings first appear as short leafless shoots since, on germination of the seeds, the seed-leaves are retained within the nut. At its tip, the shoot develops obscurely lobed juvenile leaves, which sometimes have an opposite arrangement. Occasionally more than one seedling grows from a single acorn, but usually one is stronger than the others and survives at their expense.

The wood is hard, heavy, and strong in most species. It has clearly defined annual rings separated by bands of large vessels. In some species, individual vessels are so large that they are easily visible when viewed in cross-section. Oak wood is in much demand for furniture and floors, but the supply has never been plentiful.

The oaks fall naturally into three groups, with three species in each group:

GROUP	COMMON NAME
White oaks	White Oak
	Garry Oak
	Bur Oak
Chestnut oaks	Swamp White Oak
	Chinquapin Oak
	Chestnut Oak
Red or black oaks	Red Oak
	Black Oak
	Pin Oak

White oaks have leaves with rounded lobes and teeth, and without bristles at their tips. The fruit matures in one season, is sweet to taste, and has a shell with a hairless inner surface. The bark is usually loosely scaly.

Chestnut oaks are similar to the white oaks in fruit and bark features, but have leaves which are usually regularly toothed rather than lobed — a characteristic that makes them quite unlike the other oaks. The teeth do not have bristle tips.

Red or black oaks have leaves with sharp-pointed lobes and teeth that have bristle tips. Their fruits are bitter, take two years to mature, and the inner shell is hairy. The bark is firm and ridged — not scaly as in the other groups.

180

WHITE OAK

Quercus alba L.

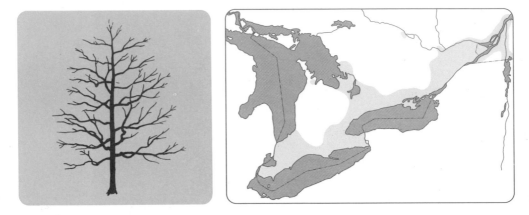

FORM—This tree, when growing in a dense stand, tends to produce a long trunk with little taper, and which is usually branch-free for two-thirds or more of its height. When growing in the open, the trunk divides near the ground into a few large limbs with many wide-spreading lateral branches which become gnarled and twisted and which give the crown a quite rugged appearance. The tree is firmly anchored by a deep tap-root and several deep, spreading lateral roots.

HABITAT—White Oak is a characteristic tree of the Deciduous Forest Region in southern Ontario and extends into the southern parts of the Great Lakes-St. Lawrence Forest Region in Ontario and Quebec. It rarely forms pure stands, but usually associates with other oaks, Basswood, Black Cherry, hickories, Sugar Maple, White Ash and occasional conifers such as Eastern White Pine and Eastern Hemlock. It makes its best growth on deep moist soils with good drainage, but will grow well on a variety of soils.

SIZE—Except near the northern limit of its range, where it may be stunted, White Oak can grow up to 100 ft. in height by 4 ft. or more in diameter. It is a slow-growing tree.

LEAVES—About 6-ins. long by 3-ins. wide; downy and pinkish when unfolding, later hairless on both surfaces; seven to nine narrow lobes, some with one or two large blunt teeth; notches between lobes usually deeply cut. (While the lobes on typical leaves have notches that are cut more than half-way to the midrib, there is considerable variation in the lobing. Some leaves have broad lobes with notches cut less than half-way to the midrib, other trees have leaves that are only slightly lobed or merely wavy on the margin. Some of these have been named varieties or forms.)

FRUIT—Acorn ½- to ¾-in. long, about one-quarter enclosed in a bowl-shaped cup covered with knob-like scales; no marginal fringe.

TWIGS—Moderately stout, greyish-brown, mostly hairless; buds blunt, ⅛- to 3⁄16-in. long, usually hairless, the end one rounded and larger than those along the side of the twig, which point away at a wide angle.

BARK—Pale grey and scaly.

WOOD—Light brown, nearly white sapwood.

IMPORTANCE—This is the most important species of the white oak group and the one that produces most of the wood marketed under that name. The wood is used for furniture, flooring, interior finishing, boat-building, wine casks and barrels for other liquids.

NOTES—The acorn is edible and was often cooked and eaten by the Indians to supplement their normal diet. The oil, which can be extracted, is reputed to soothe painful joints.

HAS DEEPLY CUT, NARROW LOBES

BUDS BLUNT, CLUSTERED TOWARDS TWIG END

BARK IS LIGHT COLOURED

ACORN IS ELONGATED

ALL OAKS HAVE MALE (LEFT) AND FEMALE FLOWERS ON THE SAME TREE

GARRY OAK

Oregon White Oak

Quercus garryana Dougl.

FORM—When growing in the open, this tree has a short stout trunk, often branching into a few large limbs within 15 ft. of the ground. The crown becomes broad and rounded and is composed of numerous twisted and gnarled branches. When forest grown, the crown is reduced in size and the trunk is short, relative to that of other associating species, and is seldom straight. The root system is wide-spreading with little or no tap-root.

HABITAT—This is the only oak native to British Columbia. It is confined to that section of the Coast Forest Region along the east coast of Vancouver Island and the adjacent islands, with two locations on the mainland: on Sumas Mountain and at Yale in the Fraser Canyon. It makes its best growth on deep, rich, loamy soils where drainage is good, but is more often found on dry rocky knolls and shallow soils which are protected from inundation by the sea. On these sites, it forms small, open, pure stands. Being very intolerant of competition from other species, it seldom grows in a mixed stand, but, when it does, there are only a few trees in any given area. Arbutus and Douglas-fir (its closest associates) may be found bordering some stands.

SIZE—On good soils Garry Oak may grow to 75 ft. in height and up to 5 ft. in diameter, but, on the poor rocky sites where it is more often found, it is usually a small crooked tree or even a coarse shrub.

LEAVES—About 5-ins. long by 3-ins. wide; dark green above with a slightly pebbled shiny surface; dull yellowish-green below, with a brownish hairiness; rather thicker and stiffer than other oak leaves and often with a slightly inrolled margin; five to seven rounded or elongated lobes separated by rather narrow but deep notches, the lobes often notched at the tip to appear as if there are one or two teeth.

FRUIT—Acorn 1- to 1¼-ins. long, only the base enclosed in a shallow, somewhat saucer-shaped cup covered with slightly thickened hairy scales; no marginal fringe.

TWIGS—Stout, densely hairy the first season, becoming hairless and dark reddish-brown; buds elongated and pointed, ¼- to ½-in. long, covered with narrow, rather loose, densely hairy, pale brown scales, those along the side of the twig pointing away at a slight angle.

BARK—Greyish-brown and scaly.

WOOD—Light yellowish-brown with almost white sapwood.

IMPORTANCE—The tree is too scarce and usually too poor in form to have any commercial value.

NOTES—In the past, Garry Oak has been used for fence posts (guaranteed for 20 years), insulator pins for telephone equipment, stirrups, saddle trees and hatch wedges for ships.

LEAF HAS ROUNDED LOBES

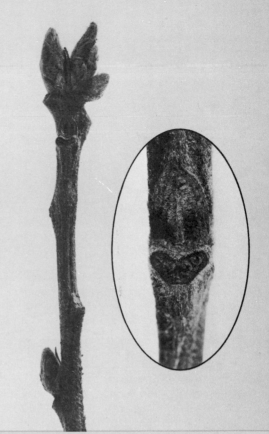

TWIG AND BUDS ARE DENSELY HAIRY

CUP COVERED WITH DENSE HAIRS

MATURE BARK IS SCALY

CROWN BROAD AND ROUNDED WITH TWISTED BRANCHES

BUR OAK

Quercus macrocarpa Michx.

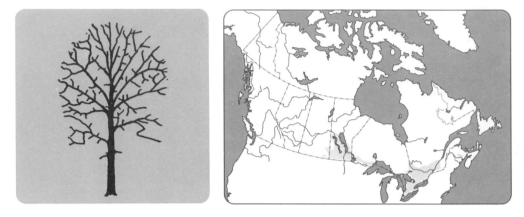

FORM—When open-grown, the crown usually has a rounded outline (although it is quite irregular), and the trunk divides into a number of radiating, crooked and gnarled branches. When in a stand with other trees, the trunk is straight and tall and extends into the top of a short conical crown which is composed of many horizontal branches. The lower part of the trunk often produces small sprouts. The root system consists of a deep tap-root and a number of deep, spreading lateral roots which all help to make the tree windfirm. In Manitoba and Saskatchewan, when in exposed locations, the tree is often stunted or even reduced to the extent of becoming a shrub.

HABITAT—This is the most wide-ranging species of oak. It is found in the Deciduous Forest Region, in scattered localities through most of the Great Lakes-St. Lawrence Forest Region, in the central part of the Acadian Forest Region and in the Boreal Forest Region in the zone of transition to the prairies. It makes its best growth on deep soils in rich bottomlands, where it grows with other hardwood species and scattered conifers. It may also grow on some upland soils.

SIZE—In Canada, Bur Oak seldom reaches the large sizes that it attains farther south. Usually it does not grow over 50 ft. in height by 2 ft. in diameter.

LEAVES—About 7-ins. long by 3½-ins. wide, extremely variable in outline, but the commonest type has a broadly expanded, toothed upper portion separated from the lower half of the leaf by a few short, rounded lobes which gradually reduce in length to the base of the leaf. The outstanding feature is the very fine white hairiness on the undersurface. Some trees have quite deeply lobed leaves while others have leaves that are toothed and merely wavily lobed. Some of these extreme types have been named varieties or forms of Bur Oak.

FRUIT—Acorn ¾- to 1¼-ins. long, approximately half, or more, enclosed in a deep cup covered with large knobby scales, those on the edge of the cup forming a conspicuous fringe.

TWIGS—Stout, yellowish-brown, somewhat hairy, often with corky ridges; buds with blunt tips, hairy, end bud ⅛- to ¼-in. long and longer than the laterals which are pressed against the twig.

BARK—Rough, becoming deeply furrowed into scaly darkish ridges.

WOOD—Pale brown, nearly white sapwood.

IMPORTANCE—Commercially, the wood is not separated from that of the White Oak and therefore is used for furniture, interior finishing, flooring, boat-building and barrels to hold liquids.

NOTES—The Bur Oak is an excellent tree for town planners to plant in city parks, because it transplants readily and is little affected by air pollution from automobile exhausts.

BUR OAK

LATERAL BUDS
FLATTENED
AGAINST TWIG

BRANCHLETS
HAVE CORKY
BARK

...VES VARIABLE; UNDERSURFACE COVERED WITH FINE HAIRS

DEEP KNOBBY CUP WITH FRINGE

MALE FLOWERS (LEFT); FEMALE FLOWERS (RIGHT)

SWAMP WHITE OAK

Quercus bicolor Willd.

FORM—When growing in the open, this species develops a broad, open, roundish-topped crown (with relatively slender branches for an oak) and a short limby trunk. The upper branches are ascending while the lower ones usually droop, with the larger branches and the trunk bearing many small, crooked, hanging branchlets. Since the tree does not shed its branches readily, the lower part has an untidy appearance which is quite typical of the species. When growing in a stand, the trunk is clear of large branches for most of the tree's height, but many of the smaller branches are retained for years and result in knots which lower the quality of the wood.

HABITAT—This oak is found in the Deciduous Forest Region and part of the Great Lakes-St. Lawrence Forest Region along the St. Lawrence Valley in the vicinity of Montreal. It makes its best growth on moist bottomlands and the margins of swamps. It is not an abundant species in Canada.

SIZE—Swamp White Oak is a small to medium-sized tree reaching heights of 50 to 60 ft. and diameters of 2 to 3 ft.

LEAVES—About 5½-ins. long by 3- or 4-ins. wide, with the broadest part of the leaf above the middle and from there gradually tapering to a wedge-shaped base; shiny dark green above and pale greyish-green and velvety beneath, with abundant white hairs; on the margin the pattern varies from uneven and

shallow lobes, to edges that are irregular and wavy-toothed.

FRUIT—Acorn ¾- to 1¼-ins. long, one-third to one-half enclosed in a deep saucer-shaped cup covered with swollen scales that often have recurved tips, those on the edge usually forming a slight marginal fringe; fruit generally borne on a stalk 1- to 3-ins. long. (Normally, the length of fruit-stalks is an unreliable feature when identifying oaks, since any of the species may have fruits with stalks. It has been included in this description, however, because the Swamp White Oak has a particularly long stalk, whereas long stalks are uncommon in the other species.)

TWIGS—Stout, usually without hairs or only slightly downy; buds blunt, seldom exceeding ⅛-in. long, usually hairless, the end bud rounded and larger than the side buds which tend to point away from the twig.

BARK—Greyish-brown and scaly.

WOOD—Light brown, nearly white sapwood.

IMPORTANCE—The wood of this species is sold with that of other white oaks and is used for flooring, interior finishing, cabinet work, furniture, boat-building and barrels for liquids.

NOTES—Oaks have long held a special place in the minds of men and have often been the object of worship or legend. Some are living monuments to historical events.

F HAS VELVETY UNDERSURFACE

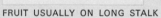

FRUIT USUALLY ON LONG STALK

URE BARK IS SCALY

TWIG AND BUDS USUALLY HAIRLESS

CHINQUAPIN OAK

Quercus muehlenbergii Engelm.

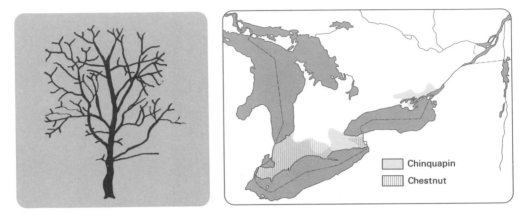

Chinquapin

Chestnut

FORM—This species usually has a straight tapering trunk that extends well into the crown and is commonly broadly buttressed at its base. The crown is made up of many rather short branches and tends to be narrow, with a rounded or somewhat flattish top. The root system is shallow.

HABITAT—Chinquapin Oak is confined to the Deciduous Forest Region, except for a small area northeast of Lake Ontario. It is found on dry rocky ridges, especially on limestone soils.

SIZE—In the forest, this oak may attain a height of 90 ft., but in the open it seldom exceeds 40 ft. in height or 2 ft. in diameter.

LEAVES—About 5-ins. long by 2½-ins. wide; often somewhat lance-shaped with a long narrow tip, but usually broadened slightly above the middle; regularly toothed with about 10 sharp-pointed teeth to a side, with sharp notches separating the teeth and with straight veins extending to each tooth; yellowish-green and glossy above, pale greyish-green and finely downy beneath.

FRUIT—Acorn ½- to ¾-in. long, approximately half enclosed in a decidedly deep cup covered with small hairy scales that are only slightly knobby, and without a marginal fringe.

TWIGS—Slender, hairless, greyish-brown to orangey-brown; buds rather sharp pointed, ³⁄₁₆-in. long, mostly hairless, light chestnut-brown, the laterals similar to the end bud.

BARK—Pale grey to nearly white; scaly.

WOOD—Heartwood dark brown, sapwood nearly white.

IMPORTANCE—One of the least important of the Canadian oaks. The wood is sold as "white oak" and is used for furniture, flooring, interior finishing, boat-building and barrels for holding liquids.

CHESTNUT OAK
Quercus prinus L.

This small tree, usually under 40 ft. in height and confined to the Deciduous Forest Region in southern Ontario, is similar in many of its characteristics to the Chinquapin Oak. It is found on dry, stony, limestone ridges where it occasionally forms small pure stands. Sometimes it is found on rich bottomlands in mixture with other species.

It is distinguishable from Chinquapin Oak by its leaves having blunt teeth and the notches between the teeth being rounded rather than sharp. Also, the buds are of greater size, being ¼- to ⅓-in. long. The end bud is larger than the laterals which spread at a wide angle from the twig.

There are often intermediate forms between Chestnut Oak and Chinquapin Oak, and between these and the Dwarf Chinquapin Oak (*Quercus prinoides* Willd.). The identification of any of these oaks is difficult for the amateur botanist.

QUAPIN OAK HAS SHARP TEETH

CHESTNUT OAK HAS
ROUNDED TEETH

CHINQUAPIN OAK (LEFT) CHESTNUT OAK (RIGHT)

NUT OAK HAS DISTINCTIVE BARK

CHINQUAPIN OAK (LEFT) CHESTNUT OAK (RIGHT)

RED OAK

Quercus rubra L.

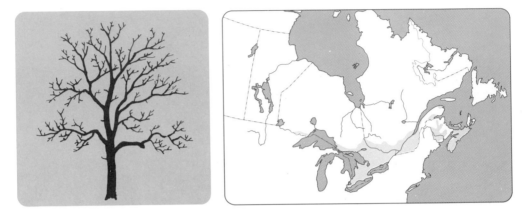

FORM—The open-grown tree of this species generally develops a short sturdy trunk, divided into a few large branches that support a wide-spreading uneven-shaped crown with a more or less rounded outline. Forest trees have straight trunks free of branches for half or more of the tree's height, and rather symmetrically rounded narrow crowns. The root system is deep and spreading, and may include a tap-root. The species is variable in many of its characteristics, particularly its fruits. The common type in southern Ontario has quite large acorns seated in shallow saucer-shaped cups, and is accepted by some botanists as a variety with the name *Quercus rubra* var. *borealis* (Michx. f.) Farw.

HABITAT—Red Oak is a common tree in the Deciduous Forest Region and throughout the Great Lakes-St. Lawrence and the Acadian Forest regions. It is rather intolerant of competition, and characteristically grows on rocky or gravelly uplands in pure stands, or in mixture with other hardwoods and occasional conifers. Two common associates are Trembling Aspen and Eastern White Pine. Towards its northern limit of growth, the Red Oak typically forms pure stands on rocky ridge-crests.

SIZE—Usually a medium-sized tree 60 to 80 ft. in height and 1 to 3 ft. in diameter but, under ideal growing conditions, may exceed 100 ft. in height and 4 ft. in diameter.

LEAVES—About 7-ins. long by 3- or 4-ins. wide; yellowish-green, dull or sometimes lustrous, hairless except for occasional tufts of inconspicuous hairs on the underside at the junctions of the veins; seven to nine lobes, tapered from base to tip and separated by V-shaped notches (the lobes are approximately equal in length, to the broadest part of the leaf between opposite notches).

FRUIT—Acorn ¾- to 1¼-ins. long and almost as broad, about one-third enclosed in a shallow bowl-shaped cup or less than one-quarter enclosed in a saucer-shaped cup (southern Red Oak); cup covered with overlapping, closely fitting, thin, hairless, reddish-brown scales on both types.

TWIGS—Moderately stout, reddish-brown, hairless; buds ¼-in. long, sharp pointed, shiny, reddish-brown, smooth except for a few brownish hairs at the tip.

BARK—Smooth, slate-grey on young trunks, later grooved by shallow cracks into long flattish ridges which become checked across; normally the checking is confined to the base of the tree.

WOOD—Pink to reddish-brown with nearly white sapwood.

IMPORTANCE—The wood is not as resistant to decay as that of the white oaks and is suitable for making barrels to hold dry goods, but not liquids. It is used extensively, however, for flooring, interior finishing and furniture.

NOTES—This North American species is popular in Europe as an ornamental.

VES HAVE BRISTLE-TIPPED LOBES AND TEETH

MALE AND FEMALE (ARROW) FLOWERS

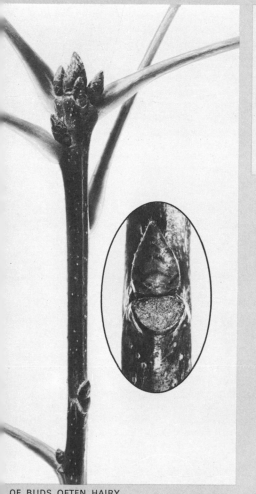

VARIETY (RIGHT) HAS SHALLOWER CUP

OF BUDS OFTEN HAIRY

MATURE BARK HAS VERTICAL PATTERN

BLACK OAK

Quercus velutina Lam.

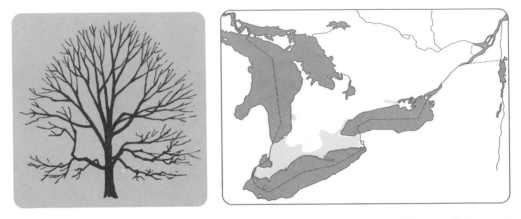

FORM—Black Oak is a variable species with a trunk that usually tapers only slightly as it extends well into the crown. The branches in the lower part of the crown are horizontal; in the upper part, they are ascending. The crown is often quite irregular and can be narrow or wide-spreading, elongated or rounded. In the forest, the trunk is usually branch-free for half the height of the tree. The root system is characterized by a deep tap-root and some wide-spreading and deep lateral roots. Several different forms of the species have been named on the basis of the variable lobing on the leaf and its degree of hairiness, and a number of hybrids between this species and Red Oak or Pin Oak have also been recorded. Some examples of Black Oak, therefore, may not correspond exactly with the detailed descriptions given below.

HABITAT—Black Oak is almost wholly confined to the Deciduous Forest Region, except for one small outlying area north of the eastern end of Lake Ontario. It is intolerant of competition and is usually found growing on poor gravelly or sandy soils, but rarely in pure or dense stands.

SIZE—Although further south, in the United States, Black Oak can reach a height of 150 ft. and a diameter of 4 ft., in Canada it is usually less than 70 ft. in height and 3 ft. in diameter.

LEAVES—About 6-ins. long by 4-ins. wide; downy when unfolding, later hairless except along the veins on the undersurface; shiny dark green above, yellowish-green below and rather roughened; five to seven oblique to horizontal lobes, somewhat rectangular, and separated by deep U-shaped notches (lobes usually at least twice as long as the width of the broadest part of the leaf between opposite notches).

FRUIT—Acorn ½- to ¾-in. long and almost as broad, approximately half enclosed in a bowl-shaped cup covered with overlapping, loosely fitting, thin, slightly hairy, dull, brownish scales; slight marginal fringe.

TWIGS—Moderately stout, dark reddish-brown, hairless or faintly hairy; buds ¼-in. long, sharp pointed, dull, greyish-brown, usually densely covered with greyish-white woolly hairs.

BARK—Smooth and dark grey on young trunks, becoming grooved by deep cracks into irregular, short, rounded ridges which check across into more or less square segments; bark on old trees almost black.

WOOD—Light brown, nearly white sapwood.

IMPORTANCE—The wood is sold as "red oak" and is used for flooring, interior finishing and furniture.

NOTES—The bark of the Black Oak contains tannin in sufficient quantities to make commercial extraction worthwhile.

A yellow dye suitable for colouring most natural fibres can be obtained by boiling shredded pieces of inner bark in water.

LEAVES ARE VARIABLE

BUDS
ARE
WOOLLY

CUP HAS
SLIGHT FRINGE

RIDGES CHECKED
ACROSS INTO
SHORT
SEGMENTS

PIN OAK

Quercus palustris **Muenchh.**

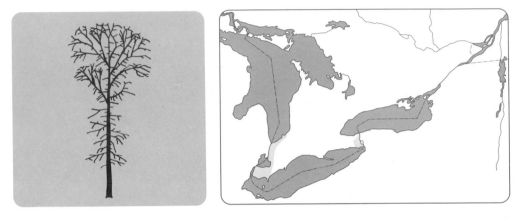

FORM—The trunk of this tree is straight, with a gradual taper, and extends well up into a crown of rather slender branches (for an oak). In the upper portion of the crown, the branches ascend, in the centre they project horizontally and, in the lower part, they tend to droop slightly. The outline is that of a symmetrical cone or pyramid. A characteristic feature, and one that has an effect in reducing the quality of the wood, is the numerous small stiff branchlets that stand out like pins or hang from the trunk and larger branches. These are not readily shed and perhaps account for the common name "Pin Oak". The root system is shallow. This species is one of the earliest oaks to bloom; the flowers appear when the leaves are about one-third developed.

HABITAT—Pin Oak is confined to relatively small areas in the Deciduous Forest Region in southern Ontario. It grows typically in damp, poorly drained, clay soils bordering swamps or along streams, but flourishes on well-drained loamy soils. Usually it is found in association with other hardwoods, including other oaks, White Elm, Slippery Elm and willows.

SIZE—A small to medium-sized tree reaching heights of 50 to 60 ft. and diameters of 1 to 2 ft. on good sites.

LEAVES—About 4½-ins. long and as wide or sometimes wider than they are long; dark green and shiny above, paler on the undersurface and without hairs except for tufts in the joints between the veins; five to seven (commonly five) wide-spreading, horizontal lobes that are narrowly rectangular and separated by deep U-shaped notches (the lobes are usually three times as long, or longer, than the width of the broadest part of the leaf between opposite notches).

FRUIT—Acorn ½ in., or less, in length (the smallest of the tree oaks), nearly spherical, enclosed only at the base in a shallow saucer-shaped cup covered with overlapping, closely fitting, thin scales with minute hairs and brownish margins.

TWIGS—Slender, hairless, reddish-brown; buds ⅛- to ³⁄₁₆-in. long (the smallest of the red oaks), sharp pointed, light chestnut-brown, almost hairless.

BARK—Greyish-brown, rather thin, smooth; with age the bark checks into narrow ridges, but these are so shallow that it appears to remain smooth.

WOOD—Light brown, sapwood nearly white.

IMPORTANCE—The wood is sold with that of other red oaks and is used for flooring, interior finishing and furniture. Because of the symmetrical shape of the tree, its clean appearance and attractive leaves, it has some use as an ornamental.

NOTES—A black ink can be made from insect-formed twig galls on Pin Oak by steeping the galls in a small quantity of water to which iron filings have been added.

FRUIT SMALLEST OF TREE-SIZE OAKS

BUDS SMALLEST IN
RED OAK GROUP

MATURE BARK HAS LOW NARROW RIDGES

ERSURFACE OF LEAF HAS TUFTS OF HAIR

WN IS CONICAL

ELM

Ulmus L.

There are approximately 18 species of elm, six of which are native to North America. The remainder are widely distributed in temperate and northern Eurasia. Of the American species, all are found east of the Rocky Mountains, three of them in Canada.

The elms are among the best-known eastern hardwood trees and in many parts of the country form a conspicuous and pleasing part of the landscape. All attain tree size; one species, the White Elm, occasionally grows very large. They are fast-growing trees, easily transplanted and are much favoured for planting along streets and as shade trees.

The leaves of the elms are shed at the end of the growing season and a new crop appears each spring. They are simple, short-stalked, alternate, in two rows along the twigs, oval, asymmetrical at the base, prominently straight-veined with coarse teeth of two sizes on the margin — the largest ones at the ends of the veins and the smaller ones between the veins.

The elms are among the earliest of the trees to flower; the flowers appear in the spring some time before the leaves unfold. The individual flowers contain both sexes (perfect) and are arranged in clusters.

The fruit is a small flat seed with a broad wing surrounding it and, in all the native species, is provided with some hairs. It matures early, before the leaves are fully grown, and is shed within a few days.

The twigs are slender and distinct from those of most other trees in having their buds arranged in two rows, with the bud-scales in two rows on the buds. Only lateral buds appear on the twigs, since at the end of each growing season the twigs die back as far as one of the fully formed lateral buds. The leaf-scars are prominent because of their light-brown colour and their three sunken bundle-scars. The pith is solid and round in cross-section.

Elm bark is dark grey to reddish-brown and, on mature trees, becomes divided by vertical cracks into elongated, somewhat flat-topped, rough, irregular ridges.

The wood is hard, heavy and tough and, because of its good bending properties, has several specialized uses, including the manufacture of hockey sticks. Locally, it is used extensively on farms or wherever a low-cost wood is needed. It is a difficult wood to split, however, and is not a favourite fuel for wood-burning stoves.

In addition to the three native elms, a few introduced species and their varieties are commonly planted on city streets, in parks and along highways in some areas. They are easily separated from the native species and from one another. The Scotch, or Wych, Elm (*Ulmus glabra* Huds.) has leaves that resemble those of the native Slippery Elm, but it bears fruit which is quite different from any other species. The fruit is the largest of all the elms, being approximately 1-in. across, and differs from native elms in being completely free of hairs, and from other introduced species in having the seed centrally located in the seed-wing. A number of grafted forms of this species are fairly common. The well-known Umbrella Elm (*Ulmus glabra* var. *camperdownii* (Henry) Rehd.) and another form with dark purple leaves, *Ulmus glabra* var. *atropurpurea* (Spaeth) Rehd., are the most popular.

The English Elm (*Ulmus procera* Salisb.), often conspicuous because of a growth of suckers along the trunk and larger branches, has smaller leaves than those of any native elm (about 2½-ins. long) and hairless fruits about ½-in. long. Some forms of English Elm with corky ridges on the branchlets resemble the native Rock Elm, but the leaf shows several of the main lateral veins forking, whereas the Rock Elm leaf rarely shows any forked veins. Siberian Elm (*Ulmus pumila* L.), or Chinese Elm as it is often improperly called, has the smallest leaves of all the elms. They are narrow and almost symmetrical at the base. This tree is popular for hedges.

WHITE ELM

American Elm

Ulmus americana L.

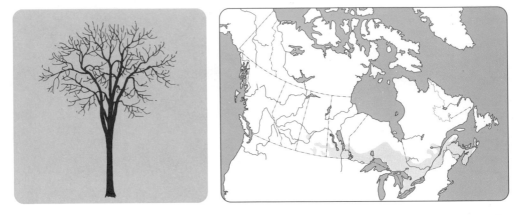

FORM—From a distance, White Elm is one of the most easily recognized trees. The trunk, usually straight (although sometimes buttressed at the base), forks several feet above the ground into a few large, ascending limbs which divide repeatedly until lost in many outwardly fanning branchlets to form a graceful, spreading, vase-like or umbrella-like crown. The branchlets are often drooping, even on relatively young trees. A shallow but wide-spreading root system gives the tree good support on all but the wettest sites. Several forms of this species have been named.

HABITAT—White Elm is found throughout the Deciduous, the Great Lakes-St. Lawrence, and the Acadian Forest regions and extends for considerable distances into the southern part of the Boreal Forest Region. It is a common tree on wet sites and alluvial flats, where water often lies in the spring, but does best on rich, moist, sandy or gravelly loams where the water table is close to the surface and drainage is good.

SIZE—One of the largest trees of eastern Canada, sometimes reaching a height of 125 ft. and a diameter of 7 ft. or more, though heights of 60 to 80 ft. and diameters of 3 to 4 ft. are more usual.

LEAVES—About 4½-ins. long by 2- to 3-ins. wide, dark green, smooth or slightly rough above, paler green on the undersurface; the lateral veins average four to the inch of midrib at the mid-portion of the leaf, with seldom more than one or two forking to end in two or more of the largest teeth (these usually towards the base of the leaf).

FLOWERS—On slender undivided stalks that are ½-in. long.

FRUIT—Oval, about ¼-in. wide; the wing notched deeply at the tip and fringed with hairs round the edge, otherwise hairless.

TWIGS—Often decidedly zigzag, greyish-brown, slightly hairy or without hairs; leaf-buds ³⁄₁₆-in. long, sharp pointed, pale reddish-brown with slightly hairy scales, somewhat flattened and lying close to the twig; flower-buds (when present) are below the leaf-buds, and are larger and plumper than the leaf-buds.

BARK—Dark greyish-brown with broad, deep, intersecting ridges, or often scaly; outer bark when broken across shows layers of a whitish-buff colour alternating with thicker dark layers. With weathering, whitish and dark areas are exposed, making the trunk somewhat mottled and ash-grey.

WOOD—Heartwood pale yellowish-brown, sapwood nearly white.

IMPORTANCE—A useful ornamental; the wood is used for barrels to hold dry goods, boxes, crates, furniture, panelling, caskets and boat-building; the unpolished veneer is used for fruit and vegetable containers.

NOTES—In many a farm kitchen, the white, scrubbed, elm-topped table was a symbol of the housewife's insistence on cleanliness.

WHITE ELM

PROMINENT DOUBLE TEETH

BOTH SEXES ARE IN THE SAME FLOWER

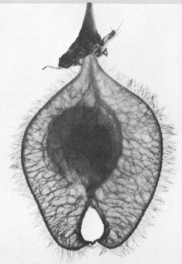

FRUIT ALMOST MATURE BEFORE LEAVES APPEAR

BUDS IN TWO ROWS
ON TWIG; BUD-SCALES
IN TWO ROWS

MATURE BARK HAS
DEEP INTERSECTING
RIDGES; SOME TREES
ARE SCALY

ROCK ELM

Cork Elm

Ulmus thomasii Sarg.

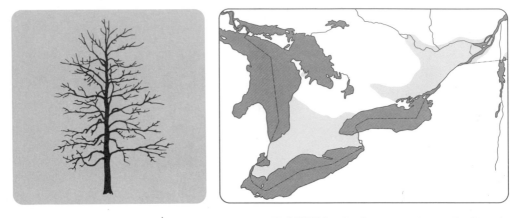

FORM—In this species, the trunk of the tree continues undivided almost to the top of the crown which is cylindrical or somewhat oval and is supported by a number of arching branches. The branches project obliquely or almost horizontally from the trunk; the smaller ones are often crooked and have a gnarled, thick, ridged bark. The coarse bark on small branches (a rather uncommon feature on Canadian trees) results from the tendency of this species to form a cork, similar to that of Bur Oak. As a result, the Rock Elm has quite a rough shaggy appearance, especially in winter when the tree is leafless. On good soils, the root system is deep and wide-spreading.

HABITAT—Rock Elm is confined to the Deciduous Forest Region and the central part of the Great Lakes-St. Lawrence Forest Region. It usually grows on limestone ridges, but can be found in a variety of soils, usually in association with other hardwoods, such as Basswood, Butternut and the maples.

SIZE—Similar in size to the Slippery Elm, usually attaining heights of 50 to 70 ft. and diameters of up to 2½ ft.

LEAVES—About 3½-ins. long by 2-ins. wide, very dark green, shiny and smooth above, slightly paler and faintly hairy on the undersurface; there is an average of six lateral veins to the inch of midrib at the mid-portion of the leaf; the veins rarely fork as they approach the margin; the base of the leaf is usually nearly symmetrical.

FLOWERS—On ½-in. slender stalks branching from a main stem about 1½-ins. long.

FRUIT—Oval, about ⅓-in. wide, the wing pointed at both ends, only slightly notched at the tip, covered with hairs over both the seed and the poorly defined wing.

TWIGS—Slender, becoming strongly ridged with corky bark, light yellowish-brown, may be covered with fine hairs or without hairs; leaf-buds sharp pointed (not flattened as in some elms), pointing away from the twig, dark chestnut-brown; bud-scales have marginal hairs.

BARK—Dark grey, furrowed and forming broad intersecting ridges; the outer bark when broken across shows layers of a whitish-buff colour alternating with darker thicker layers; with weathering, whitish and dark areas of bark are exposed, making the trunk somewhat mottled and ash-grey.

WOOD—Rock Elm wood is the hardest, toughest and strongest of the Canadian elms; heartwood light brown, sapwood nearly white to light brown.

IMPORTANCE—Although the wood is used especially for piano frames, boat frames and dock fenders, its major use is for hockey sticks.

NOTES—Rock Elm is a very difficult wood to work, but it holds nails exceptionally well, takes a good polish and accepts paint and other types of surface finishes.

ROCK ELM

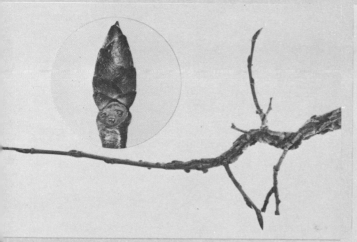

NCHLET CORKY; BUD-SCALES IN TWO ROWS

MANY CLOSELY-SPACED, STRAIGHT VEINS

TS HAIRY; ATTACHED TO A CENTRAL STEM

TYPICAL TREE HAS
SINGLE TRUNK
CONTINUING TO TOP
OF CROWN

FLOWERS ARE ON SLENDER
STALKS

MATURE BARK
HAS BROAD INTERSECTING RIDGES

SLIPPERY ELM

Red Elm

Ulmus rubra Mühl.

FORM—Although this species resembles White Elm in general appearance, the trunk divides into wide-spreading limbs rather high up on the tree, giving the Slippery Elm a greater length of branch-free trunk in relation to crown depth. The crown is broad and rather flat-topped. Also, the branchlets tend to be ascending or spreading, not drooping as is common with White Elm. The root system is shallow but wide-spreading, and the tree is considered to be quite windfirm.

HABITAT—Slippery Elm is found in the Deciduous Forest Region and the southern parts of the Great Lakes-St. Lawrence Forest Region. It makes its best growth on rich soils along streams and on low slopes, but may also be found as a smaller tree on dry rocky ridges. Like other species of elm, it does not form pure stands, but grows with other hardwoods, including maples, Basswood and Butternut.

SIZE—Slippery Elm reaches 70 ft. in height and 2 ft. in diameter; occasionally it is larger.

LEAVES—About 5½-ins. long by 3-ins. wide, often widest above the middle, dark green above with very rough hairs (which, when the leaf is dry, are sufficiently abrasive to mark the surface of a thumb nail), paler green and hairy on the undersurface; lateral veins average four to the inch of midrib at the mid-portion and several fork near the margin to end in two or more of the largest teeth; leaf fragrant.

FLOWERS—In densely packed clusters which are made up of almost stalkless flowers.

FRUIT—Almost circular in outline, approximately ½-in. across, the wing shallowly notched at the tip and hairy only over the seed.

TWIGS—Moderately stout, greyish-brown and hairy; buds dark brown, fairly blunt and coated at the ends with long rusty hairs. The bark of the twigs when chewed has a slippery consistency, and is said to be a thirst quencher.

BARK—Reddish-brown, shallowly furrowed into rather irregular, vertical, scaly ridges; outer bark when broken across does not show different coloured layers (see White Elm), but is a uniform dark reddish-brown and retains this colour with weathering.

WOOD—Inferior to other native elms; heartwood reddish-brown, sapwood greyish-white.

IMPORTANCE—The wood is usually sold as "White Elm" and is used for the same purposes: barrels for dry goods, boxes, crates, furniture, panelling, caskets and boat-building.

NOTES—The bark was used by some Indians for canoe-building, but was much less suitable than the more popular and lighter birch bark.

The bark has some medicinal properties in that when the inner bark is steeped in warm water, a substance is produced that can be used as a poultice for minor injuries.

SLIPPERY ELM

BOTH SURFACES OF LEAF ARE HAIRY

FLOWERS ARE IN DENSE STALKLESS CLUSTERS

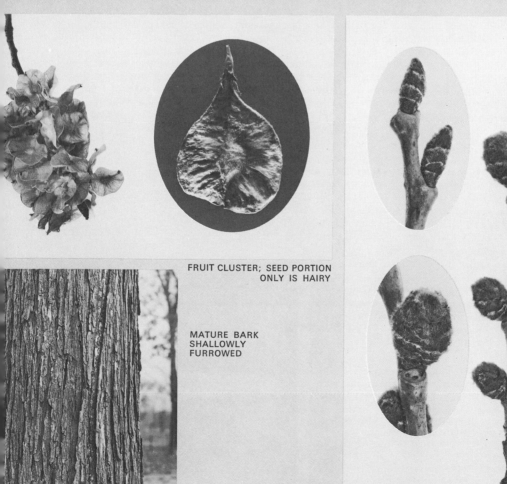

FRUIT CLUSTER; SEED PORTION
ONLY IS HAIRY

MATURE BARK
SHALLOWLY
FURROWED

TWIGS AND
BUDS HAIRY;
FLOWER BUDS PLUMP

HACKBERRY

Celtis occidentalis L.

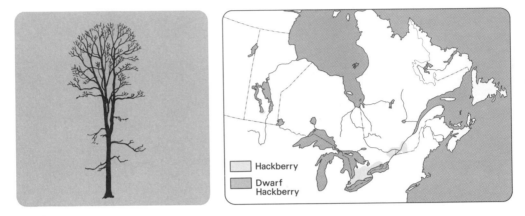

Hackberry
Dwarf Hackberry

FORM—The Hackberry resembles the elms in general appearance. The crown has a broad top of ascending arching branches, often with drooping branchlets. The tree grows in a variety of forms, some of them scarcely larger than shrubs. One, referred to as Dwarf Hackberry (*Celtis tenuifolia* Nutt.), is reported in the Port Franks and Point Pelee areas of Ontario. It is described as a coarse shrub, or small tree up to 25 ft. in height, with leaves that are very symmetrical and broader and shorter than those of the Hackberry. The Dwarf Hackberry leaves seldom exceed 2¼ ins. in length and are either toothless or have no more than 15 teeth to a side; the fruits are small. In addition, two varieties have been segregated on the basis of leaf-shape, *Celtis occidentalis* var. *pumila* (Pursh) Gray, with very asymmetrical leaves more than half as wide as they are long; and *Celtis occidentalis* var. *canina* (Raf.) Sarg., with narrow almost symmetrical leaves less than half as wide as they are long. Since both these varieties (and the Dwarf Hackberry) may be found in the same areas as the species, the separation of the different forms is at best uncertain.

HABITAT—Hackberry is scattered throughout the Deciduous Forest Region and part of the Great Lakes-St. Lawrence Forest Region. One isolated report shows that it grows near Delta, on the south shore of Lake Manitoba.

SIZE—Usually a medium-sized tree seldom over 60 ft. in height or 2 ft. in diameter.

LEAVES—Shed at the end of each growing season, simple, short-stalked, alternate in two rows along the twig, variable in size and shape, 2- to 6-ins. long, 1½- to 3½-ins. wide, long tapering tip, asymmetrical base, deep bluish-green and rough or smooth above, paler beneath and hairy on the veins (which make an acute angle with the midrib), the lowest pair of veins project below the base and suggest a three-forked stalk; 15 to 40 single teeth on either side, except at the oblique base.

FLOWERS—Appear with the leaves; perfect and one-sexed, both sexes on the same tree.

FRUIT—Single on ¾-in. stalks, fleshy like a cherry but with a thin flesh and pitted stone, edible, reddish-purple, ⅓-in. across, hanging on the tree in winter.

TWIGS—Slender, green or tinged with brown, finely downy; as in the walnuts, the pith shows cavities separated by partitions; buds arranged in two rows with two rows of bud-scales on each bud.

BARK—Greyish-brown; ridges narrow with corky thickenings.

WOOD—Heavy, hard, coarse-textured, weak; yellowish with paler sapwood.

IMPORTANCE—Some forms useful ornamentally. Wood of no commercial importance.

NOTES—A coarse thread suitable for ropes and matting is obtained when the bark is steeped in water until the fibres separate.

STALK DIVIDES INTO THREE
V LEAF-BLADE

END BUD IS OFTEN BENT

MALE FLOWER CLUSTERS ILLUSTRATED

THICKENINGS ON NARROW RIDGES

SINGLE LONG-STALKED FRUIT AT JUNCTION OF LEAF-STALK

RED MULBERRY

Morus rubra L.

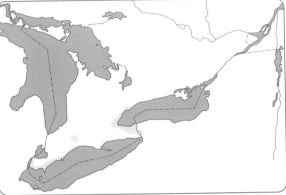

FORM—This tree has a short trunk which seldom reaches 6 ft. in height before dividing into stout spreading branches that form the dense rounded crown. The tree has a golden tinge which is largely hidden in the summer by the yellowish-green foliage. Though the only representative of the family *Moraceae* native to Canada, other species of this family have been introduced, and two of them are common in some areas of Ontario. White Mulberry (*Morus alba* L.), from eastern Asia, is identified by the high lustre of its leaves, the absence of hair on the leaf undersurface, and by its whitish or reddish fruit. Osage-orange (*Maclura pomifera* (Raf.) Schneid.) from the southern United States, is easily recognized by its small oval leaves which narrow abruptly into long slender tips, and also by its zigzag twigs which commonly bear a stiff thorn at each bend just above the leaf. The fruit resembles an orange, but is green and not edible.

HABITAT—Although native to only a few districts within the Deciduous Forest Region, Red Mulberry has been planted as an ornamental or as a fruit tree in other parts of Canada, and has escaped locally in southern Ontario and British Columbia. It does not form pure stands, and grows best on deep moist soils scattered among other hardwoods.

SIZE—A small tree seldom more than 30 ft. in height, although forest-grown trees may reach heights of 50 to 60 ft. and diameters of approximately 3 ft.

LEAVES—Shed annually, simple, on 1-in. stalks, alternate, approximately 5-ins. long, coarsely single toothed, unlobed to variously lobed on the same tree, sinuses between lobes without teeth, prominently three-veined at the base (like the Hackberry), short pointed, yellowish-green above, rough hairy beneath.

FLOWERS—Male and female in separate clusters, occasionally mixed in a cluster, appearing before or with the leaves, both kinds usually on the same tree.

FRUIT—A compact cluster resembling a blackberry, about 1-in. long, dark reddish-purple to almost black, sweet, juicy and edible.

TWIGS—Slender, exude a milky juice when cut, orangey-brown; buds in two rows on the twig (all lateral buds as in elms, but leaf-scars show several bundle-scars whereas elm leaf-scars show only three bundle-scars).

BARK—Reddish-brown, separating into long flaky plates like the bark of the Hop-hornbeam.

WOOD—Heavy, hard, durable, straight-grained; orangey-brown with yellow sapwood.

IMPORTANCE—The quantity of this wood in Canada is negligible, but, where available, it is valued for its durability for posts, barrel-making and boat-building.

NOTES—Bird watchers living in the relatively small area where Red Mulberry can be grown are well advised to plant this tree.

RED MULBERRY

-STALK DIVIDES INTO THREE

SOME LEAVES ARE LOBED

T IS A COMPACT CLUSTER OF FLESH-COVERED SEEDS

ON RAISED PROJECTION
E LEAF-SCAR

LEAF-SCAR SHOWS SEVERAL
BUNDLE-SCARS

TWIG HAS NO TRUE TERMINAL BUD (SEE INSERT)

CUCUMBER-TREE

Magnolia acuminata L.

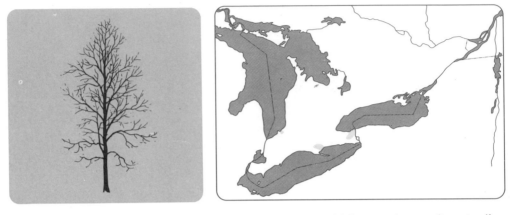

FORM—Of about 35 species of the genus *Magnolia* distributed in North America, Central America, and eastern and southern Asia, nine are native to North America and one of these has been able to extend its range into Canada. Although the Canadian species is rare in the natural state, many representatives and several ornamental forms have been planted. Most of the ornamentals have very showy tulip-like flowers which have made the magnolias well known in the milder parts of the country. When growing in the forest, the native tree develops a straight trunk free of branches for 40 ft. or more, but, in the open, the crown extends to within a few feet of the ground and is broadly pyramidal. The root system is deep and wide-spreading.

HABITAT—The Cucumber-tree can be found in a few locations within the Deciduous Forest Region, usually on rich well-drained soils along streams or on protected hillsides. It does not form pure stands, but grows singly or in scattered colonies among other hardwoods.

SIZE—A medium-sized tree seldom over 70 ft. in height or 2 ft. in diameter. In the United States, it may reach heights of 100 ft. and diameters of up to 4 ft.

LEAVES—Shed each autumn; on 1-in. long stalks; simple, alternate, approximately 7-ins. long by 3½-ins. wide, broadest near the middle, abruptly tapered to a short sharp tip, rounded to slightly tapered at the base, slightly hairy on the undersurface, greenish; margin without teeth, often slightly wavy; veins prominent, widely spaced, not quite extending all the way to the margin.

FLOWERS—Solitary, at the ends of the twigs, appearing after the leaves; both sexes in the same flower; bell-shaped, about 2-ins. across, greenish-yellow; not colourful.

FRUIT—An aggregate of small fleshy pods on a stout short stem, 2- to 3-ins. long, green until mature and somewhat resembling a cucumber, turning reddish at maturity when the pods split along their backs to shed one or two large, scarlet seeds which hang for a time on fine, white, tensile threads.

TWIGS—Stout, usually bright reddish-brown to greyish, encircled at each horseshoe-shaped leaf-scar by a line-like mark; terminal bud ½- to ¾-in. long, lateral buds much smaller, all coated with greyish silky hairs.

BARK—Greyish-brown and furrowed into long, narrow, flattish, scaly ridges.

WOOD—Moderately soft, heavy, weak, close-grained; greenish-yellow to brown; sapwood thin, nearly white.

IMPORTANCE—This tree is too rare in Canada to be of much importance, though it does have some value as an ornamental.

NOTES—Fossils have been discovered which show that magnolias once bloomed on the banks of the Red Deer River in Alberta.

There are reports of an extract from the fruit being used as a medicine.

CAL LEAF HAS A ROUNDED BASE

FLOWER PETALS LARGE AND FLESHY

AT ST. WILLIAMS FOREST STATION,
RIO

DISCARDED FLOWER PARTS
LEAVE MARKS BELOW FRUIT

MATURE BARK FURROWED

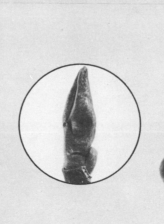
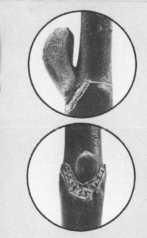

BUDS VELVETY; TWIG RINGED AT LEAF-SCARS

TULIP-TREE

Yellow-poplar

Liriodendron tulipifera L.

FORM—Only two species of this genus are known; one a small tree in China (*Liriodendron chinense* (Hemsl.) Sarg.), and this one which grows over much of eastern and southern North America. It is one of Canada's most distinctive trees. When the tree is growing in the forest, the tall massive trunk may make up two-thirds or more of the tree's height by rising 60 ft. to the first branch. It is straight, branch-free, has little taper, and supports a small, narrow, compact crown. In the open, the crown is more irregular and occupies most of the tree's height. The root system is deep and wide-spreading.

HABITAT—The Tulip-tree is confined to the Deciduous Forest Region, where it grows on deep, rich, moist soils along streams or around swampy areas. It is usually mixed with other hardwoods or with some conifers (particularly Eastern Hemlock) and rarely forms pure stands.

SIZE—One of the largest hardwood trees, commonly reaching heights of 50 to 75 ft. and diameters of 2 ft. or more; but can grow to 175 ft. and 10 ft. or more in diameter.

LEAVES—Shed each autumn, simple, alternate; approximately 4-ins. long by 4½-ins. wide, on slender stalks usually longer than the leaf-blades (which permit the leaves to tremble in the wind in much the same way as certain poplar leaves), four-lobed but occasionally six-lobed, with a broad shallow notch at the top which makes the leaf appear as if the tip had been cut off; no teeth on the lobes.

FLOWERS—Solitary, at the ends of the twigs, appearing after the leaves; both sexes in the same flower, cup-shaped, approximately 2-ins. across, greenish-yellow; colourful, but not conspicuous on large trees.

FRUIT—An aggregate of winged nutlets, 2- to 3-ins. long, spindle-shaped; each nutlet has an elongated wing with a small angled seed-case at its base (sometimes the seed-case does not completely enclose the one or two seeds), shed from the central stalk when ripe leaving the stalk erect on the branchlets.

TWIGS—Stout, brownish, shiny, encircled at each leaf-scar by a line-like mark; terminal bud ½-in. long, flattened, with two outer scales face to face; lateral buds much smaller, with a slight bloom; pith solid but in longitudinal section crossed at intervals with bands of a different colour.

BARK—Brownish; furrowed into close, interlacing, rounded ridges which are separated by greyish crevices.

WOOD—Light, soft, weak, close-grained; yellow to greenish-brown with sapwood which is nearly white.

IMPORTANCE—Too scarce to be of much importance; typical use is for core-stock in the manufacture of furniture and fixtures.

NOTES—In 1886, a popular heart stimulant was first extracted from the inner bark of the root of the Tulip-tree.

APPEARS CUT OFF AT THE TOP

NOTE SWOLLEN LEAF-STALK BASES, LINES ENCIRCLING TWIG AND FLATTENED TERMINAL BUD

MATURE BARK HAS ROUNDED RIDGES

FLOWER BUD TULIP-LIKE; FLOWER SINGLE AND LARGE

ATURE FRUIT IS SPINDLE-SHAPED

MATURE FRUIT; CENTRAL STALK (LEFT) REMAINS AFTER WINGED SEEDS (RIGHT) ARE DISPERSED

PAWPAW

Asimina triloba (L.) Dunal

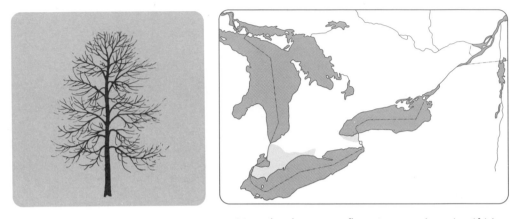

FORM—The Pawpaws do not grow outside North America, and most of the trees in the genus *Asimina* are tropical or subtropical. Of the known species, only one extends into Canada. When Pawpaw reaches tree size, it has a short slender trunk with a rather broad, but high, crown formed by straight spreading side-branches.

HABITAT—Pawpaw grows sparingly in the Deciduous Forest Region. It can be found on the rich, moist, better-drained soils in river valleys near streams and on low slopes. Being very tolerant of shade, it tends to grow under higher hardwoods. It is not a common tree, but occasionally forms small dense thickets in the open. More often Pawpaw is found singly or in small groups.

SIZE—As a tree, Pawpaw may attain heights of 20 to 40 ft. with diameters of 10 to 12 ins., but more often it is an upright shrub under 8 ft. in height.

LEAVES—Shed each autumn, simple, alternate, on short stalks, thin and tend to hang from the twigs owing to their thinness; light green above, paler on the undersurface which is without hairs; 4- to 12-ins. long by 2- to 4-ins. wide, broadest near the top then tapering abruptly to a short sharp tip, gradually narrowing from the broadest part to a long wedge-shaped base; margin without teeth; prominent rusty veins not extending to the margin but looped together near it.

FLOWERS—Solitary, on the previous year's twigs, appearing with the leaves; both sexes in the same flower; approximately 1½-ins. across, reddish-purple and quite showy.

FRUIT—Fleshy, pale greenish-yellow becoming nearly black when ripe, elongated or almost circular but of many shapes and of different sizes up to 5-ins. long, contains several dark brown, flattish seeds embedded in a pulp which is sweet and pleasant to eat.

TWIGS—Rather slender, brownish but streaked with fine whitish, line-like grooves, hairy; terminal bud without scales, ⅓-in. long and flat, covered with dark rusty-red hairs; lateral buds similar but very small, flattened and pressed against the twig, often two or more above a leaf-scar, the lowest hard to see; pith whitish and solid, but barred across at intervals with hard partitions.

BARK—Thin, smooth, shiny, dark brown with greyish blotches when young; becoming rough and slightly scaly.

WOOD—Light, soft, weak; yellow with a visible tinge of green.

IMPORTANCE—Has no commercial value other than as an ornamental.

NOTES—The raccoons usually succeed in eating the fruit of the few natural-growing trees long before they become ripe enough for human consumption. Small boys are prone to play a similar role in relation to ornamentals.

The botanical name *triloba* refers to part of the calyx of the flower.

214

PAWPAW

... LOOP TOGETHER NEAR THE MARGIN

FRUIT; SEED (LEFT) IS EMBEDDED IN PULP (RIGHT)

...MER TWIG
...THREE FLOWER BUDS VISIBLE

WINTER TWIG
WITH LEAF
AND FLOWER BUDS

LEAVES HANG LIMPLY

...G TREES HAVE SMOOTH BLOTCHED BARK

SASSAFRAS

Sassafras albidum (Nutt.) Nees

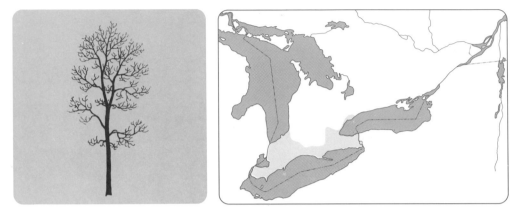

FORM—The genus *Sassafras* belongs to a family that is mainly tropical and subtropical; three species are known — two in eastern Asia and one in North America. The Sassafras is distinct from other trees because of its pleasant spicy fragrance which is derived from the leaves, twigs, branches and bark when these are crushed or broken. The tree is unusual in that the trunk bears many abruptly spreading, crooked, brittle branches which, in the upper part of the tree, form a flat-topped, irregular, columnar crown. The branchlets have a stag-horn appearance caused by the twigs on the sides being much longer than the twig on the end. The root system has a deep tap-root and a few spreading, lateral roots. Thickets of root sprouts often surround the base of the tree.

HABITAT—Sassafras is confined to the Deciduous Forest Region. It grows best on rich sandy loams, but can be found on a variety of sites. It is tolerant of shade and may grow underneath other hardwoods.

SIZE — Often reduced to a shrub in dry sandy areas, but may reach 30 to 40 ft. in height and 12 to 18 ins. in diameter; rarely larger.

LEAVES—Shed each autumn, simple, alternate, on short stalks; oval, 3- to 6-ins. long by 1½- to 3-ins. wide, blunt tipped; without teeth on the margin, hairless or slightly hairy on the undersurface, with two strong lateral veins arising a little distance above the wedge-shaped base, a few other lateral veins branching off irregularly from the midrib at remote intervals and curving towards the tip of the leaf (in addition to this type, some leaves are deeply notched with one to three lobes; usually all kinds are on the same tree).

FLOWERS—In loose terminal clusters which appear as the leaves unfold; small, greenish-yellow; male and female flowers in different clusters and usually on different trees.

FRUIT— Small, dark blue, berry-like, approximately ½-in. long, containing a large stone-like seed; borne on a stout, fleshy, red, club-shaped stalk; several to a cluster.

TWIGS—Stout, smooth, glossy, yellowish-green, brittle; with plump greenish buds, terminal bud ⅓- to ⅖-in. long, lateral buds smaller; leaf-scar has one dash-like bundle-scar.

BARK—Dark and brownish, deeply grooved and forming heavy corky ridges that are easily cut across with a knife.

WOOD—Light, soft, weak, coarse-grained, durable; orangey-brown with thin yellow sapwood; aromatic.

IMPORTANCE—Occasionally used for cabinet work and locally for fence posts. The "oil of sassafras" used for flavouring comes from the roots of this tree.

NOTES—An orange dye can be extracted by boiling the inner bark.

The Indians exploited the wood's durability by using it for dugout canoes.

SASSAFRAS

LEAVES ARE LOBED
OR UNLOBED;
THE VEINS BRANCH
IRREGULARLY

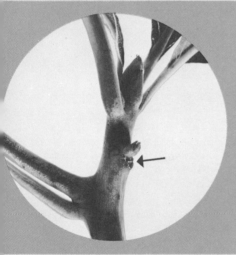

...AF-SCAR HAS A SINGLE DASH-LIKE
...NDLE-SCAR

DEEPLY RIDGED BARK OF
MATURE TREE

...OT SPROUTS SURROUNDING THE BASE
... THE TREE

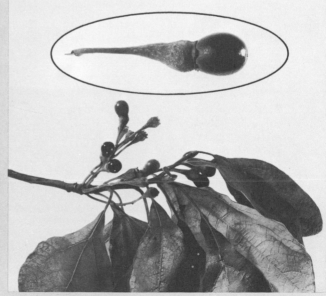

BERRY-LIKE FRUITS GROW IN CLUSTERS ON CLUB-SHAPED STALKS

WITCH-HAZEL

Hamamelis virginiana L.

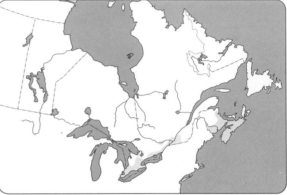

FORM—Of the six known species of the genus *Hamamelis*, three of which grow in North America, this is the only one found in Canada. It has a low-spreading irregular crown supported by a leaning and crooked trunk. Witch-hazel is conspicuous because of its rather sprawling appearance, its unusual-looking leaves and its habit of flowering in the autumn when other trees are losing their leaves. A variety, *Hamamelis virginiana* var. *parvifolia* Nutt., is reported to grow from Nova Scotia southwards along the Atlantic seaboard of the United States. This variety can be identified by its smaller leaves (4 ins. or less in length) which are leathery in texture and covered with dense hairs on the undersurface; the hairiness extends along the leaf-stalk and onto the twigs.

HABITAT—Witch-hazel is found in the Deciduous Forest Region, the Great Lakes-St. Lawrence Forest Region and the Acadian Forest Region. It makes its best growth on moist shaded sites, such as in wooded ravines.

SIZE—Usually a coarse thicket-forming shrub, but may grow into a small tree which will reach heights of 20 to 25 ft. and diameters of up to 6 ins.

LEAVES—Shed each autumn, simple, alternate, on short stalks; 3- to 6-ins. long, markedly asymmetrical at the base, pronounced irregularly wavy to almost coarse-toothed margin, very thin texture, dark green above, paler and hairless on the undersurface (or hairy only on the widely spaced veins); there are approximately six noticeable, ascending veins on each side of the midrib.

FLOWERS—Appear in September to October as the leaves are falling, in clusters of three; 1- to 1½-ins. across, both sexes in the same flower, four bright-yellow, strap-like petals which are often twisted, quite showy.

FRUIT—A two-beaked, woody, buff-coloured, hairy pod which remains on the tree over winter until the tree is in flower again before maturing and splitting open to eject two small, black, shiny seeds; clusters of empty pods remain on the tree for one more year.

TWIGS—Slender, sometimes downy, yellowish; buds stalked, without scales, densely covered with yellowish-brown hairs, terminal bud ½-in. long, flat and curved, lateral buds much smaller, commonly more than one bud at a leaf-scar.

BARK—Smooth or slightly scaly, light brown, often mottled; inner bark reddish-purple.

WOOD—Heavy and hard; light brown with almost white sapwood.

IMPORTANCE—The wood is not used commercially in Canada.

NOTES—A forked Witch-hazel twig is the favourite "tool" of the water diviner or "well witcher" who seems to have the gift of finding underground sources of water.

The bark, twigs and leaves contain the famous Witch-hazel astringent which is processed for its medicinal properties.

218

VES ARE IRREGULAR IN SHAPE AND HAVE
GULAR MARGINS

FRUIT PODS ARE HAIRY; SEED (RIGHT) IS
SHINY BLACK

VER BUDS ON SUMMER TWIGS OPEN IN OCTOBER

FLOWERS HAVE STRAP-LIKE TWISTED PETALS

; LATERAL BUDS ARE ON STALKS

WITCH-HAZEL USUALLY GROWS IN CLUMPS

SYCAMORE

Plane-tree, Buttonball

Platanus occidentalis L.

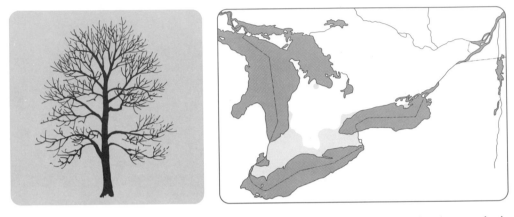

FORM—There are approximately seven species of *Platanus*, three of them are native to the United States and one has spread into Canada. The others are found in Mexico, southeastern Europe and India. London Plane (*Platanus acerifolia* (Ait.) Willd.), which is considered to be a hybrid between Oriental Plane (*Platanus orientalis* L.) and the Canadian Sycamore, is commonly planted on streets in southern Ontario. It is identified by the end lobe of its leaf which is as long as or longer than it is broad, and by having two or three ball-like fruits on each fruit-stalk. Sycamores stand out among other trees because of their bark which is strikingly mottled, and because of their open spreading crowns of massive crooked branches supported by a thick central trunk. The root system is shallow and spreads just below the ground.

HABITAT—Sycamore is mainly confined to the Deciduous Forest Region, and is usually found scattered among other hardwoods on rich bottomlands. Beyond its natural range, there are planted examples growing as far north as Ottawa.

SIZE—One of the largest hardwood trees of eastern North America, reaching heights of 150 ft. and diameters of 7 or 8 ft., but usually less than half that size.

LEAVES—Shed each autumn, simple, alternate, usually over 5-ins. long and slightly wider; three to five wavy-toothed lobes, end lobe shorter than it is broad; leaf-stalks hollow at the base and completely enclosing the bud.

FLOWERS—Appear with the leaves; both sexes in separate ball-like clusters on the same tree.

FRUIT—A single ball-like aggregate hanging at the end of a long stem; individual fruits small, elongated, with stiff brownish hairs at the base which stand apart when the fruit is released from the ball; fruits remain on the tree throughout the winter; the ball disintegrates gradually.

TWIGS—Brownish, without hairs, encircled at each leaf-scar by a line-like mark; buds all laterals, concealed in the base of the leaf-stalks until after leaf-fall, reddish, bluntly cone-shaped, covered with a single scale and almost surrounded by the narrow leaf-scar.

BARK—Mostly smooth, brownish, flaking off in large, irregular, thin pieces and exposing the greyish to cream-coloured inner bark which gradually becomes whitish and produces the strikingly mottled appearance.

WOOD—Medium heavy and hard, weak; rays wide, causing a prominent wood-ray figure on quarter-sawn surfaces; heartwood brownish, sapwood lighter in colour.

IMPORTANCE—Not of great importance. The wood has been used for cabinet work and interior finishing.

NOTES—Many of the old-fashioned solid butchers' blocks were made by sawing a section directly from the trunk of a Sycamore and mounting the debarked log on four wooden legs.

WIDTH IS SLIGHTLY GREATER THAN LENGTH

FRUIT; HAIRS ON INDIVIDUAL
FRUITS AID DISPERSAL

TWIG; NARROW LEAF-SCAR
ALMOST ENCIRCLES BUD

...WAY LEAF-STALK (LEFT), SHOWS CONCEALED BUD

...RE BARK IS MOTTLED

MASSIVE CROWN OF MATURE TREE

MOUNTAIN-ASH

Sorbus L.

This genus, along with hawthorns, cherries, plums, serviceberries and crab apples, belongs to the family of plants known as the *Rosaceae* — a very large family of approximately 90 genera and 1,500 species. Many of the members furnish us with delicious fruits and beautiful flowers. Some of these fruits are strawberries, raspberries, blackberries, apples, pears, peaches and sweet cherries. Foremost among the flowers are the roses, often acclaimed as our most beautiful flower. The mountain-ashes include more than 80 species, of which six are thought to be native to Canada. The exact number is in doubt because of the difficulty of separating the related forms.

Of the Canadian species, only American Mountain-ash (*Sorbus americana* Marsh.) and Showy Mountain-ash (*Sorbus decora* (Sarg.) Schneid.) regularly become clearly defined trees and are given full descriptions in this book. *Sorbus occidentalis* (S. Wats.) Greene, a tall shrub or sometimes a small tree of the far west, is distinguishable because of its short, blunt, dull bluish-green leaflets which are toothed only near the tips. *Sorbus sitchensis* Roem., and *Sorbus scopulina* Greene are shrubby species of the Rocky Mountains and prairies; *Sorbus cascadensis* G. N. Jones is a shrub in British Columbia.

One exotic species, European Mountain-ash or Rowan Tree (*Sorbus aucuparia* L.), is widely planted in many of its horticultural forms, and in some places has escaped and is growing wild. In some localities, it may be in sufficient numbers to appear as if it were a native species. The Rowan Tree can be identified by its winter buds which are not gummy, but densely covered with white woolly hairs, especially on the upper portion. Also, it has very short-tipped, scarcely tapering leaflets which are often coarsely toothed (except near the base), usually hairy, and whitish on the undersurface. The fruit is larger than in the native species (often almost ½-in. across) and the fruit cluster is round-topped. The great variety of forms of this tree, however, causes a considerable variation in the leaf and fruit characteristics.

The leaves of mountain-ashes are alternate, 6- to 10-ins. long, composed of 7 to 17 similar leaflets on very short stalks, opposite, in pairs along each side of the main leaf-stalk, with one leaflet at the end. At the base of each leaf-stalk are two small, leaf-like structures (stipules) that are usually shed before the leaves are fully grown. The leaves are shed each autumn, and are replaced the following spring on new twigs that develop from the leaf-buds of the previous year's twigs. The leaflets are 2- to 4½-ins. long by ½- to 1-in. wide, sharp tipped, toothed along the margin (at least on the half nearest the tip), smooth on the upper surface and slightly hairy or hairless on the underside.

The flowers are quite small, seldom more than ¼-in. across and appear in many-flowered, flat-topped or rounded, showy clusters at the ends of the twigs after the leaves are mature. Both sexes are in the same flower.

The fruit is of the apple type but is berry-like in size and appearance, ¼- to ½-in. across, orange or red, has a bitter taste and remains on the branches after the leaves fall. Since the fruit provides food for some birds, it is often removed early in the season.

The bark is thin and smooth, light grey, with conspicuous, elongated, widely separated, horizontal markings (lenticels). Sometimes the bark on mature trees becomes scaly.

The wood of the mountain-ashes is moderately light, low in strength, with pale-brown heartwood and nearly white sapwood. It is of no commercial value.

The mountain-ash is not a true ash and is easily distinguishable from the ashes by its leaves which are not in opposite pairs. It is one of our most attractive trees with its handsome foliage, showy flowers and bright reddish fruits. It is not very large, seldom exceeds 25 ft. in height and has a clean smooth trunk and a well-formed rounded crown which make it suitable for ornamental planting.

AMERICAN MOUNTAIN-ASH

Sorbus americana **Marsh.**

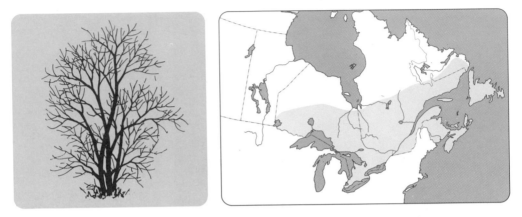

FORM—American Mountain-ash, more often referred to simply as Mountain-ash, has a short trunk with spreading slender branches that form a narrow, rather open, round-topped crown, when the tree is growing in the open. In the forest, a longer branch-free trunk is developed which usually reaches or exceeds twice the length of the live crown.

HABITAT—This tree grows in the southern parts of the Boreal Forest Region eastwards from the Manitoba / Ontario border and throughout the Great Lakes-St. Lawrence Forest Region. There is some representation in the Deciduous Forest Region, with the tree becoming common again in the Acadian Forest Region. It is usually found in rather moist situations on the borders of swamps and rocky hillsides, but it can grow well in a stunted form on relatively dry soils.

SIZE—This is a small tree, 10 to 30 ft. in height and with a diameter of 4 to 10 ins. Occasionally a tree may be somewhat larger, but most individuals are of tall-shrub size, rather than of tree size.

LEAVES—Up to 10-ins. long, with 11 to 17 thin, narrow, gradually tapering, sharp-pointed leaflets, 3- to 4½-ins. long by approximately ¾-in. wide, finely and sharply toothed almost to the base, dull green above, pale green and hairless or almost so on the undersurface. Small leafy structures (stipules) at the base of the leaf-stalk are shed early.

FLOWERS—Appear in May and June; individuals less than ¼-in. across, on short, stout, hairless stems and arranged in flat-topped terminal clusters which appear after the leaves are fully grown.

FRUIT—Matures in August, ¼-in. across, glossy, bright orangey-red, almost circular with a thin fleshy part; seeds about ⅛-in. long.

TWIGS—Stout, dark reddish-brown to greyish, with a skin that weathers off, hairless; buds very dark reddish-brown, narrowly cone-shaped, with sharp tips; terminal bud ½-in. long, often curved at the tip, otherwise similar to the laterals which are smaller, shiny and gummy and have a few scattered hairs.

BARK—Smooth, thin, greyish-green, becoming slightly scaly with age.

WOOD—Light, soft, weak, close-grained; the heartwood is a pale brown with a lighter-coloured sapwood.

IMPORTANCE—Of no commercial importance. Its fruit and inner bark have been used for medicinal purposes. The fruit is also a favourite food for many species of overwintering birds. Although the tree is not as handsome as its relative, *Sorbus decora*, it is also useful for ornamental planting.

NOTES—The common name "mountain-ash" seems to have been given to this tree by immigrants from Europe who improperly identified its slender leaflets.

The fruit, although eaten by birds and some animals, is not palatable to most people; home-made jelly is the usual food form.

224

FRUIT IS BRIGHT ORANGEY-RED

LEAFLETS NARROW WITH LONG TIPS

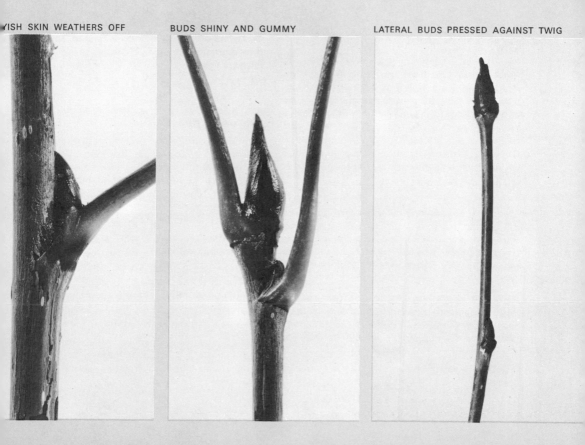

ISH SKIN WEATHERS OFF   BUDS SHINY AND GUMMY   LATERAL BUDS PRESSED AGAINST TWIG

SHOWY MOUNTAIN-ASH

Sorbus decora (Sarg.) Schneid.

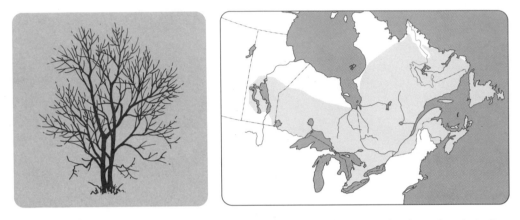

FORM—This is usually a very attractive bushy-looking tree but, when growing in the forest, it develops a long branch-free trunk and a short rounded crown. Many nature-lovers consider the bushy form to be the most beautiful of the mountain-ashes. Where it grows in association with the American Mountain-ash, it can often be identified by the attitude of its leaves which are held horizontally. Those of the American Mountain-ash tend to be "on edge" and arching. Also, the Showy Mountain-ash flowers about 10 days later than the American Mountain-ash. In the far north, there is a variety with rather wide but very long-pointed leaflets which are not greyish on the undersurface. It has been named *Sorbus decora* var. *groenlandica* (Schneid.) G. N. Jones, and ranges from the Gaspé peninsula to northern Quebec, Newfoundland and Labrador. This variety also extends into southern Greenland.

HABITAT—The Showy Mountain-ash grows within the Boreal Forest Region from central Manitoba to Newfoundland, with scattered representation southward to the Deciduous Forest Region. It is particularly common in the Acadian Forest Region. Throughout this wide range, the tree grows in many different soils and under a variety of conditions.

SIZE—A small tree, 15 to 35 ft. in height with a diameter of 4 to 12 ins. On the best sites, it may attain a height of 75 ft. and a diameter of up to 20 ins. In the far north it is often reduced to a shrub.

LEAVES—Up to 10-ins. long, with 11 to 15 firm, scarcely tapered, sharp-tipped leaflets 2- to 3½-ins. long by about ½- to 1-in. wide, mostly with fine teeth from the tip to the middle or below the middle, greyish and slightly hairy on the undersurface; the small leaf-like structures at the base of the leaf-stalk are shed early.

FLOWERS—Appear in June and early July; individuals approximately ½-in. across, on short, stout, hairy stems, arranged in flat-topped terminal clusters, bloom after the leaves are fully grown.

FRUIT— Matures in August; individuals ¼- to ⅓-in. across, glossy, scarlet or vermilion, almost circular with a medium-thick fleshy part; seeds ⅛-in. long.

TWIGS—Stout, reddish-brown to greyish, with a skin that weathers off, hairless; buds dark reddish-brown, narrowly cone-shaped with sharp tips; terminal bud ½-in. long, often curved at the tip, otherwise similar to the laterals which are smaller, shiny and gummy and have a few scattered hairs.

BARK—Smooth, thin, greyish-green, becoming slightly scaly with age.

WOOD—Light, soft, weak, close-grained; the heartwood is a pale brown with a lighter-coloured sapwood.

IMPORTANCE—Of no commercial importance, but a useful ornamental.

NOTES—Unlike Europeans, the Indians in their folklore did not attribute magical powers to the North American mountain-ashes.

SHOWY MOUNTAIN-ASH

FLOWERS OF ALL MOUNTAIN-ASHES ARE VERY SHOWY

LET MARGINS ALMOST PARALLEL BUT
RING TO A SHARP TIP

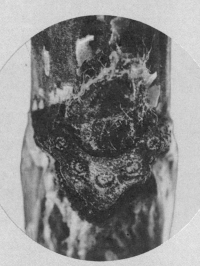

LEAF-SCAR HAS FIVE BUNDLE-SCARS

OTH BARK BECOMES SCALY

FRUITS ARE BRIGHT SCARLET OR VERMILION

HAWTHORN

Crataegus L.

This is a very large genus of small trees and coarse shrubs which has its greatest concentration of species in eastern North America. Over 100 of the 1,000 or more recognized species grow on this continent and about 25 or 30 different hawthorns grow in various locations across Canada. The most common species is the Golden-fruited Hawthorn (*Crataegus chrysocarpa* Ashe) which has a range that extends from Alberta to Nova Scotia. British Columbia has only two native species, Black Hawthorn (*Crataegus douglasii* Lindl.) and Columbia Hawthorn (*Crataegus columbiana* Howell); the latter rarely attains tree size. The remaining native hawthorns inhabit the southeastern parts of the country, mainly southern Ontario and southern Quebec.

Extensive clearance of the forests of eastern North America during the ice age greatly increased the area of open soil which the hawthorns are so well adapted to exploit. This led to rapid spreading and mixing of many isolated populations of hawthorn, and accelerated the evolution of new races and species by crossbreeding and natural selection. The process is still going on, and although hawthorns are easily recognized, the many forms in which the different kinds appear make their identification and classification difficult.

In addition to the native trees, two European species are often planted as ornamentals, and either of them (or their varieties) may be found in the southern-most parts of each province in Canada. They are the May Thorn or One-seeded Hawthorn (*Crataegus monogyna* Jacq.) and the English Hawthorn (*Crataegus oxycantha* L.). Both have very short thorns and deeply lobed leaves; the leaves of the May Thorn are cut nearly to the midrib. Their flowers may be rose-coloured, dark red, bright scarlet, pink or white and some of the trees are very showy when in full flower. The fruit of the English Hawthorn has two seeds; that of the May Thorn only one seed.

With the introduction of these foreign species and some of their varieties, there is additional opportunity for hybridization. Thus, the probability of encountering individual trees that do not correspond to the descriptions given in any of the tree books is greatly increased. The easiest solution, then, is to refer to such hybrids simply as "hawthorn" without attempting to isolate their specific identity. Only a few of the most distinctive species are described in this edition.

The hawthorns have low, wide-spreading, somewhat rounded or flat-topped crowns and short often crooked trunks. Few of them attain heights above 25 or 30 ft. Their branches are characterized by having rather zigzag twigs and branchlets often with two rounded buds side by side at each bend in the twig. One of these buds develops into a thorn, while the other produces the new twig which bears leaves, or flowers, or perhaps both. The thorns are not roughened by leaf-scars, do not produce buds (as in the plums and crab apples), but are smooth and usually shiny as though polished. They are generally very rigid and sharp pointed; some may be branched.

The leaves are simple, alternate, coarsely toothed and sometimes lobed and toothed; often with two toothed, leaf-like structures (stipules) at the base of the stalk, which persist until autumn. The leaves are shed at the end of each growing season.

The flowers are arranged in flat-topped clusters on the ends of short twigs, each with five greenish sepals, five white or occasionally pink petals, 5 to 25 stamens and one to five pistils. Since both sexes are in the same flower, the flowers are said to be "perfect". They are often very showy, like apple blossoms.

The fruit resembles a small apple with a thin flesh, and is often called a "haw". It is edible, although usually eaten only by birds.

The bark is shreddy, somewhat like that of the Hop-hornbeam, but more evenly separated into firm shreds that become loose at both ends.

The wood is hard and heavy but never of large enough size to be commercially important; however, it is suitable for wood carving.

HAWTHORNS

Crataegus L.

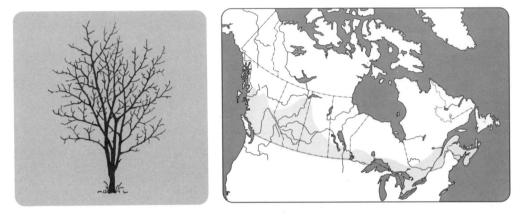

INTRODUCTION—Hawthorns are easily distinguishable from other native trees by the spines, or thorns, on their branches and the unmistakable winter buds which are almost as broad as they are long, round on top, smooth, shiny and covered with overlapping close-fitting scales. Other thorn-bearing trees that might be confused with hawthorns are plums and crab apples. Their thorns bear buds which are longer than they are broad (sharp pointed in plums, and usually blunt but very elongated and hairy in crab apples). The following species are typical of the hawthorns that grow across Canada.

COLUMBIA HAWTHORN—*Crataegus columbiana* Howell is a small tree or shrub which grows in the dry Interior of British Columbia and on Vancouver Island. Thorns stout; leaves distinctly lobed and irregularly toothed, almost hairless; fruit red.

BLACK HAWTHORN—*Crataegus douglasii* Lindl. is the only hawthorn that regularly grows as a tree in British Columbia. Its range extends through Alberta into Saskatchewan, with scattered examples in the Lake Superior area of Ontario. Thorns very short; leaves coarsely double toothed to shallowly lobed, almost hairless; fruit black.

GOLDEN-FRUITED HAWTHORN—*Crataegus chrysocarpa* Ashe is commonly a shrub or may be a small tree. It ranges from Newfoundland to the Rocky Mountains, and north to the Peace River in Alberta. Thorns slender; leaves almost circular, shallowly lobed and toothed, almost hairless; fruit reddish-orange.

DOTTED HAWTHORN—*Crataegus punctata* Jacq. is a small tree which is conspicuous because of its horizontal branches. It is found in southern Quebec and Ontario. Thorns stout, sometimes branched; leaves broadest near the top, gradually tapering to the base, toothed to slightly lobed, with many veins ascending obliquely; fruit dull red, conspicuously dotted.

QUEBEC HAWTHORN—*Crataegus submollis* Sarg. is a showy species because of its large white flowers. It grows in the southern parts of eastern Canada. Thorns slender, straight; leaves broadest below the middle, abruptly tapered to the base, coarsely toothed to shallowly lobed; fruit bright orangey-red.

DOWNY HAWTHORN—*Crataegus mollis* Scheele is very showy. It grows in southern Ontario. Thorns thick, straight, not numerous; leaves broadest below the middle, abruptly tapered to the base, coarsely double toothed to shallowly lobed, very downy; fruit scarlet.

COCKSPUR HAWTHORN—*Crataegus crusgalli* L. is a small tree with wide-spreading horizontal branches (similar to those of Dotted Hawthorn), found in southern Quebec and Ontario. Thorns slender, numerous; leaves usually rounded at the broad top, sharply toothed, hairless, leathery, shiny on the upper surface; fruit dull red.

HOLMES HAWTHORN—*Crataegus holmesiana* Ashe is a small variable tree or coarse shrub of southern Ontario and Quebec. Thorns stout, not numerous; leaves broad, widest below the middle, sharp pointed, double toothed to shallowly lobed; fruit reddish.

230

LEAVES OF DOTTED (LEFT), COCKSPUR (CENTRE) AND DOWNY (RIGHT)

FLOWERS HAVE BOTH MALE AND FEMALE PARTS

HAS DOME-SHAPED BUDS; THORNS SHARP
AND HORN-LIKE

BARK IN THIN NARROW SHREDS

FRUITS LOOK LIKE SMALL APPLES

WILD CRAB APPLE

Malus coronaria (L.) Mill.

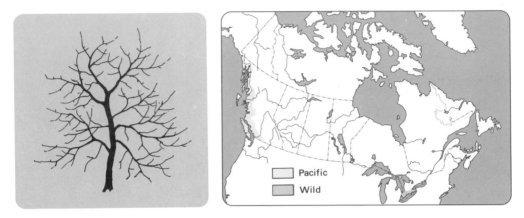

Pacific

Wild

FORM—About 25 species of the genus *Malus* are known; two are native to Canada, Wild Crab Apple, and its western counterpart, Pacific Crab Apple (*Malus diversifolia* (Bong.) Roem.). Both are very similar, except for their fruits. Those of the western tree are ½- to ¾-in. long, oval and red or yellowish flushed with red; those of the eastern tree are usually broader than they are long, almost round, about 1½-ins. across, and green. The Pacific Crab Apple grows only in British Columbia in the wet or swampy woods of the coastal forest. In addition to the two native species, several exotics are planted as ornamentals and for their fruits. The best known is the common domestic apple (*Malus pumila* Mill.) which includes most varieties of edible apples. These are widely planted and often spread into adjacent forests. They differ from the native species in having unlobed finely toothed leaves which are whitish and downy on the undersurface, the leaf-stalks, and often on the twigs and buds. They do not have thorns, the spur-like growths on their branches being blunt — not thorn-like.

HABITAT—Wild Crab Apple is mainly confined to the Deciduous Forest Region, where it grows in the shade of larger hardwood trees and in the open along fences and roadsides.

SIZE—The tree is always small — up to 30 ft. in height with a maximum trunk diameter of 14 ins. It usually has a crooked trunk and an irregular spreading crown. The western species is the larger, but both grow more commonly

as thicket-forming shrubs, rather than trees.

LEAVES—Variable, shed each autumn, simple, alternate, usually widest below the middle; 3½-ins. long, coarsely toothed, the teeth increasing in size from the tip downwards to become almost lobe-sized near the base which is roundish to heart-shaped, almost hairless on the undersurface.

FLOWERS—In small clusters, appearing at the same time as the leaves; both sexes in the same flower, approximately 1½-ins. across, white, streaked with pink, very showy.

FRUIT—An apple, green, almost round, 1½-ins. across, as broad or broader than it is long, hard, wax-coated, sour, remaining on the tree into winter.

TWIGS—Slender, reddish-brown with a greyish skin which gradually flakes off; buds elongated, mostly blunt, bright red, hairy, laterals pressed against the twig; branchlets with rough thorn-like spurs which bear buds.

BARK—Reddish-brown, scaly.

WOOD—Hard, heavy, even-textured, brownish.

IMPORTANCE—Of no commercial importance; the wood is suitable for carving and hobby-shop turning of small articles. The tree is useful as an ornamental.

NOTES—Many of the original grist mills in rural Ontario had gear wheels and conveyor screw-blades carved from crab apple wood.

WIDEST BELOW THE MIDDLE

FLOWER CLUSTERS ARE VERY SHOWY

T OF PACIFIC CRAB APPLE
VAL

FRUIT OF EASTERN TREE IS
ALMOST ROUND

NOTE THORN-LIKE SPURS BEARING BUDS

IN TYPICAL HEDGEROW HABITAT

BARK IS SCALY

SERVICEBERRY

Amelanchier Med.

This is a genus of shrubs and small trees, many of which are not clearly defined. Of about 24 recognized species, 18 are found in North America, with approximately 13 species having ranges that extend into Canada; every province has at least one species of serviceberry. The identification of the different species is difficult owing to the uncertainty of separating many closely related groups. Only two of the four species described here regularly reach tree size — the Downy Serviceberry (*Amelanchier arborea* (Michx. f.) Fern.) and the Allegheny Serviceberry (*Amelanchier laevis* Wieg.). The other two, Mountain Juneberry (*Amelanchier bartramiana* (Tausch) Roem.) and Saskatoon-berry (*Amelanchier alnifolia* (Nutt.) Nutt.) occasionally become trees. One other species that may also be encountered as a very small tree in the area from Lake Superior to southern Quebec is the Roundleaf Serviceberry (*Amelanchier sanguinea* (Pursh) DC.). It is not described in this edition because its features (except for a permanent hairiness on the undersurface of its leaves) are almost the same as those given for the Saskatoon-berry.

In addition to the problems of separating the main species of serviceberry, hybrids between different species have been reported. One variation of Allegheny Serviceberry, with dark shiny leaves, grows in Newfoundland and Nova Scotia and has been named variety *nitida* (Wieg.) Fern. Variations in the Saskatoon-berry have been considered varieties of either that species or the Pacific Serviceberry (*Amelanchier florida* Lindl.), a shrubby species in British Columbia. These add to the difficulties of identifying serviceberries.

Serviceberries, when of tree size, are usually under 30 ft. in height with diameters of 3 to 12 ins., but, occasionally, a tree may reach a height of 60 ft. and a diameter of 1 or 2 ft. The trunk is usually straight and slender with very little taper, and has a smooth greyish bark that is conspicuously marked by slightly twisted vertical lines of a darker colour. On old trees, the bark may become roughened by shallow longitudinal depressions which split into narrow strips that check across

and become scaly, especially near the base of the tree. The crown is usually narrow with rising branches that tend to droop because of their slenderness. Occasionally, branches extend beyond the general crown outline to give the tree an irregular appearance, and the abundance of fine branchlets that are developed make the crown very dense.

The leaves of serviceberries are shed annually. They are usually less than 3-ins. long, simple, alternate, oval to almost circular, on slender stalks, singly and regularly toothed along the margin (at least over the portion near the tip), and have sharp-pointed teeth.

The flowers, which are showy, appear early in the spring before the leaves are fully grown. They are borne on slender stalks and are arranged along a central stem; the lowest flower stalks are usually much longer than the upper ones and the whole cluster is erect or slightly drooping. Individual flowers have five green sepals, five elongated white petals, 10 to 20 stamens and a central pistil which appears indistinctly five-celled.

The fruit is small, reddish or purplish, contains several hard seeds and (on most species) is sweet and juicy and good to eat. It ripens in late July or early August.

The twigs are very slender, with a pith that is five-sided in cross-section, and bear conspicuous, usually much-elongated, cylindrical buds. These, except for the terminal buds, are closely pressed against the twig. The scars left by the fallen leaves show three large bundle-scars, and, on most species, a ridge extends down the twig for a short distance on each side of the leaf-scar.

The wood is hard, heavy and suitable for turnery, but, because of the scattered distribution of the trees and their small size, is of no commercial importance. Some of the species are useful as ornamentals or as grafting stock for some domestic fruit trees, such as pear and quince. The fruits provide food for birds and animals and, in the case of the Saskatoon-berry, are used locally for making pies and jam.

SERVICEBERRIES

Amelanchier Med.

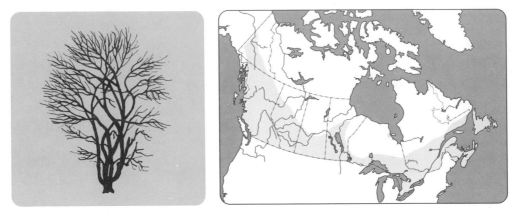

INTRODUCTION—The features of the leaves of serviceberries (although characteristic of the genus) are not always reliable for separating the species, since the range of variation within a species is often greater than the difference between average forms in related species. Usually, the features of the flowers and fruits must be combined with those of the leaves before a positive identification of a species can be made. The four most common serviceberries are described below.

ALLEGHENY SERVICEBERRY — *Amelanchier laevis* Wieg. is the most common species in Canada. It is found throughout the Acadian Forest Region, the Great Lakes-St. Lawrence Forest Region and the southern portion of the Boreal Forest Region from Newfoundland to Lake Superior. The leaves are oval, 2- to 3-ins. long, abruptly tapered to a sharp tip, about 25 teeth to a side, hairless on the undersurface (even when young), at least half-grown at flowering time; flowers in drooping clusters, petals ½- to ¾-in. long; fruit juicy and sweet, the lowest in the cluster on a stalk 1- to 2-ins. long.

DOWNY SERVICEBERRY—*Amelanchier arborea* (Michx. f.) Fern. is scattered throughout the Deciduous Forest Region and the Great Lakes-St. Lawrence Forest Region. The leaves are oval, 2- to 3-ins. long, abruptly tapered to a sharp tip, about 25 teeth to a side, usually hairy on the undersurface, still small and folded at flowering time; flowers usually in erect clusters, petals approximately ½-in. long; fruit dry and tasteless, the lowest in the cluster on a stalk approximately ½-in. long.

SASKATOON-BERRY—*Amelanchier alnifolia* (Nutt.) Nutt. ranges from the Alaska border south along the coast to the southern part of British Columbia and eastwards to the upper Great Lakes area, with scattered representation in central Ontario. The leaves are broadly oval to almost circular, 1- to 3-ins. long, rounded at the tip, about 15 teeth to a side, usually without hairs, still folded at flowering time; flowers few, in erect clusters, petals approximately ¼-in. long; fruit juicy and sweet, the lowest in the cluster on a stalk ⅜-in. long.

MOUNTAIN JUNEBERRY—*Amelanchier bartramiana* (Tausch) Roem. is reported to attain tree size in Nova Scotia, but is more usually a small bushy shrub ranging through the Boreal Forest Region from Labrador to Lake Superior and south through the Great Lakes-St. Lawrence Forest Region and the Acadian Forest Region. The leaves are oval, 1- to 2-ins. long, usually tapered to both ends, hairless, not folded when emerging; flowers unlike those of the other species, the cluster consisting of a terminal flower with up to three others between the upper leaves, usually not more than three in a cluster; fruit longer than it is broad, sweet but dry.

SERVICEBERRIES

TYPICAL SERVICEBERRY LEAVES

FLOWER CLUSTERS ARE SHOWY

T USUALLY SWEET; CONTAIN LARGE SEEDS

BUDS ELONGATED;
PRESSED AGAINST
THE SLENDER TWIG

YOUNG BARK SMOOTH
AND MARKED WITH VERTICAL LINES

CHERRIES AND PLUMS

Prunus L.

Nearly 200 species of this genus are known, but fewer than 30 are native to North America; of these, seven grow in Canada — five cherries and two plums. Some authorities consider the plums to be one species — *Prunus americana* Marsh. — with *Prunus americana* var. *nigra* (Ait.) Waugh as a variety, but in this book they are treated as separate species. Sand Cherry (*Prunus pumila* L.) is always a low shrub and is not described. The others attain tree size, but only one, the Black Cherry (*Prunus serotina* Ehrh.), grows large enough to be classed as a timber-producing tree.

Many kinds of *Prunus* have been introduced from other countries and are in cultivation for their fruits, or edible seeds, and for the beauty of their flowers. Some examples of fruit trees are the Peach (*Prunus persica* Batsch), the Sweet Cherry (*Prunus avium* L.), the Apricot (*Prunus armeniaca* L.), the Garden Plum (*Prunus domestica* L.) and the Sloe (*Prunus spinosa* L.). The Almond (*Prunus amygdalus* Batsch) is grown for its seeds, and the Flowering Almond (*Prunus triloba* Lindl.) is a favourite and attractive ornamental.

The leaves of *Prunus* are simple, and are arranged alternately on the twigs. They are shed annually at the end of the growing season and are replaced the following spring on new twigs that emerge from the leaf-buds formed the previous summer. Varying from oval to narrowly oval, the leaves usually have margins with sharp single teeth, and often have one or more glands on the leaf-stalk near the base of the leaf. The teeth on the leaf margins are so distinctive that the species can be identified by this feature alone, provided there is no doubt that the tree in question belongs to the genus *Prunus*.

The flowers bear both male and female reproductive organs (perfect), and the circles of organs composed of sepals, petals, stamens and pistils are in five's or multiples of five. Usually the blooms are white, but on the plums they are often pinkish. They appear in the spring or early summer as, or after, the tree comes into leaf, and in most species are showy, particularly when the petals are pink or include shades of red.

The fruit is one-stoned, with a juicy edible flesh (at least in the native species) and is sometimes used for preserves, jams or jellies. The floral remains, unlike those of the apple, are found at the base of the fruit.

The twigs of all species are relatively slender. The plums bear a few twigs that fail to develop properly and grow into thorn-like spurs which bear leaves and show leaf-scars while they remain alive. (The hawthorns and locusts have a similar feature but with a different development.) All of the twigs, except those of the Choke Cherry, are covered with a greyish skin that gradually weathers away and is easily rubbed off. The twigs have a bitter almond taste and smell. The buds are scaly with more than two rows of bud-scales.

The bark shows conspicuous markings (lenticels) which are helpful in the identification of the different species.

The genus is divided into several subgenera, and the Canadian species fall naturally into three of these categories. The plums (subgenus *Prunophora*) have large fruits with an oval and rather flattened stone, like a prune stone, and their twigs do not have terminal buds. The cherries differ in having nearly round fruit stones, like the fruit itself, and twigs which have true terminal buds. Often there will be a cluster of buds at the end of a twig. The species with few flowers to a cluster on stems arising at one point on the twig (umbel), produce red sour fruits and are in the subgenus *Cerasus*. Those with many-flowered clusters, each on a short stem along a central flower-stalk (raceme), and which bear blackish, sweet fruits are in the subgenus *Padus*. The first two species to be described, Black Cherry (*Prunus serotina* Ehrh.) and Choke Cherry (*Prunus virginiana* L.), are in the subgenus *Padus*.

BLACK CHERRY

Prunus serotina Ehrh.

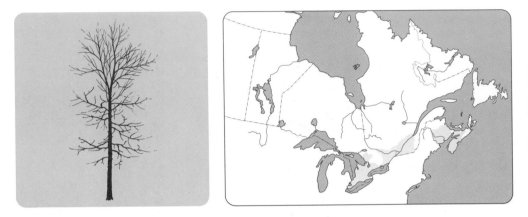

FORM—When growing in the forest, this tree develops a straight branch-free trunk with little taper. The crown becomes narrow and has a rounded top supported by slender arching branches which often droop at the ends. Open-grown trees have shorter trunks with more taper and a longer and broader, but more irregular, crown.

HABITAT—The Black Cherry ranges throughout the Deciduous Forest Region, the southern parts of the Great Lakes-St. Lawrence Forest Region, and most of the Acadian Forest Region. It grows on a variety of soils, but makes its best growth on rich, alluvial soil formations when in association with other hardwood species, such as White Ash, Basswood, Yellow Birch, White Oak, Shagbark Hickory and (in the south) the Tulip-tree.

SIZE—Black Cherry is the largest member of the genus *Prunus* in Canada. Heights of 60 to 70 ft., with diameters of 18 to 24 ins. are common, but there have been reports of trees reaching heights of 100 ft. on the best of the southerly sites. Towards its northern limit of growth, the Black Cherry may be shrub size.

LEAVES—Narrowly oval with a gradual taper to both ends, sharp pointed, 3- to 5-ins. long, thick and leathery; shiny bright green on top, paler on the undersurface, with a mat of fine brown hairs along each side of the midrib; narrow but distinctly elongated slightly curved teeth with sharp incurved tips which, under magnification, resemble birds' beaks.

FLOWERS—Appear at the ends of the new twigs after the first leaves are fully developed; individuals approximately ¼-in. across on ¼-in. stems (but not packed tightly together like the flowers of the Choke Cherry).

FRUIT—Approximately ⅜-in. across, almost black, slightly bitter but edible; retains the lower whorl of flower parts (calyx) at its base (a good recognition feature); matures in late August or early September.

TWIGS—Slender, reddish-brown; buds reddish-brown with darker scale-ends, blunt tipped, approximately ⅛-in. long, spreading slightly from the twig.

BARK—Smooth on young trees, very dark reddish-brown to almost black, with conspicuous, horizontal, dash-like, greyish markings (lenticels); with age, breaking into squarish scales that curve outwards at their vertical edges and retain the horizontal smooth-bark markings for several years.

WOOD—Moderately heavy, hard and strong; light to dark reddish-brown; semi-ring porous.

IMPORTANCE—The wood is valuable for furniture, but now-a-days the supply is very limited because of the scarcity of the tree. Many of the pieces of furniture produced in the early days of Canada's development are fine examples of the value of this species for cabinet work.

NOTES—Wilted leaves contain prussic acid and are poisonous to browsing farm animals.

BLACK CHERRY

CALYX AT BASE OF FRUIT LARGE

HAS BEAKED TEETH; MIDRIB HAIRY

BUDS SPIRAL
AROUND TWIG

RE BARK
KS INTO SQUARE SCALES

FLOWERS ARE ON CENTRAL STEM

CHOKE CHERRY

Prunus virginiana L.

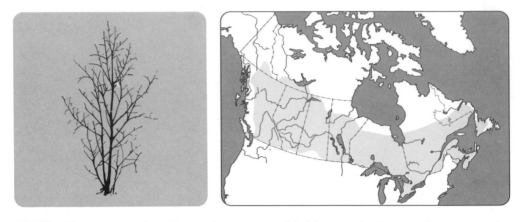

FORM—When of tree size, this species generally has a slender, inclined or twisted trunk that does not taper much, but is often crooked. The crown is narrow and irregular, and is composed of mostly upright to slightly spreading slender and crooked branches. Choke Cherry is a variable species with several recorded varieties and forms. One variety from the Pacific Coast of British Columbia, the Western Choke Cherry (*Prunus virginiana* var. *demissa* (Nutt.) Torr.), has leaves that are often heart-shaped at the base and downy beneath. Young twigs are also downy. Another variety, perhaps the most common form in the Interior of southern British Columbia, is the Black Choke Cherry (*Prunus virginiana* var. *melanocarpa* (A. Nels.) Sarg.). This tree has leaves of the same shape as the Choke Cherry, but much smaller and thicker; the fruit is almost black and is less astringent than that of the species.

HABITAT—In its different forms, this species is transcontinental in distribution. Relatively intolerant of shade, it is commonly found on rich moist soils in open situations, such as fence lines, along streams, on cleared land and bordering wooded areas.

SIZE—Usually a shrub, but in favourable situations becomes a tree up to 30 ft. in height and 6 ins. in diameter.

LEAVES—Broadly oval to broadest above the middle, rather abruptly tapered to both ends, particularly to the short sharp tip, 3- to 4-ins. long, quite thin, dull green on top, greenish and hairless on the lower surface, except for occasional tufts of hair at the junctions of the veins; margins with fine, sharp, closely spaced, even-sized teeth, each tooth ending in a straight hair-like point.

FLOWERS—Appear at the ends of the new twigs after the first leaves are almost fully developed; individuals approximately ¼-in. across on ¼-in. stems and packed closely to make a solid-looking cylindrical cluster.

FRUIT— Approximately ⅜-in. across, varying from crimson to black, astringent but edible; at the base the lower whorl of flower parts (calyx) is minute and scarcely noticeable; matures in late August or early September.

TWIGS—Slender to moderately stout, greyish-brown, smooth; the only member of the genus without a greyish skin that weathers off; buds chocolate-brown, sharp pointed, approximately ¼-in. long, spreading slightly from the twig; bud-scales with pale edges.

BARK—Smooth, or with fine scales, dark greyish-brown becoming almost black on old trees; horizontal markings common to most cherries and plums not noticeable.

WOOD—Hard, heavy, weak; light brown; diffuse porous.

IMPORTANCE—Of no commercial importance. The tree is too small and scattered for profitable harvesting.

NOTES—The fruit was used in pemmican, after being pounded into a mush.

CHOKE CHERRY

LEAF HAS FINE TEETH WITH LONG TIPS; GLANDS ON LEAF-STALK

FRUIT; CALYX MINUTE

FLOWERS IN ERECT CLUSTERS

TWIG HAS SHARP BUDS; BUD-SCALES HAVE PALE MARGINS

PIN CHERRY

Red Cherry
Bird Cherry
Fire Cherry

Prunus pensylvanica **L.f.**

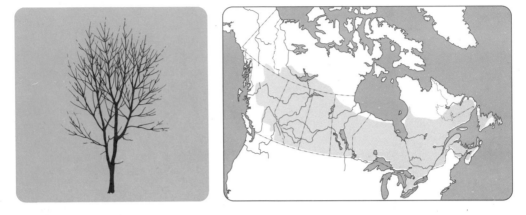

FORM—This tree develops a fairly straight trunk that extends to the top of a narrow round-topped crown. The branches, at first ascending, become more or less horizontal and spreading as the tree ages. In the open, the trunk is usually short, with a crown that becomes rather flat-topped. In the forest, the tree soon becomes over-shadowed, often takes on a dead or unhealthy appearance and has a crown that is much reduced in length. One variation of the species, *Prunus pensylvanica* var. *saximontana* Rehd., is recognized in the western part of the tree's range. This variety has much broader leaves which are widest near the mid-portion, are less shiny and have blunter tips than those of the species. It is usually found in shrub form.

HABITAT—Pin Cherry is an inhabitant of most of the wooded parts of Canada and grows singly or in groves along the rivers in the western prairies. It is a scattered and rather sparse tree in the Deciduous Forest Region. In central British Columbia its range meets that of the Bitter Cherry (*Prunus emarginata* Dougl.) and hybrids between them are not uncommon. The tree is intolerant of shade, and therefore seldom grows in the mature forest, but may be found in clearings and in burned-over or recently cut-over areas.

SIZE—A small tree attaining heights of 40 to 50 ft. and diameters of 4 to 12 ins., but usually of much smaller size. In soils deficient in moisture, it may be reduced to a shrub.

LEAVES—Lance-shaped with a long gradual taper to a slender sharp tip, broadest below or near the middle, 3- to 4-ins. long, thin and fragile, with minute uneven teeth, appearing as though gnawed by an insect along the margin, shiny yellowish-green on both surfaces, hairless, commonly curving downwards from the twig and slightly folded along the midrib, often turning bright red in autumn.

FLOWERS—Appear from lateral buds with the leaves, five to seven in a cluster on stalks ¾-in. long; individuals about ½-in. across.

FRUIT—Approximately ¼-in. across, bright red, with a thin, sour but edible flesh which matures in late August or early September.

TWIGS—Very slender, reddish; buds small, approximately ⅟₁₆-in. long, rounded, several clustered at the end of the twig in addition to the laterals along the twig (clustered buds are also a feature of Bitter Cherry), the buds along the sides spread slightly from the twig.

BARK—Smooth on young trees; dark reddish-brown with conspicuous, large, widely spaced, orange, powdery, horizontal markings (lenticels) on mature trees.

WOOD—Light, moderately soft, low in strength; brownish; porous.

IMPORTANCE—Occasionally used for fuel. A useful "nurse" tree for conifer seedlings.

244

LEAF; TEETH UNEVEN AND MINUTE   SMALL FRUIT ON LONG STALK   BARK MARKED BY WIDELY SPACED LENTICELS

FLOWERS FIVE TO A CLUSTER   BUDS PROTRUDE FROM ALL SIDES, WITH SEVERAL CLUSTERED AT END OF TWIG

BITTER CHERRY

Prunus emarginata Dougl.

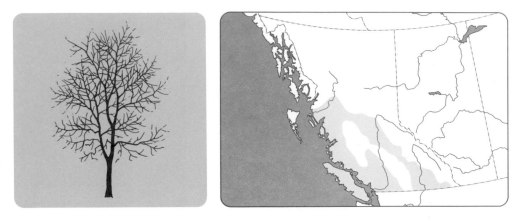

FORM—This species usually has a straight slender trunk extending well up to the top of a narrow crown of slender ascending branches. Generally the branch-free portion of the trunk is short compared to the length of the crown, largely because the tree usually grows in the open. Like its close relative the Pin Cherry, the Bitter Cherry does not do well in the shade of other trees, and therefore does not have the trunk of a typical forest tree. In the North Thompson and Shuswap river valleys, where the two species overlap, hybrids between them have been reported. Also, one variety has been named *Prunus emarginata* var. *mollis* (Dougl.) Brewer. It grows on the Pacific Coast, and can be identified by the dense coating of down on the underside of its leaves, leaf-stalks and flower-stalks. To some authors, it is the separate species *Prunus prunifolia* (Greene) Shafer.

HABITAT—The Bitter Cherry is found in the southern part of British Columbia, in the Coast and Columbia Forest regions and the moister parts of the Montane Forest Region. It does well in moist sparsely wooded areas along streams, but is also often found on cut-over and burned-over areas as an early arrival.

SIZE—A small tree, not more than 40 to 50 ft. in height by 12 ins. in diameter, although usually much smaller. On dry or exposed situations, it may be found as a shrub.

LEAVES—Oval or broadest towards the top, with a long gradual taper to the base, rounded at the tip, 1- to 3-ins. long, approximately 1-in.

wide at the widest point, thin and fragile, with minute uneven-sized teeth that appear as if they have been gnawed by an insect, dull yellowish-green on both surfaces, hairless or downy on the undersurface, ascending or standing stiffly from the twig, and slightly folded along the midrib.

FLOWERS—Appear when the leaves are almost half grown; 5 to 12 in a cluster on short stems; individuals ½-in. across.

FRUIT—Approximately ¼- to ½-in. across, dark red, with a thin, bitter, astringent flesh, matures in July or August.

TWIGS—Slender, downy becoming smooth, dark reddish; buds pointed, several clustered at the end of the twig in addition to the buds along the side (similar to the Pin Cherry), approximately ⅛-in. long, spreading slightly from the twig.

BARK—Smooth on young trees, very bitter taste, dark reddish-brown with conspicuous, large, widely spaced, orange, powdery horizontal markings (lenticels).

WOOD—Soft, low in strength, close-grained; brownish; porous.

IMPORTANCE—Occasionally used locally for fuel, but more useful as a "nurse" tree for conifer seedlings.

NOTES—Narrow strips of bark are ideal for ornamental basket-work.

BITTER CHERRY

LEAVES
TAPER TO
BOTH ENDS

BUDS
POINTED;
A FEW
CLUSTERED
AT END
OF TWIG

LOWER FLOWER-STALKS ARE LONGEST

CROWN NARROW; BRANCHES ASCENDING

CANADA PLUM

Prunus nigra Ait.

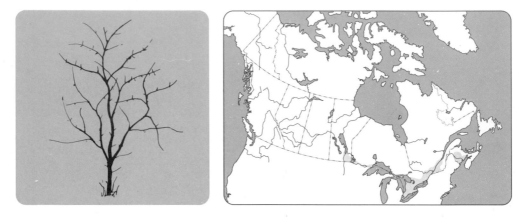

FORM—This is a straggling tree with a short crooked trunk which is often divided a few feet above the ground into several stiff, upright but crooked branches. The crown is irregular, rather narrow and flat-topped and is made up of slender, twisted and zigzag branches.

HABITAT—Canada Plum grows as a scattered, but widespread, tree in eastern Canada. It makes its best growth in water-formed soils of river valleys, and in limestone soils on hillsides throughout the Great Lakes-St. Lawrence Forest Region (except in the northern parts).

SIZE—This species is usually found as a small tree up to 30 ft. high, with a diameter which seldom exceeds 10 ins.

LEAVES—Broadly oval to broadest above the middle, narrowing abruptly into a long slender tip, widely wedge-shaped, rounded or heart-shaped at the base, 3- to 5-ins. long, fairly thin and fragile, doubly toothed with prominent rounded teeth, the smaller ones usually gland-tipped, dull dark green on top, slightly paler on the undersurface; a strong midrib with slender lateral veins; stalks stout, with two large, dark glands just below the leaf-base.

FLOWERS—Appear along the branchlets on the spur-like thorns or dwarf twigs at the same time as or just before the tree comes into leaf; three or four in a cluster on slender reddish stalks, ½- to ¾-in. long; blossoms approximately 1¼-ins. across, petals white, turning to pink, often very showy.

FRUIT—Slightly over 1-in. long, with a thick orange-red skin which has no bloom, and with a yellow, juicy, sour flesh which ripens during the period mid-August to early September.

TWIGS—Slender, smooth, reddish-brown; buds greyish-brown, approximately ⅛- to ¼-in. long, pressed tightly against the twig; bud-scales thin at the ends (ends are often frayed) and paler than the bud; buds on the sides of the twigs only, the absence of a terminal bud marked by a small scar at the end of the twig.

BARK—Black, with slightly elongated greyish markings (lenticels); with age, splits vertically on the trunk, the two separated parts curling back only slightly to reveal the inner bark which gradually becomes scaly.

WOOD—Moderately heavy, hard, fairly strong, close-grained; rich reddish-brown with paler to almost white sapwood; porous.

IMPORTANCE—The wood is of no commercial importance because of the smallness and scarcity of the tree. The Canada Plum is a useful ornamental, however, because of its attractive leaves and showy flowers. Several cultivated forms have been developed.

NOTES—Potatoes should not be planted near a plum tree because of an aphid which sometimes overwinters in the tree. The aphid can carry a potato disease, but does not harm the tree or its fruit.

F HAS GLANDS ON TEETH AND LEAF-STALK

TREE HAS PROFUSION OF FLOWERS IN SPRING

FRUIT IS SOUR

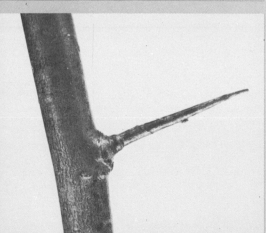

ORN-LIKE TWIGS HAVE LEAF-SCARS AND BUDS

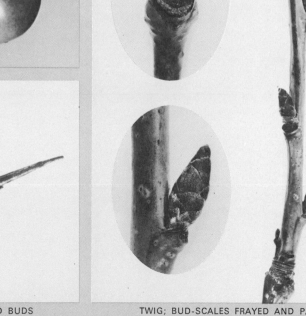

TWIG; BUD-SCALES FRAYED AND PALE AT EDGES

WILD PLUM

Prunus americana **Marsh.**

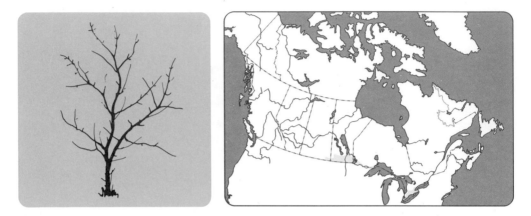

FORM—Like its close relative the Canada Plum, the Wild Plum has a short crooked trunk with stiff lateral branches which spread horizontally to form a wide, low, flattish-topped, irregular crown.

HABITAT—Wild Plum is native only to southern Ontario, southern Manitoba and the extreme southeastern portion of Saskatchewan. There are many instances, however, of the tree having been planted for decorative purposes around homesteads and in communities far beyond its natural range. In some of these places, the tree has escaped and become established. The Wild Plum grows on rich soils along streams and at the borders of swamps. The ranges of the two native plums overlap and there is some difficulty in deciding whether an individual tree is a Canada Plum or a Wild Plum. The Wild Plum, however, being a more southerly tree than the Canada Plum is considered to inhabit the southern portion of their common range. The range maps for the two species show the probable distribution of the plums in Canada.

SIZE—It is perhaps more often found as a shrub than a tree, but it may grow to heights of 30 ft. and diameters of 12 ins.

LEAVES—Narrowly oval, but usually broadest slightly below the middle, tapering gradually to a long, narrow, sharp tip, fully rounded at the base or with a slight taper towards the leaf-stalk, 3- to 5-ins. long, fairly thin and fragile, doubly or singly toothed along the margin, with sharp-pointed teeth, usually not gland-tipped, dull green on top, paler on the undersurface, without hairs or slightly hairy; strong midrib but fainter veins; leaf-stalk with or without glands near the leaf-base.

FLOWERS—Appear before, or with, the leaves along the branchlets on the spur-like thorns and dwarf branches, usually five to a cluster, on slender greenish-brown stems; blossoms approximately 1-in. across, petals white, showy.

FRUIT—Approximately 1¼-ins. long, orange or reddish with a slight bloom, the flesh juicy, sweet or sour; ripening about the end of August or early in September.

TWIGS—Slender, smooth, greyish to reddish-brown; buds greyish, pointed, ⅛- to ¼-in. long, pressed against the twigs; bud-scales two shades of pale greyish-brown; buds on the side of the twig only, the absence of a terminal bud is marked by a small scar.

BARK—Reddish-brown or dark grey to nearly black, with short horizontal markings (lenticels); splits vertically and curls horizontally; the inner bark becomes scaly.

WOOD—Moderately heavy, hard, moderately strong; heartwood dark brown with nearly white sapwood; porous.

IMPORTANCE—The wood is of no commercial value. The fruit can be made into preserves and the tree may occasionally be used for horticultural or decorative purposes.

TAPERS GRADUALLY TO A LONG
T; TEETH ARE SHARP POINTED

TYPICAL FLOWER SHOWING FLOWER PARTS

CLUMP OF WILD PLUM

G BARK SMOOTH AND

FRUIT ORANGE OR REDDISH WITH SLIGHT BLOOM

HONEY-LOCUST

Gleditsia triacanthos L.

FORM—Honey-locust, along with Kentucky Coffee-tree and Redbud, belongs to the *Leguminosae*, a very large family of some 13,000 species in over 500 genera, including herbaceous plants, shrubs and trees. The herbaceous plants are of great economic importance. Among them are pea, bean, vetch, clover, alfalfa and many others that provide food. The Honey-locust has a short crooked trunk divided near the ground into a few spreading branches that form a broad, open, flat-topped crown. The trunk and larger branches are often armed with long, extremely sharp, branched thorns. A variety that may be found in southern Ontario, *Gleditsia triacanthos* var. *inermis* Willd., does not have thorns (or has only a few thorns) and is slender in form. Black-locust (*Robinia pseudoacacia* L.), an introduced species also called False-acacia, has been planted as an ornamental in Canada and has seeded itself in many localities. It has singly compound leaves comprising an odd number of oval-shaped untoothed leaflets, and short broad-based thorns at the base of the leaf-stalks. The flowers are similar to pea flowers in shape, white, fragrant, showy and hang in clusters. The fruit resembles a pea-pod, is about 4-ins. long and there are several on a central stalk.

HABITAT—This species grows naturally only along the Lake Erie shore of Essex County, Ontario, from Point Pelee to Amherstburg, and on the islands in the lake. Being a popular tree for planting, because of its delicate foliage,

it has become established as an ornamental far beyond its natural range.

SIZE—Occasionally reaching 100 ft. in height and 3 ft. in diameter, but usually much smaller.

LEAVES—Alternate, about 6-ins. long, divided into an even number of leaflets arranged along a central stalk, often doubly compound. Leaflets about 1-in. long, minutely toothed, or sometimes without teeth.

FLOWERS—Greenish-white, about ¼-in. across, arranged along a central stalk.

FRUIT—A flat, twisted, brownish pod, about 1-ft. long by 1¼-ins. across, containing bean-like seeds; fall in winter without opening.

TWIGS—Zigzag, brownish; buds in a vertical row, mostly hidden beneath the bark, no terminal bud; branchlets usually armed with sharp reddish thorns.

BARK—Smooth, brownish, becoming broken into scaly ridges.

WOOD—Heavy, hard, strong, decay-resistant; golden-brown.

IMPORTANCE—Of little commercial value because of its scarcity in the natural state. Sometimes the wood is used for fence posts, rails, general construction and furniture, but the tree's widest use is for landscaping.

NOTES—Immature seed pods have sweet-tasting pulp between the seeds and are enjoyed by cattle. Some small animals and birds also eat the fruit by tearing open the pods when they fall to the ground during the winter.

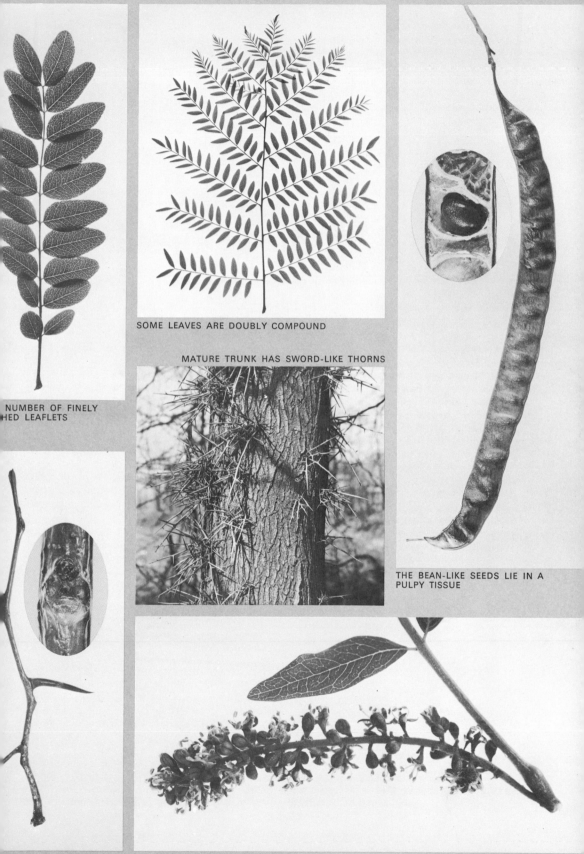

SOME LEAVES ARE DOUBLY COMPOUND

MATURE TRUNK HAS SWORD-LIKE THORNS

NUMBER OF FINELY
HED LEAFLETS

THE BEAN-LIKE SEEDS LIE IN A
PULPY TISSUE

NED TWIG; BUDS
ALLY SUNKEN IN THE
CAR

A FLOWER CLUSTER. (NOTE THAT SOME LEAFLETS LACK TEETH.)

KENTUCKY COFFEE-TREE

Gymnocladus dioicus (L.) K. Koch

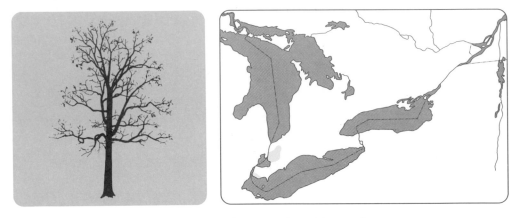

FORM—There are only two species of *Gymnocladus* in the world, this one and one in China. The generic name refers to the naked appearance of the tree when it is in its winter condition (see Appendix "B"). The Kentucky Coffee-tree loses its leaves early in the autumn and does not leaf-out until late in the spring, which means that it is leafless for nearly half the year. The small number of branches, their coarseness and the sparseness of their twigs add to the naked look. The trunk is usually short, and divides into three or four sharply ascending limbs that support a narrow crown. In summer, the tree is quite striking because of the large size of the leaves displayed on so few branches.

HABITAT—This species grows naturally only in Essex and Lambton counties in Ontario, but it has been planted as an ornamental far beyond its range. Some examples can be found as far north as Ottawa.

SIZE—The Kentucky Coffee-tree is usually small, but may reach 80 ft. in height and approximately 2 ft. in diameter.

LEAVES—The largest of any Canadian tree, 1- to 3-ft. long and up to 2-ft. wide; doubly compound (except at the base, where there are one or two pairs of single leaflets); leaflets broadest below the middle, without teeth, about 2-ins. long, seldom opposite each other, no end leaflet.

FLOWERS—Greenish-white, in large, open, unattractive, terminal clusters; usually the male and female flowers are on separate trees.

FRUIT—A hard, dark, reddish-brown, leathery pod, usually with a slight bloom, about 5-ins. long by 1½-ins. wide containing a few, large, blackish-brown, slightly flattened, hard-shelled, rounded seeds imbedded in a sweet sticky pulp; pods hang on stout stalks 1-in. long, and remain on the tree through the winter.

TWIGS—Very stout, blunt-ended, with only a few on the branches, smooth or downy, greyish-brown with a large deep-orange pith; leaf-scars large, heart-shaped; buds minute, blackish, silky-haired, two or three in a row, the upper one larger and placed well above the leaf-scar, the lowest one close to it; no terminal buds.

BARK—Greyish, with hard, thin, firm and scaly ridges curling outwards along their edges.

WOOD—Moderately heavy, hard, decay-resistant; light reddish-brown with yellowish-white sapwood.

IMPORTANCE—Of no commercial value but, as with all legumes, the roots bear nodules containing nitrogen-fixing bacteria which, on decaying, enrich the soil. Useful as an ornamental because of its strikingly different appearance when in leaf.

NOTES—The seeds cannot be recommended as a substitute for coffee. The name refers to the appearance of the seed rather than to its taste which is bitter and unpleasant.

KENTUCKY COFFEE-TREE

GE LEAF IS DIVIDED INTO MANY LEAFLETS

MALE FLOWER CLUSTER

; LEAF-SCAR HEART SHAPED;
HAIRY

LEATHERY FRUIT POD CONTAINS ROUNDED SEEDS

; SCALY RIDGES ARE LOOSE AT THE ENDS

MEDIUM-SIZED TREE GROWING IN OTTAWA

REDBUD

Cercis canadensis L.

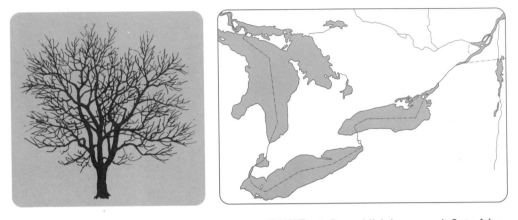

FORM—Of the seven known species of *Cercis*, two are found in North America and the range of one of these extends into Canada. In the form of a mature tree, it has a low spreading crown of horizontal branches supported by a short, erect or leaning trunk.

HABITAT—The Redbud grows in the extreme southern part of Ontario. It has been reported on the mainland shore of Lake Erie in Kent County and on Pelee Island, but the only substantiated record of natural growth is from Pelee Island. Recently it has been reintroduced in Point Pelee National Park, Ontario, where it was thought to be extinct.

SIZE—It is a small tree, usually under 25 ft. in height and with diameters of up to 10 ins.

LEAVES—Broadly heart-shaped with a short blunt tip, 3- to 5-ins. long by 3- to 5-ins. wide, without teeth on the margin, pale bluish-green; lighter on the undersurface and hairless or slightly downy, five to seven prominent veins radiate from the leaf-stalk which is quite noticeably swollen below the leaf-blade.

FLOWERS—Appear in the spring in small clusters, usually before the leaves unfold; individual flowers approximately ½-in. long, somewhat like a pea flower in shape, pink to reddish, on stalks ½-in. long which extend from opened buds on the old wood to display the flowers; when the flowers are massed along the branches the tree is very colourful.

FRUIT—A flat reddish-brown pod, 2- to 4-ins. long, a few hanging from the same point on the stem, each with a paler narrow wing along the side where the seeds are attached, this side curving at the base in a direction opposite to the direction of its curve at the tip; seeds are flat and nearly circular in outline (not bean-shaped).

TWIGS—Slender, dark reddish-brown; buds dark red, often placed one above the other, the lower ones very small; twig has only leaf-buds which are small, pressed against it and somewhat flattened; no terminal bud; flower-buds larger, blunt, roundish, but slightly flattened and often swollen at the end; flower-buds appear only on the old wood, and occasionally there are a few just below the twig-bases.

BARK—Reddish-brown, scaly, sometimes divided into long narrow scaly ridges.

WOOD—Hard, heavy, weak; dark brown.

IMPORTANCE—Of no importance for the wood, but of value throughout most of the Deciduous Forest Region as an ornamental because of its beautiful appearance when in bloom in the early spring, particularly when planted next to evergreens.

NOTES—Fossilized Redbuds have been found in the Don River Valley near Toronto.

A yellow dye can be obtained by boiling pieces of the twigs in water.

256

STALK IS SWOLLEN BELOW LEAF-BLADE

FLOWERS RADIATE FROM THE BASE OF THE CLUSTER

SEED POD AND
SEEDS ARE FLAT

RIDGES ON MATURE BARK

SMALL TREE AT ST. WILLIAMS FOREST STATION,
ONTARIO

TWIGS LACK TERMINAL BUDS

HOP-TREE

Ptelea trifoliata L.

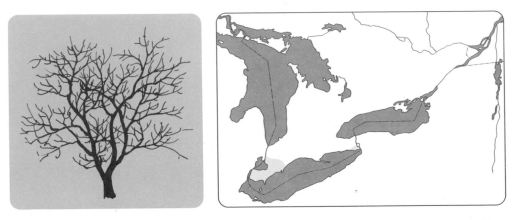

FORM—*Ptelea* comprises a group of about ten species of small trees and shrubs which are restricted to North America. Two species reach tree size and one, the Hop-tree, extends into Canada. It has a slender, often crooked trunk that divides near the ground and supports a broad round-topped crown of many short, twisted and interwoven, but ascending, branches. Prickly-ash (*Zanthoxylum americanum* Mill.) is a member of the *Rutaceae* to which the Hop-tree belongs. The Prickly-ash is a thorny plant which, although rarely attaining tree size, could be mistaken for one of the native thorn-trees mentioned elsewhere in this book. For that reason, its salient recognition features are given here. It has alternate leaves divided into five to eleven leaflets which have translucent dots similar to those on Hop-tree leaves; it is the only thorn-tree with that unusual feature. The thorns are in pairs (like those of Black-locust), but the buds are exposed, whereas those of Black-locust are hidden under the leaf-scar.

HABITAT—The Hop-tree ranges as far south as Mexico, but the northern extremity of its range only reaches the southern part of Ontario. It is found at a few places along the shore of Lake Erie, on Pelee Island and near Thamesville west of London. The tree grows sparsely in open stands of other species along sandy beaches and on dry rocky soils bordering wooded areas. Only occasionally will it be found as an understory tree.

SIZE—A small tree up to 25 ft. in height with a diameter usually under 6 ins.

LEAVES—Alternate, shed each autumn, 4- to 6-ins. long, divided into three nearly stalkless parts, on a long stalk almost as long as the end leaflet; leaflets without teeth or faintly toothed, sharp pointed, narrowing below the middle to a wedge-shaped base, shiny dark green above, much paler and slightly downy on the undersurface, marked by a profusion of tiny translucent dots which can be seen by holding the leaf against a strong light.

FLOWERS—In greenish-white clusters at the ends of the twigs.

FRUIT—A two-chambered, one- or two-seeded body surrounded by a veined wing, in dense clusters which remain on the tree throughout most of the winter.

TWIGS—Slender, with or without hairs, dark reddish-brown; buds small, roundish, yellow, woolly, partly sunk into the bark and not visible until after leaf-fall, more than one above a leaf-scar.

BARK—Dark grey to reddish-brown, smooth or with a slight roughness.

WOOD—Moderately heavy, hard, of medium strength; yellowish-brown.

IMPORTANCE—Of no commercial value, but occasionally planted as an ornamental.

NOTES—When crushed, the leaves have a strong orange-like odour.

The fruit can be substituted for hops in flavouring beer, hence the name Hop-tree.

TRANSLUCENT DOTS ARE VISIBLE
NLARGEMENT

PERFECT AND IMPERFECT FLOWERS ARE TOGETHER IN CLUSTER

IS IN A DENSE CLUSTER

MENT-LIKE WING SURROUNDS SEED

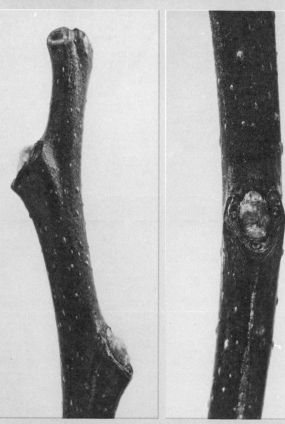

PARTIALLY SUNKEN, WOOLLY BUDS

STAGHORN SUMAC

Rhus typhina L.

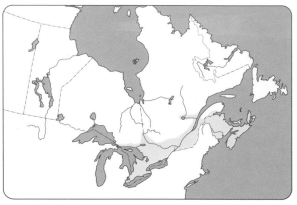

FORM—The Staghorn Sumac is a small tree with a flat crown supported by a short, crooked, often leaning trunk that divides near the ground into a few ascending branches. The branches fork into stout woolly branchlets and, in winter, they resemble the antlers of a deer in velvet. The root system is shallow but widespreading, and produces new stems from rootsuckers; thus the species is generally found in thickets. A closely related shrubby species, *Rhus glabra* L., has a wide range that extends from Lake Huron to central British Columbia. Normally, it is easily distinguishable by its hairless twigs and leaves, but it has been reported to cross with Staghorn Sumac to produce hybrid forms. An introduced species, the Tree-of-Heaven or Chinese Sumac (*Ailanthus altissima* (Mill.) Swingle), a member of the *Quassia* family and not related to Staghorn Sumac, has become naturalized in southern Ontario. It differs from Staghorn Sumac in having coarse hairless twigs and leaves with a few teeth only at the base of the leaflets. Each tooth has a large gland on the underside.

HABITAT—Staghorn Sumac grows throughout the Deciduous, Great Lakes-St. Lawrence and Acadian Forest regions. It is usually found in open areas, characteristically on sandy or rocky soils, but occasionally in swamps.

SIZE—Often only a shrub, but, as a tree, normally reaches heights of 15 ft., and diameters of 4 ins.

LEAVES—Alternate, shed in autumn, 1- to 2-ft. long, divided into 11 to 31 leaflets on a densely hairy stalk which is often reddish on top; leaflets almost without stalks, long pointed, 2- to 5-ins. long, the middle pairs considerably longer than those at either end of the leaf, sharply toothed, dark green above, paler on the undersurface with fine hairs on the midrib and main veins; in autumn turns bright scarlet with shades of crimson.

FLOWERS—Appear in July in large, dense, yellowish-green, upright clusters at the ends of the branches; male and female generally on separate trees, the male clusters about 1-ft. long, the female clusters shorter.

FRUIT—A large, cone-shaped, dense cluster of small single-seeded bodies, each covered with bright red hairs; the clusters stand upright at the ends of the branches and remain attached throughout most of the winter.

TWIGS—Very stout, densely covered with dark velvety hairs, exude a milky sap if broken and disclose a thick yellowish-brown pith; leaf-scars narrow and almost encircling the small, roundish, velvety buds; no terminal bud.

BARK—Dark yellowish-brown, thin, smooth, becoming scaly with age.

WOOD—Light, soft, brittle; orange with broad greenish rays.

IMPORTANCE—The wood is occasionally used for decorative finishing and novelties. The tree is sometimes planted as an ornamental for its brilliant autumn foliage.

DENSELY HAIRY TWIGS HAVE HORSESHOE-SHAPED LEAF-SCARS

...NUMBER OF LEAFLETS; UNDERSURFACE
...ELY HAIRY

TREE IS UNMISTAKABLE IN ITS FALL COLOURS

...ER OF DENSELY HAIRY
...S

MALE FLOWERS ARE IN
LARGE CLUSTERS

FEMALE FLOWERS ARE IN SMALLER,
MORE COMPACT CLUSTERS

POISON SUMAC

Poison-dogwood
Poison-elderberry

Rhus vernix L.

FORM—This is one of the three poisonous species of *Rhus* that are native to Canada, and the only one that attains tree size. It has a slender trunk and a small rounded crown of moderately stout branches; the twigs are lightly clothed with large compound leaves. The other two poisonous species of *Rhus* are small shrubs or vines which sometimes twist around rocks and plants, or climb up into trees. One lives in eastern Canada and the other is in British Columbia. The eastern one is the true Poison-ivy (*Rhus radicans* L.) and the western one, called Poison-oak (*Rhus diversiloba* Torr. & Gray), is very similar to it. They are mentioned here because of their poisonous properties and common habit of climbing tree-trunks, where they could be handled if not recognized as being potentially dangerous. Both differ from Poison Sumac mainly in size and in having leaves divided into only three parts. Also, their leaflets can have a few or many coarse teeth, and sometimes may even be lobed. Flowers, fruits and twigs of all three species are similar.

HABITAT—The Poison Sumac is uncommon in Canada, but can be found in the southern parts of the Deciduous Forest Region and a few places in the southern area of the Great Lakes-St. Lawrence Forest Region. It grows in open swampy woodlands where it associates with other lowland species, such as willows, poplars, Black Ash, White Elm, Silver Maple and Eastern White Cedar.

SIZE—A tall shrub or small tree, 5 to 20 ft. in height and usually under 3 ins. in diameter.

LEAVES—Alternate, shed in autumn, 7- to 15-ins. long, ascending on the twigs; divided into seven to thirteen stalked leaflets which are long-pointed at the tip and wedge-shaped at the base, 3- to 4-ins. long, without teeth, lustrous dark green above, whitened and without hairs on the undersurface; the leaf-stalk is often reddish.

FLOWERS—Small, in open clusters arising in the axils of the leaves.

FRUIT— White or ivory, hairless, single-seeded, thin-fleshed, glossy, pearl-like, about ¼ in. in diameter, in open clusters, usually persisting throughout the winter. (The fruits of this species and of the two shrubby types are often useful in the recognition of these poisonous plants in winter.)

TWIGS—Stout, mottled, brownish-yellow, hairless, dotted with raised markings; leaf-scars broad, shield-shaped with many dot-like bundle-scars more or less in three groups; buds small, brown, hairy; the twig has a terminal bud.

BARK—Dark grey, smooth.

WOOD—Light and moderately soft, low in strength, porous; heartwood greenish-brown, sapwood yellowish-white.

IMPORTANCE—Of no known usefulness, but important in that everyone should learn to recognize and avoid these poisonous plants.

R PORTION OF TREE SHOWING LEAVES
ED INTO LEAFLETS

POISON-IVY LEAF HAS ONLY THREE LEAFLETS

THIS LEAF HAS NINE LEAFLETS

THE WHITE FRUIT IS IN OPEN CLUSTERS

VINE-LIKE FORM OF POISON-IVY

MAPLE

Acer L.

Although about 150 species of maple are known, most grow in eastern Asia and only 13 are native to North America; ten grow in Canada. The native maples are large trees, with the exception of four species, Mountain Maple and Striped Maple in eastern Canada, and Vine Maple and Douglas Maple in western Canada. These four are nearly always coarse shrubs or small bushy trees.

All the native species shed their leaves at the end of the growing season and produce a new crop the following spring. All have an opposite leaf arrangement and, with the exception of the Manitoba Maple, the leaves are simple, with three to nine veins radiating from the top of the leaf-stalk. Usually there is an equal number of lobes on the margin.

The flowers are very diverse. In several species they lack the petals usually associated with flowers. Some are composed of male organs only, others of female organs only and some have both sexes in the same flower. Also, there may be different kinds on the same tree. Some flowers are nectar-producing and insect-pollinated, others are wind-pollinated, and still others are various intermediate forms between the two.

The fruit is distinct from that of other species. It consists of two seed-cases, each containing one seed and a long wing. The two seeds are joined on a single stalk and are displayed in clusters. The angle at which the two wings are spread, and the type of fruit cluster, are useful in identifying the species.

The twigs display their leaf-scars and buds in an opposite arrangement. The bud-scales are also opposite. In the two "hard maples" (Sugar Maple and Black Maple) there are four to eight pairs of scales, and in the "soft maples" there are one to four pairs of scales.

Of outstanding commercial importance, the maple is also Canada's national tree. Maples contribute valuable wood products, sustain the maple sugar industry and beautify the landscape. The wood is variable in hardness, toughness and in other properties, depending on the species. It is in demand for flooring, furniture, interior woodwork, plywood, veneer, small woodenware, etc., and supports several flourishing industries throughout its range in eastern Canada. The hard maples have the stiffer, stronger, tougher and more sought-after wood. Also, they often provide the wood characterized by curly grain and birds-eye figure, so highly prized in furniture-building and cabinet-making.

Several introduced maples are planted in Canada as ornamentals and street or road-side trees. The most important of these is Norway Maple (*Acer platanoides* L.) in different varieties and forms. The typical form of this exotic species is easily distinguishable from the native maples by its leaf which, although resembling a Sugar Maple leaf in general outline, has teeth with bristle-like tips and an undersurface that is a lustrous green. As with Bigleaf Maple, a milky juice can be squeezed out of a cut leaf-stalk. The fruit is large (2 ins. or more in length) and the two wings are spread in a nearly straight line.

Other favourite ornamentals include Sycamore Maple (*Acer pseudoplatanus* L.) with large thick leaves which are wrinkled above and whitish or often purplish on the undersurface. The fruits are large, and several are arranged along a central stem similar to those of Bigleaf Maple, but without the dense hairiness of the Bigleaf Maple fruits. The buds are green. Two Japanese maples, *Acer palmatum* Thunb. and *Acer japonicum* Thunb., have many-lobed leaves like their Canadian relative Vine Maple, but with sharper lobes and deeper clefts separating them. There are a great many varieties of Japanese Maple. Also commonly found is the Amur Maple (*Acer ginnala* Maxim.) which has narrow leaves almost twice as long as they are wide (3 ins. by $1\frac{1}{2}$ ins.) with three shallow lobes. Some leaves are unlobed, but all have coarse teeth. The tree is usually made up of many limbs projecting from a common trunk near the ground, and is characterized by its strikingly brilliant foliage in the autumn.

SUGAR MAPLE

Hard Maple

Acer saccharum **Marsh.**

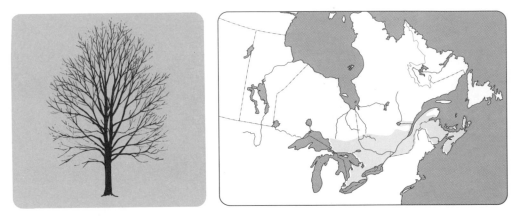

FORM—This tree, when growing in the forest, develops a straight trunk free of branches for two-thirds or more of its height. The trunk supports a narrow round-topped crown of short, but sturdy, branches. In the open, the branch-free trunk is short and divides near the ground into a few large, spreading limbs that support a wide full crown which narrows rather gradually to a rounded top. The root system is wide-spreading, but relatively deep compared to that of most maples.

HABITAT—The Sugar Maple is a characteristic tree of hardwood stands in the Deciduous Forest Region and is a common constituent of the forest throughout most of the Great Lakes-St. Lawrence, and the Acadian Forest regions. It makes its best growth on deep, fertile, moist, well-drained soils, especially where there is lime in the substratum. It may form pure stands or grow in mixture with other hardwoods, or with hardwoods and scattered conifers. Since it is very tolerant of shade, the Sugar Maple can grow successfully in the understory of the forest and often remains small for many years, until released by a break in the canopy.

SIZE—One of the largest Canadian maples; commonly reaches heights of 80 to 90 ft. and diameters of 2 to 3 ft.; occasionally attains 130 ft. in height and 5 ft. in diameter.

LEAVES—Usually five-lobed, but occasionally found with only three lobes, 3- to 5-ins. across, deep yellowish-green above, paler and without hairs on the undersurface; lobes have only a few irregular, wavy teeth, end lobe almost square, separated from the two side lobes by wide open notches which are rounded at the bottom; turns yellow to brilliant orange and scarlet in the fall.

FLOWERS—Appear with the unfolding leaves; small, without petals, hanging on long slender stalks in tassel-like clusters.

FRUIT—Matures in autumn; approximately 1¼-ins. long with a plump seed; borne on slender stalks which are usually longer than the fruits; the seed wings are almost parallel or diverge slightly.

TWIGS—Reddish-brown, shiny, without hairs; buds reddish-brown, sharp pointed with several pairs of faintly hairy scales.

BARK—Dark grey, divided into long, vertical, firm, irregular strips that usually curl outwards along one side, occasionally somewhat scaly.

WOOD—Heavy, hard, strong; pale yellowish-brown; diffuse porous.

IMPORTANCE—One of the most valuable commercial hardwoods in Canada. Typical uses are for furniture, flooring, farm tools, turnery, veneer, plywood, dies and cutting blocks. The sap is the principal source of the maple syrup and maple sugar of commerce.

NOTES—One of the earliest recorded descriptions of the Indian's method of extracting a syrup from maple was published in the "Philosophical Transactions of the Royal Society", London, England, in 1684.

SUGAR MAPLE

SPREADING WINGS SHORTER THAN FRUIT STALKS

TWIG SHINY AND HAIRLESS

...ES HAVE ONLY A FEW WAVY TEETH

...K; FIRM
...GES CURL OUTWARDS ALONG ONE SIDE

BUDS POINTED WITH NUMEROUS SCALES

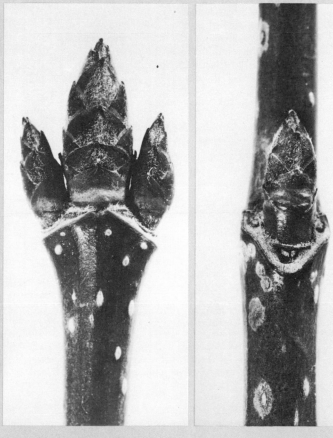

BLACK MAPLE

Acer nigrum Michx. f.

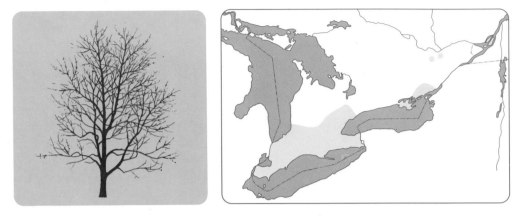

FORM—This species is similar in general form to the Sugar Maple and is considered by some authors to be a variety of that species, or a subspecies of it. Classified in this way, the tree has been named *Acer saccharum* var. *nigrum* (Michx. f.) Britton, or *Acer saccharum* Marsh. ssp. *nigrum* (Michx. f.) Desmarais. Unlike the Sugar Maple, the Black Maple has a rather wilted appearance when in leaf. The ends of the lobes of the quite flimsy leaves curve downwards and give the appearance of a tree needing water. Another difference between the two is that Black Maple bark is narrowly ridged and of a darker colour. Other differences are indicated below.

HABITAT—The Black Maple's centre of distribution is in the mid-eastern United States, with the northern range extending through the Deciduous Forest Region of Ontario and along the St. Lawrence Valley to Montreal Island. A few grow in Ottawa and at Almonte in the Ottawa Valley. The tree thrives best on sites that are moister than those where Sugar Maple makes its best growth. Like Sugar Maple, it is very tolerant of shade and is able to survive as an understory tree for many years, until an opening in the canopy gives it the opportunity to gain a place in the main stand.

SIZE — Similar to Sugar Maple; attains heights of 80 to 90 ft. and diameters of 2 to 3 ft.

LEAVES—Three to five shallow lobes with a few irregular and indistinct teeth, 3- to 5-ins. across, dark green above, yellowish-green on the undersurface with dense, brownish, velvety hairs which extend along the leaf-stalk; end lobe almost square, separated from the two side lobes by wide open notches which are shallow and rounded at the bottom; turns yellow to brownish-yellow in the fall, not as showy as Sugar Maple.

FLOWERS—Appear with the unfolding leaves; small, without petals, hanging on slender stalks in tassel-like clusters.

FRUIT— Matures in autumn; approximately 1¼-ins. long with a large plump seed, borne on a slender stalk about as long as the fruits; the seed wings are almost parallel or converge noticeably.

TWIGS—Reddish-brown, dull, hairy; buds greyish-brown, pointed, with several pairs of blunt hairy scales.

BARK—Blackish-grey, divided into long, narrow, vertical, firm, irregular sections, occasionally scaly.

WOOD—Heavy, hard, strong; pale yellowish-brown; diffuse porous.

IMPORTANCE—The wood has the same physical properties as that of Sugar Maple and is not graded separately by the lumber industry. The two are sold under the trade name "hard maple", and are used for furniture, fixtures, flooring, farm tools, turnery, veneer, plywood, dies and cutting blocks. The sap is also used in making maple syrup products.

ERSURFACE OF LEAF DENSELY HAIRY

FOLIAGE HAS WILTED APPEARANCE

GS ABOUT SAME LENGTH AS FRUIT STALKS

. IS NARROWLY RIDGED

OPEN-GROWN TREE

BIGLEAF MAPLE

Broadleaf Maple

Acer macrophyllum **Pursh**

FORM—In the forest, this maple develops a narrow crown supported by a trunk free of branches for one-half or more of its length. Trees growing in the open have broad rounded crowns supported by a few, large, spreading and ascending limbs that arise low down on the trunk, leaving only a small portion free of branches. The bark retains moisture well and the trunk and larger branches may be almost completely covered with mosses, liverworts and ferns. The root system is shallow and wide-spreading.

HABITAT—Bigleaf Maple is confined to the area of the Coast Forest Region in British Columbia and adjacent islands south of latitude 52 degrees North. It generally grows in coarse, gravelly, moist soils, but can be found in other types of moist soils scattered among hardwoods and conifers such as Red Alder, Black Cottonwood, Douglas-fir, Western Red Cedar and Western Hemlock. Occasionally it occupies clearings where, later, it will be succeeded by conifers.

SIZE—This is the largest and fastest growing maple in western Canada. Commonly attaining heights of 50 to 70 ft. and diameters of 2 ft. or more, it may reach heights of 100 ft. on the best sites.

LEAVES—The largest leaf of any Canadian maple and the largest undivided leaf of any Canadian tree species; 6- to 12-ins. across, almost as long, deeply five-lobed, shiny, dark green above, paler and without hairs on the undersurface; lobes with only a few, irregular, bluntish, wavy teeth, end lobe narrows inwardly towards its base, separated from the two side lobes by narrow U-shaped notches which are sometimes closed by overlapping of the lobes; turns yellow in autumn; leaf-stalk exudes a milky sap when broken.

FLOWERS—Appear with the unfolding leaves; on short stalks, many arranged along a single hairy stem at the ends of the twigs, $\frac{1}{4}$-in. across, with greenish-yellow petals.

FRUIT—Matures in autumn; $1\frac{1}{4}$- to $2\frac{1}{2}$-ins. long with a swollen hairy seed; the seed wings are not spread very far apart.

TWIGS—Stout, reddish-brown, without hairs; buds blunt, greenish to reddish with three to four pairs of scales; leaf-scars show five to nine dot-like bundle-scars (the highest number for any Canadian maple).

BARK—Greyish-brown, shallowly furrowed into scaly ridges.

WOOD—Moderately hard, not strong; light brown; diffuse porous.

IMPORTANCE—The limited supply of hardwoods in British Columbia makes this tree of some local importance for furniture, musical instruments, interior panelling and other uses where a hardwood is preferred.

NOTES—The various Ice Ages caused the peculiar range patterns exhibited by maples throughout the northern hemisphere. Many immediate relatives of the Bigleaf Maple grow in Europe, but it is the only surviving representative on the North American Continent.

BIGLEAF MAPLE

SEED IS HAIRY

IS UNMISTAKABLE BECAUSE OF ITS SIZE

FLOWERS ARRANGED
ALONG CENTRAL STEM

-GROWN TREE,
ICHAN BAY, B.C.

TWIG; BUDS HAVE
ONLY A FEW SCALES

SILVER MAPLE

Soft Maple

Acer saccharinum L.

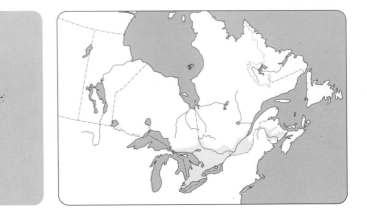

FORM—This tree has a short trunk which divides near the ground into a number of limbs which again divide and give rise to a broad crown that is rounded at the top. The branches from the trunk ascend sharply and the larger ones arch outwards and downwards before turning upwards at the ends. In the forest, the crown is narrow and much less spreading, and the trunk is more elongated. The root system is usually quite shallow.

HABITAT—Silver Maple grows best on rich moist bottomlands along streams and the shores of lakes, and is less common than Sugar Maple or Red Maple. It is seldom found at high elevations. The tree grows throughout the Deciduous Forest Region, the southeastern parts of the Great Lakes-St. Lawrence Forest Region in Ontario and Quebec, and in the Acadian Forest Region in New Brunswick.

SIZE—A large fast-growing tree; commonly 80- to 90-ft. high and up to 3 ft. in diameter. Under good growing conditions, it may reach heights of 125 ft. and diameters of up to 5 ft.

LEAVES—Five-lobed with deep notches, usually extending more than half-way to the centre of the leaf-blade, 3- to 5-ins. across, light green above, whitened and without hairs on the undersurface; lobes have coarse, sharp, irregular, double teeth, end lobe narrows inwardly towards the centre of the leaf, separated from the two side lobes by rather narrow, deep, U-shaped notches; turns pale yellow or brownish in autumn.

FLOWERS—Appear before the leaves in dense almost-stalkless clusters; male and female flowers usually in separate clusters on the same tree, or on different trees; without petals.

FRUIT—Matures early about the time the leaves are fully developed, sheds at once and germinates soon after falling; 1¼- to 2¼-ins. long with a ribbed, thick, swollen seed (often only one seed develops); wings spread at an angle of approximately 90 degrees.

TWIGS—Fairly stout, shining red to greyish-brown, without hairs; differ from those of other maples (except Red Maple) in bearing clusters of plump flower-buds ringing the twigs; leaf-buds blunt, less than twice as long as they are broad, reddish, smooth, shiny, usually four pairs of scales.

BARK—Dark reddish-brown, separated into long, thin, narrow flakes fastened at the centre and free at both ends, which give the tree a somewhat shaggy appearance.

WOOD—Moderately hard, heavy, not strong; light yellowish-brown.

IMPORTANCE—The wood is used for furniture, flooring, boxes, crates, pulpwood and wherever strength is not important. This species is widely used for street planting and as an ornamental.

NOTES—The Silver Maple often has a hollow trunk which makes the tree appealing to small boys, animals and birds.

SILVER MAPLE

LOBE NARROWS TO
RE OF LEAF

TWIGS SIMILAR TO THOSE OF RED MAPLE; FLOWER BUDS (RIGHT);
FLOWERS EARLY IN SPRING

-GROWN TREE

MALE (LEFT) AND FEMALE FLOWER CLUSTERS

RE BARK HAS THIN LOOSE FLAKES

SEED ELONGATED; OFTEN ONLY ONE MATURES

RED MAPLE

Soft Maple

Acer rubrum L.

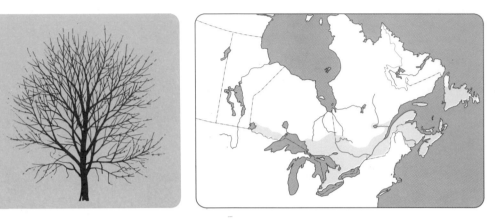

FORM—When growing in the open, this tree divides near the ground into a few ascending limbs which bear widely diverging and ascending branches to form a rather deep dense crown. In the forest, the trunk is usually free of branches for half its length, or more, and the crown is short and narrow. The root system is shallow and wide-spreading. The commonest variety is *Acer rubrum* var. *tridens* Wood, which can be identified by its small three-lobed leaves with rounded bases.

HABITAT—The range is similar to that of Sugar Maple, but extends farther north. The tree grows throughout the Deciduous, Great Lakes-St. Lawrence, and Acadian Forest regions and northwards into the eastern fringe of the Boreal Forest Region. The Red Maple prefers moist soils round the borders of swamps, but is also found on dry upland soils that may be rocky.

SIZE—Reaches heights of 90 ft. and diameters of up to 4 ft., but usually is much smaller.

LEAVES—Three to five lobes with shallow notches and irregular, sharp, double teeth, 3- to 5-ins. across, light green above, whitened on the undersurface, both surfaces hairless; end lobe with its two sides almost parallel to the midrib which (not including the tapered apex) makes it almost square, separated from the two side lobes by wide open notches which are V-shaped at the base, the sides of the two lobes often form a right angle; turns a brilliant scarlet in autumn.

FLOWERS—Red, appear before the leaves in dense slender-stalked clusters; male and female flowers usually in different clusters on the same tree, or on different trees; flowers have very small petals.

FRUIT—Matures in midsummer, ¾-in. long with a swollen seed; wings spread at an angle of about 60 degrees.

TWIGS—Fairly stout, shining red to greyish-brown, without hairs; differ from those of other maples (except Silver Maple) in bearing clusters of plump flower-buds ringing the twigs; leaf-buds blunt, less than twice as long as they are broad, reddish, smooth, shiny, usually four pairs of scales.

BARK—Similar to that of Silver Maple, but more flaky; dark greyish-brown, separated into scaly ridges fastened at the centre and loose at the ends.

WOOD—Moderately heavy, moderately hard, moderately strong; light brown.

IMPORTANCE—Red Maple is not an important timber producer. Its wood is used for furniture, veneer, plywood, boxes, crates, railway ties and pulpwood, and the tree is sometimes planted as an ornamental.

NOTES—Maple lumber can be identified as "hard" or "soft" by applying any solution of ferric salt to the sapwood — blue stain, soft maple; green stain, hard maple.

Red Maple is appropriately named, for its twigs, buds, flowers, immature fruits, and leaf-stalks are often bright red. In autumn its leaves also turn red.

RED MAPLE

FLOWER BUDS RING MOST TWIGS
IN LATE WINTER

MATURE BARK IS SIMILAR TO
THAT OF SILVER MAPLE

LOBE ALMOST SQUARE

TREE GROWS SLOWLY ON DRY ROCKY HILLS

MALE (LEFT) AND FEMALE FLOWER CLUSTERS

MOUNTAIN MAPLE

Acer spicatum **Lam.**

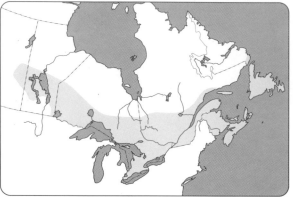

FORM—This small tree has a short often crooked trunk which is irregularly divided into a few ascending, slender, rather straight branches that form an unevenly rounded open crown. The root system is very shallow, with most of the roots being close to the surface.

HABITAT—Mountain Maple is an understory tree in the forests of eastern Canada, and ranges throughout the Deciduous, Great Lakes-St. Lawrence and Acadian Forest regions. It also extends through the southern portion of the Boreal Forest Region eastwards from Saskatchewan. The tree grows well on well-drained moist soils along streams, bordering ravines and on moist rocky hillsides. It may produce thickets from prostrate branches, and is a common species on recently cut-over forest land, but it seldom thrives in the open.

SIZE—This is the smallest of the eastern maples. Usually grows as a coarse shrub, but sometimes reaches heights of up to 25 ft. and diameters of 3 to 7 ins.

LEAVES—A little longer than they are wide, on slender reddish stalks usually longer than the leaf-blades, three-lobed (sometimes indistinctly five-lobed), 2¾- to 3½-ins. across, yellowish-green above, soft whitish hairs on the undersurface; end lobe triangular, with wedge-shaped notches separating it from the side lobes, coarsely and irregularly single-toothed, with the edges of the teeth usually curved outwards; turns shades of red, yellow or brown in autumn.

FLOWERS—Appear after the leaves are fully grown in dense upright clusters at the ends of the branchlets; individual flowers ¼-in. across, pale yellowish-green, on slender stalks which are often branched and which are arranged along a central stem; male and female organs in separate flowers on the same tree, and usually in the same flower cluster.

FRUIT—Matures in autumn, often brilliant red, later turning yellow or pinkish-brown, some remaining on the tree into winter, ¾-in. long, on short stalks in the cluster; seed portion indented on one side, angle separating the wings less than 90 degrees.

TWIGS—Slender, yellowish-green to reddish-brown or pink, coated with very short grey hairs giving a somewhat dull velvety look; buds slender, stalked, two to three times as long as they are broad, with one pair of visible scales which meet along their edges but do not overlap, covered with grey hairs.

BARK—Thin, dull, reddish to greyish-brown, smooth or slightly grooved.

WOOD—Moderately light, soft, low in strength; pale brown, nearly white sapwood.

IMPORTANCE—The wood has no economic value. The tree is sometimes planted for ornamental purposes, particularly certain forms with strikingly reddish fruits.

NOTES—Although of little commercial value, this tree provides food for deer and birds.

276

MOUNTAIN MAPLE

END LOBE TRIANGULAR

FRUIT INDENTED ON ONE SIDE

FLOWERS ARE
IN UPRIGHT CLUSTERS

COVERED WITH SHORT HAIRS

BARK IS DARK AND FINELY
GROOVED

TREE SMALL WITH A FEW ASCENDING BRANCHES

STRIPED MAPLE

Acer pensylvanicum L.

FORM—This tree has a short trunk which is divided into a few irregular, ascending and arching branches that form a broad but very uneven, flat-topped to rounded crown. The branchlets are straight and slender. The root system is shallow and wide-spreading.

HABITAT—Like Mountain Maple, with which it is commonly associated, Striped Maple is an understory tree. It grows throughout the forests of eastern Canada within the Great Lakes-St. Lawrence and Acadian Forest regions, but not in the Deciduous Forest Region. The tree grows best on well-drained moist soils in deep valleys, and on northern slopes when shaded by overhead trees and where the soil is cool and moist. When seen with its arching branches, striped bark and large drooping leaves, the Striped Maple adds a great deal to the attractiveness of the forest interior. The leaves and young shoots provide a favourite food for moose and deer, which accounts for the second name "Moosewood".

SIZE—A small tree or coarse shrub which, under conditions favourable to good growth, may attain a height of 40 ft. and a diameter of up to 10 ins.

LEAVES—The largest leaf of the eastern Canadian maples, 4- to 7-ins. across, about the same in length, or a little shorter than it is wide, three-lobed towards the upper part of the blade, but sometimes unlobed on fast growing shoots, pale yellowish-green on both surfaces, hairless; end lobe broadly triangular, with shallow wide notches separating it from the two side lobes, uniformly double-toothed, with many fine sharp teeth on each lobe, ends of lobes drawn out into long, narrow, finely toothed tips; turns yellow in autumn.

FLOWERS—Appear after the leaves are fully grown in dense drooping clusters at the ends of the branchlets; individuals yellow, approximately $\frac{1}{4}$-in. across on slender stalks arranged along a central stem; male and female organs usually in separate flowers and separate clusters, both are usually on the same tree.

FRUIT—Matures in autumn, 1-in. long on short stalks in the cluster; seed portion indented on one side; angle separating the wings 90 degrees, or more.

TWIGS—Rather stout, smooth, reddish-brown, shiny, hairless; buds stalked, one to two times as long as they are broad, showing two visible scales which meet along their edges, hairless.

BARK—Thin, smooth, greenish-brown; when young, conspicuously marked by long, vertical, greenish-white stripes which eventually turn grey and darken.

WOOD—Moderately light, soft, low in strength; light brown, sapwood nearly white.

IMPORTANCE—The wood is of no commercial value, but the species has some use as an ornamental because of its unusually large leaves and attractive bark markings.

NOTES—In winter, birds feed on the buds.

STRIPED MAPLE

NOTE FINE SHARP DOUBLE TEETH

YOUNG BARK HAS DISTINCTIVE VERTICAL STRIPES

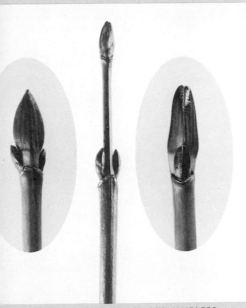

: BUDS STALKED, TWO-SCALED AND HAIRLESS

MARKED
NTATION ON FRUIT; FRUIT CLUSTER (INSERT)

FLOWERS ARE IN DROOPING CLUSTERS

DOUGLAS MAPLE

Rocky Mountain Maple

Acer glabrum Torr. var. *douglasii* (Hook.) Dipp.

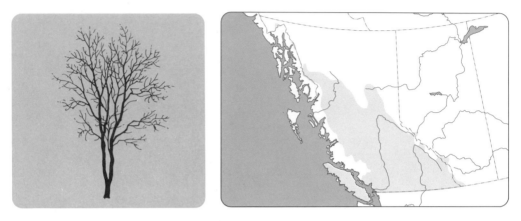

FORM—This tree has a short trunk which is divided into a few slender and sharply ascending limbs which are again divided into many small branches that form an irregular and uneven-topped crown. The root system is shallow and wide-spreading.

HABITAT—Douglas Maple is found on cliffs, bluffs and ledges of rocky hills along the Pacific Coast, from Alaska south through British Columbia. South of latitude 56 degrees North, it extends inland along streams and in sheltered ravines through the Rocky Mountains into Alberta, where it is found in the foothill country. Inland, it grows in tree form only in the extreme south. Douglas Maple does not grow in the Queen Charlotte Islands, but it is found on Vancouver Island and some of the smaller islands along the coast. *Acer glabrum* Torr., the species, is not believed to extend across the border into Canada.

SIZE—Douglas Maple is usually a tall shrub, but it does become a tree under favourable growing conditions and may attain heights of up to 35 ft. and diameters of up to 10 ins.

LEAVES—On long, slender, often reddish stalks; 3- to 4-ins. wide and about the same in length, three-lobed to indistinctly five-lobed, dark green above, greyish-green on the undersurface, both surfaces hairless; notches separating lobes usually shallow, but occasionally extending to the top of the leaf-stalk and separating the blade into three leaflets; end lobe narrows inwardly towards the centre of the

leaf and is separated from the two side lobes by notches that narrow to sharp slits, coarsely double-toothed, outer edges of the teeth often curved outwards; turns a dull red in autumn.

FLOWERS—Appear with the unfolding leaves in loose-flowered drooping clusters at the ends and along the sides of the branchlets; individual flowers approximately ⅛-in. long, on short stalks within the cluster, greenish-yellow, with petals; male and female organs in separate flowers and usually on separate trees.

FRUIT—Matures in midsummer, approximately 1-in. long, green, often rose-coloured, turning light brown in autumn, hairless, on medium-length stalks in the cluster; seed portion strongly wrinkled and indented; wings at a very narrow angle or almost parallel.

TWIGS—Slender, smooth, pale green to reddish-brown or purplish, often faintly many-sided in cross-section; buds blunt, bright red or occasionally yellow, ⅛- to ¼-in. long, smooth with one visible pair of opposing scales.

BARK—Thin, smooth, dark reddish-brown, roughened on larger branches and old trunks.

WOOD—Moderately hard and heavy, close-grained; light brown or often nearly white.

IMPORTANCE—The wood is of no commercial value, but may be used locally for fuel.

NOTES—Douglas Maple is suitable for use as an ornamental in small gardens because of its size and attractive autumn colouring.

DOUGLAS MAPLE

F IS INDISTINCTLY FIVE-LOBED

TWIG HAIRLESS;
BUDS HAVE
TWO VISIBLE SCALES

SEEDS WRINKLED; WINGS ALMOST PARALLEL

E IS USUALLY SHRUBBY

BARK CHECKS WITH AGE

VINE MAPLE

Acer circinatum **Pursh**

FORM—Vine Maple normally has a short crooked trunk with a few twisted, spreading limbs that support a low, broad, irregular crown. Often the trunk is prostrate or arching, and roots where it touches the ground.

HABITAT—This tree characteristically grows in water-formed soils along the banks of streams and is often found in moist soils, even when these are rocky. It may grow in clumps or patches, but is also found scattered amongst other species. Vine Maple endures shade well and is a constituent of the forest understory within parts of its range, but it may also be found in openings in the forest, particularly on recently logged-over areas. Its range is confined to the southern part of the Coast Forest Region, on the mainland of British Columbia, and to two small areas on Vancouver Island.

SIZE—Vine Maple is often a coarse shrub, but, under good conditions, it will grow into a tree and sometimes attain heights of up to 30 ft. and diameters of up to 6 ins.

LEAVES—Almost circular, 2½- to 4½-ins. across, normally with seven to nine radiating lobes, but occasionally with five lobes; bright yellowish-green above, undersurface pale green and downy but becoming free of hairs; lobes narrowly triangular with sharp single or double teeth, lobes separated by V-shaped notches; veins radiate conspicuously from the top of the stout leaf-stalk; turns red or yellow in autumn.

FLOWERS—Appear when the leaves are nearly half grown, in loose drooping clusters that hang from the ends of the branchlets; individual flowers have petals and are on long slender stalks that branch frequently; male and female organs are in the same flower, but in each flower only the male organs or the female organs are functional, thus only a few flowers in each cluster develop into fruits.

FRUIT—Ripens late in autumn, red or rose-coloured during the summer, 1- to 1½-ins. long; seed portion swollen, ridged, hairless; seed wings spread widely to form a straight line.

TWIGS—Slender, hairless, green, often becoming red in autumn; the only species of maple lacking terminal buds (except when there are flower-buds); leaf-buds small with one or two pairs of scales, red, hairless; the inner scales are hairy.

BARK—Thin, greenish becoming bright reddish-brown, smooth, or sometimes marked by shallow crevices.

WOOD—Heavy, hard, moderately weak, close-grained; pale brown, often nearly white.

IMPORTANCE—The wood, which is of little commercial value, is used locally for tool handles and fuel.

NOTES—The common name "Vine Maple" probably originated from the tree's gnarled and crooked appearance.

The Indians carved spoons, bowls, platters and other small household utensils out of the wood, but there are better woods available now-a-days for hobby carving.

F HAS LARGEST NUMBER OF LOBES OF ANY NATIVE MAPLE

IT WINGS SPREAD WIDELY

TREE IS OFTEN A COARSE SHRUB

MANITOBA MAPLE

Acer negundo L.

FORM—The Manitoba Maple has an irregular form. The trunk divides near the ground into a few long, spreading, rather crooked limbs which branch irregularly to support a broad uneven crown. When growing among other trees, the undivided portion of the trunk is much longer and usually straighter, and the crown it supports is small and more frequently divided than that of the open-grown tree. Several varieties have been named, the most common being *Acer negundo* var. *interius* (Britt.) Sarg., which is recognized by its leaves having only three leaflets and by its hairy leaf-stalks and twigs.

HABITAT—The tree grows in southern Ontario and northwestward through Manitoba, usually along lakeshores and the banks of streams. It is a favourite tree for planting, and has established itself far beyond its natural range in many parts of Canada.

SIZE—Occasionally attains heights of 70 ft. and diameters of 3 ft., but more often it is a small to medium-sized tree 40- to 50-ft. high by 1 to 2 ft. in diameter.

LEAVES—This is the only Canadian maple with leaves that are normally divided into several parts, although the Douglas Maple occasionally displays the same feature. The leaf is composed of three to seven leaflets (rarely undivided), 6- to 15-ins. long, light green above, greyish-green on the undersurface, usually without hairs; leaflets shallowly lobed or coarsely toothed; turns yellow in the fall.

FLOWERS—Appear with or before the leaves, pale green, without petals; male organs in separate flowers on slender stalks in loose clusters; the female flowers arranged along a central stem; the two kinds of flowers on separate trees.

FRUIT—Matures in autumn and remains on the tree well into the winter; approximately 1½-ins. long; seed portion two to three times as long as it is broad and markedly wrinkled; the angle separating the two wings is less than 60 degrees.

TWIGS—Stout, light-green to purplish or brownish with a polished look, or often covered with a whitish bloom that is easily rubbed off, hairless; buds blunt, ⅛- to ¼-in. long with one or two pairs of scales, coated with fine white hairs.

BARK—Light grey, smooth, becoming furrowed into narrow firm ridges, darkening with age.

WOOD—Moderately light, soft, low in strength, close-grained; nearly white.

IMPORTANCE—The wood is used locally for boxes and rough construction. The fast growth of the tree, its hardiness and suitability to the climate have made Manitoba Maple popular on the prairies for street and ornamental planting and for shelter-belts.

NOTES—To gardeners, this is a "dirty" tree because it sheds. Small boys, however, seem to thrive among its hospitable branches and they, rather than nature, may be partly to blame for the gardeners' prejudiced attitude.

MANITOBA MAPLE

COMPOUND LEAF HAS THREE TO SEVEN LEAFLETS

TWIGS HAIRLESS;
BUDS WOOLLY;
SCALES PARTIALLY
OPEN IN THIS
ILLUSTRATION

MALE (LEFT) AND FEMALE FLOWER CLUSTERS ARE ON DIFFERENT TREES

FRUIT VERY LONG AND WRINKLED; GROWS IN CLUSTERS

MATURE BARK IS DEEPLY RIDGED

CASCARA

Rhamnus purshiana DC.

FORM—*Rhamnus* is a genus of about 90 species of trees and shrubs, but only 12 species are known in North America and two of these grow in Canada. Of the Canadian species, only the Cascara becomes a tree. It has a slender trunk which divides about 10 ft. above the ground into numerous ascending or sometimes nearly horizontal branches which form a compact rounded crown. The other species which might be confused with Cascara, Alder-leaved Buckthorn (*Rhamnus alnifolia* l'Her.), is a low spreading shrub ranging across Canada. It is readily distinguishable in summer by its finely toothed leaves which have only six to eight pairs of veins, and in winter by its scaly buds. In addition to the native species, two small trees have been introduced from Europe and they may be found growing wild as coarse shrubs or small trees. The European Buckthorn (*Rhamnus cathartica* L.) has spine-tipped branchlets, toothed leaves with three to five pairs of veins and scaly winter buds. The Alder Buckthorn (*Rhamnus frangula* L.) does not have spines, has leaves without teeth, has five to eight pairs of veins and buds without scales.

HABITAT—Cascara is native to the southern parts of the Coast and Columbia Forest regions in British Columbia. The best growth is made on rich bottomlands, but the tree also grows on coarse, sandy or gravelly soils. It is found as an understory tree in forests of conifers, and as an associate of alders, maples, birches and a few conifers on burned-over areas and clearings.

SIZE—Usually a tree about 20-ft. high by 6 to 12 ins. in diameter, Cascara may reach a height of 40 ft. with a diameter of 30 ins. On poor sites it may be reduced to a low shrub.

LEAVES—Shed each year, single, alternate (or occasionally opposite), 2- to 7-ins. long by 1- to 2½-ins. wide, usually broadest just above the middle, finely and evenly toothed, short or blunt tip, rounded at the base, slightly hairy on the undersurface, 10 to 15 pairs of veins which bend upwards at the ends to form a part of the margin.

FLOWERS—Appear in June; yellowish-green, inconspicuous, in small clusters along twigs.

FRUIT—Blackish, rounded, ¼- to ½-in. across, containing two to three small nutlets.

TWIGS—Slender, reddish-brown, bitter tasting; leaf-scars raised, crescent shaped; buds without scales, hairy, usually in four rows along the twig.

BARK—Thin, dark greyish-brown, smooth, becoming scaly with age.

WOOD—Light, soft, close-grained; brown tinged with red.

IMPORTANCE—The wood is of no commercial value, but the bark is the source of the drug cascara.

NOTES—Pursh first described Cascara, but by mistake selected the already-used name *Rhamnus cathartica*.

FRUIT IS ROUND
AND
BERRY-LIKE

TWIG; BUDS HAVE NO SCALES

HAS TEN OR MORE PAIRS OF VEINS;
S OF VEINS FORM PART
EAF MARGIN

HAS A COMPACT ROUNDED CROWN

BASSWOOD

Lime
Linden
Whitewood

Tilia americana L.

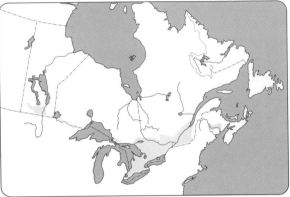

FORM—Of the 20 or more species of *Tilia* that are known, six or seven are found in North America and one grows in Canada. Normally, the Canadian species develops a straight trunk which is branch-free in the lower part and reaches well into the upper part of the crown. The branches are slender, ascending and arching, or they spread outwards and turn upwards towards the ends to form a uniformly rounded crown having the appearance of being shaped by pruning. Basswood often regenerates by producing sprouts around the base of old stumps, and some of these survive to form a clump of trunks. The root system is wide-spreading and deep, which makes the tree windfirm. Several introduced species of basswood are often planted along streets, in parks and as ornamentals on private property. The Small-leaved Lime (*Tilia cordata* Mill.) has roundish leaves about 2 ins. in diameter that are hairless, except in the angles between the veins and the midrib. The White Lime (*Tilia tomentosa* Moench) is easily recognized by its dense coating of silvery white hairs on the undersurface of the leaves. These are the two most common exotics.

HABITAT—Basswood is found throughout the Deciduous and Great Lakes-St. Lawrence Forest regions as far east as western New Brunswick, and westwards along the rivers into the Grasslands in Manitoba. It grows in mixture with other hardwoods, and makes its best growth on deep fertile soils. It does not form pure stands anywhere throughout its range.

SIZE—Usually 60 to 70 ft. in height and 2 to 2½ ft. in diameter, this tree occasionally exceeds 100 ft. in height and 4 ft. in diameter.

LEAVES—Shed annually, alternate, approximately 4½-ins. wide and slightly longer, heart-shaped, one side lower than the other below the top of the leaf-stalk, single-toothed with coarse gland-tipped teeth.

FLOWERS—Appear in July; creamy-yellow, ½-in. across, both sexes in the same flower, fragrant, in small flat-topped clusters at the end of long stalks extending from the midrib of a long, narrow, leaf-like structure.

FRUIT—A woody roundish body, ¼-in. across, coated with brownish hairs, usually containing only one seed, a few in a cluster, hanging on the tree into winter.

TWIGS—Stout, yellowish-brown, hairless; buds broad, ¼-in. long, hairless, often reddish, in two rows along the twig, lopsided, two or three visible scales.

BARK—Dark greyish-brown, broken into many long, narrow, flat-topped, scaly ridges.

WOOD—Light, soft, low in strength; heartwood pale brown, sapwood lighter.

IMPORTANCE—The wood is one of the softest and lightest in weight of the Canadian hardwoods and is valued for hand-carving, modelling, turnery, interior trim, veneer, plywood and furniture parts.

NOTES—The Indians wove strong tangle-free ropes from the long fibres in the bark.

288

BASSWOOD

HAS ASYMMETRICAL BASE; FRUIT CLUSTER ATTACHED TO MIDDLE OF ELONGATED LEAF-LIKE STRUCTURE

AND FEMALE PARTS ARE COMBINED IN EACH FLOWER

RE BARK BROKEN INTO
FLAT SCALY RIDGES

DENSE CLUMP OF SPROUTS
FROM OLD STUMP

TWIG; LARGE SCALE MAKES BUDS
LOPSIDED

BLACK GUM

Tupelo
Sour Gum
Pepperidge

Nyssa sylvatica Marsh.

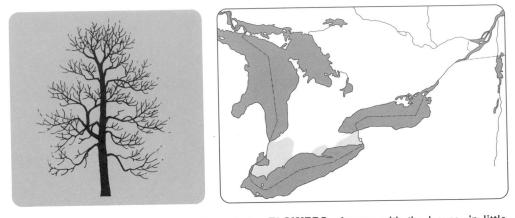

FORM—This is the only species of *Nyssa* that is native to Canada, although there are five others growing elsewhere in North America. The Black Gum has an upright trunk which extends well into the crown. Above the trunk, the many crooked branches spread nearly horizontally and branch, almost as an entanglement, to form a broadly elongated and flattish-topped crown. A variation of the species, bearing leaves that are very thin and covered with minute pimple-like swellings on their lower surfaces, has been named *Nyssa sylvatica* var. *caroliniana* (Poir.) Fern. It is not generally separated from the species.

HABITAT—Restricted to the Deciduous Forest Region, Black Gum makes its best growth on low wet ground along streams or in swamps, but may also be found on well-drained upland soils. It is usually scattered and rather sparsely distributed in some hardwood stands.

SIZE—A medium-sized tree which attains heights of 40 to 50 ft. and diameters of 1 to $2\frac{1}{2}$ ft. Some individuals may be larger.

LEAVES—Shed at the end of the growing season, simple, alternate, on stalks about one-quarter the length of the blade, 2- to 5-ins. long by $\frac{1}{2}$- to 3-ins. wide, variable in shape but usually broadest above the middle, without teeth, often wavy along the margin (especially near the short tip), deep green and shiny above, pale on the undersurface and sparsely hairy on the veins, turn scarlet in autumn.

FLOWERS—Appear with the leaves, in little clusters at the end of long stalks, small, greenish-white with minute fleshy petals, inconspicuous, the sexes normally in separate flowers on separate trees.

FRUIT—A single-stoned fleshy body, approximately $\frac{3}{8}$-in. long, the flesh thin, oily and sour, the stone indistinctly ribbed; usually one to three fruits mature in each cluster, cluster at the end of a long stalk.

TWIGS—Reddish-brown with a greyish skin, slender; buds dark reddish-brown, pointed, end bud $\frac{1}{4}$-in. long with the tip curved and often hairy, side buds smaller, spread widely from the twig. When cut lengthwise the twig shows a pith with hard greenish bars; this is a good identification feature.

BARK—Dark grey, broken into thick irregular ridges which are checked across into short segments, giving it a block-like appearance.

WOOD—Moderately heavy, hard, relatively strong, close-grained; brownish-grey with wide lighter-coloured sapwood.

IMPORTANCE—Black Gum is an uncommon tree in Canada and rarely reaches commercial size. The wood, when it is available, is suitable for concealed parts of furniture, planing-mill products, boxes and crates.

NOTES—Some unusual uses in the past for this wood were: pipes in a salt factory, hatters' blocks, pistol grips and rollers for glass.

BLACK GUM

LEAF SHAPE VARIABLE

LL FRUIT
STERS ARE AT
S OF LONG STALKS

WINTER TWIG AND SUMMER TWIG; BUDS POINTED AND HAIRY

ES ON MATURE
CHECKED IN SHORT SEGMENTS

DOGWOOD

Cornus L.

This genus comprises about 50 species which are widely distributed throughout the temperate zones of the Northern Hemisphere. Only one species is native to the Southern Hemisphere. About 15 species grow in North America; most of them are found in Canada.

The Canadian dogwoods are extremely diverse in character. Two are small herbs, three are small trees and the remainder are shrubs, although two of these shrubs may occasionally reach tree size. The smallest species, and perhaps the best known, is the Bunchberry (*Cornus canadensis* L.). It is a common plant in the ground-cover of many conifer stands across Canada, and is very attractive when in flower because of its four white, petal-like floral leaves centred in a whorl of shiny green leaves at the top of a short upright stem 6- to 8-ins. high. In late summer it is equally appealing when the flowers have matured into a "bunch" of bright red, berry-like fruits—hence its name "Bunchberry". None of the shrubs are of much importance except as ornamentals, but, because there are several kinds across Canada and a few may be mistaken for the tree forms, the main recognition features of the more common ones are given here.

Two dogwoods that are commonly found as shrubs but may occasionally attain tree size are the Roughleaf Dogwood (*Cornus drummondii* C. A. Meyer) and the Roundleaf Dogwood (*Cornus rugosa* Lam.). The Roughleaf Dogwood has leaves that are rough above and have scattered stiff hairs. Other features are white fruits and greyish-brown branchlets with a slender brown pith. It is restricted to a few places along the shores of Lake Erie and owing to its scarcity is seldom seen. The Roundleaf Dogwood has almost circular leaves, with a white woolly texture on the undersurface. The fruits are blue, the branchlets are greenish red (usually blotched with purple) and the pith is white. It extends across the eastern half of Canada from southern Manitoba to the maritime provinces.

A common shrub is the Panicled Dogwood (*Cornus racemosa* Lam.) which has small, narrow, long-pointed leaves, white fruits on red stems and very slender grey branchlets with a pale brown pith. Another, the Red Osier (*Cornus stolonifera* Michx.), with its smooth bright red twigs and branchlets and dull white fruits, is found all across Canada.

Of all shrub and tree species, only the Alternate-leaved Dogwood (*Cornus alternifolia* L.f.) has alternate leaves and should not be mistaken for one of the shrubs.

Among the exotics are the Cornelian Cherry (*Cornus mas* L.) which is cultivated for its yellowish branchlets, yellow flowers and leaves that remain green into late autumn; and Red-branched Dogwood (*Cornus sanguinea* L.) which is cultivated for its dark red branches in winter and its dark red leaves in the autumn. Forms with variegated leaves are also planted.

The leaves of the dogwoods are shed at the end of the growing season and replaced with a new crop the following spring. They are arranged opposite on the twigs (except in the Alternate-leaved Dogwood), are simple, without teeth along the margin and with veins strongly tending to follow the margin towards the leaf-tips. This type of venation is uncommon on native trees, but is found on some of the buckthorns (except Cascara).

The flowers are small, white, greenish-white or yellow and are grouped into compact or open clusters, the individual flowers containing organs of both sexes (perfect). In a few species, each cluster of flowers is encircled by two to eight large, white, petal-like floral leaves (enlarged bud-scales, called bracts) which are very showy.

The fruit is a small plum-like body with a single stone which contains two seeds in separate cavities.

The winter buds are usually slender and pointed, with two pairs of scales showing in most species.

The branchlets divide into short twigs at the end and long twigs at the side, which make the leaves appear to be clustered at the ends of the branches.

The wood is hard, tough and horn-like in texture and wears smooth under friction.

EASTERN FLOWERING DOGWOOD

Cornus florida L.

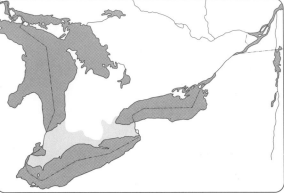

FORM—This tree has a short trunk and a wide-spread crown when growing in the open. The branches are slender, upright at first, but then spread almost horizontally into many divided branchlets that turn up at the ends. The tree has quite a bushy appearance and is often as wide as it is high, but, when growing in mixture with other trees, the crown is often reduced to a narrow irregularly rounded shape near the top of a long trunk which is often slightly crooked. The root system is moderately deep and not wide-spreading. Different forms based mainly on differences in flower colour have been named. Forma *rubra* (West.) Palmer & Steyerm., with pink floral leaves encircling the flower clusters, is occasionally seen as an ornamental. Forma *xanthocarpa* Rehd., has yellow fruits; and one with many floral leaves (instead of four) is named forma *pluribracteata* Rehd. The native ranges of these forms are not known with certainty.

HABITAT—The Eastern Flowering Dogwood is native only to the Deciduous Forest Region where it is seen in open clearings in the southern hardwood forests. Since it is fairly tolerant of shade, the tree may be widely scattered in the understory of some hardwood stands. It grows best on deep, rich, well-drained soils.

SIZE—A small tree, but may reach heights of 30 ft. or more and diameters of 4 to 8 ins.; occasionally a tree may grow larger.

LEAVES—Arranged opposite on the twigs; tapering to a long narrow tip, broadest about the middle, rounded at the base or tapered to a broad wedge-shaped base, dark greyish-green above, whitish on the under-surface, with or without hairs, slight waviness along the margin, turning an attractive red in autumn and remaining on the trees for some days before falling.

FLOWERS—Appear before the leaves, ⅛-in. across, greenish-white, inconspicuous, grouped into compact clusters, each encircled by four white floral leaves (bracts) which give the cluster the appearance of a single flower with white petals; floral leaves approximately 1-in. long, almost as broad at the outer end, where there is a prominent purple notch; the whole cluster approximately 2½-ins. across and strikingly attractive.

FRUIT—Plum-like, ⅓-in. across, bright red.

TWIGS—Dull, dark red, with whitish hairs; side buds minute, hairy, terminal bud larger, flattish, showing one pair of downy scales; the flower buds are completely enclosed by the floral leaves in winter.

BARK—Reddish-brown, broken into roundish or squarish small segments, giving a block-like appearance.

WOOD—Hard, heavy, fine-grained; white.

IMPORTANCE—A popular ornamental in areas where it is hardy.

NOTES—The wood was particularly well suited for shuttles in textile mills.

A red dye can be extracted from the bark by boiling small pieces in water.

LEAF; VEINS BEND AND FOLLOW THE MARGIN

NOT ALL OF THE FRUITS DEVELOP

INCONSPICUOUS FLOWERS
ROUNDED BY FOUR WHITE
FLORAL LEAVES

FLOWER BUD SHOWING BUD-SCALES
WHICH FORM THE FLORAL LEAVES

TWIG; SMALL
PORTION OF
LEAF-STALK
REMAINS
AND ELEVATES
THE LEAF-SCAR

BLOCK-LIKE
MENTS ON
TURE BARK

WESTERN FLOWERING DOGWOOD

Cornus nuttallii **Audubon**

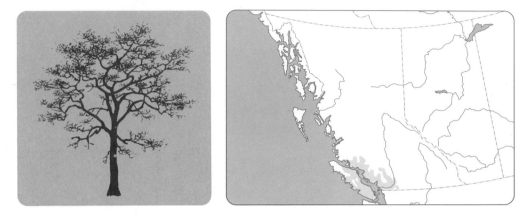

FORM—When forest grown, this tree has a slightly tapered trunk that extends to the top of a narrow short crown. On open-grown trees, the trunk is quite short, the crown is large and about as high as it is broad, and the top is rounded. The branches usually ascend at first, then spread horizontally; the branchlets often droop, but bear twigs that turn upwards. The root system is rather deep and often there is a tap-root. A form with pink floral leaves encircling the flower clusters has been reported from Vancouver Island.

HABITAT—The Western Flowering Dogwood is known throughout the southern part of the Coast Forest Region, south of Knight Inlet on the mainland, and including most of Vancouver Island. It grows best on deep, coarse, well-drained soils, including old water-formed terraces, banks of rivers and lower parts of valleys. The tree often forms the understory in conifer stands, and is conspicuous along the edge of the forest, when in flower.

SIZE—Normally 20 to 30 ft. in height by 6 to 12 ins. in diameter, but under good growing conditions may reach a height of 60 ft. and a diameter of 2 ft.

LEAVES—Arranged opposite on the twigs; broadest near the middle, tapered to both ends with a broad wedge-shaped base and a short sharp tip, deep green above, greyish-green on the undersurface with fine hairs on both surfaces, wavy margin, turning dull red in autumn.

FLOWERS—Appear in April to June and sometimes again in September; individual flowers minute, dull shades of purple or green and inconspicuous, grouped into compact clusters, each cluster encircled by four to six white floral leaves (bracts) which give the cluster the appearance of a single flower with white petals. The floral leaves are approximately 2-ins. long by 1½-ins. wide at the middle and taper to a sharp tip. The whole cluster with its floral leaves is approximately 4-ins. across, and the tree in full bloom is very attractive.

FRUIT—Plum-like, ⅓-in. across, slightly longer, somewhat flattened or angular from the pressure of one against another in the cluster, bright red.

TWIGS—Dull, greyish-green to brownish, with fine white hairs; side buds minute, terminal bud larger, long tipped, showing one pair of downy scales; flower buds not enclosed during the winter by the floral leaves.

BARK—Thin, light grey, rarely breaking into small plates (as in the Eastern Flowering Dogwood) even when old.

WOOD—Heavy, hard, fine-grained; whitish.

IMPORTANCE—Where hardy, grown as an ornamental for its attractive blossoms.

NOTES—There is a small demand for the wood of this tree for piano keys.

Early settlers on the west coast used trunk sections for maul and mallet heads.

E TYPICAL VEIN PATTERN ON LEAF

FRUIT; NOTE FLATNESS CAUSED BY
DENSE CLUSTERING

THE TREE IS SHOWY WHEN FLOWERING

LL FLOWER SURROUNDED
ARGE WHITE, PETAL-LIKE FLORAL LEAVES

ALTERNATE-LEAVED DOGWOOD

Cornus alternifolia L.f.

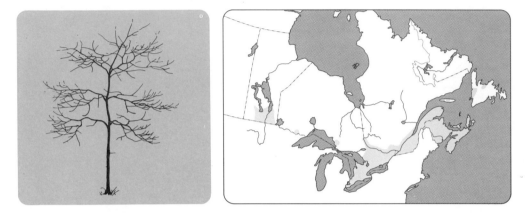

FORM—The trunk of this small tree divides near the ground into several branches that spread horizontally in tiers and grow unevenly in length. The crown is made up of several uneven, spreading, flattish sections which give the tree an irregular outline and a noticeably flat layered appearance. The trunk is short and usually straight.

HABITAT—Alternate-leaved Dogwood is found throughout the Deciduous, the Great Lakes-St. Lawrence and the Acadian Forest regions, and extends northwards in eastern Canada into the southern fringe of the Boreal Forest Region. The tree grows best on well-drained deep soils, usually mixed with other species and is commonly found in fertile open woodlands, along streams, bordering swamps and near the bottom of steep slopes.

SIZE—A small tree seldom attaining heights above 25 ft. or diameters over 2 to 6 ins. — often a shrub with several stout limbs.

LEAVES—Arranged alternately on the twigs, but, because of the shortness of many of the twigs, some leaves appear to be opposite; noticeably clustered at the ends of the branchlets, variable in size on the tree, but averaging approximately 3½-ins. long by 2¼-ins. wide, gradually narrowing to a long slender tip, broadest near the middle, rounded at the base or abruptly tapered to a broad wedge shape, dark green above, whitish on the undersurface, hairless, slightly wavy along the margin.

FLOWERS—Small, white or cream-coloured, each flower on a jointed stalk and arranged in large, open, irregularly rounded clusters that are flattened at the top; no whitish showy floral leaves encircle the cluster as in the Eastern Flowering Dogwood.

FRUIT—Berry-like, round, ⅓ in. in diameter, dark blue or bluish-black, on red stems.

TWIGS—Shiny as though polished, greenish-red to dark reddish-brown, or dark purplish-red; buds small, pointed, showing two or three brownish-red scales, the outer ones not tight against the bud, pith white; many branchlets will show long slender side twigs much longer than the stout end twigs (in this unusual branching very similar to the branching on Sassafras, but easily distinguishable from it because the Sassafras has large green buds and a spicy fragrance).

BARK—Thin, reddish-brown, smooth when young, becoming broken into shallow ridges as the tree matures.

WOOD—Heavy, hard, uniform in structure, withstands abrasion and wears smooth under friction; light-coloured.

IMPORTANCE—The wood is of no commercial value, but the tree is occasionally used as an ornamental, when its layered form can be displayed to the best advantage.

NOTES—During the construction of grist and seed mills by pioneering families, this tree was one of the species required for a home-built mill. The wood's ability to cope with friction made it a premium material for long-life bearings and shaker slides.

FRUIT IS ON SHORT STALKS

NO FLORAL LEAVES AROUND
FLOWER CLUSTERS

; VEIN PATTERN IS TYPICAL
LL DOGWOODS

BRANCHLET OF FIVE LONG, SLENDER SIDE TWIGS AND SHORT,
LEAF-BEARING END TWIGS

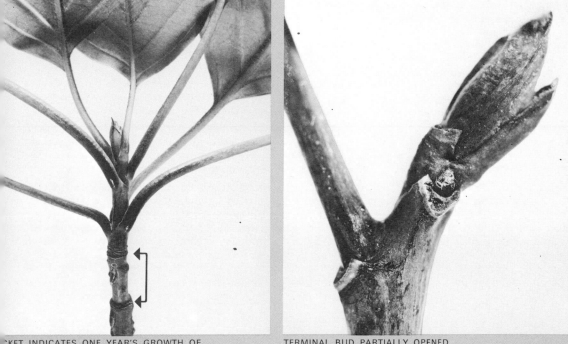

CKET INDICATES ONE YEAR'S GROWTH OF
-BEARING END TWIG

TERMINAL BUD PARTIALLY OPENED

ARBUTUS

Madrona, Madrone

Arbutus menziesii **Pursh**

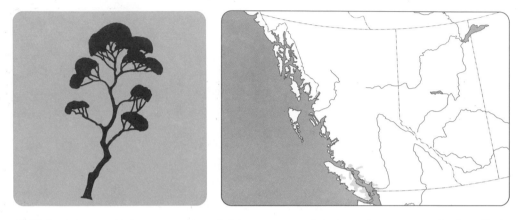

FORM—Of about 12 known species of *Arbutus* in Eurasia and North America, only one grows in Canada and it is the only broad-leaved evergreen tree native to Canada. It can be recognized by this feature alone, particularly in winter. The Arbutus is a small scraggly tree with a trunk that is nearly always crooked, often leaning and usually extending well up into the rounded and irregular crown. Quite often the trunk divides low down into several twisting, upright branches.

HABITAT—The range of the Arbutus is restricted to a narrow belt along the Pacific Coast where it is seldom found more than five miles inland or at heights above 1,000 ft. It makes its best growth on well-drained soils near sea level, but characteristically grows on exposed rocky bluffs overlooking the sea. Inland, it is found on stony well-drained soils and, since the tree is very intolerant of shade, it seldom grows in stands. The Arbutus, however, is one of the first species to occupy newly cleared land.

SIZE—Often a very small tree, seldom more than 30 to 40 ft. in height by 1 to 2½ ft. in diameter. In Canada, the maximum dimensions are about 90-ft. high by 3 ft. in diameter.

LEAVES—Alternate on the twigs, simple, 3- to 5-ins. long, on short stout leaf-stalks, functioning for more than one growing season (evergreen), usually shed in May of the second year, thick, leathery texture, broadest near the middle with the two sides almost parallel, rounded at both ends, normally without teeth but on vigorous growth often finely toothed, dark glossy green above, lighter on the undersurface, hairless; veins numerous and often branching.

FLOWERS—White, approximately ⅓-in. long, in drooping branched clusters at the ends of the branchlets, both sexes in each flower.

FRUIT—Berry-like, ¼-in. across, orangey-red with a granular surface; several seeds.

TWIGS—Stout, pale green becoming reddish-brown, hairless; buds red with many overlapping scales; leaf-scar with one bundle-scar.

BARK—Thin, smooth, reddish-brown, peeling in papery flakes and strips, newly exposed surfaces yellowish-green, soon reddening, thickening on old trunks and breaking into many small flakes.

WOOD—Heavy, hard, moderately strong; pale brown or reddish-brown; sapwood nearly white; checks badly on drying.

IMPORTANCE—The tree is too scarce to be of commercial importance, but is often planted as an ornamental. The wood is used locally for fuel, small cabinet work and turnery.

NOTES—When the famous Scottish botanist and traveller, Archibald Menzies, first collected specimens of this tree in 1792, he described it as the "oriental strawberry tree". His description probably stemmed from the colour of the fruit.

The flowers have a strong honey odour and are very attractive to bees.

THICK AND LEATHERY WITH MANY FINE VEINS

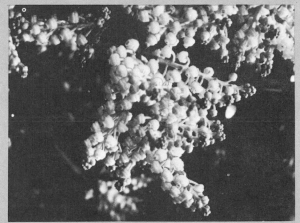

WHITE FLOWERS HANG IN DENSE CLUSTERS

SURFACE OF FRUIT IS GRANULAR

PEELS IN PAPERY STRIPS

SCRAGGLY CROOKED-TRUNKED TREE ON ROCKY BLUFF

ASH

Fraxinus L.

The ashes comprise almost 60 species of trees and shrubs of which there are 16 in North America and four in Canada. In earlier editions of *Native Trees*, Oregon Ash (*Fraxinus latifolia* Benth.) was included in the Canadian group, but reports of its existence in Canada have never included identifiable material.

Most of the native ashes grow in eastern Canada, although there are forms of Red Ash extending west of Manitoba to the southeastern corner of Alberta. The ashes occupy a variety of situations, but make their best growth on rich moist soils. Some forms may be found in swamps or along streams, or on poor dry upland soils.

In addition to the native species, the European Ash (*Fraxinus excelsior* L.), in different forms, is commonly planted in eastern Canada as an ornamental. In some characteristics it is similar to the Black Ash; for example, its leaves have leaflets without stalks and its fruits have a wide wing extending to the base of the seed portion. Two main differences are that its leaves lack the rusty hairiness at the joints of each pair of leaflets, and the buds are inky-black. Also, the bark on the European Ash is firm and ridged, not scaly and soft to the touch like Black Ash bark. A few of the different forms of the species used as ornamentals include types with white- or yellow-margined leaflets, or leaves that are variegated in whites or yellows. One form has undivided leaves, or leaves that are in three parts; other forms have different-coloured branchlets.

The native ashes are all of medium height with generally slender straight trunks which often extend almost to the top of the crown. The crown is formed of ascending and spreading straight branches which bear a few coarse branchlets and twigs.

The leaves of all ashes are shed at the end of the growing season and are replaced the following spring with a new crop, on new twigs that emerge from the leaf-buds. As in the maples, the leaves are opposite on the twigs, but, unlike maples (except Manitoba Maple), are divided into an odd number of leaflets. There are from five to eleven of these leaflets, all generally of the same size, or with the lowest pair sometimes slightly smaller. The leaflets are stalked (except in the Black Ash and on a few of the introduced forms).

The flowers are small and dark and are arranged in compact many-flowered clusters. They appear in early spring before the leaves, or, in a few species, with the unfolding leaves. The male and female organs are in different flowers and usually on different trees, although there may be flowers comprising both sexes. The flowers of the native species lack petals; the sepals are minute or missing altogether.

The fruit has a single seed with a long wing extending from the seed portion (like the maples, but the seed part is more elongated, and the fruits are alone in the clusters, not joined in pairs). After maturing in the autumn, the fruit of all except Blue Ash hangs on the tree well into the winter.

The twigs are stout, with conspicuous leaf-scars and the buds are arranged in the same way as the leaves. The terminal buds are broadly triangular or pyramidal and have one or two pairs of scales with a soft, granular surface-texture. The leaf-scars show many small markings (called bundle-scars) which are arranged in a curve and more or less follow the outline of the leaf-scar.

The bark varies from being finely furrowed into firm ridges to a scaly type that rubs off easily with hand pressure.

The ashes are noted for the high quality of their wood which is tough, hard, straight-grained and valuable for many purposes. One of the species, White Ash, is an important timber-producing tree.

In China, the production of Chinese Insect Wax for candles and polish depends on the exudations of a parasitic insect on an ash.

WHITE ASH

Fraxinus americana L.

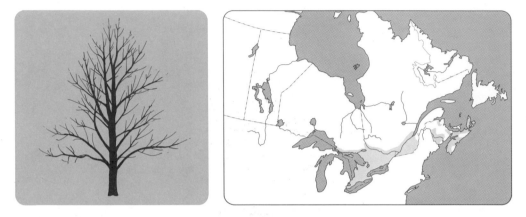

FORM—This is a slender graceful tree which, in the forest, has a long straight trunk free of branches for most of the tree's height. The crown is narrow and pyramidal. Open-grown trees tend to develop quite a broad round-topped crown which is supported by a short thick trunk. The root system is deep in well-drained soils, but may be shallow and wide-spreading in some soils.

HABITAT—White Ash grows throughout the Deciduous, Great Lakes-St. Lawrence and Acadian Forest regions, except in their most northerly parts. It makes its best growth on deep, well-drained but moist soils, in mixture with other hardwoods and occasional conifers. Some common associates are Beech, Sugar Maple, Basswood, Black Cherry, White Oak, Eastern Hemlock and Eastern White Pine. White Ash does not form pure stands.

SIZE—The tree attains heights of 60 to 70 ft. with diameters of 1½ to 2 ft., but may attain a height of 100 ft. and a diameter of 3 ft.

LEAVES—Each leaf is 8- to 15-ins. long with usually seven oval leaflets that are 3- to 5-ins. long by 1½- to 3-ins. wide, gradually tapered to each end; leaflets on ¼- to ½-in. long stalks (the longest of any ash) without teeth or with inconspicuous ones, dark green above, very pale on the undersurface, hairless; leaves turn dull purple or yellowish in autumn.

FLOWERS—The male and female organs are in separate flowers on separate trees; the stalks are without hairs.

FRUIT—Wing extends from a little below the top of the seed-portion and is slightly wider than the seed; seed cylindrical with a minute collar (remnants of flower parts) at its base.

TWIGS—Stout, light-brown, shiny, or with a greyish skin, hairless; terminal bud ¼-in. long, four-sided, blunt, broader than it is long; the two uppermost side buds almost at the same level as the terminal bud, preventing any bark showing between the terminal bud and the side buds. (See difference between this species and Black Ash on page 310.)

BARK—Light grey, furrowed into firm irregular ridges that are broken across, run into one another and give a somewhat diamond-shaped surface pattern on the trunk.

WOOD—Hard, heavy, tough and strong, coarse-grained; light brown with sapwood which is nearly white.

IMPORTANCE—All species of ash (except Black Ash) are sold as "white ash" and it is difficult to place a value on the different species. Most ash lumber is sawn from White Ash and is used where strength is needed for items such as sporting goods, handles, agricultural tools and furniture.

NOTES—There are reports that the juice from a White Ash leaf rubbed immediately on a mosquito bite will afford some measure of relief from the usual swelling and itching.

LEAFLETS HAVE LONG STALKS

MALE FLOWERS (LEFT); FEMALE FLOWERS (RIGHT)

TWIG;
NO SPACE BETWEEN
TERMINAL BUD AND
UPPERMOST SIDE
BUDS; LEAF-SCAR
HAS NUMEROUS
BUNDLE-SCARS

MATURE BARK
HAS IRREGULAR
INTERSECTING
RIDGES

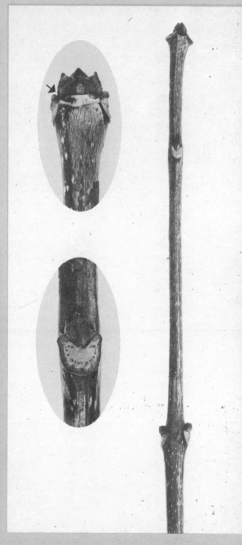

CLUSTER; SEED-WING EXTENDS A LITTLE BELOW TOP OF SEED

RED ASH

Fraxinus pennsylvanica **Marsh.**

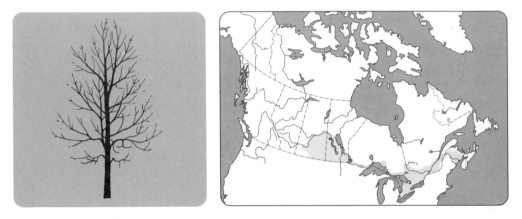

FORM—This is a very variable species which may grow as a small shrubby tree with a leaning or twisted trunk in one place, and as a slender tree with a straight trunk like a White Ash in another. Several varieties have been named, the commonest being *Fraxinus pennsylvanica* var. *subintegerrima* (Vahl) Fern. (synonym var. *lanceolata* (Borkh.) Sarg.) which has been called Green Ash. It differs from the typical Red Ash in that its leaf-stalks, leaves, twigs, flower-stalks and fruit-stalks are almost hairless. It is reported as the common ash on the western prairies. Another form with prominently toothed leaflets, shorter fruits, and broader spatula-shaped fruit-wings has been named Northern Red Ash (*Fraxinus pennsylvanica* var. *austini* Fern.) and is reported to be more common in eastern Canada than the species.

HABITAT—Red Ash is a wide-ranging tree which grows throughout the Deciduous, Great Lakes-St. Lawrence and Acadian Forest regions (except in Nova Scotia where it is rare). Its range also extends into the southern fringe of the Boreal Forest Region in Manitoba and Saskatchewan where it grows along the river-banks across the prairies. Red Ash is typically a riverbank or lakeshore tree and is often found with such species as Silver Maple and Eastern Cottonwood. The tree also inhabits upland areas where competition from other species is not too great, but it does not grow in pure stands.

SIZE—Normally a tree 30 to 40 ft. in height by 1 to 1½ ft. in diameter, but occasionally reaches a height of 85 ft. and a diameter of 2½ ft. on good sites.

LEAVES—Each leaf is 10- to 12-ins. long with usually seven oval leaflets that are 3- to 5-ins. long by 1- to 1½-ins. wide, gradually tapered to each end, without teeth or faintly toothed, yellowish-green above, paler and downy on the undersurface, turning yellowish-brown in autumn.

FLOWERS—Male and female organs in separate flowers on separate trees; stalks hairy.

FRUIT—Wing extends from the middle or slightly below the middle of the slender cylindrical seed portion and widens out above it; a minute collar (remnants of flower parts) at the base of the fruit.

TWIGS—Moderately stout, greyish-brown, typically downy; buds reddish-brown, hairy, terminal bud flattish, the two adjoining side buds almost at the same level on the twig.

BARK—Greyish-brown often tinged with red, becoming broken into firm, narrow, irregular, slightly raised ridges running into one another and giving a somewhat diamond-shaped pattern.

WOOD—Hard, heavy, moderately strong, coarse-grained; light brown, with nearly white sapwood; ring porous.

IMPORTANCE—Sold as "white ash" and used for much the same purposes where strength is required: sporting goods, handles, agricultural tools and furniture.

RED ASH

...FLET STALKS ARE SHORTER THAN THOSE
...WHITE ASH

MALE (LEFT) AND FEMALE FLOWERS ARE ON HAIRY STALKS

FRUIT CLUSTER; SEED-WING EXTENDS FROM ABOUT THE MIDDLE OF THE SEED

...ILLUSTRATING DENSE HAIRINESS
...ED ASH

BARK HAS IRREGULAR INTERSECTING RIDGES

BLUE ASH

Fraxinus quadrangulata Michx.

FORM—This is a medium-sized tree with a slender, straight, slightly tapered trunk which supports a narrow, rounded, often irregular crown of spreading branches.

HABITAT—The Blue Ash is restricted to the Deciduous Forest Region in Ontario where it can be found on Point Pelee, Pelee Island and in the valley of the Thames River in the south-western part of the province. It grows as a scattered tree, usually mixed with other southern hardwoods on beaches and bottomlands. Some common associates are the White Ash, Chinquapin Oak, Black Oak and other oak species, Black Walnut, Rock Elm, Butternut and, occasionally, hickories.

SIZE—Seldom exceeds 70 ft. in height and 1 ft. in diameter; usually in smaller sizes.

LEAVES—Each leaf is 8- to 12-ins. long with five to eleven elongated oval leaflets that are 3- to 5-ins. long by 1- to 2-ins. wide; leaflets on short stalks, unequally rounded at the base and tapered from near the middle to a long slender tip, prominent coarse teeth, dark green above and lighter green on the undersurface, hairless or with small tufts of hair where the veins meet the midrib.

FLOWERS—Male and female organs in the same flower (perfect); stalks without hairs.

FRUIT—The wing is broad, often twisted, sometimes notched at the tip and extends all the way to the base of a flat seed portion, completely surrounding it. There is no minute collar (remnants of flower parts) at the base of the fruit as on White Ash and Red Ash fruits.

TWIGS—Stout, light greyish-brown, conspicuously four-sided with ridges or low wings extending from the two sides of each leaf-scar to the pairs of leaf-scars below; buds dark brown, with fine hairs, terminal bud slightly flattened, the two adjoining side buds almost at the same level on the twig, in this feature similar to all the ashes, except Black Ash.

BARK—The unusual scaly bark is a feature that at once attracts attention. On old trees, the bark is broken into scaly plates, and because of these loose hanging plates it appears very shaggy and reminds one of the Shagbark Hickory. The inner bark contains a sticky substance which turns blue when exposed.

WOOD—Hard, heavy, strong, coarse-grained; yellowish-brown with nearly white sapwood.

IMPORTANCE—The scarcity of this species makes it of little commercial importance in Canada. When sawn, the wood is sold as "white ash" and is used for the same purposes: sporting goods, handles, agricultural tools and furniture.

NOTES—A blue dye can be extracted from the tree by chopping the bark into small pieces, steeping them in water over night and concentrating the colour by boiling.

LETS HAVE LONG SLENDER TIPS

A YOUNG BLUE ASH IN THE ROYAL BOTANICAL
GARDENS, HAMILTON, ONTARIO

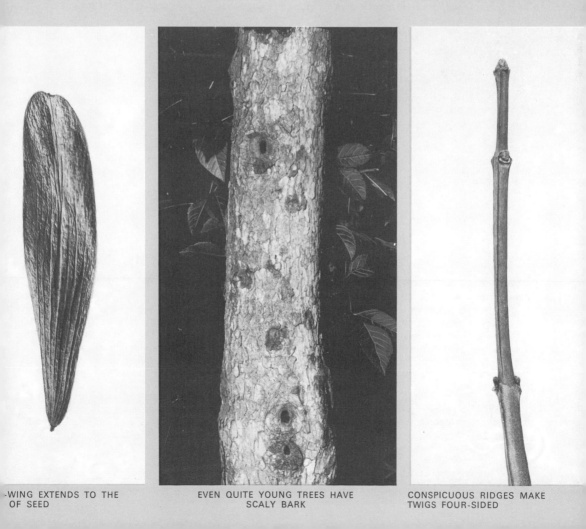

-WING EXTENDS TO THE
OF SEED

EVEN QUITE YOUNG TREES HAVE
SCALY BARK

CONSPICUOUS RIDGES MAKE
TWIGS FOUR-SIDED

BLACK ASH

Swamp Ash

Fraxinus nigra Marsh.

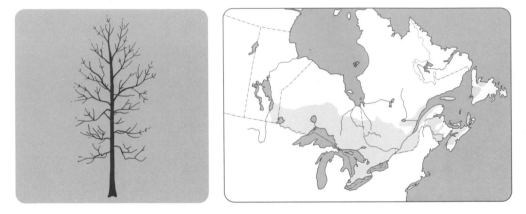

FORM—This tree has a slender, sometimes bent or leaning trunk which extends almost to the top of a narrow open crown of coarse ascending branches. The root system is quite shallow and wide-spreading.

HABITAT—The Black Ash ranges throughout the Deciduous, Great Lakes-St. Lawrence and Acadian Forest regions, and extends into the southeastern portion of the Boreal Forest Region. It is the only ash that grows in New-foundland. To the west, it just reaches the edge of the Grasslands. Typically a tree of swampy woodlands, the Black Ash may form small pure stands, or grow in association with White Elm, Eastern White Cedar, Speckled Alder, Red Maple, Silver Maple and other hardwoods that grow in rich soils.

SIZE—A small tree 40 to 60 ft. in height and 1 to 2 ft. in diameter, but occasionally may reach 90 ft. in height.

LEAVES—Each leaf is 10- to 16-ins. long, with seven to eleven elongated oval leaflets that are 4- to 5-ins. long by 1- to 2-ins. wide; leaflets without stalks, unequally rounded or broadly wedge-shaped at the base, tapered from well above the middle to a long slender tip, finely and sharply toothed, both surfaces dark green and hairless, except for dense tufts of rusty hairs at the joints where the leaflets are attached to the main leaf-stalk.

FLOWERS—Male and female organs in the same flower (perfect) or in separate flowers, all three kinds may appear on the same tree, or the unisexual flowers may be on separate trees along with some perfect ones; the stalks are without hairs.

FRUIT—The wing is broad, often twisted, sometimes slightly notched at the tip and extends all the way to the base of a flat seed portion, completely surrounding it. There is no minute collar (remnants of flower parts) at the base of the fruit.

TWIGS—Very stout, light grey, dull, hairless, round in cross-section; buds dark brown to nearly black, side buds small, the uppermost pair distinctly below the terminal bud with the bark of the twig clearly visible above them.

BARK—Light grey, scaly, soft, developing into soft corky ridges which are easily rubbed off by hand pressure.

WOOD—Moderately heavy, medium hard, not strong, coarse-grained; dark greyish-brown, sapwood nearly white.

IMPORTANCE—Black Ash wood is not as strong nor as hard as White Ash wood because of its narrow growth rings, and therefore cannot be used for many of the purposes for which White Ash is acceptable. It is used for interior finishing, certain types of furniture and cabinet work.

NOTES—Baskets can be woven from Black Ash wood which is prepared by pounding a block until it separates into slats along the annual growth rings. The wood must be wet.

310

HAS TUFTS OF HAIRS AT THE STALKLESS
LET JUNCTIONS

SEED-WING EXTENDS TO BASE OF SEED AS IN BLUE ASH

IS SCALY

TWIG HAS WIDE SPACE BETWEEN TERMINAL BUD AND
UPPERMOST SIDE BUDS

NANNYBERRY

Sweet Viburnum
Sheepberry

Viburnum lentago L.

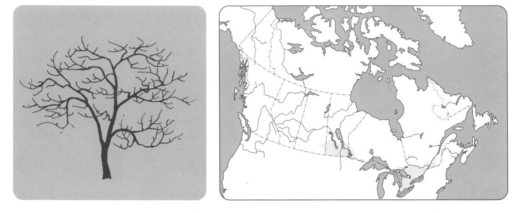

FORM—The Nannyberry has a slender crooked trunk and a very open irregular crown of a few arching branches. This species is a member of the Honeysuckle family (*Caprifoliaceae*) which is a large family of at least 10 genera, comprising nearly 300 species. The majority are shrubs. The Nannyberry (in the genus *Viburnum*) occasionally becomes a tree in Canada, but, since it is found more often as a shrub than a tree, it may be mistaken for one of the other eight shrubby species in this genus. Only one of the shrubs need be troublesome, and that is the closely related Wild Raisin or Witherod (*Virburnum cassinoides* L.). It is a tall shrub which can be identified by the short or blunt tips on its leaves and by its golden or yellowish buds. Also, its leaves are often wavy margined rather than toothed.

HABITAT—This species ranges from southwestern New Brunswick to eastern Saskatchewan, within the Deciduous and Great Lakes-St. Lawrence Forest regions and the southern parts of the Boreal Forest Region. It grows along riverbanks and the shores of lakes, in mixture with other species of trees and shrubs.

SIZE—Occasionally attains a height of 30 ft. and a diameter of 6 ins., but more often found as a tall shrub.

LEAVES—Leaves of all species of *Viburnum* are shed annually, and are opposite on the twigs in the same way as the leaves of maples, ashes, elderberries, dogwoods (except Alternate-leaved Dogwood) and some buckthorns.

The leaves are 2- to 5-ins. long, simple, egg-shaped to narrowly oval, drawn out at the end to a slender tip, rounded at the base, hairless, finely and sharply toothed, yellowish-green above, with tiny dark brown dots on the under-surface; leaf-stalk grooved, bordered along each side by narrow extensions of the leaf-blade.

FLOWERS—Small, creamy-white, male and female organs in the same flower, a large number arranged in round-topped clusters.

FRUIT—Berry-like, bluish-black, ⅓- to ½-in. long, with thin, sweet, edible flesh and a flat black stone.

TWIGS—Slender, smooth, pale brown, disagreeable smell when broken; leaf-buds slender, ½- to ¾-in. long, with one pair of scales, greyish-brown, granular looking; flower buds at the end of the twig, with a bulbous base and a long slender tip.

BARK—Greyish-brown, broken into small irregular scales.

WOOD—Hard, heavy, close-grained; dark brown, sapwood nearly white.

IMPORTANCE—The wood has no commercial value, but the tree is sometimes used for landscaping purposes.

NOTES—Although the Nannyberry is occasionally planted as an ornamental in city parks, it is not recommended for the average suburban garden because of its undesirable habit of spreading by sprouting from the roots.

FLOWER CLUSTERS ARE ROUND-TOPPED

UNDERSURFACE DISTINCTLY DOTTED;
-STALK WINGED

FRUIT HAS SINGLE STONE

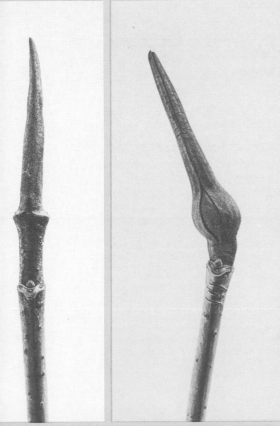

-BUD (LEFT); FLOWER-BUD (RIGHT) HAS SWOLLEN BASE

SCALES ON BARK ARE IRREGULAR

BLUE ELDER

Blue Elderberry

Sambucus glauca Nutt.

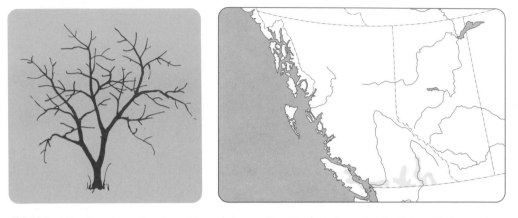

FORM—Like the preceding tree, Nannyberry, this species is a member of the Honeysuckle family, *Caprifoliaceae.* Twenty or more species of the genus *Sambucus* are known, but most of them are shrubs. Of the four species in Canada, only the Blue Elder becomes a tree. Usually, it has a very short trunk which branches near the ground into a few, stout, arching and spreading branches that form a broad rounded crown. Two of the other three species, the Elderberry (*Sambucus canadensis* L.) and the Red-berried Elder (*Sambucus pubens* Michx.) are not likely to be mistaken for Blue Elder since they are not found west of Manitoba. The Black-berried Elder (*Sambucus melanocarpa* Gray) grows in British Columbia, however, and can readily be confused with the Blue Elder. The Black-berried Elder differs in having flowers and fruits in roundish clusters, 2¾-ins. across and usually deeper than they are broad, and branchlets with a brownish pith.

HABITAT—Blue Elder is a species which is confined to the southern British Columbia mainland and Vancouver Island. It grows in clearings in the forest and along streams and ravines, usually on gravelly or stony soils.

SIZE—Usually found as a tall coarse shrub, but occasionally it attains a height of 30 ft. and a diameter of 8 ins.

LEAVES—Shed in autumn and replaced the following spring, opposite on the twigs, 6- to 8-ins. long, on grooved stalks, divided into five to nine elongated leaflets with long, slender, sharp tips and uneven bases, occasionally doubly compound (particularly the lower leaflets) coarsely and sharply toothed, bluish-green above, paler on the undersurface, hairless, rank-smelling when crushed.

FLOWERS—Small, ⅛-in. across, creamy-white, male and female organs in the same flower, a large number in dense, nearly flat-topped, five-rayed clusters, 3- to 6-ins. across, approximately 1½-ins. deep.

FRUIT—Berry-like, bluish-black, round, ¼-in. across, thin fleshed, with three minute stones, juicy, sweet and edible.

TWIGS—Very stout, often ribbed, pale green to brownish, weak; the woody part thin and surrounding a thick white pith; buds large, with two or three pairs of greenish or brownish scales, terminal bud usually absent; leaf-scars large, with five to seven bundle-scars.

BARK—Thin, light brown often tinged with red, has narrow, intersecting, scaly ridges.

WOOD—Light, soft, not strong, coarse-grained; brownish-yellow, sapwood thin, lighter-coloured; diffuse porous.

IMPORTANCE—The wood is of no commercial value, but the tree is sometimes planted as an ornamental. The fruit is edible and is used for making jams, jellies, pies and wine; it also supplies food for many birds.

NOTES—A fragrant, light, white wine can be made from the flowers of the Blue Elder.

LEAF-STALKS ARE GROOVED

FLOWER-STALK DIVIDES INTO FIVE STEMS

USUAL FORM IS A TALL COARSE SHRUB

SMALL ROUND FRUIT IS EDIBLE

I

J

K

Basswood
Largetooth Aspen
Ponderosa Pine
Black Cherry
Tulip-Tree
Willow
Hop-Tree

H Striped Maple
I Canada Plum
J White Elm
K Shagbark Hickory
L Wild Crab Apple
M Ponderosa Pine
N Redbud

L

M

N

Acknowledgements

■ DEPARTMENT OF THE ENVIRONMENT, CANADA

Graphic design, layout and production	Mrs. Iris Gott, Mr. Bing-Lin Wong Mr. A. Lang, Mr. G. Guillet
Cover design	Mr. Bing-Lin Wong
Cartography	Mr. J. Brittain, Mr. M. Hayne, Mr. G. Leclair
Manuscript analysis (English — French)	Mr. A. Potvin
Manuscript preparation	Mrs. A. Miles
Additional photography	Mr. K. McVeigh, Mr. P. S. Debnam, Miss A-M. Nosch, Mr. E. Rayner Mr. J. M. Robinson, Mr. F. D. Mac Andrews Mr. S. Gosewitz, Mr. E. Campbell, Mr. J. Scrimger Dr. R. C. Dobbs, Dr. E. T. Oswald
Photographic processing	Mr. M. Fokkema, Mr. J. McAuley
Wood uses	Mr. E. Perem
General assistance	Mr. D. R. Monk, Mr. L. Cameron Mrs. M. Boucher, Mr. T. C. Jones, Miss C. Kotlarsky Mr. R. Ficht, Mr. D. Finnigan, Miss C. Price, Miss S. Marchand Miss S. L. Lacasse, Mrs. P. W. Grey Mrs. E. Harris, Mr. W. Morse, Mr. J. Sheridan, Miss M. Lenz Mrs. A. Sample, Mr. G. P. Atkinson, Mr. E. L. Hughes Dr. J. S. Maini, Dr. E. B. Peterson, Dr. A. Jablanczy, Mr. V. Hildahl Mr. R. M. Waldron, Mr. J. C. Boynton Mr. M. Boulerice, Miss E. McFarlane, Mr. S. A. Farooqui Miss S. J. Wilson, Mr. J. Santon Mr. A. Bickerstaff, Mr. R. Bailey, Mr. S. Zubrowski Mrs. M. I. Moore, Mr. J. Wiebe

■ CANADA DEPARTMENT OF AGRICULTURE
Dr. B. Boivin, Dr. W. G. Dore, Mr. R. P. Cooper, Mr. A. R. Buckley
Mr. W. S. Condy, Mr. W. J. Cody

■ CANADIAN GOVERNMENT TRAVEL BUREAU
Mr. A. Shearer

■ NATIONAL CAPITAL COMMISSION
Mr. M. M. Outhet

■ NATIONAL FILM BOARD
Mr. D. Hopkins

■ PUBLIC PRINTING AND STATIONERY DEPARTMENT
Mr. J. D. Shaw, Mr. J. J. Pennylegion, Mr. J. R. G. Patenaude
Mr. I. Young

■ SECRETARY OF STATE DEPARTMENT
Dr. J. H. Soper, Mr. P. LeQuellec, Dr. G. M. Day

■ DEPARTMENT OF MINES, AGRICULTURE AND RESOURCES OF
NEWFOUNDLAND AND LABRADOR
Mr. E. R. Bearns

■ DEPARTMENT OF LANDS AND FORESTS OF ONTARIO
Mr. W. Edwards, Mr. A. Heald

■ NIAGARA PARKS COMMISSION
Mr. C. Dalby, Mr. R. Woods

■ ROYAL BOTANICAL GARDENS
Dr. Pringle, Dr. Vrugpman, Mr. W. J. Lamoureux, Mr. R. Halward

■ BRITISH COLUMBIA FOREST SERVICE
Miss B. Davies, Mr. A. McMinn, Mr. H. Lyons, Mr. A. Grooner

■ OTHERS WHO HELPED
Mr. and Mrs. K. L. Volmer, Mr. W. Filsinger
Mr. S. Koluk, Mr. L. Walsh, Dr. E. E. Gaertner, Dr. J. M. A. Franco
Dr. E. Rouleau, Mr. and Mrs. B. McLean, Mrs. D. M. Ling
Mr. H. Gillatt, Mrs. B. Barber, Miss N. Purdy, Miss V. G. Smith

APPENDICES

APPENDIX A

Martin Frobisher was the last of the China-bound explorers whose short-sighted pursuit of known riches caused them to overlook the far greater rewards awaiting on the North American Continent. To Frobisher, Hudson, Cabot and the others, Canada was a frustration. Even Jacques Cartier was seeking a passage to Asia when he remarked on the "goodly meadows and trees" of what is now Prince Edward Island. The importance of the new land was recognized eventually by Champlain, but, at his death in 1635, France had only a bare handful of settlers established along the fringes of the St. Lawrence. In a few more years, furs became the treasure to seek and the reason for pushing further and further into a hostile hinterland. Communication and trade during this period depended on river arteries, or on dangerous travel along Indian trails in the deep forest.

By the beginning of the eighteenth century, the most plentiful product of the land, timber, was being exported to Europe in the form of squared timber for ship's masts, planks and spars. Laws protected oak and white pine throughout New France. Later, British policy extended government protection, not only to the trees themselves, but to "any area particularly suited to the growing of these species". Conservation, then, is not a new idea, but one that was born of a need to have at hand the materials of war. Ironically, war stifled the policy for, in the turbulence of the period, the new laws lost their meaning and wanton destruction of the forests continued for almost a hundred years.

Other eyes were looking at the forests however — almost from the beginning. Jacques Cartier was probably the first to record his astonishment at the number of different trees he found, and he was certainly the first to carry specimens home to France. His reports so stimulated French interest in the plants of the New World that, by the year of Champlain's death, a description of the plants of Canada had been published in Paris (*Canadensium Plantorum Aliarumque nondum editarum historia* by Jacques Phillipe Cornut). All early research work was done in Europe, for in Europe was centred the learning of the day.

The following list of botanists who gave their names to Canadian trees presents yet another glimpse into the history of North America, and, indeed, the world. For example the collections made by Dr. Michel Sarrasin of Quebec City, up to 1734, are represented here in the many trees bearing the name code, "L", for Carl Linnaeus. Also, the co-operation between Professor Peter Kalm of Sweden and Dr. Gaultier, Sarrasin's replacement, ensured classification of numerous Canadian species during Kalm's journey to New France in 1749. Kalm was a pupil of the great Swedish botanist, Linnaeus, who founded the modern system of plant classification. Then, there are the explorer-botanists who followed Indian trails far into the interior and returned to publish their findings. André Michaux (1792) and, later, David Douglas (1824) have their travels recorded in the ranges of the species they named, and Archibald Menzies (See Appendix "B") was the first European to record having sighted the Douglas-fir.

Unfortunately many of the major contributors to Canadian botany are not included in this list because they were "collectors" who left classification to others. The German names in the list reflect the importance of Berlin as the centre of the greatest botanical collection of the period, while Switzerland has representation because of French botanists fleeing from the Revolution. The long association of John Bartram of Philadelphia with Peter Collinson of London is yet another example of co-operation between the Old World and the New in the field of botany. During this period, Sir William Hooker's *Flora Boreali Americana* (1840) described the botanical collections of many famous explorers.

After 1850, Canadian botanists began to publish in Canada. Abbé Léon Provancher wrote *Flore canadienne* in 1862, and during the period 1883 to 1902 John Macoun issued his seven volume *Catalogue of Canadian Plants*.

More recently, botanical surveys have included detailed descriptions of Canadian species within a limited geographical region. Probably the most famous of these is *Flore laurentienne* written by Frère Marie-Victorin of Montreal and published in 1935. Since then, most of the botanical research in Canada has been sponsored by the federal government and the universities. Some of the outstanding names of the last few years are: E. H. Moss (*Flora of Alberta*); A. E. Roland (*Flora of Nova Scotia*); A. E. Porsild (*Illustrated Flora of the Canadian Arctic Archipelago*); J. H. Soper (*100 Shrubs of Ontario*); H. J. Scoggan (*Flora of Manitoba*); and Bernard Boivin of the Plant Research Institute, Canada Department of Agriculture. Others who have made valuable contributions in their specialized fields are: T. M. C. Taylor, T. C. Brayshaw, C. Frankton, W. J. Cody, W. G. Dore, Marcel Raymond, Ernest Lepage, Ernest Rouleau and W. K. W. Baldwin.

The identification of the authors whose names appear in the following list is based on material published in Volume 2 of the *International Plant Index*. Anyone compiling a list of botanical authors, however, is faced with the historical fact that nomenclature before 1907 was rudimentary, and that chance may have given credit to the wrong person. The names given here and the short biographical sketches are as accurate as present information allows. Research continues and, with the prospect of progress in information retrieval, more complete information may be available for the next edition of *Native Trees of Canada*.

Abbreviation	Identification and Biography

A. Dietr.

Albert Dietrich (1795-1856).
Prolific writer and botanist who published nearly 50 works in Germany between 1824 and 1856 on subjects ranging from the cactus to a handbook for amateur gardeners.

Ait.

William Aiton (1731-1793).
Scottish botanist who, in 1759, became director of Kew Gardens in London. Published a catalogue of the plants cultivated at Kew, entitled *Hortus Kewensis*. Was a pupil of Philip Miller.

Anderss.

Nils Johan Andersson (1821-1880).
Swedish botanist who became Professor of Botany at the University of Lund, Stockholm. He specialized in willows and in the flora of Lapland.

A. Nels.

Aven Nelson (1859-1952).
Professor of Botany, University of Wyoming, Laramie, Wyoming, U.S.A. Specialized in the flora of western America, particularly of the Rocky Mountains.

Arnold

Johann Franz Xaver Arnold (1785- • •).
The Austrian botanist who classified the Austrian Pine, an exotic which is commonly planted in Canada.

Ashe

William Willard Ashe (1872-1932).
Chairman of the U.S. Forest Service Tree Name Committee. Published many botanical works during a lifetime devoted to forestry. Best known for his assistance in preparing *Flora of the Southeastern United States* and *Standardized Plant Names*.

Audubon

John James Laforest Audubon (1785-1851).
Famous American naturalist and ornithologist best known for his great work *The Birds of America*. Born in Haiti of French parents, he settled in New York.

Barratt

Joseph Barratt (1796-1882).
American botanist who specialized in the study of willows. Author of notes and observations describing the types of willows most suited for crafts and ornamental planting.

Bartr.

John Bartram (1699-1777).
Called the "Father of American Botany", Bartram lived in Philadelphia where he cultivated a garden full of interesting specimens that he collected during a lifetime of travel through the then unknown regions of North America. Sent many botanical specimens to London to be identified and named.

Bartr.

William Bartram (1739-1823).
Son of John Bartram, known as a botanist, ornithologist, writer and traveller. See "John and William Bartram" in Appendix "C".

Batsch

August Johann Georg Carl Batsch (1761-1802).
Among 38 books, papers and studies on botanical subjects published between 1786 and 1802, the German botanist, Batsch, chose to write one in French for the ladies. Its title was *Botanique pour les femmes* and it appeared in 1795.

B. Ehrh.

Johann Balthasar Ehrhart (1700-1756).
German botanist who, in 1732, published his *Botanologiae juvenilis mentissa* and, in 1753, *Plant History* in the form of notes for what today would be called nature walks.

Beissn.

Ludwig Beissner (1843-1927).
Inspector of the Royal Gardens in Germany. Teacher at the Academy of Land Research. Special research in conifers.

Abbreviation	Identification and Biography

Benth.

George Bentham (1800-1884).
English botanist commissioned by the British Government in 1857 to publish a series of books on the flora of British Colonies and possessions.

Blanch.

William Henry Blanchard (1850-1922).
Vermont school teacher who specialized in the collecting and classification of blackberries. Travelled extensively in eastern Canada and United States, but concentrated on the flora of south-western Maine.

Boiss.

Edmond Pierre Boissier (1810-1885).
Swiss botanist and author of *Flora Orientalis*. Donated his herbarium to the Faculty of Sciences at the University of Geneva.

Boivin

Bernard Boivin (1916-   ).
Research Scientist, Plant Research Institute, Canada Department of Agriculture, Ottawa. Specializes in taxonomy, floristics and nomenclature. Author of *Enumération des plantes du Canada; Flora of the Prairie Provinces* and *Flore du Québec méridional et du Canada oriental.*

Bong.

August Heinrich Gustav Bongard (1786-1839).
One of the German botanists attracted to St. Petersburg, Russia, by the Czar's interest in the sciences. Published his memoirs while a member of the Académie des Sciences de St. Petersburg.

Borkh.

Moritz Balthasar Borkhausen (1760-1806).
German botanist whose two-volume work *Theoretisch-praktisches Handbuch der Forstbotanik und Forsttechnologie* was published between 1800 and 1803.

Brewer

William Henry Brewer (1828-1910).
American botanist and Professor of Agriculture at Yale University. Known for his writings *On the forests of Sequoia gigantea*, published in 1865, and *On the forests of Sequoia (Wellingtonia)* of the same year.

Britt.
Britton

Nathaniel Lord Britton (1859-1934).
Director-in-chief of the New York Botanical Garden, who specialized in North American flora. Author of *Illustrated Flora of the Northern United States and Canada*. Co-operated with Sterns and Poggenburg.

B.S.P.

Nathaniel Lord Britton (1859-1934).

Emerson Ellick Sterns (1846-1926).

Justus Ferdinand Poggenburg (1840-1893).
Britton, Sterns and Poggenburg co-operated in a *Preliminary catalogue of Anthophyta and Pteridophyta reported as growing spontaneously within 100 miles of New York City*, which was published in 1888.

C. A. Meyer

Carl Anton Andrejewicz von Meyer (1795-1855).
German botanist who lived in Russia and who reported at length on the flora of the different regions of Russia. Published papers on *Cornus* in 1845.

Carr.

Elie Abel Carrière (1816-1896).
Director of the nurseries of the Jardin des plantes de Paris. Spent his life studying conifers. Noted for his *Traité général des conifères.*

325

Abbreviation	*Identification and Biography*
DC.	**Augustin Pyrame de Candolle (1778-1841).** Swiss botanist whose life-work was connected with the classification of plants. Collaborated with a collector, Dr. Thomas Coulter, who arrived on the West Coast of North America in 1831.
D. Don	**David Don (1799-1841).** Botanist who became librarian of the Linnaean Society in 1822. Published his *Prodromus Florae Nepalensis*, in 1825.
Desmarais	**Yves Desmarais (1918-).** Dr. Desmarais was Professor of Ecology at Laval University, Quebec, before he was appointed director of the Montreal Botanical Garden.
Dipp.	**Leopold Dippel (1827-1914).** German botanist who, in the latter half of the 19th century, published many papers on botanical subjects. His interests varied from *Studies of the Histology of Plants* (1865) to *Handbuch der Laubholzkunde*, published in 1889.
Dode	**Louis Albert Dode (1875-1943).** Specialized in the study of poplars and willows while working at the Forestry Laboratory in Toulouse, France. In 1905, Dode published an important monograph on the genus *Populus*, in which many new species were described.
Donn	**James Donn (1758-1813).** English botanist and curator of the Cambridge Botanical Garden. Best known for having named *Claytonia perfoliata* and for having published a catalogue of the plants growing at Cambridge.
Dougl.	**David Douglas (1798-1834).** Scottish botanist who, as a collector for the Royal Historical Society, discovered many new plants, trees and birds in British Columbia. Douglas kept a diary of his travels throughout western Canada.
Dunal	**Michel Félix Dunal (1789-1856).** French botanist who studied under Candolle and later took over Candolle's chair of botany at Geneva University.
Du Roi	**Johann Philipp Du Roi (1741-1785).** German botanist who made a special study of trees, shrubs and bushes, which included some of the flora of North America. Published a two-volume work on his findings, in 1771.
Ehrh.	**Jakob Friedrich Ehrhart (1742-1795).** Swiss botanist best known for his interesting observations in *Suppléments à l'Histoire naturelle*.
E. J. Hill	**Ellsworth Jerome Hill (1833-1917).** In the last decade of the 19th century, this American botanist wrote about the flora of the middle west. His *Quercus ellipsoidalis in Iowa* was published in 1899.
Endl.	**Stephen Friedrich Ladislaus Endlicher (1804-1849).** Noted Hungarian botanist and linguist who was Professor of Botany at Vienna University. Published *Genera plantarum* during the ten years from 1831 to 1841.
Engelm.	**George Engelmann (1809-1884).** German-American botanist who amassed a large collection of plants and botanical notes, all of which are in the Missouri Botanical Gardens, St. Louis. Published many monographs on different families of American plants (*Pinaceae, Juncaceae*, etc.).

Abbreviation	Identification and Biography

Farw.

Oliver Atkins Farwell (1867-1944).
Curator of the Herbarium and Drug Inspector, Parke, Davis and Co., Lake Linden, Michigan. Specialized in the flora of Michigan.

Fern.

Merritt Lyndon Fernald (1873-1950).
Director of the Gray Herbarium and for over 40 years one of the greatest authorities on the flora of northeastern America. Author of the 8th edition of *Gray's Manual of Botany* (1950) and long-time Editor-in-Chief of the botanical magazine *Rhodora*.

Forbes

James Forbes (1773-1861).
Gardener at Woburn Abbey, home of the Dukes of Bedford. Achieved his greatest fame for having described *Epipactis purpurator*.

Franco

João Manuel António Pais do Amaral Franco (1921-   ).
Professor and Agronomical Engineer at the College of Agronomy, Lisbon, Portugal. An international authority on botanical nomenclature. Author of *Dendrologia Flosestal* and contributor to *Flora Europaea*.

Gaertn.

Joseph Gaertner (1732-1791).
German botanist who became director of the Botanical Gardens at St. Petersburg in Russia. He wrote a standard work on the morphology of fruits and seeds.

Glend.

Robert Glendinning (• • .- • •).
English horticulturist who, in 1849, described methods of transplanting large evergreen trees.

G. N. Jones

George Neville Jones (1904-   ).
Professor of Botany and Curator of the Herbarium, University of Illinois. Author of *Flora of Illinois*, published in 1963.

Gord.

George Gordon (1806-1879).
Horticultural writer. His most important work was *Pinetum*. Foreman of the Arboretum of the horticultural society of Chiswick, England.

Gray

Asa Gray (1810-1888).
Famous American writer-botanist who, with John Torrey, published Torrey and Gray's *Flora*. Creator of the Harvard Herbarium which became the largest and most valuable collection in the United States.

Greene

Edward Lee Greene (1843-1915).
Specialized in plants of California and the western and southwestern States. Published *Native Shrubs of California*, in 1889 — one of many titles produced during his working life.

Griscom

Ludlow Griscom (1890-   ).
Research ornithologist and biologist, Museum of Comparative Zoology, Harvard. A member of many scientific expeditions to South America and Canada, including a botanical expedition to Quebec in 1923.

Hemsl.

William Botting Hemsley (1843-1924).
Keeper of the Herbarium and Library at the Royal Botanical Gardens, Kew, England. Author of many books on botanical subjects including *Handbook of Hardy Trees and Shrubs, and Herbaceous Plants* which was published in 1873 and revised in 1877.

327

Abbreviation	Identification and Biography

Henk. **Johann Baptist Henkel (1815-1871).**
Although trained in medicine, Dr. Henkel turned his attention to pharmacology (Medizinisch-pharmaceutische Botanik) and in 1865 published *Synopsis der Nadelhölzer* in co-operation with Wilhelm Hochstetter.

Henry **Louis Henry (1853-1913).**
From the age of 30, Professor Henry produced a steady stream of botanical writings on a wide range of subjects. Henry was a native of France.

Hochst. **Wilhelm Hochstetter (1825-1881).**
German botanist who, among other works dealing with conifers, published a guide to the botanical gardens at the University of Tubingen.

Hook. **Sir William Jackson Hooker (1785-1865).**
Regius Professor of Botany at Glasgow University until 1841 when he became Director of the Royal Botanical Gardens at Kew, London. Published *Flora Boreali Americana* between 1833 and 1840.

Howell **Thomas Jefferson Howell (1842-1912).**
American botanist, best known for his work in the Pacific northwest. Published *New Species of Pacific Coast Plants*, in 1895, and *A Flora of Northwest America*, in 1897.

Huds. **William Hudson (1730-1793).**
English botanist who published *Flora anglica*, in 1762, and a second, two-volume edition, in 1778. A third edition was published in 1798 after Hudson's death.

Hultén **Oskar Eric Gunnar Hultén (1894-).**
Swedish professor and curator of the Herbarium in the Botanical Museum at the University of Lund. Best known for his *Flora of Alaska and Yukon* which was published in 1941.

Hylander **Nils Hylander (1904-).**
Assistant professor and Chief Horticultural Inspector, Uppsala, Sweden. Specializes in philosophy and botany. Author of *Studies of northern potted plants, Northern potted plant flora* and *The Genus Hosta in Swedish Gardens*.

Jacq. **Baron Nicolaus Joseph von Jacquin (1727-1817).**
Austrian pupil of the French botanist Antoine de Jussieu. Best known for his *Flora Austriaca* which he published between 1773 and 1778.

James **Edwin James (1797-1861).**
American explorer, naturalist and physician who wrote an *Account of an expedition from Pittsburg to the Rocky Mountains* in the years 1819 and 1820.

Karst. **Gustav Karl Wilhelm Hermann Karsten (1817-1908).**
German botanist and traveller in South America. Professor of Botany at Vienna University. Author of *Beiträge zur Anatomie und Physiologie der Pflanzen*.

K. Koch **Karl Heinrich Emil Koch (1809-1879).**
German naturalist and traveller who became director of the Potsdam Botanical Gardens. His principal work was *Dendrology* published between 1869 and 1873.

Abbreviation	Identification and Biography

L.

Carl Linnaeus (1707-1778).
Swedish botanist who, in his *Genera Plantorum*, founded the modern conception of systematic botany. First to use specific names in nomenclature. Raised to the nobility in 1757 and became known as Carl von Linné. Linnaeus is probably the most famous historical figure in the botanical world.

L.f.

Carl von Linné (1741-1783).
Son of Carl Linnaeus who carried on his father's work after Linnaeus died in 1778. Carl von Linné only outlived his father by five years.

Lam.

Jean Baptiste Pierre Antoine de Monnet Lamarck (1744-1829).
French naturalist, founder of Lamarkism and the first zoologist to distinguish vertebrate from invertebrate animals. Author of *Dictionnaire de Botanique*.

Lamb.

Aylmer Bourke Lambert (1761-1842).
English botanist who was vice-president of the Linnaean Society. Specialized in research on pines. Published his *Description of the Genus Pinus* in 1803.

Laws.

Peter Lawson (17 · · -1820).
Peter Lawson & Sons were nurserymen in Edinburgh, Scotland. Peter introduced many species into cultivation. Sir Charles Lawson, his son, was a leader in Scottish agriculture.

Ledeb.

Karl Friedrich von Ledebour (1785-1851).
German botanist who was Director of the Botanical Gardens and Professor of Botany at Creifswald and then at Dorpat. Famous for his *Flora Rossica*.

Lemm.

John Gill Lemmon (1832-1908).
American who specialized in the conifers of the Pacific northwest and west. Published numerous papers on conifers during his lifetime, including *Cone-bearers of California,* in 1890.

l'Her.

Charles Louis l'Heritier de Brutelle (1746-1800).
French botanist who, from 1784 to 1798, published several papers on botanical subjects. Named several species collected by André Michaux and other botanists who visited Canada.

Liebl.

Franz Kaspar Lieblein (1744-1810).
Best known for his *Flora fuldensis* which was published in Frankfort, Germany, in 1784.

Lindl.

John Lindley (1799-1865).
Professor of Botany at University College, London. Assisted in writing the *Encyclopedia of Plants,* published *An Introduction to the Natural System of Botany* and edited *Edward's Botanical Register.*

Loud.

John Claudius Loudon (1783-1843).
Scottish botanist and landscape gardener. Famous for his *Encyclopaedia of Gardening* and *Encyclopaedia of Agriculture.*

Marsh.

Humphry Marshall (1722-1801).
American botanist famous for his work *Arbustrum Americanum* published in 1785.

Mattuschka

Heinrich Gottfried, Graf von Mattuschka (1734-1779).
German nobleman who wrote *Flora silesiaca* which was published in Breslau in 1776.

Abbreviation	Identification and Biography

Maxim.

Karl Johann Maximovicz (1827-1891).
Maximovicz was a German botanist who took advantage of the Czar's offer to work in Russia. He described many new species during extensive travels in Japan and Mongolia. Published his findings from 1857 to 1889.

Med.

Friedrich Casimir Medicus (1736-1808).
During the latter part of his life, the German-born Medicus wrote many papers on various botanical subjects. One interesting title was his *History of Botany in our Time*, published in 1793.

Michx.

André Michaux (1746-1802).
Michaux was sent to North America by the French Government in 1785. After several years of botanical exploration, he arrived in Montreal in 1792 and spent the next five months travelling throughout Quebec. The results of his work were published in Paris after his return to France in 1797, but he did not live to see his most famous book, *Flora Boreali-Americana*.

Michx. f.

François André Michaux (1770-1855).
Son of André Michaux and author of *Histoire des arbres forestiers de l'Amérique septentrionale*. François spent much of his time searching for plants in the southern Appalachian region of the United States.

Mill.

Philip Miller (1691-1771).
English botanist whose *Dictionary of Gardens* was published in 1731 and was translated into all the principal languages of Europe. Curator of the Physic Garden, Chelsea, which became the foremost botanical garden of its time.

Mirb.

Charles François Brisseau Mirbel (1776-1854).
Professor at the Sorbonne in Paris, who was celebrated for his work on cellulose. His most important publication was *Histoire naturelle des végétaux classés par familles*.

Moench

Conrad Moench (1774-1805).
Moench studied pharmacy, botany, chemistry and mineralogy and was Professor of Botany in the Collequim Medicum, Germany. Noted for his *Methodus Plantas Horti botanici et Agri Marburgensis a Staminum Situ Describendi*.

Muenchh.

Otto, Freiherr von Muenchhausen (1716-1774).
Published a six-volume work entitled *Der Hausvater* in the years 1765 to 1773. Volume 5, issued in 1770, deals with trees and shrubs.

Mühl.

Gotthilf Heinrich Ernst Mühlenberg (1753-1815).
In 1806, working from notes made by the German botanist, Professor Willdenow, and from his own observations, Mühlenberg published a paper on North American willows. Botany was a hobby; by profession he was a minister in Pennsylvania, U.S.A.

Nees

Christian Gottfried Daniel Nees von Esenbeck (1776-1858).
Professor of Botany at the University of Breslau, Germany, until 1851.

Nutt.

Thomas Nuttall (1784-1859).
The pioneer of American paleontology and curator of the Harvard Botanical Gardens. Author of *The Genera of North American Plants*. Nuttall, who was born and died in England, was also known as an ornithologist.

Abbreviation	Identification and Biography

Palmer
Ernest Jesse Palmer (1875-1962).
Collector and Research Assistant, Arnold Arboretum, Jamaica Plain, Massachusetts. Specialized in plant geography and forest distribution. Studied hawthorns.

Parl.
Filippo Parlatore (1816-1877).
Italian naturalist whose most important but unfinished work was *Flora Italiana*, to which he devoted forty years of his life. Caruel completed the publication.

Parry
Charles Christopher Parry (1823-1890).
First to hold the post of Botanist in the United States Department of Agriculture. His many botanical papers were rather brief and of a special character.

Peck
Raymond Elliot Peck (1904-   ).
Professor of Geology at the University of Missouri. Researcher and member of the American Science Advisory Commission.

Poir.
Jean Louis Marie Poiret (1755-1834).
French naturalist who collaborated with Lamarck. With others he published a dictionary of botany entitled *l'Encyclopédie*.

Pursh
Frederick Traugott Pursh (1774-1820).
German botanist whose contribution to botany is among the most valuable of the early North American botanists. Died in Montreal while collecting material for a publication on the flora of Canada.

Raf.
Constantine Samuel Rafinesque-Schmaltz (1784-1842).
Professor of Botany and Modern Languages at Transylvania University, Kentucky, U.S.A. His published works include *New Flora and Botany of North America*.

Raup
Hugh Miller Raup (1901-   ).
Formerly director of the Harvard Forest, Harvard University, Petersham, Massachusetts. Has taken part in many botanical expeditions to the Yukon and Northwest Territories.

Reg.
Eduard August von Regel (1815-1892).
German botanist who was one of the scientists attracted to St. Petersburg by the Czar's interest in botany. Regel's main work was connected with birches.

Rehd.
Alfred Rehder (1863-1949).
Curator of the Arnold Arboretum and Professor of Dendrology at Harvard. Best known for his *Manual of Cultivated Trees and Shrubs in North America*.

Roem.
Max J. Roemer (· · · · ·).
From 1835 to 1840 Roemer published a *Handbook of German Botany*. Another *Handbook* of botany was published in London in 1836.

Roth
Albrecht Wilhelm Roth (1757-1834).
German botanist who, in 1830, published a three-volume *Manual of Botany* which was his last work after a steady output of material from 1778.

Rupr.
Franz Josef Ivanovich Ruprecht (1814-1870).
From 1841 until his death, Ruprecht reported on the flora of various regions of Russia and other countries. His main work was concerned with bamboo.

Abbreviation	Identification and Biography

Rydb.

Per Axel Rydberg (1860-1931).
Swedish-American botanist who was curator of the New York Botanical Gardens. Author of *Flora of the Prairies and Plains of Central North America* which was not published until one year after his death.

Salisb.

Richard Anthony Salisbury (1761-1829).
For nearly 30 years Salisbury made observations on the plants he studied. He published papers in his native England on many different genera, from conifers to peaches.

Sarg.

Charles Sprague Sargent (1841-1927).
Professor of Horticulture and Arboriculture at Harvard University. Director of the Arnold Arboretum. Author of *Manual of the Trees of North America* and *The Silva of North America*.

S. Brown

Stewardson Brown (1867-1921).
Botanist and Assistant to the Curator of the herbarium at the Philadelphia Academy, Pennsylvania. Member of the commission appointed to establish a code of botanical nomenclature.

Scheele

Georg Heinrich Adolph Scheele (1808-1864).
Although a German botanist, Scheele published observations on the flora of Texas, in 1848. At this time, Berlin was the centre of botanical learning.

Schneid.

Camillo Karl Schneider (1876-1951).
German botanist who studied coniferous and deciduous trees in Europe and North America. His published works included *Dendrologische Winterstudien, Handbuch der Laubholzkunde* and *Unsere Freiland — Nadelhölzer*.

Shafer

John Adolph Shafer (1863-1918).
Co-author with his fellow-American, Nathaniel Lord Britton, of *North American Trees* which was published in 1908.

Sieb.

Philipp Franz von Siebold (1796-1866).
Explored Japan from 1823 to 1830. Published several works on his botanical findings, including *Flora Japonica*. Siebold was German.

Spach

Edouard Spach (1801-1879).
In 1835, the French botanist, Spach, published his *Synopsis monographiae onagrearum* in the *Nouvelles Annales des Sciences Naturelles*. Also published a monograph on the maples.

Spaeth

Franz Ludwig Spaeth (1839-1913).
Berlin nurseryman, botanist and writer who, between 1883 and 1900, published 23 papers and profusely illustrated books on many botanical subjects. In 1892 he studied maples.

Spreng.

Kurt Polykarp Joachim Sprengel (1766-1833).
German botanist and physician. Professor of Medicine at Halle. Among his works was *Geschichte der Botanik* — a history of botany.

Starker

Thurman James Starker (1890-   ).
Professor of Forestry, Oregon State College, Corvallis, Oregon. Specialized in silviculture and wood preservation.

Steyerm.

Julian Alfred Steyermark (1909-   ).
Associate Curator, Chicago Natural History Museum. Specialized in the flora of Missouri, the Ozarks and Central and South America.

Abbreviation	Identification and Biography

Stokes

Jonathan S. Stokes (1755-1831).
Stokes published a four-volume work, in 1812, which listed the plants used in food and medical preparations of the day. His only other published work (1830) was a volume of botanical commentaries.

S. Wats.

Sereno Watson (1826-1892).
A prolific writer on botanical subjects — mostly concerned with flora of the southwestern United States and parts of Mexico and Guatemala. Began a bibliographical index to North American botany, but only completed one volume.

Sweet

Robert S. Sweet (1783-1835).
Sweet was well-known in England for the many books he wrote on botanical and horticultural subjects. His hot-house and green-house manual, published in its fifth edition in 1831, was a standard reference for many years.

Swingle

Walter Tennyson Swingle (1871-1952).
Dr. Swingle was a botanist with the U.S. Department of Agriculture, Washington, D.C. Among many other interests connected with plant life, a favourite subject was research in hybridizing *Citrus* and related genera.

Tausch

Ignaz Friedrich Tausch (1793-1848).
Austrian botanist who, for 31 years, maintained an interest in the flora around him. The author of some 20 papers on various botanical subjects.

Thunb.

Carl Pehr Thunberg (1743-1828).
Swedish botanist, traveller and pupil of Linnaeus. Author of *Flora Japonica, Flora Capensis* and *Icones plantarum Japonicarum,* etc.

Torr.

John Torrey (1796-1873).
American botanist who, in 1843, published *Flora of the State of New York.* Worked with his pupil, Asa Gray, on *A Flora of North America* which was published between 1838 and 1843.

Turra

Antonio Turra (1730-1796).
Best known for his list of Italian flora which was published in 1780. Turra was not a prolific writer, his only other recorded work being on horse-chestnuts.

Vahl

Martin Hendriksen Vahl (1749-1804).
Norwegian botanist who studied under Linnaeus and later became Professor of Botany and Inspector of the Botanical Gardens at Copenhagen. He wrote seven parts of *Flora Danica* and a work entitled *Enumeratis Plantarum.*

Voss

Andreas Voss (1857-1924).
German horticulturist and naturalist who, in the latter part of the 19th century and the early 20th century, published several botanical studies. In 1903 he edited *Salomon's Dictionary of Botany.*

Walt.

Thomas Walter (1740-1788).
Walter was an American who gained fame in the last year of his life when he published his *Flora caroliniana.*

Wang.

Friedrich Adam Julius Wangenheim (1747-1800).
Among other botanical papers relating to Germany and central Europe, Wangenheim published notes on North American species, in 1781.

333

Abbreviation	Identification and Biography
Waugh	**Frank Albert Waugh (1869-1947).** Professor of Horticulture and Landscape Gardening, Massachusetts State College, Amherst, Massachusetts. Specialized in United States National and State Forests and Parks.
West.	**Richard Weston (1733-1806).** Weston worked in England on a major publication which ran to four volumes. His *Catalogue of Trees and Shrubs* which described the flora cultivated in European nurseries was issued in 1771.
Wieg.	**Karl McKay Wiegand (1873-1941).** American botanist who, in co-operation with F. W. Foxworthy, published *A key to the genera of woody plants in winter* (1906). Professor Wiegand taught at Cornell University and was a close collaborator of M. L. Fernald.
Wight	**William Franklin Wight (1874-1954).** Botanist in the Horticultural Crops and Diseases Division of the United States Department of Agriculture, Bonsall, California. Specialized in the flora of Alaska.
Willd.	**Karl Ludwig Willdenow (1765-1812).** German botanist whose name is perpetuated in the Willdenow Oak. Author of over 30 botanical papers and books, but best known for *Anleitung zum Selbststudium der Botanik,* published in 1804.
Wood	**Alphonso Wood (1810-1881).** Author of the *Class-book of Botany* (1845), an important landmark in botanical texts. Later, in 1879, Wood wrote *Flora atlantica.*
Zenari	**Silvia Zenari (1896-).** Professor at the Royal Institute in Padova, Italy. Specialized in botany and ecology.
Zucc.	**Joseph Gerhard Zuccarini (1797-1848).** Best known for his work on conifers which culminated in the publication, in 1843, of *Studies of the Morphology of the Conifers.* Zuccarini lived in Germany.

APPENDIX B
MEANINGS OF TREE NAMES

a

Abies
the classical Latin name of the fir; probably derived from *abeo* "arising".

Acer
Latin for maple; derived from the Celtic.

acerifolia
with leaves like those of a maple; from the Latin *acer* "maple" and *folium* "leaf".

acuminata
sharp-pointed — referring to the leaves; from the Latin *acuminare* "to make sharp".

Aesculus
the ancient Latin name of the oak or any mast-bearing tree.

Ailanthus
from *ai lanto* or *Aylanto*, the native name of the Tree-of-Heaven, an exotic species introduced from the East Indies.

alaskana (alaskensis)
Latin form of Alaskan.

alba
Latin for white.

albertiana
Latin form of Albertan.

albicaulis
white-stemmed; from the Latin *albus* "white" and *caulis* "stem".

albidum
whitish.

alleghaniensis
Latin form of "from the Allegheny Mountains".

alnifolia
with leaves like those of the alder; from the Latin *alnus* "alder" and *folium* "leaf".

Alnus
the classical Latin name of the alder.

alternifolia
with alternate leaves; from the Latin *alternus* "other" and *folium* "leaf".

altissima
Latin for very high or the highest.

amabilis
Latin for lovely.

Amelanchier
from the French name for a European species.

americana (americanum)
Latin form of American.

amygdalus (amygdaloides)
almond, almond-like — referring to the shape of the leaves; from the Greek *amugdalos* "almond" and *öides* "appearing like".

angustifolia
with narrow leaves; from the Latin *angustus* "narrow" and *folium* "leaf".

arborea
tree-like; from the Latin *arbor* "tree".

Arbutus
the classical Latin name of the Strawberry Madrone; possibly from the Celtic *arboise*.

armeniaca
Latin for "belonging to Armenia".

aromatica
with a pleasant smell; Latin for "fragrant", from the Greek *aroma* "a spice".

Asimina
possibly from the Illinois Indian *assi* "hidden" and *mina* "berry".

atropurpurea
dark purple — referring to the colour of the fruit; from the Latin *ater* "black" and *purpureus* "purple".

aucuparia
used by bird hunters — presumably referring to the attractiveness of the tree to birds; from the Latin *aucupari* "to catch birds".

austini
after Coe Finch Austin (1831-1880), an American botanist from New York.

avium
of the birds—presumably referring to the tree's attractiveness to birds; from the Latin *avis* "bird".

b

babylonica
of Babylon—the Weeping Willow was thought to be the tree in Babylon under which exiled Jews wept; from the Greek *babulon*.

baccata
berried; from the Latin *bacca* "berry".

balsamea
pertaining to balsam — a fragrant resin; from the Hebrew *balsam*, the Greek *balsamon* and the Latin *balsamum* referring to the resinous pockets in the bark of Balsam Fir.

balsamifera
balsam bearing, with the odour of balsam; from the Latin *balsamum* "resin" and *ferre* "to bear".

banksiana
dedicated to Sir Joseph Banks (1743-1820), president of the Royal Society of London.

bartramiana
after William Bartram (1739-1823), who sent Mountain Juneberry seeds to Europe. William was the son of John Bartram (1699-1777), the pioneer of American botany. (See Appendix "A".)

bebbiana
after Michael Schuck Bebb (1833-1895), an authority on willows.

Betula
the classical Latin name of the birch.

*All genus names are written with an initial capital. — Since the meanings of many of the genus names have been lost in antiquity, only probable sources can be given. — See references marked with an asterisk in Appendix "C" for more information about the meanings and use of botanical names.

335

bicolor
Latin for two-coloured — referring to the leaves; from *bis* "two" and *color* "colour".

borealis
Latin for northern; from *Boreas* the Greek god of the north wind.

brevifolia
short-leaved; from the Latin *brevis* "short" and *folium* "leaf".

C

caerulea
Latin for dark-coloured— specifically bluish-green.

camperdownii
named for Camperdown House near Dundee, Scotland, where Umbrella Elm was first described.

canadensis
Latin form of Canadian.

candicans
whitish; from the Latin *candicare* "to shine".

canina
Latin for pertaining to a dog — usually used in the sense of "of little value".

Caprifoliaceae
the honeysuckle family; from the medieval Latin *caprifolium* "goat leaf".

carolinia (caroliniana)
Latin form of "from the Carolinas".

Carpinus
the classical Latin name of the hornbeams; possibly from the Celtic *car* "wood" and *pin* an old word meaning "yoke".

Carya
from the Greek *karua* "walnut tree". First proposed for use in 1818 by Thomas Nuttall. (See Appendix "A".)

cascadensis
Latin form of "from the Cascade Mountains".

cassinoides
shaped like a helmet; from the Greek *cassis* "helmet" and *öides* "appearing like".

Castanea
Latin for the chestnut tree; from the Greek *kastanea* "chestnut tree" which may have been named after Castane, a town in Thessaly.

cathartica
Latin for purging; from the Greek *katharo* "to cleanse".

Celtis
the classical Latin name of the African Lotus and applied to the hackberries because of their sweet fruit.

Cerasus
the Latin name for a cherry tree originating in Asia.

Cercis
from the Greek *kerkis,* the ancient name for the Judas-tree (from its legendary biblical association).

Chamaecyparis
from two Greek words *chamai* "ground" and *kuparissos* "cypress".

chinense
Latin form of Chinese.

chrysocarpa
golden or yellow fruited; from the Greek *chrysos* "golden" and *karpos* "fruit".

cinerea
ashy or ash coloured — referring to the bark of the White Walnut; from the Greek *konis* and the Latin *cineris* "ashes".

circinatum
Latin for rounded or circular — referring to the leaves.

coccinea
Latin for scarlet.

columbiana
Latin form of Columbian; from the Columbia River east of the Cascade Mountains.

communis
Latin for common — referring to the wide range of the Common Juniper.

commutata
changeable; from the Latin *commutare* "to change".

concolor
of uniform colour — referring to the needles of the White Fir which are pale bluish-green on both sides; from the Latin prefix *con* "together" and *color* "colour".

contorta
Latin for contorted or twisted — alluding to the twisted branches of the typical scrubby Shore Pine of the west coast.

cordata (cordiformis)
heart-shaped; from the Latin *cordis* "of the heart" and *forma* "shape".

cordifolia
with heart-shaped leaves; from the Latin *cordis* "of the heart" and *folium* "leaf".

Cornus
Latin for horn — referring to the hard wood.

coronaria
from the Latin *corona* "crown" or "wreath" — referring to the attractive flowers of the Wild Crab Apple.

Crataegus
the classical Greek name of the hawthorns; from *kratos* "strength".

crebra
Latin for close, frequent or repeated.

crispa
Latin for curled or crimped.

crus-galli
with thorns like a cock's spurs; from the Latin *crus* "shin" or "leg", and *gallus* "cock".

spidata
with a sharp stiff point; from the Latin *cuspis* "point".

cidua
deciduous, with leaves shed the same year, falling away; from the Latin *decidere* "to fall".

cora
showy, or ornamental — referring to the colourful fruit of the Showy Mountain Ash; from the Latin *decor* "elegance" or "beauty".

ltoides
triangular — referring to the shape of the leaves; from the Greek letter Δ (delta) and *öides* "appearing like".

missa
Latin for low or weak.

ntata
having teeth; from the Latin *dens, (dentis)* "a tooth" — referring to the toothed leaf-margins of the Chestnut.

icus
two dwellings — referring to the male and female flowers being on separate trees; from the Greek *di* "two", and *oikos* "dwelling".

color
with two or more colours — referring to the leaves of the Pussy Willow; from the Greek prefix *dis* "two" and *color* "colour".

ersifolia
separated leaves — referring to the Pacific Crab Apple; from the Latin *diversus* "divergent" and *folium* "leaf".

ersiloba
with lobes turned in different directions; from the Latin *diversus* "divergent" and the Greek *lobos* "lobe".

domestica
Latin for domesticated.

douglasii
after David Douglas (1798-1834), Scottish botanist and explorer. (See Appendix "A".)

drummondii
after Thomas Drummond (1780-1835), Scottish botanist and explorer.

e

Elaeagnus
from the Greek *elaia* "olive" and *agnos,* the name of a plant like a willow.

ellipsoidalis
Greek for "in the shape of an ellipse" — referring to the acorns.

emarginata
having a notched edge — referring to the shallow notch at the apex of the petals and sepals of the Bitter Cherry; from the Latin *emarginare* "to deprive of its edge".

engelmannii
after George Engelmann (1809-1884), German-born physician and botanist of St. Louis, who was an authority on conifers.

excelsior
Latin for taller, or higher.

f

Fagus
the classical Latin name of the beeches; from the Greek *fagein* "to eat" — referring to the fruit.

flexilis
Latin for reflexed, or bent back — referring to the scales of the open cones of Limber Pine.

florida
flowering, or abounding in flowers; from the Latin *flos* "blossom".

fontinalis
Latin for fountain-like or fountain-shaped.

fragilis
Latin for fragile — referring to the easily broken twigs of the Crack Willow.

frangula
the name of the drug that is obtained from Alder Buckthorn; from the Latin *frango* "to weaken or diminish".

fraxinifolia
with leaves like the ash from the Latin *fraxinus* "ash" and *folium* "leaf".

Fraxinus
the classical Latin name of the ash.

fruticosa
from the Latin *fruticari* "to sprout" or "to become bushy".

g

garryana
after Nicholas Garry, Director and Deputy Governor of the Hudson's Bay Company, who gave his name to Fort Garry, now Winnipeg.

ginnala
possibly from the Greek *ginnos* "a small mule" — referring to the size and hardiness of the tree.

glabra (glabrum)
Latin for smooth, without hairs or bald.

glauca
glaucous, or covered with a bloom — referring to the bluish-green foliage; from the Greek *glaukos* "bluish".

Gleditsia
sometimes spelled Gleditschia — named in 1753 after the German botanist Johann Gottlieb Gleditsch (1714-1786).

glutinosa
Latin for sticky or full of glue.

grandidentata
Latin for large-toothed.

337

grandifolia
Latin for large-leaved, with large leaves.

grandis
Latin for large or great.

groenlandica
Latin form of "from Greenland".

Gymnocladus
naked branch; from the Greek *gymnos* "naked" and *klados* "branch".

h

Hamamelis
refers to the Witch-hazel's late blooming when other trees are in fruit; from the Greek *hama* "together with" and *melon* "apple" or "fruit".

heterophylla
Latin for various-leaved, or with leaves of different sizes and shapes; from the Greek *heteros* "different" and *phullon* "leaf".

hippocastanum
horse-chestnut; from the Greek *hippos* "horse" and *kastanon* "chestnut".

holmesiana
after Joseph Austin Holmes(1859-1915), a geologist who lived in North Carolina.

hookeriana
after William Jackson Hooker (1785-1865), noted Scottish botanist. (See Appendix "A".)

horizontalis
Latin for growing horizontally.

humilis
Latin for base or low.

i

incana
Latin for pale grey or hoary.

inermis
Latin for unarmed, without thorns.

interius
Latin for "of the interior".

italica
Latin for Italian.

j

japonicum
Latin form of Japanese.

Juglans
Jupiter's nut — the classical Latin name of the walnut tree; from *Jovis* "Jupiter's" and *glans* "nut".

Juniperus
classical Latin name of the junipers.

l

laciniata
Latin for in strips.

laciniosa
Latin for full of lappets or folds — referring to the bark of Big Shellbark Hickory.

laevis
Latin for smooth.

lanceolata
Latin for lance-shaped, armed with a little lance or point.

laricina
Latin for larch-like.

Larix
the classical Latin name of the European Larch.

lasiandra
having woolly stamens; from the Greek *lasios* "shaggy" or "woolly" and *andron* "male".

lasiocarpa
hairy-fruited; from the Greek *lasios* "shaggy" or "woolly" and *karpos* "fruit".

latifolia
Latin for "with broad leaves".

Leguminosae
Latin for a pod-bearing family of plants.

lenta (lentago)
flexible or supple; from the Latin *lentus* "pliant".

leptolepis
fine scaled; from the Greek *leptos* "fine" and *lepis* "scale" or "flake".

Liriodendron
lily tree; from the Greek *leirion* "lily" and *dendron* "tree".

lucida
Latin for bright, lustrous or shining.

lutea
Latin for golden-yellow; from the colour of a plant used in dyeing.

lyallii
after Auchinblae-born David Lyall (1817-1895), Scottish surgeon and naturalist who accompanied various British expeditions and surveys.

m

Maclura
after William Maclure (1763-1840), American geologist.

macrocarpa
with large fruit; from the Greek *makros* "large" and *karpos* "fruit".

macrophyllum
large-leaved; from the Greek *makros* "large" and *phullon* "leaf".

magnifica
Latin for magnificent — referring to the cones of the Shasta Fir.

Magnolia
after Pierre Magnol (1638-1715), professor of medicine and director of the botanical gardens at Montpellier, France.

Malus
the classical Latin name of the apple; from the Greek *melon* "apple" or "fruit".

mariana
Latin form of "from Maryland". To Philip Miller, "Maryland" epitomized North America — hence *Picea mariana*, although Black Spruce does not grow in Maryland. (See Appendix "A".)

mas
Latin for male.

melanocarpa
Latin for black-fruited; from the Greek *melas* "black" and *karpos* "fruit".

menziesii
after Archibald Menzies (1754-1842), Scottish physician and naturalist who, in 1791, discovered Douglas-fir at Nootka Sound on Vancouver Island.

mertensiana
after Karl Heinrich Mertens (1796-1830), German naturalist and physician who discovered Mountain Hemlock at Sitka, Alaska.

mollis
Latin for soft.

monogyna
having a single ovary; from the Greek *monos* "single" and *gyne* "woman".

monticola
Latin for inhabiting mountains; from *montis* "mountain" and *colere* "to dwell".

Moraceae
Latin for the mulberry family.

Morus
the classical Latin name of the mulberry.

muehlenbergii (mühlenbergii)
after Gotthilf Henry Ernst Mühlenberg (1753-1815). (See Appendix "A".)

mughus (mugo)
of unknown origin.

n

negundo
the native name given to the Chaste Tree of India, also applied to the Manitoba Maple because of the similarity of the leaves.

neoalaskana
new Alaskan — referring to *Betula papyrifera* var. *neoalaskana* which Sargent originally named *Betula alascana*, a name that had already been allocated to a type of tree found in fossilized form.

nigra (nigrum)
Latin for black.

nitida
Latin for shiny, smooth and clear, lustrous or glittering.

nootkatensis
named for Nootka Sound, on Vancouver Island, British Columbia, where Yellow Cypress was first described.

nuttallii
after Thomas Nuttall (1784-1859), English-American botanist and ornithologist. (See Appendix "A".)

Nyssa
from Mount Nyssa in Asia Minor, the legendary home of the *naiads* or water nymphs who brought fruitfulness to plants, herbs and mortals.

o

occidentalis
Latin for western, of the Western Hemisphere; from *occidere* "to set", as with the sun.

Oleaster
Latin name of the wild olive tree.

oregona
Latin form of "from Oregon".

orientalis
Latin for eastern, of the Orient.

Ostrya
either from the Greek *ostrua*, a tree with very hard wood, or *ostruos* "a scale" — referring to the fruit.

ovalis (ovata)
Latin for egg-shaped or oval — referring to the leaves; from *ovum* "egg".

oxyacantha
with sharp thorns; from the Greek *oxys* "sharp" or "pointed", and *akantha* "thorn".

p

Padus
name given to a group of cherries; from the Greek *pados* "tree".

palmatum
Latin for "bearing the mark of a hand with the fingers spread".

palustris
Latin for "of marshes, swamps or wet places".

papyrifera
Latin for paper bearing, with a papery bark; from the Greek *papyros* "paper reed", and the Latin *ferre* "to bear".

parvifolia
Latin for small-leaved; from *parvis* "small" and *folium* "leaf".

pendula
Latin for hanging or drooping; from *pendere* "to hang".

pennsylvanica (pensylvanica) (pensylvanicum)
Latin forms of "from Pennsylvania". The one "n" commemorates an old spelling of the former colony.

pentandra
Latin for five-stamened; from the Greek *penta* "five" and *andron* "male".

persica
Latin for Persian.

petraea
Latin for rock-loving or belonging to rocks; from the Greek *petra* "rock".

phanerolepis
with visible scales — referring to the exposed bracts on the cones of Bracted Balsam Fir; from the Greek *phaneros* "visible" and *lepis* "scale" or "flake".

Picea
from the Latin *pix* "pitch" — referring to a pine; later applied to spruces as the genus name.

pinnatisecta
cut down to the mid-rib in a pattern like a feather; from the Latin *penna* "feather" and *sectare* "to cut".

pinsapo
old Spanish Andalusian word used by local farmers and meaning pine-fir, from *pino* "pine" and *sapino* "fir".

Pinus
the classical Latin name of the pine tree.

platanoides
resembling a plane tree; from the Greek *platus* "broad" and *öides* "appearing like".

Platanus
plane-tree; from the Greek *platus* "broad"—referring to the leaves.

plicata
Latin for folded — referring to the flattened twigs, with regularly arranged scale-like leaves, of Western Red Cedar.

pluribracteata
with several bracts — referring to the many floral leaves of Eastern Flowering Dogwood; from the Latin *pluribus* "many" and *bractea* "a thin metal plate or leaf".

pomifera
Latin for apple bearing — referring to the large ball-like fruits of the Osage-orange tree.

ponderosa
Latin for "of great weight", or imposing — referring to the massive appearance of Ponderosa Pine.

populifolia
with leaves like the poplar; from the Latin *populus* "poplar" and *folium* "leaf".

Populus
the classical Latin name of the poplars.

porsildii
after Alf Erling Porsild (1901-   ), noted Canadian botanist and public figure.

prinoides
with leaves resembling those of the Chestnut Oak; from the Greek *prinos* "the great scarlet oak" and *öides* "appearing like".

prinus
the classical Latin name of a European oak.

procera
Latin for tall or high.

prunifolia
with leaves like those of the plum tree; from the Latin *prunus* "plum tree" and *folium* "leaf".

Prunophora
a term applied to the plum family; from the Greek *prunos* "plum" and *phoros* "bearing".

Prunus
the classical Latin name of the plum tree; from the Greek *prunos* "plum".

pseudoacacia
Latin for False-acacia; from the Greek *pseudos* "falsehood" and *akakia* the Greek name for the Egyptian pod-thorn tree.

pseudoplatanus
Latin for false plane-tree.

Pseudotsuga
false hemlock; from the Greek *pseudos* "falsehood", and the Japanese *tsuga* "hemlock".

Ptelea
Greek for elm — given to the Hop-tree because of the similarity of their fruit.

pubens (pubescens)
downy, with soft, short hairs; from the Latin *pubes* "covered with soft hair" (when referring to plants) and *escens* "becoming".

pumila
Latin for dwarf, small or diminutive.

punctata
Latin for covered with dots — referring to the fruit of Dotted Hawthorn.

pungens
sharp-pointed — referring to the needles of Blue Spruce; from the Latin *pungere* "to prick".

purpurea
Latin for purple.

purshiana
after Frederick Pursh (1774-1820), German-American botanist. (See Appendix "A".)

q

quadrangulata
Latin for four-angled.

Quercus
the classical Latin name of the oaks; probably from the Celtic *quer* "fine" and *cuez* "a tree".

r

racemosa
Latin for full of clusters— usually referring to fruit or flowers.

radicans
taking root or rooting — referring to the habit of Poison-ivy which takes root as it grows over the ground; from the Latin *radix* "root".

regia
royal, magnificent or kingly; from the Latin *regis* "of the king".

resinifera
resin-bearing; from the Latin *resina* "resin" and *ferre* "to bear".

resinosa
Latin for full of resin.

Rhamnus
either from the Greek *rhamnos* "buckthorn", or from the Celtic *rham* "a tuft of branches".

rhombifolia
with rhombic leaves; from the Latin *rhombus* "rhombic" and *folium* "leaf".

Rhus
Latin for sumac; from the classical Greek *rhous* which is apparently from the Celtic *rhudd* "red".

rigida
Latin for rigid, or stiff — referring to the cone-scales of Pitch Pine.

Robinia
after Jean Robin (1550-1629) and his son Vespasien Robin (1579-1662), herbalists to Henri IV of France, who first cultivated the locust tree in Europe.

robur
Latin for hard tree or hard wood — applied specifically to the oak.

rosaceae
a term applied to the rose family; from the Latin *rosa* "a rose".

rubens
Latin for reddish — referring to the reddish-brown cones of Red Spruce.

rubra (rubrum)
Latin for red.

rugosa
Latin for wrinkled.

rutaceae
a term applied to the rue family; from the Latin *rutaceus* "of the rue".

S

saccharinum (saccharum)
sweet or sugary — referring to the sap; from the Sanskrit *sarkarà* "grit" or "sugar", through the Greek *sakcharon*, the sweet liquid obtained from bamboo joints.

Salix
the classical Latin name of the willows; probably from the Celtic *sal* "near" and *lis* "water".

Sambucus
the classical Latin name of the elder; from the Greek *sambuke,* an ancient musical instrument — referring to the bark of the elder which can easily be removed in tubes to make a flute or whistle.

sanguinea
Latin for bloody.

sargentii
after Charles Sprague Sargent (1841-1927). (See Appendix "A".)

Sassafras
the name presumed to have been given by early Spanish explorers to this North American tree.

sativa
Latin for sown or planted.

saximontana
from the Rocky Mountains; from the Latin *saxeus* "rocky" and *montis* "mountain".

scopulina
shrubby or broom-like; from the Latin *scopula* "little broom" and *ina* "resembling".

scopulorum
Latin for "of rocky cliffs or crags" — referring to the habitat of Rocky Mountain Juniper.

scouleriana
after John Scouler (1804-1871), Scottish naturalist and physician who made collections of plants on the northwest coast of North America.

serotina
Latin for late — referring to the late maturing fruit of Black Cherry.

shastensis
Latin form of "from Mount Shasta" or Shasta County in California.

sibirica
Latin form of Siberian.

sieboldiana
after Philipp F. von Siebold (1796-1866), who introduced the Japanese Walnut to Europe in 1860. (See Appendix "A".)

sinuata
wavy margined — referring to the leaves of Sitka Alder; from the Latin *sinuare* "to bend" or "to wave".

sitchensis
Latin form of "from Sitka Sound" in south-eastern Alaska, where Sitka Spruce was first described.

Sorbus
the classical Latin name of the mountain-ash.

spicatum
Latin for provided with spikes, spike-like.

spinosa
Latin for thorny or prickly.

stolonifera
with runners that take root; from the Latin *stolo* "a shoot" and *ferre* "to bear".

strobus
the ancient name of an incense-bearing pine; related to the Latin *strobilus* "pine cone", and the Greek *strobos* "whirling around".

subcordata
slightly heart-shaped; from the Latin *sub* "under" or "less than" and *cordis* "of the heart".

subintegerrima
with an almost even margin; from the Latin *sub* "under" or "less than" and *integer* "complete".

submollis
partly covered with soft hairs; from the Latin *sub* "under" or "less than" and *mollis* "soft".

sylvatica
of the woods or trees; from the Latin *sylva* "a forest".

sylvestris
Latin for "of the forest".

t

Taxus
the classical Latin name of the yew.

tenuifolia
thin-leaved; from the Latin *tenuo* "to make thin" and *folium* "leaf".

thomasii
after David Thomas (1776-1859), American civil engineer and horticulturist who first named Rock Elm.

Thuja (Thuya)
a form of *thya,* the Latin name for an aromatic tree; from the Greek *thuia* an aromatic cedar.

Tilia
the classical Latin name of the Linden or Lime tree.

tomentosa
covered with woolly hairs; from the Latin *tomentum* "of wool" and *osus* "full of".

tremuloides
having a tendency to tremble; from the Latin

tremulus "trembling" and the Greek *öides* "appearing like".

triacanthos
three-thorned; from the Greek *treis* "three" and *akantha* "a spine".

trichocarpa
hairy fruited; from the Greek *thrix* "a hair" and *karpos* "fruit".

tridens
with three lobes; from the Latin *tres* "three" and *dens* "tooth".

trifoliata
three-leaved; from the Latin *tres* "three" and *folium* "leaf".

triloba
three-lobed; from the Greek *treis* "three" and *lobos* "lobe".

Tsuga
hemlock; from the Japanese name for the native hemlocks of Japan.

tulipifera
tulip-bearing; from the Turkish *tulbend* "a turban", and the Latin *ferre* "to bear".

typhina
like the cattail *(typha);* from the Greek *typhe* "reed mace" and the suffix *ina* "resembling".

u

Ulmus
the classical Latin name of the elms.

v

velutina
velvet-like — referring to the young leaves of the Black Oak; from the Latin *vellus* "a fleece" and *ina* "resembling".

vernix
Latin for varnish — so named because Poison Sumac was mistakenly thought to be the same tree from which Japanese lacquer is obtained.

Viburnum
the classical Latin name of the Wayfaring tree of Eurasia.

virginiana
Latin form of Virginian.

vitellina
like an egg yolk — referring to the colour; from the Latin *vitellus* "egg yolk" and *ina* "resembling".

x

xanthocarpa
with yellow fruit; from the Greek *xanthos* "yellow" and *karpos* "fruit".

z

Zanthoxylum
yellow wood; from the Greek *xanthos* "yellow" and *xylon* "wood".

APPENDIX C

For many readers, interest in the native trees of Canada will extend beyond identification of the species and their general characteristics. To assist those who wish to pursue their studies and those whose natural curiosity leads them further afield, a modest bibliography of interesting references is offered. The list which follows does not pretend to be comprehensive. The titles have been selected with the intention of providing a starting point for every taste. Included is history, fantasy, even poetry, and for the culinary-minded a recipe book. Some of the older publications may not be readily available, but second-hand bookshops may harbour these and other hidden treasures which the tree-lover can profitably explore. All books listed can be borrowed through local library services.

A FIELD GUIDE TO TREES AND SHRUBS
George A. Petrides. 1958. One of the Peterson Field Guide Series. Houghton Mifflin Company, Boston, Massachusetts, U.S.A. 431 pages.

*A GLOSSARY OF BOTANIC TERMS
B. D. Jackson. Fourth Edition, 1928. Gerald Duckworth and Co. Ltd., 3 Henrietta Street, London W.C.2, England. 481 pages.

A NATURAL HISTORY OF TREES OF EASTERN AND CENTRAL NORTH AMERICA
Donald Culross Peattie. 1950. Houghton Mifflin Company, Boston, Massachusetts, U.S.A. 606 pages.

A NATURAL HISTORY OF WESTERN TREES
Donald Culross Peattie. 1953. Houghton Mifflin Company, Boston, Massachusetts, U.S.A. 751 pages.

*BOTANICAL LATIN
William T. Stearn. 1966. Thomas Nelson and Sons (Canada) Ltd., 81 Curlew Drive, Don Mills, Ontario. 566 pages.

CHECK LIST OF NATIVE AND NATURALIZED TREES OF THE UNITED STATES (INCLUDING ALASKA)
Elbert L. Little, Jr. 1953. United States Forest Service, Tree and Range Plant Name Committee, U.S. Department of Agriculture, Washington, D.C., U.S.A. Agriculture Handbook No. 41. Available from the Superintendent of Documents, U.S. Government Printing Office, Washington 25, D.C., U.S.A. 472 pages.

CONE BEARING TREES OF THE PACIFIC COAST
Nathan A. Bowers. 1965. Pacific Books, Palo Alto, California, U.S.A. 169 pages.

CULTURE OF ORNAMENTAL TREES FOR CANADIAN GARDENS
R. W. Oliver. 1965. Central Experimental Farm, Canada Department of Agriculture, Ottawa. Publication No. 994. Available from the Information Division, Canada Department of Agriculture, Ottawa, Ontario. 30 pages.

*See footnote on page 335.

DOUGLAS OF THE FIR

A. G. Harvey. 1947. Harvard University Press, Cambridge, Massachusetts, U.S.A. 290 pages.

FANTASTIC TREES

Edwin A. Menninger. 1967. The MacMillan Company of Canada Ltd., 70 Bond Street, Toronto 2, Ontario. 304 pages.

FIFTY TREES OF CANADA EAST OF THE ROCKIES

J. L. Van Camp and T. E. Shaw. 1952. Canadian Forestry Association. Available from The Book Society of Canada Ltd., Agincourt, Ontario. 64 pages.

FOREST REGIONS OF CANADA

J. S. Rowe. 1959. Forestry Branch, Department of Northern Affairs and National Resources, Ottawa, Ontario. Bulletin No. 123. Available from the Queen's Printer's Bookshops. 71 pages.

FOREST TREES

Rev. Joseph H. Hilts. 1888. William Briggs, 78 King Street East, Toronto, Ontario. 380 pages.

FOREST TREES OF THE PACIFIC SLOPE

George B. Sudworth. 1908. Forest Service, U.S. Department of Agriculture, Washington, D.C., U.S.A. Available from the Superintendent of Documents, U.S. Government Printing Office, Washington 25, D.C., U.S.A. 441 pages.

GRAY'S MANUAL OF BOTANY

M. L. Fernald. 1950. American Book Company, New York, New York, U.S.A. (Eighth Edition). 1632 pages.

GROWING YOUR TREES

Wilbur H. Youngman and Charles E. Randall. 1967. The American Forestry Association, Washington, D.C., U.S.A. 72 pages.

GUIDE TO SOUTHERN TREES

Ellwood S. Harrar and J. George Harrar. 1962. Dover Publications Inc., 180 Varick Street, New York 14, New York, U.S.A. 709 pages.

HARDWOOD TREES OF ONTARIO WITH BARK CHARACTERISTICS

E. J. Zavitz. 1959. Ontario Department of Lands and Forests, Province of Ontario, Parliament Buildings, Toronto, Ontario. 60 pages.

HARVEST WITHOUT PLANTING

Erika E. Gaertner. 1967. Donald F. Runge Ltd., 243 Pembroke Street West, Pembroke, Ontario. 65 pages.

IDENTIFICATION OF NOVA SCOTIA WOODY PLANTS IN WINTER

James F. Donly. 1960. Department of Lands and Forests, Province of Nova Scotia, Province House, Halifax, Nova Scotia. Bulletin No. 19. 56 pages.

I LIVE IN THE WOODS

Paul Provencher. 1953. Brunswick Press Ltd., Phoenix Square, Fredericton, New Brunswick. 188 pages.

ILLUSTRATED FOREST ACTIVITIES, NO. 4. THE PRINCIPAL COMMERCIAL TREES OF BRITISH COLUMBIA

Available from the Public Information and Education Division, British Columbia Forest Service, Department of Lands, Forests and

Water Resources, Province of British Columbia, Parliament Buildings, Victoria, British Columbia. 11 pages.

JOHN AND WILLIAM BARTRAM
Ernest Earnest. 1940. University of Pennsylvania Press, Philadelphia, Pennsylvania, U.S.A. 187 pages.

KNOWING YOUR TREES
G. H. Collingwood and Warren D. Brush. 1964. The American Forestry Association, Washington, D.C., U.S.A. 328 pages.

MANUAL OF CULTIVATED TREES AND SHRUBS HARDY IN NORTH AMERICA, EXCLUSIVE OF THE SUBTROPICAL AND WARMER TEMPERATE REGIONS
Alfred Rehder. 1940. The MacMillan Company, New York, New York, U.S.A. (Second Edition). 930 pages.

MANUAL OF THE TREES OF NORTH AMERICA. 2 VOLS.
Charles Sprague Sargent. 1949. Dover Publications Inc., 180 Varick Street, New York 14, New York, U.S.A. 910 pages.

NORTH AMERICAN TREES
Richard J. Preston, Jr. 1966. The M.I.T. Press, Massachusetts Institute of Technology, Cambridge, Massachusetts, U.S.A. 395 pages.

*PAXTON'S BOTANICAL DICTIONARY
Edited by Samuel Hereman. 1868. Bradbury, Evans & Co., Bouverie Street, London E.C.1, England. 623 pages.

PLANT LIFE THROUGH THE AGES
A. C. Seward. 1959. Hafner Publishing Co. Inc., 31 East 10th Street, New York 3, New York, U.S.A. 603 pages.

*PLANT NAMES SIMPLIFIED, THEIR PRONUNCIATION, DERIVATION AND MEANING
A. T. Johnson and H. A. Smith. 1951. W. H. & L. Collingridge Ltd., 2-10 Tavistock Street, London W.C.2, England. 120 pages.

POCKET GUIDE TO TREES AND SHRUBS IN BRITISH COLUMBIA
Revised by E. H. Garman, 1963. British Columbia Forest Service, Department of Lands, Forests and Water Resources, Province of British Columbia, Parliament Buildings, Victoria, British Columbia. 137 pages.

SAGAS OF THE EVERGREENS
Frank H. Lamb. 1938. W. W. Norton and Company Inc., 70 Fifth Avenue, New York, New York, U.S.A. 364 pages.

SILVICS OF FOREST TREES OF THE UNITED STATES
Compiled and revised by H. A. Fowells. 1965. United States Forest Service, Division of Timber Management Research, U.S. Department of Agriculture, Washington, D.C., U.S.A. Agriculture Handbook No. 271. Available from the Superintendent of Documents, U.S. Government Printing Office, Washington 25, D.C., U.S.A. 762 pages.

*See footnote on page 335.

SUMMER KEY TO THE WOODY PLANTS OF NOVA SCOTIA
A. E. Roland and D. A. Benson. 1955. Department of Lands and Forests, Province of Nova Scotia, Province House, Halifax, Nova Scotia. Bulletin No. 16. 42 pages.

TEXTBOOK OF DENDROLOGY COVERING THE IMPORTANT FOREST TREES OF THE UNITED STATES AND CANADA
William M. Harlow and Ellwood S. Harrar. 1968. One of the American Forestry Series. McGraw-Hill Book Co. Inc., Toronto, Ontario. 555 pages.

THE BOOK OF TREES
W. C. Grimm. 1962. The Stackpole Company, Harrisburg, Pennsylvania, U.S.A. 493 pages.

THE BOTANICAL COLLECTOR'S GUIDE
D. P. Penhallow. 1891. E. M. Renouf, Montreal. 125 pages.

THE FOREST TREES OF ONTARIO AND THE MORE COMMONLY PLANTED FOREIGN TREES
J. H. White. Revised by R. C. Hosie. 1968. Division of Reforestation, Ontario Department of Lands and Forests, Toronto, Ontario. (Fourth Edition). Available from the Ontario Department of Lands and Forests, Parliament Buildings, Toronto 5, Ontario. 119 pages.

THE GREAT AMERICAN FOREST
Rutherford Platt. 1965. Prentice-Hall, Inc., Englewood Cliffs, New Jersey, U.S.A. 271 pages.

THE HUMAN SIDE OF TREES
Royal Dixon and Franklyn E. Fitch. 1917. Frederick A. Stokes Co., New York, New York, U.S.A. 199 pages.

THE MESSAGE OF THE TREES
Maud Cuney Hare. 1918. The Cornhill Company, Boston, Massachusetts, U.S.A. 190 pages.

THE PICTORIAL ENCYCLOPAEDIA OF PLANTS AND FLOWERS
F. A. Novak. 1966. Crown Publishers Inc., New York, New York, U.S.A. 589 pages.

THE TREE IDENTIFICATION BOOK
George W. D. Symonds. 1958. George J. McLeod Ltd., Toronto, Ontario. 268 pages.

TREE ANCESTORS
Edward Wilber Berry. 1923. Williams and Wilkins Company, Baltimore, Maryland, U.S.A. 272 pages.

TREES AND SHRUBS OF ALBERTA
R. G. H. Cormack. Department of Lands and Forests, Province of Alberta, Legislative Buildings, Edmonton, Alberta. 76 pages.

TREES FOR ORNAMENTAL PLANTING
R. W. Oliver. 1965. Central Experimental Farm, Canada Department of Agriculture, Ottawa. Publication No. 995. Available from the Information Division, Canada Department of Agriculture, Ottawa, Ontario. 31 pages.

TREES OF THE EASTERN AND CENTRAL UNITED STATES AND CANADA
William M. Harlow. 1957. Dover Publications Inc., 180 Varick Street, New York 14, New York, U.S.A. 288 pages.

APPENDIX D

The Keys to the Trees

KEY TO THE CONIFERS

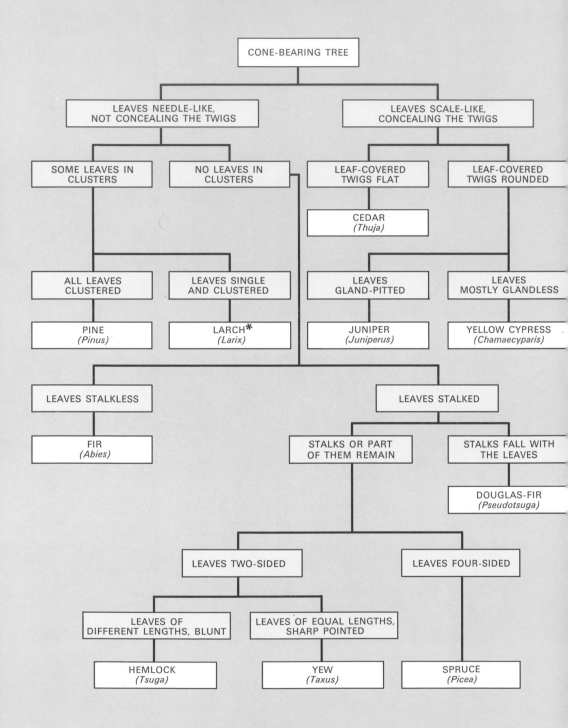

CONE-BEARING TREE

LEAVES NEEDLE-LIKE, NOT CONCEALING THE TWIGS

LEAVES SCALE-LIKE, CONCEALING THE TWIGS

SOME LEAVES IN CLUSTERS

NO LEAVES IN CLUSTERS

LEAF-COVERED TWIGS FLAT

LEAF-COVERED TWIGS ROUNDED

CEDAR
(Thuja)

ALL LEAVES CLUSTERED

LEAVES SINGLE AND CLUSTERED

LEAVES GLAND-PITTED

LEAVES MOSTLY GLANDLESS

PINE
(Pinus)

LARCH*
(Larix)

JUNIPER
(Juniperus)

YELLOW CYPRESS
(Chamaecyparis)

LEAVES STALKLESS

LEAVES STALKED

FIR
(Abies)

STALKS OR PART OF THEM REMAIN

STALKS FALL WITH THE LEAVES

DOUGLAS-FIR
(Pseudotsuga)

LEAVES TWO-SIDED

LEAVES FOUR-SIDED

LEAVES OF DIFFERENT LENGTHS, BLUNT

LEAVES OF EQUAL LENGTHS, SHARP POINTED

HEMLOCK
(Tsuga)

YEW
(Taxus)

SPRUCE
(Picea)

*LARCH IS LEAFLESS IN WINTER, BUT CAN BE RECOGNIZED THEN BY THE SPUR-LIKE DWARF BRANCHLETS ALONG THE BRANCHES, AND INNER BARK THAT IS A VIVID REDDISH-PURPLE.

KEY TO THE PINES

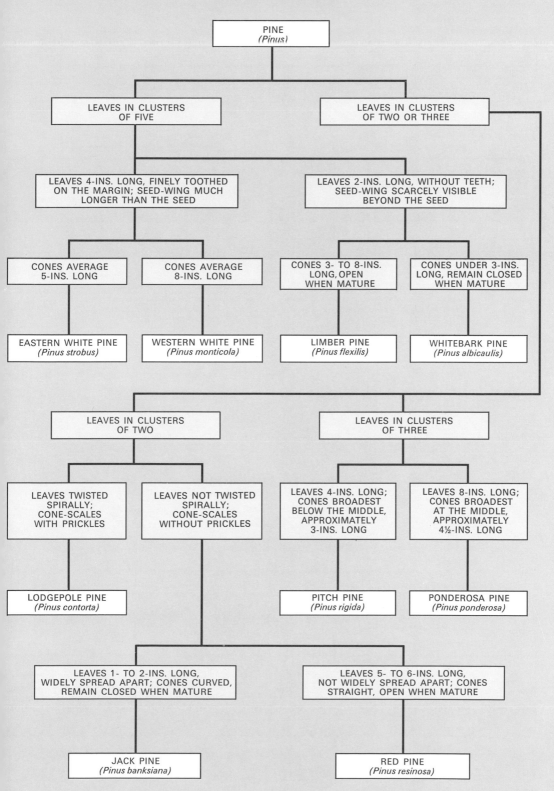

PINE
(Pinus)

LEAVES IN CLUSTERS OF FIVE

LEAVES IN CLUSTERS OF TWO OR THREE

LEAVES 4-INS. LONG, FINELY TOOTHED ON THE MARGIN; SEED-WING MUCH LONGER THAN THE SEED

LEAVES 2-INS. LONG, WITHOUT TEETH; SEED-WING SCARCELY VISIBLE BEYOND THE SEED

CONES AVERAGE 5-INS. LONG

CONES AVERAGE 8-INS. LONG

CONES 3- TO 8-INS. LONG, OPEN WHEN MATURE

CONES UNDER 3-INS. LONG, REMAIN CLOSED WHEN MATURE

EASTERN WHITE PINE
(Pinus strobus)

WESTERN WHITE PINE
(Pinus monticola)

LIMBER PINE
(Pinus flexilis)

WHITEBARK PINE
(Pinus albicaulis)

LEAVES IN CLUSTERS OF TWO

LEAVES IN CLUSTERS OF THREE

LEAVES TWISTED SPIRALLY; CONE-SCALES WITH PRICKLES

LEAVES NOT TWISTED SPIRALLY; CONE-SCALES WITHOUT PRICKLES

LEAVES 4-INS. LONG; CONES BROADEST BELOW THE MIDDLE, APPROXIMATELY 3-INS. LONG

LEAVES 8-INS. LONG; CONES BROADEST AT THE MIDDLE, APPROXIMATELY 4½-INS. LONG

LODGEPOLE PINE
(Pinus contorta)

PITCH PINE
(Pinus rigida)

PONDEROSA PINE
(Pinus ponderosa)

LEAVES 1- TO 2-INS. LONG, WIDELY SPREAD APART; CONES CURVED, REMAIN CLOSED WHEN MATURE

LEAVES 5- TO 6-INS. LONG, NOT WIDELY SPREAD APART; CONES STRAIGHT, OPEN WHEN MATURE

JACK PINE
(Pinus banksiana)

RED PINE
(Pinus resinosa)

KEY TO THE SPRUCES

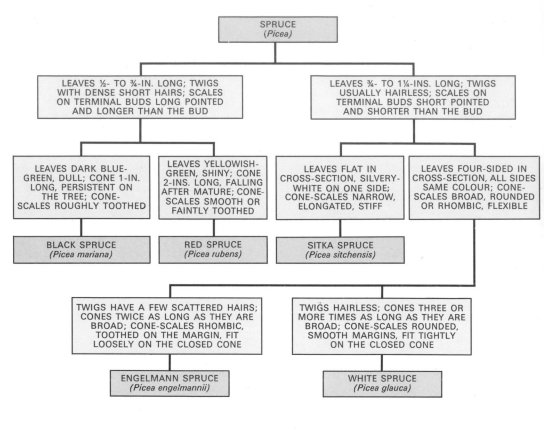

SPRUCE
(*Picea*)

LEAVES ½- TO ¾-IN. LONG; TWIGS WITH DENSE SHORT HAIRS; SCALES ON TERMINAL BUDS LONG POINTED AND LONGER THAN THE BUD

LEAVES ¾- TO 1¼-INS. LONG; TWIGS USUALLY HAIRLESS; SCALES ON TERMINAL BUDS SHORT POINTED AND SHORTER THAN THE BUD

LEAVES DARK BLUE-GREEN, DULL; CONE 1-IN. LONG, PERSISTENT ON THE TREE; CONE-SCALES ROUGHLY TOOTHED

LEAVES YELLOWISH-GREEN, SHINY; CONE 2-INS. LONG, FALLING AFTER MATURE; CONE-SCALES SMOOTH OR FAINTLY TOOTHED

LEAVES FLAT IN CROSS-SECTION, SILVERY-WHITE ON ONE SIDE; CONE-SCALES NARROW, ELONGATED, STIFF

LEAVES FOUR-SIDED IN CROSS-SECTION, ALL SIDES SAME COLOUR; CONE-SCALES BROAD, ROUNDED OR RHOMBIC, FLEXIBLE

BLACK SPRUCE
(*Picea mariana*)

RED SPRUCE
(*Picea rubens*)

SITKA SPRUCE
(*Picea sitchensis*)

TWIGS HAVE A FEW SCATTERED HAIRS; CONES TWICE AS LONG AS THEY ARE BROAD; CONE-SCALES RHOMBIC, TOOTHED ON THE MARGIN, FIT LOOSELY ON THE CLOSED CONE

TWIGS HAIRLESS; CONES THREE OR MORE TIMES AS LONG AS THEY ARE BROAD; CONE-SCALES ROUNDED, SMOOTH MARGINS, FIT TIGHTLY ON THE CLOSED CONE

ENGELMANN SPRUCE
(*Picea engelmannii*)

WHITE SPRUCE
(*Picea glauca*)

KEY TO THE FIRS

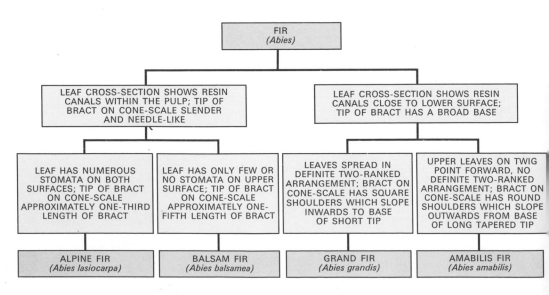

FIR
(*Abies*)

LEAF CROSS-SECTION SHOWS RESIN CANALS WITHIN THE PULP; TIP OF BRACT ON CONE-SCALE SLENDER AND NEEDLE-LIKE

LEAF CROSS-SECTION SHOWS RESIN CANALS CLOSE TO LOWER SURFACE; TIP OF BRACT HAS A BROAD BASE

LEAF HAS NUMEROUS STOMATA ON BOTH SURFACES; TIP OF BRACT ON CONE-SCALE APPROXIMATELY ONE-THIRD LENGTH OF BRACT

LEAF HAS ONLY FEW OR NO STOMATA ON UPPER SURFACE; TIP OF BRACT ON CONE-SCALE APPROXIMATELY ONE-FIFTH LENGTH OF BRACT

LEAVES SPREAD IN DEFINITE TWO-RANKED ARRANGEMENT; BRACT ON CONE-SCALE HAS SQUARE SHOULDERS WHICH SLOPE INWARDS TO BASE OF SHORT TIP

UPPER LEAVES ON TWIG POINT FORWARD, NO DEFINITE TWO-RANKED ARRANGEMENT; BRACT ON CONE-SCALE HAS ROUND SHOULDERS WHICH SLOPE OUTWARDS FROM BASE OF LONG TAPERED TIP

ALPINE FIR
(*Abies lasiocarpa*)

BALSAM FIR
(*Abies balsamea*)

GRAND FIR
(*Abies grandis*)

AMABILIS FIR
(*Abies amabilis*)

DECIDUOUS TREES
SUMMER KEY NUMBER ONE

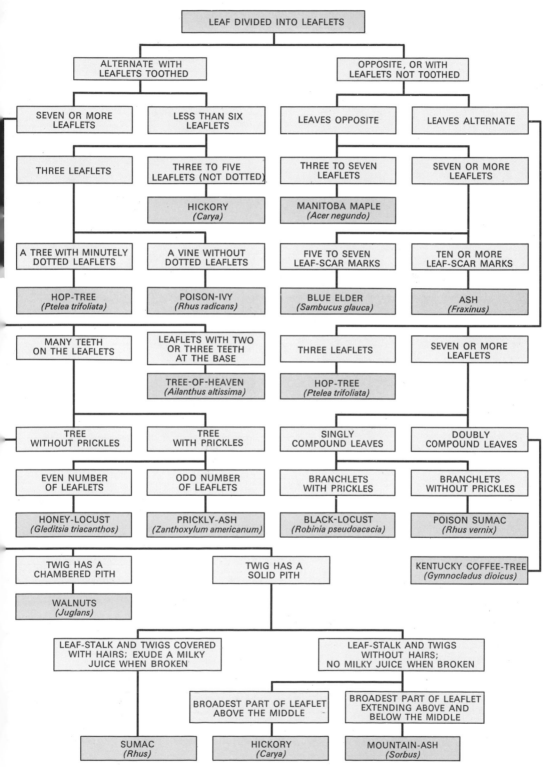

LEAF DIVIDED INTO LEAFLETS

ALTERNATE WITH LEAFLETS TOOTHED

OPPOSITE, OR WITH LEAFLETS NOT TOOTHED

SEVEN OR MORE LEAFLETS

LESS THAN SIX LEAFLETS

LEAVES OPPOSITE

LEAVES ALTERNATE

THREE LEAFLETS

THREE TO FIVE LEAFLETS (NOT DOTTED)

THREE TO SEVEN LEAFLETS

SEVEN OR MORE LEAFLETS

HICKORY
(Carya)

MANITOBA MAPLE
(Acer negundo)

A TREE WITH MINUTELY DOTTED LEAFLETS

A VINE WITHOUT DOTTED LEAFLETS

FIVE TO SEVEN LEAF-SCAR MARKS

TEN OR MORE LEAF-SCAR MARKS

HOP-TREE
(Ptelea trifoliata)

POISON-IVY
(Rhus radicans)

BLUE ELDER
(Sambucus glauca)

ASH
(Fraxinus)

MANY TEETH ON THE LEAFLETS

LEAFLETS WITH TWO OR THREE TEETH AT THE BASE

THREE LEAFLETS

SEVEN OR MORE LEAFLETS

TREE-OF-HEAVEN
(Ailanthus altissima)

HOP-TREE
(Ptelea trifoliata)

TREE WITHOUT PRICKLES

TREE WITH PRICKLES

SINGLY COMPOUND LEAVES

DOUBLY COMPOUND LEAVES

EVEN NUMBER OF LEAFLETS

ODD NUMBER OF LEAFLETS

BRANCHLETS WITH PRICKLES

BRANCHLETS WITHOUT PRICKLES

HONEY-LOCUST
(Gleditsia triacanthos)

PRICKLY-ASH
(Zanthoxylum americanum)

BLACK-LOCUST
(Robinia pseudoacacia)

POISON SUMAC
(Rhus vernix)

TWIG HAS A CHAMBERED PITH

TWIG HAS A SOLID PITH

KENTUCKY COFFEE-TREE
(Gymnocladus dioicus)

WALNUTS
(Juglans)

LEAF-STALK AND TWIGS COVERED WITH HAIRS; EXUDE A MILKY JUICE WHEN BROKEN

LEAF-STALK AND TWIGS WITHOUT HAIRS; NO MILKY JUICE WHEN BROKEN

BROADEST PART OF LEAFLET ABOVE THE MIDDLE

BROADEST PART OF LEAFLET EXTENDING ABOVE AND BELOW THE MIDDLE

SUMAC
(Rhus)

HICKORY
(Carya)

MOUNTAIN-ASH
(Sorbus)

DECIDUOUS TREES
SUMMER KEY NUMBER TWO

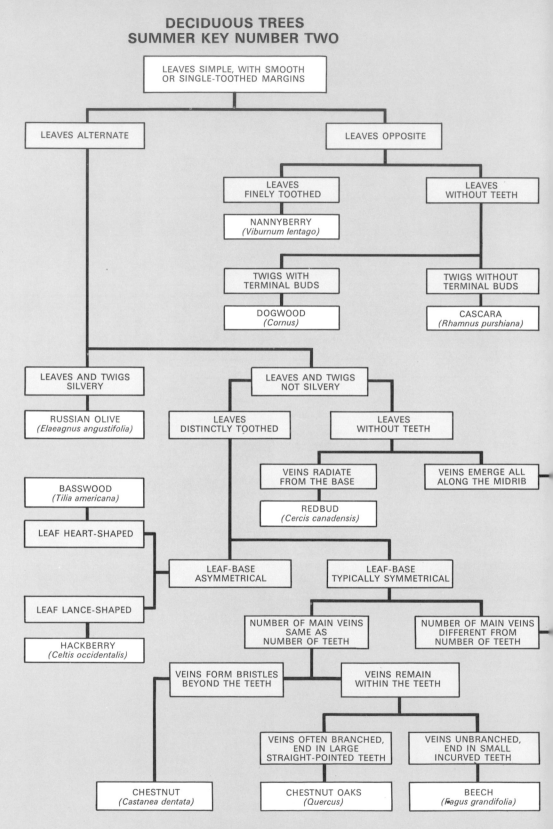

LEAVES SIMPLE, WITH SMOOTH OR SINGLE-TOOTHED MARGINS

LEAVES ALTERNATE

LEAVES OPPOSITE

LEAVES FINELY TOOTHED

LEAVES WITHOUT TEETH

NANNYBERRY
(Viburnum lentago)

TWIGS WITH TERMINAL BUDS

TWIGS WITHOUT TERMINAL BUDS

DOGWOOD
(Cornus)

CASCARA
(Rhamnus purshiana)

LEAVES AND TWIGS SILVERY

LEAVES AND TWIGS NOT SILVERY

RUSSIAN OLIVE
(Elaeagnus angustifolia)

LEAVES DISTINCTLY TOOTHED

LEAVES WITHOUT TEETH

VEINS RADIATE FROM THE BASE

VEINS EMERGE ALL ALONG THE MIDRIB

BASSWOOD
(Tilia americana)

REDBUD
(Cercis canadensis)

LEAF HEART-SHAPED

LEAF-BASE ASYMMETRICAL

LEAF-BASE TYPICALLY SYMMETRICAL

LEAF LANCE-SHAPED

NUMBER OF MAIN VEINS SAME AS NUMBER OF TEETH

NUMBER OF MAIN VEINS DIFFERENT FROM NUMBER OF TEETH

HACKBERRY
(Celtis occidentalis)

VEINS FORM BRISTLES BEYOND THE TEETH

VEINS REMAIN WITHIN THE TEETH

VEINS OFTEN BRANCHED, END IN LARGE STRAIGHT-POINTED TEETH

VEINS UNBRANCHED, END IN SMALL INCURVED TEETH

CHESTNUT
(Castanea dentata)

CHESTNUT OAKS
(Quercus)

BEECH
(Fagus grandifolia)

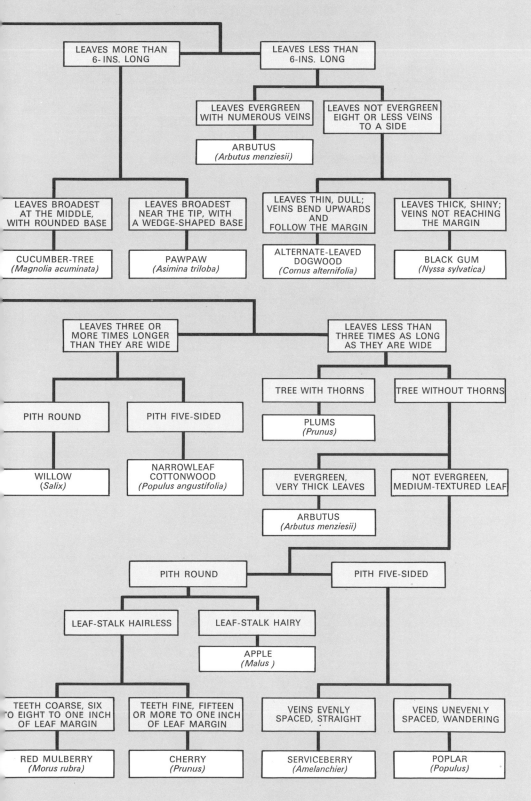

LEAVES MORE THAN 6-INS. LONG

LEAVES LESS THAN 6-INS. LONG

LEAVES EVERGREEN WITH NUMEROUS VEINS

ARBUTUS
(Arbutus menziesii)

LEAVES NOT EVERGREEN EIGHT OR LESS VEINS TO A SIDE

LEAVES BROADEST AT THE MIDDLE, WITH ROUNDED BASE

CUCUMBER-TREE
(Magnolia acuminata)

LEAVES BROADEST NEAR THE TIP, WITH A WEDGE-SHAPED BASE

PAWPAW
(Asimina triloba)

LEAVES THIN, DULL; VEINS BEND UPWARDS AND FOLLOW THE MARGIN

ALTERNATE-LEAVED DOGWOOD
(Cornus alternifolia)

LEAVES THICK, SHINY; VEINS NOT REACHING THE MARGIN

BLACK GUM
(Nyssa sylvatica)

LEAVES THREE OR MORE TIMES LONGER THAN THEY ARE WIDE

LEAVES LESS THAN THREE TIMES AS LONG AS THEY ARE WIDE

PITH ROUND

PITH FIVE-SIDED

TREE WITH THORNS

PLUMS
(Prunus)

TREE WITHOUT THORNS

WILLOW
(Salix)

NARROWLEAF COTTONWOOD
(Populus angustifolia)

EVERGREEN, VERY THICK LEAVES

ARBUTUS
(Arbutus menziesii)

NOT EVERGREEN, MEDIUM-TEXTURED LEAF

PITH ROUND

PITH FIVE-SIDED

LEAF-STALK HAIRLESS

LEAF-STALK HAIRY

APPLE
(Malus)

TEETH COARSE, SIX TO EIGHT TO ONE INCH OF LEAF MARGIN

RED MULBERRY
(Morus rubra)

TEETH FINE, FIFTEEN OR MORE TO ONE INCH OF LEAF MARGIN

CHERRY
(Prunus)

VEINS EVENLY SPACED, STRAIGHT

SERVICEBERRY
(Amelanchier)

VEINS UNEVENLY SPACED, WANDERING

POPLAR
(Populus)

353

DECIDUOUS TREES
SUMMER KEY NUMBER THREE

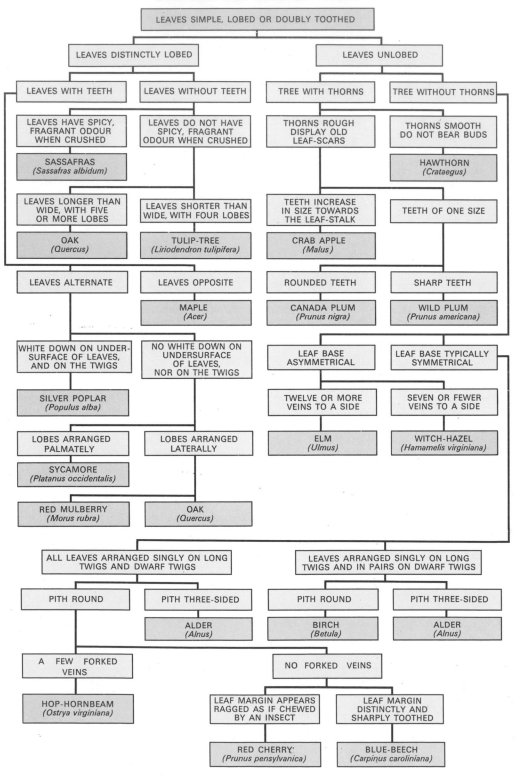

LEAVES SIMPLE, LOBED OR DOUBLY TOOTHED

LEAVES DISTINCTLY LOBED

LEAVES UNLOBED

LEAVES WITH TEETH

LEAVES WITHOUT TEETH

TREE WITH THORNS

TREE WITHOUT THORNS

LEAVES HAVE SPICY, FRAGRANT ODOUR WHEN CRUSHED

LEAVES DO NOT HAVE SPICY, FRAGRANT ODOUR WHEN CRUSHED

THORNS ROUGH DISPLAY OLD LEAF-SCARS

THORNS SMOOTH DO NOT BEAR BUDS

SASSAFRAS
(Sassafras albidum)

HAWTHORN
(Crataegus)

LEAVES LONGER THAN WIDE, WITH FIVE OR MORE LOBES

LEAVES SHORTER THAN WIDE, WITH FOUR LOBES

TEETH INCREASE IN SIZE TOWARDS THE LEAF-STALK

TEETH OF ONE SIZE

OAK
(Quercus)

TULIP-TREE
(Liriodendron tulipifera)

CRAB APPLE
(Malus)

LEAVES ALTERNATE

LEAVES OPPOSITE

ROUNDED TEETH

SHARP TEETH

MAPLE
(Acer)

CANADA PLUM
(Prunus nigra)

WILD PLUM
(Prunus americana)

WHITE DOWN ON UNDER-SURFACE OF LEAVES, AND ON THE TWIGS

NO WHITE DOWN ON UNDERSURFACE OF LEAVES, NOR ON THE TWIGS

LEAF BASE ASYMMETRICAL

LEAF BASE TYPICALLY SYMMETRICAL

SILVER POPLAR
(Populus alba)

TWELVE OR MORE VEINS TO A SIDE

SEVEN OR FEWER VEINS TO A SIDE

LOBES ARRANGED PALMATELY

LOBES ARRANGED LATERALLY

ELM
(Ulmus)

WITCH-HAZEL
(Hamamelis virginiana)

SYCAMORE
(Platanus occidentalis)

RED MULBERRY
(Morus rubra)

OAK
(Quercus)

ALL LEAVES ARRANGED SINGLY ON LONG TWIGS AND DWARF TWIGS

LEAVES ARRANGED SINGLY ON LONG TWIGS AND IN PAIRS ON DWARF TWIGS

PITH ROUND

PITH THREE-SIDED

PITH ROUND

PITH THREE-SIDED

ALDER
(Alnus)

BIRCH
(Betula)

ALDER
(Alnus)

A FEW FORKED VEINS

NO FORKED VEINS

HOP-HORNBEAM
(Ostrya virginiana)

LEAF MARGIN APPEARS RAGGED AS IF CHEWED BY AN INSECT

LEAF MARGIN DISTINCTLY AND SHARPLY TOOTHED

RED CHERRY
(Prunus pensylvanica)

BLUE-BEECH
(Carpinus caroliniana)

DECIDUOUS TREES
WINTER KEY NUMBER ONE

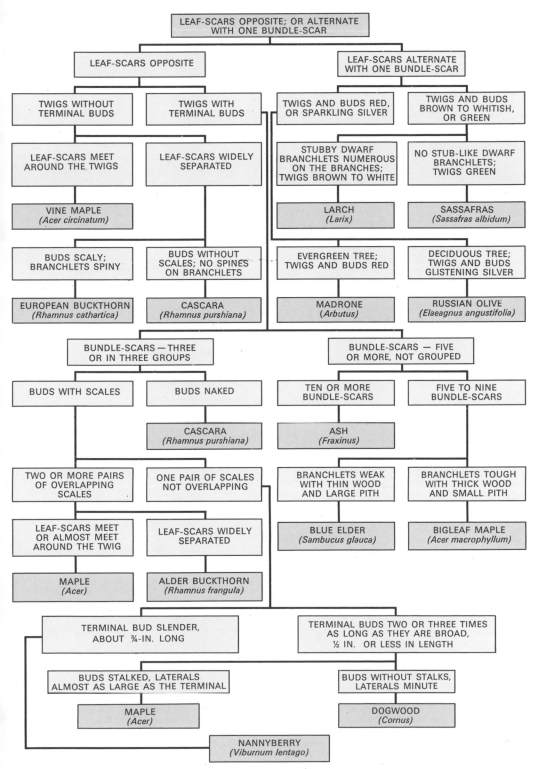

LEAF-SCARS OPPOSITE; OR ALTERNATE WITH ONE BUNDLE-SCAR

LEAF-SCARS OPPOSITE

LEAF-SCARS ALTERNATE WITH ONE BUNDLE-SCAR

TWIGS WITHOUT TERMINAL BUDS

TWIGS WITH TERMINAL BUDS

TWIGS AND BUDS RED, OR SPARKLING SILVER

TWIGS AND BUDS BROWN TO WHITISH, OR GREEN

LEAF-SCARS MEET AROUND THE TWIGS

LEAF-SCARS WIDELY SEPARATED

STUBBY DWARF BRANCHLETS NUMEROUS ON THE BRANCHES; TWIGS BROWN TO WHITE

NO STUB-LIKE DWARF BRANCHLETS; TWIGS GREEN

VINE MAPLE
(Acer circinatum)

LARCH
(Larix)

SASSAFRAS
(Sassafras albidum)

BUDS SCALY; BRANCHLETS SPINY

BUDS WITHOUT SCALES; NO SPINES ON BRANCHLETS

EVERGREEN TREE; TWIGS AND BUDS RED

DECIDUOUS TREE; TWIGS AND BUDS GLISTENING SILVER

EUROPEAN BUCKTHORN
(Rhamnus cathartica)

CASCARA
(Rhamnus purshiana)

MADRONE
(Arbutus)

RUSSIAN OLIVE
(Elaeagnus angustifolia)

BUNDLE-SCARS — THREE OR IN THREE GROUPS

BUNDLE-SCARS — FIVE OR MORE, NOT GROUPED

BUDS WITH SCALES

BUDS NAKED

TEN OR MORE BUNDLE-SCARS

FIVE TO NINE BUNDLE-SCARS

CASCARA
(Rhamnus purshiana)

ASH
(Fraxinus)

TWO OR MORE PAIRS OF OVERLAPPING SCALES

ONE PAIR OF SCALES NOT OVERLAPPING

BRANCHLETS WEAK WITH THIN WOOD AND LARGE PITH

BRANCHLETS TOUGH WITH THICK WOOD AND SMALL PITH

LEAF-SCARS MEET OR ALMOST MEET AROUND THE TWIG

LEAF-SCARS WIDELY SEPARATED

BLUE ELDER
(Sambucus glauca)

BIGLEAF MAPLE
(Acer macrophyllum)

MAPLE
(Acer)

ALDER BUCKTHORN
(Rhamnus frangula)

TERMINAL BUD SLENDER, ABOUT ¾-IN. LONG

TERMINAL BUDS TWO OR THREE TIMES AS LONG AS THEY ARE BROAD, ½ IN. OR LESS IN LENGTH

BUDS STALKED, LATERALS ALMOST AS LARGE AS THE TERMINAL

BUDS WITHOUT STALKS, LATERALS MINUTE

MAPLE
(Acer)

DOGWOOD
(Cornus)

NANNYBERRY
(Viburnum lentago)

DECIDUOUS TREES
WINTER KEY NUMBER TWO

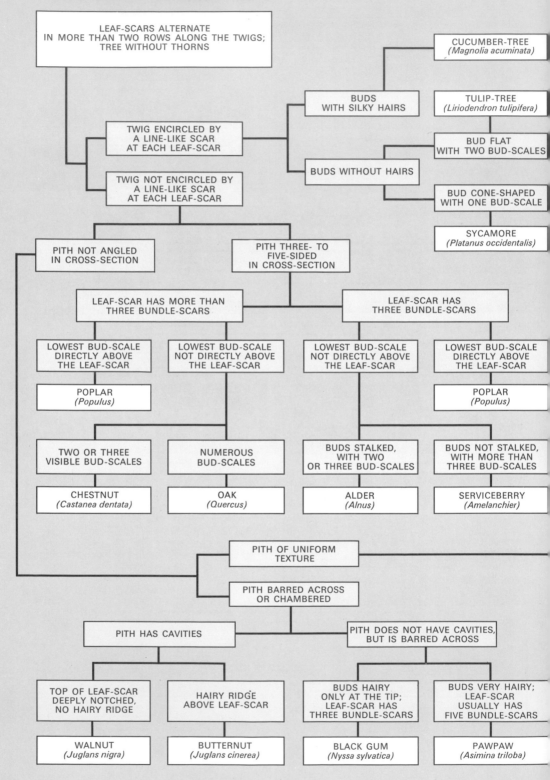

LEAF-SCARS ALTERNATE IN MORE THAN TWO ROWS ALONG THE TWIGS; TREE WITHOUT THORNS

CUCUMBER-TREE
(Magnolia acuminata)

BUDS WITH SILKY HAIRS

TULIP-TREE
(Liriodendron tulipifera)

TWIG ENCIRCLED BY A LINE-LIKE SCAR AT EACH LEAF-SCAR

BUD FLAT WITH TWO BUD-SCALES

BUDS WITHOUT HAIRS

TWIG NOT ENCIRCLED BY A LINE-LIKE SCAR AT EACH LEAF-SCAR

BUD CONE-SHAPED WITH ONE BUD-SCALE

SYCAMORE
(Platanus occidentalis)

PITH NOT ANGLED IN CROSS-SECTION

PITH THREE- TO FIVE-SIDED IN CROSS-SECTION

LEAF-SCAR HAS MORE THAN THREE BUNDLE-SCARS

LEAF-SCAR HAS THREE BUNDLE-SCARS

LOWEST BUD-SCALE DIRECTLY ABOVE THE LEAF-SCAR

LOWEST BUD-SCALE NOT DIRECTLY ABOVE THE LEAF-SCAR

LOWEST BUD-SCALE NOT DIRECTLY ABOVE THE LEAF-SCAR

LOWEST BUD-SCALE DIRECTLY ABOVE THE LEAF-SCAR

POPLAR
(Populus)

POPLAR
(Populus)

TWO OR THREE VISIBLE BUD-SCALES

NUMEROUS BUD-SCALES

BUDS STALKED, WITH TWO OR THREE BUD-SCALES

BUDS NOT STALKED, WITH MORE THAN THREE BUD-SCALES

CHESTNUT
(Castanea dentata)

OAK
(Quercus)

ALDER
(Alnus)

SERVICEBERRY
(Amelanchier)

PITH OF UNIFORM TEXTURE

PITH BARRED ACROSS OR CHAMBERED

PITH HAS CAVITIES

PITH DOES NOT HAVE CAVITIES, BUT IS BARRED ACROSS

TOP OF LEAF-SCAR DEEPLY NOTCHED, NO HAIRY RIDGE

HAIRY RIDGE ABOVE LEAF-SCAR

BUDS HAIRY ONLY AT THE TIP; LEAF-SCAR HAS THREE BUNDLE-SCARS

BUDS VERY HAIRY; LEAF-SCAR USUALLY HAS FIVE BUNDLE-SCARS

WALNUT
(Juglans nigra)

BUTTERNUT
(Juglans cinerea)

BLACK GUM
(Nyssa sylvatica)

PAWPAW
(Asimina triloba)

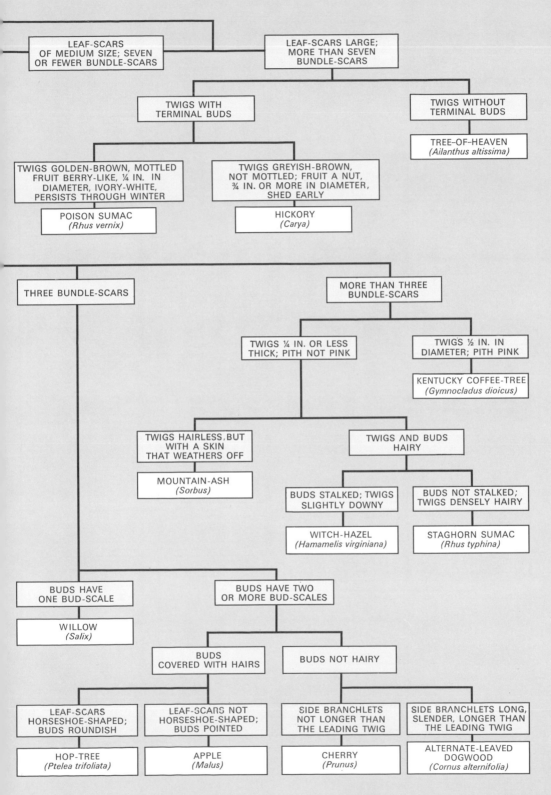

LEAF-SCARS OF MEDIUM SIZE; SEVEN OR FEWER BUNDLE-SCARS

LEAF-SCARS LARGE; MORE THAN SEVEN BUNDLE-SCARS

TWIGS WITH TERMINAL BUDS

TWIGS WITHOUT TERMINAL BUDS

TREE–OF–HEAVEN
(Ailanthus altissima)

TWIGS GOLDEN-BROWN, MOTTLED FRUIT BERRY-LIKE, ¼ IN. IN DIAMETER, IVORY-WHITE, PERSISTS THROUGH WINTER

POISON SUMAC
(Rhus vernix)

TWIGS GREYISH-BROWN, NOT MOTTLED; FRUIT A NUT, ¾ IN. OR MORE IN DIAMETER, SHED EARLY

HICKORY
(Carya)

THREE BUNDLE-SCARS

MORE THAN THREE BUNDLE-SCARS

TWIGS ¼ IN. OR LESS THICK; PITH NOT PINK

TWIGS ½ IN. IN DIAMETER; PITH PINK

KENTUCKY COFFEE-TREE
(Gymnocladus dioicus)

TWIGS HAIRLESS, BUT WITH A SKIN THAT WEATHERS OFF

MOUNTAIN-ASH
(Sorbus)

TWIGS AND BUDS HAIRY

BUDS STALKED; TWIGS SLIGHTLY DOWNY

WITCH-HAZEL
(Hamamelis virginiana)

BUDS NOT STALKED; TWIGS DENSELY HAIRY

STAGHORN SUMAC
(Rhus typhina)

BUDS HAVE ONE BUD-SCALE

WILLOW
(Salix)

BUDS HAVE TWO OR MORE BUD-SCALES

BUDS COVERED WITH HAIRS

BUDS NOT HAIRY

LEAF-SCARS HORSESHOE-SHAPED; BUDS ROUNDISH

HOP-TREE
(Ptelea trifoliata)

LEAF-SCARS NOT HORSESHOE-SHAPED; BUDS POINTED

APPLE
(Malus)

SIDE BRANCHLETS NOT LONGER THAN THE LEADING TWIG

CHERRY
(Prunus)

SIDE BRANCHLETS LONG, SLENDER, LONGER THAN THE LEADING TWIG

ALTERNATE-LEAVED DOGWOOD
(Cornus alternifolia)

DECIDUOUS TREES
WINTER KEY NUMBER THREE

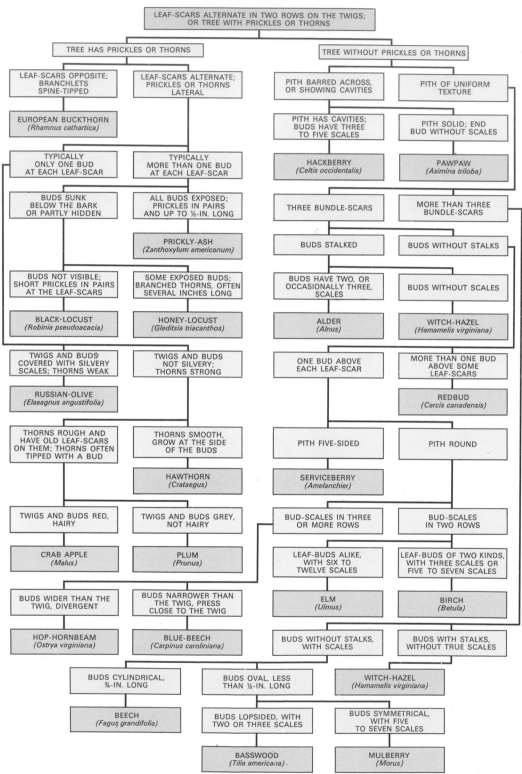

LEAF-SCARS ALTERNATE IN TWO ROWS ON THE TWIGS; OR TREE WITH PRICKLES OR THORNS

TREE HAS PRICKLES OR THORNS

TREE WITHOUT PRICKLES OR THORNS

LEAF-SCARS OPPOSITE; BRANCHLETS SPINE-TIPPED

LEAF-SCARS ALTERNATE; PRICKLES OR THORNS LATERAL

PITH BARRED ACROSS, OR SHOWING CAVITIES

PITH OF UNIFORM TEXTURE

EUROPEAN BUCKTHORN
(Rhamnus cathartica)

PITH HAS CAVITIES; BUDS HAVE THREE TO FIVE SCALES

PITH SOLID; END BUD WITHOUT SCALES

TYPICALLY ONLY ONE BUD AT EACH LEAF-SCAR

TYPICALLY MORE THAN ONE BUD AT EACH LEAF-SCAR

HACKBERRY
(Celtis occidentalis)

PAWPAW
(Asimina triloba)

BUDS SUNK BELOW THE BARK OR PARTLY HIDDEN

ALL BUDS EXPOSED; PRICKLES IN PAIRS AND UP TO ½-IN. LONG

THREE BUNDLE-SCARS

MORE THAN THREE BUNDLE-SCARS

PRICKLY-ASH
(Zanthoxylum americanum)

BUDS STALKED

BUDS WITHOUT STALKS

BUDS NOT VISIBLE; SHORT PRICKLES IN PAIRS AT THE LEAF-SCARS

SOME EXPOSED BUDS; BRANCHED THORNS, OFTEN SEVERAL INCHES LONG

BUDS HAVE TWO, OR OCCASIONALLY THREE, SCALES

BUDS WITHOUT SCALES

BLACK-LOCUST
(Robinia pseudoacacia)

HONEY-LOCUST
(Gleditsia triacanthos)

ALDER
(Alnus)

WITCH-HAZEL
(Hamamelis virginiana)

TWIGS AND BUDS COVERED WITH SILVERY SCALES; THORNS WEAK

TWIGS AND BUDS NOT SILVERY; THORNS STRONG

ONE BUD ABOVE EACH LEAF-SCAR

MORE THAN ONE BUD ABOVE SOME LEAF-SCARS

RUSSIAN-OLIVE
(Elaeagnus angustifolia)

REDBUD
(Cercis canadensis)

THORNS ROUGH AND HAVE OLD LEAF-SCARS ON THEM; THORNS OFTEN TIPPED WITH A BUD

THORNS SMOOTH, GROW AT THE SIDE OF THE BUDS

PITH FIVE-SIDED

PITH ROUND

HAWTHORN
(Crataegus)

SERVICEBERRY
(Amelanchier)

TWIGS AND BUDS RED, HAIRY

TWIGS AND BUDS GREY, NOT HAIRY

BUD-SCALES IN THREE OR MORE ROWS

BUD-SCALES IN TWO ROWS

CRAB APPLE
(Malus)

PLUM
(Prunus)

LEAF-BUDS ALIKE, WITH SIX TO TWELVE SCALES

LEAF-BUDS OF TWO KINDS, WITH THREE SCALES OR FIVE TO SEVEN SCALES

BUDS WIDER THAN THE TWIG, DIVERGENT

BUDS NARROWER THAN THE TWIG, PRESS CLOSE TO THE TWIG

ELM
(Ulmus)

BIRCH
(Betula)

HOP-HORNBEAM
(Ostrya virginiana)

BLUE-BEECH
(Carpinus caroliniana)

BUDS WITHOUT STALKS, WITH SCALES

BUDS WITH STALKS, WITHOUT TRUE SCALES

BUDS CYLINDRICAL, ¾-IN. LONG

BUDS OVAL, LESS THAN ½-IN. LONG

WITCH-HAZEL
(Hamamelis virginiana)

BEECH
(Fagus grandifolia)

BUDS LOPSIDED, WITH TWO OR THREE SCALES

BUDS SYMMETRICAL, WITH FIVE TO SEVEN SCALES

BASSWOOD
(Tilia americana)

MULBERRY
(Morus)

KEY TO THE POPLARS

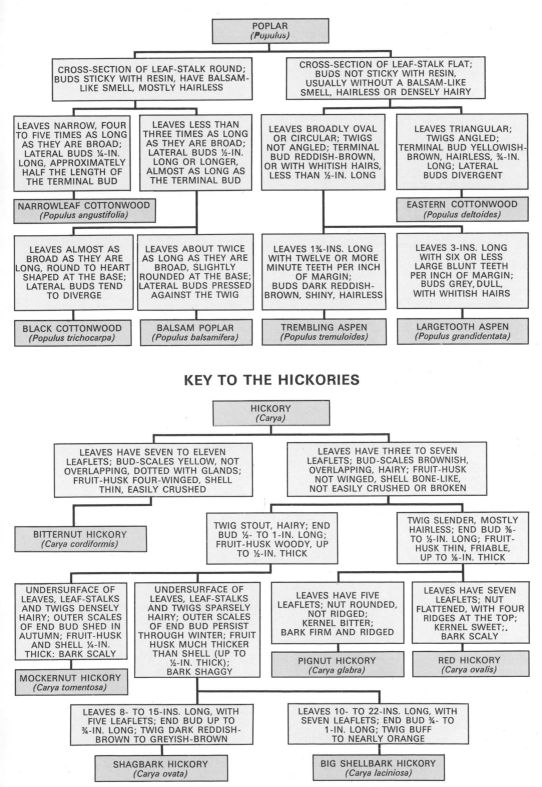

POPLAR
(Populus)

CROSS-SECTION OF LEAF-STALK ROUND; BUDS STICKY WITH RESIN, HAVE BALSAM-LIKE SMELL, MOSTLY HAIRLESS

CROSS-SECTION OF LEAF-STALK FLAT; BUDS NOT STICKY WITH RESIN, USUALLY WITHOUT A BALSAM-LIKE SMELL, HAIRLESS OR DENSELY HAIRY

LEAVES NARROW, FOUR TO FIVE TIMES AS LONG AS THEY ARE BROAD; LATERAL BUDS ¼-IN. LONG, APPROXIMATELY HALF THE LENGTH OF THE TERMINAL BUD

LEAVES LESS THAN THREE TIMES AS LONG AS THEY ARE BROAD; LATERAL BUDS ½-IN. LONG OR LONGER, ALMOST AS LONG AS THE TERMINAL BUD

LEAVES BROADLY OVAL OR CIRCULAR; TWIGS NOT ANGLED; TERMINAL BUD REDDISH-BROWN, OR WITH WHITISH HAIRS, LESS THAN ½-IN. LONG

LEAVES TRIANGULAR; TWIGS ANGLED; TERMINAL BUD YELLOWISH-BROWN, HAIRLESS, ¾-IN. LONG; LATERAL BUDS DIVERGENT

NARROWLEAF COTTONWOOD
(Populus angustifolia)

EASTERN COTTONWOOD
(Populus deltoides)

LEAVES ALMOST AS BROAD AS THEY ARE LONG, ROUND TO HEART SHAPED AT THE BASE; LATERAL BUDS TEND TO DIVERGE

LEAVES ABOUT TWICE AS LONG AS THEY ARE BROAD, SLIGHTLY ROUNDED AT THE BASE; LATERAL BUDS PRESSED AGAINST THE TWIG

LEAVES 1¾-INS. LONG WITH TWELVE OR MORE MINUTE TEETH PER INCH OF MARGIN; BUDS DARK REDDISH-BROWN, SHINY, HAIRLESS

LEAVES 3-INS. LONG WITH SIX OR LESS LARGE BLUNT TEETH PER INCH OF MARGIN; BUDS GREY, DULL, WITH WHITISH HAIRS

BLACK COTTONWOOD
(Populus trichocarpa)

BALSAM POPLAR
(Populus balsamifera)

TREMBLING ASPEN
(Populus tremuloides)

LARGETOOTH ASPEN
(Populus grandidentata)

KEY TO THE HICKORIES

HICKORY
(Carya)

LEAVES HAVE SEVEN TO ELEVEN LEAFLETS; BUD-SCALES YELLOW, NOT OVERLAPPING, DOTTED WITH GLANDS; FRUIT-HUSK FOUR-WINGED, SHELL THIN, EASILY CRUSHED

LEAVES HAVE THREE TO SEVEN LEAFLETS; BUD-SCALES BROWNISH, OVERLAPPING, HAIRY; FRUIT-HUSK NOT WINGED, SHELL BONE-LIKE, NOT EASILY CRUSHED OR BROKEN

BITTERNUT HICKORY
(Carya cordiformis)

TWIG STOUT, HAIRY; END BUD ½- TO 1-IN. LONG; FRUIT-HUSK WOODY, UP TO ½-IN. THICK

TWIG SLENDER, MOSTLY HAIRLESS; END BUD ⅜- TO ½-IN. LONG; FRUIT-HUSK THIN, FRIABLE, UP TO ⅛-IN. THICK

UNDERSURFACE OF LEAVES, LEAF-STALKS AND TWIGS DENSELY HAIRY; OUTER SCALES OF END BUD SHED IN AUTUMN; FRUIT-HUSK AND SHELL ¼-IN. THICK: BARK SCALY

UNDERSURFACE OF LEAVES, LEAF-STALKS AND TWIGS SPARSELY HAIRY; OUTER SCALES OF END BUD PERSIST THROUGH WINTER; FRUIT HUSK MUCH THICKER THAN SHELL (UP TO ½-IN. THICK); BARK SHAGGY

LEAVES HAVE FIVE LEAFLETS; NUT ROUNDED, NOT RIDGED; KERNEL BITTER; BARK FIRM AND RIDGED

LEAVES HAVE SEVEN LEAFLETS; NUT FLATTENED, WITH FOUR RIDGES AT THE TOP; KERNEL SWEET; BARK SCALY

PIGNUT HICKORY
(Carya glabra)

RED HICKORY
(Carya ovalis)

MOCKERNUT HICKORY
(Carya tomentosa)

LEAVES 8- TO 15-INS. LONG, WITH FIVE LEAFLETS; END BUD UP TO ¾-IN. LONG; TWIG DARK REDDISH-BROWN TO GREYISH-BROWN

LEAVES 10- TO 22-INS. LONG, WITH SEVEN LEAFLETS; END BUD ¾- TO 1-IN. LONG; TWIG BUFF TO NEARLY ORANGE

SHAGBARK HICKORY
(Carya ovata)

BIG SHELLBARK HICKORY
(Carya laciniosa)

KEY TO THE BIRCHES

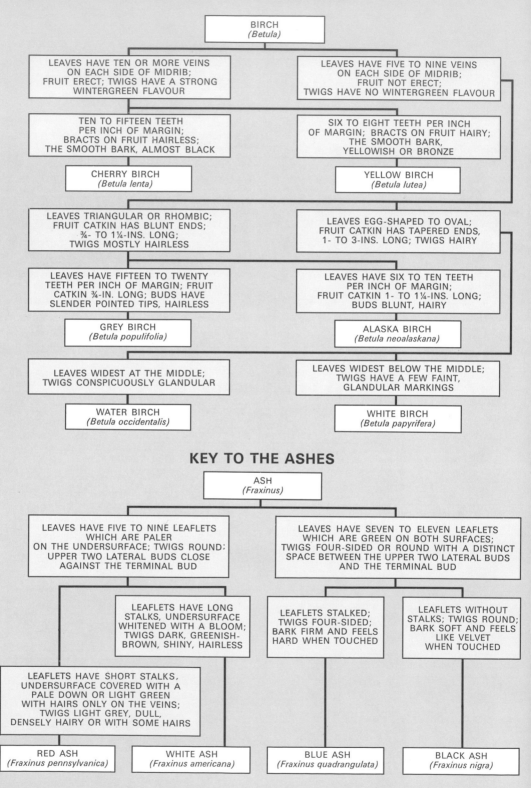

BIRCH
(Betula)

LEAVES HAVE TEN OR MORE VEINS ON EACH SIDE OF MIDRIB; FRUIT ERECT; TWIGS HAVE A STRONG WINTERGREEN FLAVOUR

LEAVES HAVE FIVE TO NINE VEINS ON EACH SIDE OF MIDRIB; FRUIT NOT ERECT; TWIGS HAVE NO WINTERGREEN FLAVOUR

TEN TO FIFTEEN TEETH PER INCH OF MARGIN; BRACTS ON FRUIT HAIRLESS; THE SMOOTH BARK, ALMOST BLACK

SIX TO EIGHT TEETH PER INCH OF MARGIN; BRACTS ON FRUIT HAIRY; THE SMOOTH BARK, YELLOWISH OR BRONZE

CHERRY BIRCH
(Betula lenta)

YELLOW BIRCH
(Betula lutea)

LEAVES TRIANGULAR OR RHOMBIC; FRUIT CATKIN HAS BLUNT ENDS; ¾- TO 1¼-INS. LONG; TWIGS MOSTLY HAIRLESS

LEAVES EGG-SHAPED TO OVAL; FRUIT CATKIN HAS TAPERED ENDS, 1- TO 3-INS. LONG; TWIGS HAIRY

LEAVES HAVE FIFTEEN TO TWENTY TEETH PER INCH OF MARGIN; FRUIT CATKIN ¾-IN. LONG; BUDS HAVE SLENDER POINTED TIPS, HAIRLESS

LEAVES HAVE SIX TO TEN TEETH PER INCH OF MARGIN; FRUIT CATKIN 1- TO 1¼-INS. LONG; BUDS BLUNT, HAIRY

GREY BIRCH
(Betula populifolia)

ALASKA BIRCH
(Betula neoalaskana)

LEAVES WIDEST AT THE MIDDLE; TWIGS CONSPICUOUSLY GLANDULAR

LEAVES WIDEST BELOW THE MIDDLE; TWIGS HAVE A FEW FAINT, GLANDULAR MARKINGS

WATER BIRCH
(Betula occidentalis)

WHITE BIRCH
(Betula papyrifera)

KEY TO THE ASHES

ASH
(Fraxinus)

LEAVES HAVE FIVE TO NINE LEAFLETS WHICH ARE PALER ON THE UNDERSURFACE; TWIGS ROUND; UPPER TWO LATERAL BUDS CLOSE AGAINST THE TERMINAL BUD

LEAVES HAVE SEVEN TO ELEVEN LEAFLETS WHICH ARE GREEN ON BOTH SURFACES; TWIGS FOUR-SIDED OR ROUND WITH A DISTINCT SPACE BETWEEN THE UPPER TWO LATERAL BUDS AND THE TERMINAL BUD

LEAFLETS HAVE LONG STALKS, UNDERSURFACE WHITENED WITH A BLOOM; TWIGS DARK, GREENISH-BROWN, SHINY, HAIRLESS

LEAFLETS STALKED; TWIGS FOUR-SIDED; BARK FIRM AND FEELS HARD WHEN TOUCHED

LEAFLETS WITHOUT STALKS; TWIGS ROUND; BARK SOFT AND FEELS LIKE VELVET WHEN TOUCHED

LEAFLETS HAVE SHORT STALKS, UNDERSURFACE COVERED WITH A PALE DOWN OR LIGHT GREEN WITH HAIRS ONLY ON THE VEINS; TWIGS LIGHT GREY, DULL, DENSELY HAIRY OR WITH SOME HAIRS

RED ASH
(Fraxinus pennsylvanica)

WHITE ASH
(Fraxinus americana)

BLUE ASH
(Fraxinus quadrangulata)

BLACK ASH
(Fraxinus nigra)

KEY TO THE OAKS

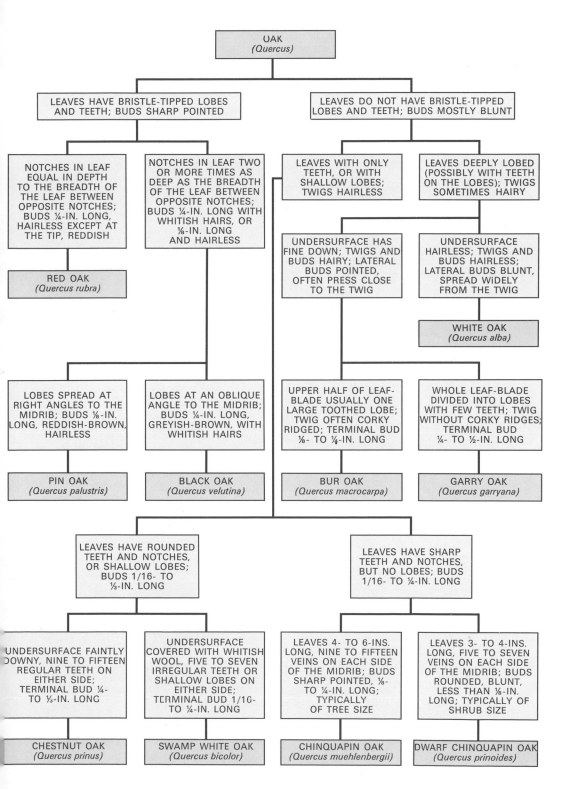

OAK
(Quercus)

LEAVES HAVE BRISTLE-TIPPED LOBES AND TEETH; BUDS SHARP POINTED

LEAVES DO NOT HAVE BRISTLE-TIPPED LOBES AND TEETH; BUDS MOSTLY BLUNT

NOTCHES IN LEAF EQUAL IN DEPTH TO THE BREADTH OF THE LEAF BETWEEN OPPOSITE NOTCHES; BUDS ¼-IN. LONG, HAIRLESS EXCEPT AT THE TIP, REDDISH

NOTCHES IN LEAF TWO OR MORE TIMES AS DEEP AS THE BREADTH OF THE LEAF BETWEEN OPPOSITE NOTCHES; BUDS ¼-IN. LONG WITH WHITISH HAIRS, OR ⅛-IN. LONG AND HAIRLESS

LEAVES WITH ONLY TEETH, OR WITH SHALLOW LOBES; TWIGS HAIRLESS

LEAVES DEEPLY LOBED (POSSIBLY WITH TEETH ON THE LOBES); TWIGS SOMETIMES HAIRY

RED OAK
(Quercus rubra)

UNDERSURFACE HAS FINE DOWN; TWIGS AND BUDS HAIRY; LATERAL BUDS POINTED, OFTEN PRESS CLOSE TO THE TWIG

UNDERSURFACE HAIRLESS; TWIGS AND BUDS HAIRLESS; LATERAL BUDS BLUNT, SPREAD WIDELY FROM THE TWIG

WHITE OAK
(Quercus alba)

LOBES SPREAD AT RIGHT ANGLES TO THE MIDRIB; BUDS ⅛-IN. LONG, REDDISH-BROWN, HAIRLESS

LOBES AT AN OBLIQUE ANGLE TO THE MIDRIB; BUDS ¼-IN. LONG, GREYISH-BROWN, WITH WHITISH HAIRS

UPPER HALF OF LEAF-BLADE USUALLY ONE LARGE TOOTHED LOBE; TWIG OFTEN CORKY RIDGED; TERMINAL BUD ⅛- TO ¼-IN. LONG

WHOLE LEAF-BLADE DIVIDED INTO LOBES WITH FEW TEETH; TWIG WITHOUT CORKY RIDGES; TERMINAL BUD ¼- TO ½-IN. LONG

PIN OAK
(Quercus palustris)

BLACK OAK
(Quercus velutina)

BUR OAK
(Quercus macrocarpa)

GARRY OAK
(Quercus garryana)

LEAVES HAVE ROUNDED TEETH AND NOTCHES, OR SHALLOW LOBES; BUDS 1/16- TO ⅓-IN. LONG

LEAVES HAVE SHARP TEETH AND NOTCHES, BUT NO LOBES; BUDS 1/16- TO ¼-IN. LONG

UNDERSURFACE FAINTLY DOWNY, NINE TO FIFTEEN REGULAR TEETH ON EITHER SIDE; TERMINAL BUD ¼- TO ⅓-IN. LONG

UNDERSURFACE COVERED WITH WHITISH WOOL, FIVE TO SEVEN IRREGULAR TEETH OR SHALLOW LOBES ON EITHER SIDE; TERMINAL BUD 1/16- TO ¼-IN. LONG

LEAVES 4- TO 6-INS. LONG, NINE TO FIFTEEN VEINS ON EACH SIDE OF THE MIDRIB; BUDS SHARP POINTED, ⅛- TO ¼-IN. LONG; TYPICALLY OF TREE SIZE

LEAVES 3- TO 4-INS. LONG, FIVE TO SEVEN VEINS ON EACH SIDE OF THE MIDRIB; BUDS ROUNDED, BLUNT, LESS THAN ⅛-IN. LONG; TYPICALLY OF SHRUB SIZE

CHESTNUT OAK
(Quercus prinus)

SWAMP WHITE OAK
(Quercus bicolor)

CHINQUAPIN OAK
(Quercus muehlenbergii)

DWARF CHINQUAPIN OAK
(Quercus prinoides)

KEY TO THE CHERRIES AND PLUMS

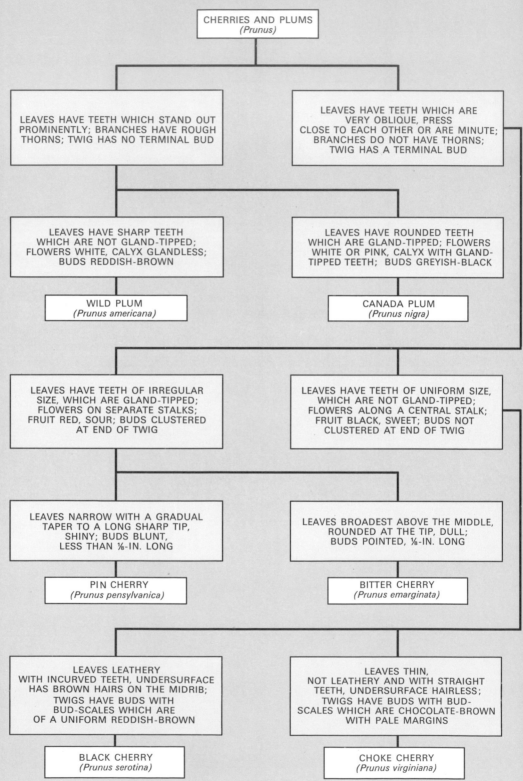

CHERRIES AND PLUMS
(Prunus)

LEAVES HAVE TEETH WHICH STAND OUT PROMINENTLY; BRANCHES HAVE ROUGH THORNS; TWIG HAS NO TERMINAL BUD

LEAVES HAVE TEETH WHICH ARE VERY OBLIQUE, PRESS CLOSE TO EACH OTHER OR ARE MINUTE; BRANCHES DO NOT HAVE THORNS; TWIG HAS A TERMINAL BUD

LEAVES HAVE SHARP TEETH WHICH ARE NOT GLAND-TIPPED; FLOWERS WHITE, CALYX GLANDLESS; BUDS REDDISH-BROWN

LEAVES HAVE ROUNDED TEETH WHICH ARE GLAND-TIPPED; FLOWERS WHITE OR PINK, CALYX WITH GLAND-TIPPED TEETH; BUDS GREYISH-BLACK

WILD PLUM
(Prunus americana)

CANADA PLUM
(Prunus nigra)

LEAVES HAVE TEETH OF IRREGULAR SIZE, WHICH ARE GLAND-TIPPED; FLOWERS ON SEPARATE STALKS; FRUIT RED, SOUR; BUDS CLUSTERED AT END OF TWIG

LEAVES HAVE TEETH OF UNIFORM SIZE, WHICH ARE NOT GLAND-TIPPED; FLOWERS ALONG A CENTRAL STALK; FRUIT BLACK, SWEET; BUDS NOT CLUSTERED AT END OF TWIG

LEAVES NARROW WITH A GRADUAL TAPER TO A LONG SHARP TIP, SHINY; BUDS BLUNT, LESS THAN ⅛-IN. LONG

LEAVES BROADEST ABOVE THE MIDDLE, ROUNDED AT THE TIP, DULL; BUDS POINTED, ⅛-IN. LONG

PIN CHERRY
(Prunus pensylvanica)

BITTER CHERRY
(Prunus emarginata)

LEAVES LEATHERY WITH INCURVED TEETH, UNDERSURFACE HAS BROWN HAIRS ON THE MIDRIB; TWIGS HAVE BUDS WITH BUD-SCALES WHICH ARE OF A UNIFORM REDDISH-BROWN

LEAVES THIN, NOT LEATHERY AND WITH STRAIGHT TEETH, UNDERSURFACE HAIRLESS; TWIGS HAVE BUDS WITH BUD-SCALES WHICH ARE CHOCOLATE-BROWN WITH PALE MARGINS

BLACK CHERRY
(Prunus serotina)

CHOKE CHERRY
(Prunus virginiana)

KEY TO THE MAPLES

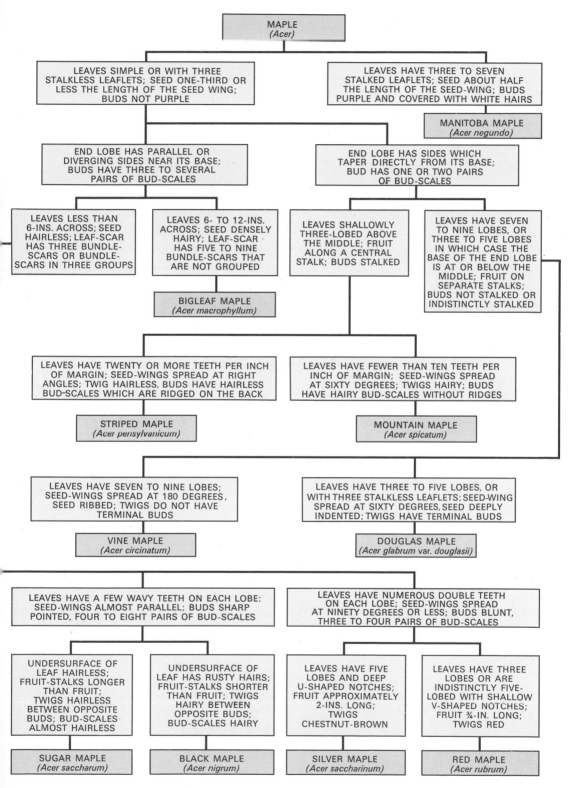

MAPLE
(Acer)

LEAVES SIMPLE OR WITH THREE STALKLESS LEAFLETS; SEED ONE-THIRD OR LESS THE LENGTH OF THE SEED WING; BUDS NOT PURPLE

LEAVES HAVE THREE TO SEVEN STALKED LEAFLETS; SEED ABOUT HALF THE LENGTH OF THE SEED-WING; BUDS PURPLE AND COVERED WITH WHITE HAIRS

MANITOBA MAPLE
(Acer negundo)

END LOBE HAS PARALLEL OR DIVERGING SIDES NEAR ITS BASE; BUDS HAVE THREE TO SEVERAL PAIRS OF BUD-SCALES

END LOBE HAS SIDES WHICH TAPER DIRECTLY FROM ITS BASE; BUD HAS ONE OR TWO PAIRS OF BUD-SCALES

LEAVES LESS THAN 6-INS. ACROSS; SEED HAIRLESS; LEAF-SCAR HAS THREE BUNDLE-SCARS OR BUNDLE-SCARS IN THREE GROUPS

LEAVES 6- TO 12-INS. ACROSS; SEED DENSELY HAIRY; LEAF-SCAR HAS FIVE TO NINE BUNDLE-SCARS THAT ARE NOT GROUPED

LEAVES SHALLOWLY THREE-LOBED ABOVE THE MIDDLE; FRUIT ALONG A CENTRAL STALK; BUDS STALKED

LEAVES HAVE SEVEN TO NINE LOBES, OR THREE TO FIVE LOBES IN WHICH CASE THE BASE OF THE END LOBE IS AT OR BELOW THE MIDDLE; FRUIT ON SEPARATE STALKS; BUDS NOT STALKED OR INDISTINCTLY STALKED

BIGLEAF MAPLE
(Acer macrophyllum)

LEAVES HAVE TWENTY OR MORE TEETH PER INCH OF MARGIN; SEED-WINGS SPREAD AT RIGHT ANGLES; TWIG HAIRLESS, BUDS HAVE HAIRLESS BUD-SCALES WHICH ARE RIDGED ON THE BACK

LEAVES HAVE FEWER THAN TEN TEETH PER INCH OF MARGIN; SEED-WINGS SPREAD AT SIXTY DEGREES; TWIGS HAIRY; BUDS HAVE HAIRY BUD-SCALES WITHOUT RIDGES

STRIPED MAPLE
(Acer pensylvanicum)

MOUNTAIN MAPLE
(Acer spicatum)

LEAVES HAVE SEVEN TO NINE LOBES; SEED-WINGS SPREAD AT 180 DEGREES, SEED RIBBED; TWIGS DO NOT HAVE TERMINAL BUDS

LEAVES HAVE THREE TO FIVE LOBES, OR WITH THREE STALKLESS LEAFLETS; SEED-WING SPREAD AT SIXTY DEGREES, SEED DEEPLY INDENTED; TWIGS HAVE TERMINAL BUDS

VINE MAPLE
(Acer circinatum)

DOUGLAS MAPLE
(Acer glabrum var. douglasii)

LEAVES HAVE A FEW WAVY TEETH ON EACH LOBE: SEED-WINGS ALMOST PARALLEL; BUDS SHARP POINTED, FOUR TO EIGHT PAIRS OF BUD-SCALES

LEAVES HAVE NUMEROUS DOUBLE TEETH ON EACH LOBE; SEED-WINGS SPREAD AT NINETY DEGREES OR LESS; BUDS BLUNT, THREE TO FOUR PAIRS OF BUD-SCALES

UNDERSURFACE OF LEAF HAIRLESS; FRUIT-STALKS LONGER THAN FRUIT; TWIGS HAIRLESS BETWEEN OPPOSITE BUDS; BUD-SCALES ALMOST HAIRLESS

UNDERSURFACE OF LEAF HAS RUSTY HAIRS; FRUIT-STALKS SHORTER THAN FRUIT; TWIGS HAIRY BETWEEN OPPOSITE BUDS; BUD-SCALES HAIRY

LEAVES HAVE FIVE LOBES AND DEEP U-SHAPED NOTCHES; FRUIT APPROXIMATELY 2-INS. LONG; TWIGS CHESTNUT-BROWN

LEAVES HAVE THREE LOBES OR ARE INDISTINCTLY FIVE-LOBED WITH SHALLOW V-SHAPED NOTCHES; FRUIT ¾-IN. LONG; TWIGS RED

SUGAR MAPLE
(Acer saccharum)

BLACK MAPLE
(Acer nigrum)

SILVER MAPLE
(Acer saccharinum)

RED MAPLE
(Acer rubrum)

INDEX

INDEX

b